N
8795
.C66
1994

Conklin, John E.

Art crime.

$49.95

DATE			
SEP 1 9 1994			

BAKER & TAYLOR

ART *Crime*

ART *Crime*

John E. Conklin

PRAEGER   **Westport, Connecticut**
London

Library of Congress Cataloging-in-Publication Data

Conklin, John E.
Art Crime / John E. Conklin.
p.   cm.
Includes bibliographical references and index.
ISBN 0–275–94771–8 (alk. paper)
1. Art thefts. 2. Art—Forgeries. I. Title.
N8795.C66   1994
364.1′6—dc20   93–11869

British Library Cataloguing in Publication Data is available.

Library of Congress Catalog Card Number: 93–11869
ISBN: 0–275–94771–8

First published in 1994

Praeger Publishers, 88 Post Road West, Westport, CT 06881
An imprint of Greenwood Publishing Group, Inc.

Printed in the United States of America

The paper used in this book complies with the
Permanent Paper Standard issued by the National
Information Standards Organization (Z39.48–1984).

10 9 8 7 6 5 4 3 2 1

For Sarah, Gillian, Lydia, Annie, and Chris,
with love

Contents

Preface

This volume focuses on a topic that has so far escaped the attention of criminologists: crime that involves works of art. Throughout the book, I use concepts developed by criminologists to examine crimes of forgery, fraud, theft, smuggling, and vandalism that involve art. I investigate the ways that those offenses are linked to the social organization of the art world.

The differences among the various types of art crimes and the lack of previous research prohibited the development of a single theory of art crime. Instead, I hope to stimulate research and theoretical work by developing a framework for the study of art crime and by showing how ideas developed by scholars can illuminate that phenomenon.

I would like to thank Peter Coveney, Senior Editor for the Humanities at the Greenwood Publishing Group, Inc., for his enthusiastic response to this project and for his efforts in getting the book published. I am also grateful for the production work of Julie Cullen and for the copyediting expertise of Patricia M. Daly.

Finally, I want to thank my wife Sarah Belcher Conklin for her love and support during the years it took me to complete this book.

ART *Crime*

Introduction

On March 19, 1990, in typeface suitable for the start of a war or the assassination of a president, a front-page headline in *The Boston Globe* announced: "$200m Gardner Museum Art Theft." Accompanied by large color photographs of paintings by Vermeer and Rembrandt, the articles that appeared that day and over the following weeks were full of speculation and questions, but little information. One question that was repeatedly asked was why anyone would steal pictures that were so famous they obviously could not be sold.

Three years earlier, an article in *Connoisseur* magazine revealed that dozens of modern sculptures produced by a Mexican had made their way into the legitimate art market as authentic pre-Columbian statues. The forgeries were owned by respected museums and esteemed collectors, and they had been written about in scholarly publications. How could the experts have been so thoroughly fooled, and how had the forgeries been marketed so successfully as ancient works of art?

In 1985, a sixty-four-year-old New Jersey woman was convicted of accepting paintings on consignment, selling them, and then failing to pay the pictures' owners. Why had collectors trusted her with their valued possessions, and how did she perpetrate her profitable fraud?

Vandals occasionally attack works of art. In 1972, a man claiming to be both Jesus Christ and Michelangelo smashed a marble sculpture by Michelangelo with a hammer. In 1914, British suffragettes slashed paintings as a protest against a social system that denied women the right to vote. Why did these people choose artworks from among all the property they could have attacked? What, if anything, did they have in common?

Scholars have done little research to help us answer these questions. Indeed, they have paid scant attention to crimes that involve works of art—theft, smuggling, forgery, fraud, and vandalism. Notable exceptions include Bonnie Burnham's book *The Art Crisis*, two papers by Gary Alan Fine on forgery and vandalism, and a study of vandalism by Dario Gamboni. Because there was little social scientific research to draw on for this book, most of the raw material comes from newspapers, art magazines, and a newsletter published by the International Foundation for Art Research. Concepts developed by criminologists are used to explore art crimes and to investigate the way that they are linked to the social organization of the art world.

WHAT IS ART CRIME?

Before defining art crime, we must define art. Everyone would call Leonardo da Vinci's *Mona Lisa* art, but how many would define as art items recently sold to collectors by auction houses such as antique toys, John Lennon's piano, Victorian wallpaper, and mummified Native American children? For our purposes, art will be limited to the kinds of objects typically displayed in museums of fine arts. To be more specific, we will focus on objects included in the following typology, which is used by the International Foundation for Art Research (IFAR) to classify works of art that are reported stolen:

1. Fine arts, including paintings, photographs, prints, drawings, and sculptures;
2. Decorative arts;
3. Antiquities;
4. Ethnographic objects;
5. Oriental and Islamic art; and
6. Miscellaneous items, including armor, books, coins, and medals.

Even this typology might cover too much. Is a rare book art? Perhaps a Gutenberg Bible is, but how about a first edition of a Hemingway novel? Whether decorative objects are art is also questionable. Old and valued furniture is on display in many museums of fine arts, but is it art? The inclusion of ethnographic objects also raises questions. Often objects created by their makers for use in religious rituals or as containers for food and drink are redefined as art by auction houses, museums, and collectors. Most of the art crimes considered in this book involve fine arts, antiquities, or ethnographic objects, but on occasion it will prove illuminating to cast our net more widely.

Art crimes are criminally punishable acts that involve works of art. Those crimes are not, however, always punished; sometimes no one reports the crime to a law-enforcement agency, sometimes the offender is not apprehended even if the crime is reported, and sometimes the offender is dealt with as if the crime were a civil wrong. Art crimes involve deceit, theft, or damage. Deceit occurs in the production and marketing of fakes and forgeries, a problem that has plagued the trade in fine art prints in recent years. Chapter 2 explores the motives for producing fakes and forgeries, the organization of that production process, and the prior question of just what constitutes an original work of art. Deceit also occurs in the distribution of authentic works of art; fraud by collectors, dealers, auction houses, and museums is the topic of Chapter 3. Another type of art crime is theft. Chapter 4 looks at motives and opportunities for the theft of artworks. The social organization of that theft is the subject of Chapter 5; there we look at techniques of theft, the reconnaissance of targets, the use of insiders and "fronts," and the "laundering" of stolen art. Chapter 6 examines the distribution of stolen art by smuggling networks and by governments that have confiscated art from vanquished enemies and subjugated colonies. Damage to and destruction of art are explored in Chapter 7. Conventional vandalism is deliberately committed for various reasons, and artworks are also harmed by thieves in the course of robberies and burglaries, by legitimate owners through neglect, and by combatants during wars. Chapter 8 explores proposals for curbing art crime, including the use of publicity to make it difficult to sell stolen art. Before beginning our investigation of art crime, however, we need to understand why art is valuable, for only if it has value will it be worth forging, stealing, or targeting for destruction. The way that value becomes attached to works of art is examined in Chapter 1.

THE EXTENT OF ART CRIME

Calculating the amount of art crime that is committed is made difficult by obstacles that have traditionally confronted criminologists seeking international data on crime. Because nations have different laws on theft, fraud, and smuggling, even if all countries gathered complete and accurate crime statistics, it would not be possible to add their figures together to get a complete count of art crimes. In addition to differences among nations in their laws and in their methods of gathering crime statistics, countries also differ in their law-enforcement emphases. Some countries, such as Italy with its eighty-person art squad, focus resources on the problem of art theft;

others, such as Peru, which are poor and face threats from terrorists or drug traffickers, devote few resources to preventing the looting of their patrimony.

Experts estimate that annual losses due to theft of art and antiquities are now at least $1 billion, second only to the cost of drug smuggling among international crimes. We would expect annual dollar losses due to art theft to have increased in recent years because of the rapid rise in the price of art; the same number of thefts of the same kinds of paintings today translates into a much larger monetary loss than it would have a decade ago. The market value of stolen art is only part of the total cost of art theft. Some thefts involve violence against museum guards, gallery owners, and private collectors; the costs of that violence—deaths, hospital expenses, lost wages, and permanent disabilities—must be added to the market value of the stolen art and antiquities to get a more complete accounting of the losses due to art theft. Moreover, losses due to art *theft* cover only part of the losses from all art *crimes*; fraud, forgery, and vandalism add a large but unknown amount to the losses due to theft.

Many art crimes are never reported. Museums fail to report thefts and acts of vandalism because they are reluctant to draw attention to the vulnerability of their holdings, fearing that this would scare off donors and attract more thieves and vandals. Collectors conceal their losses out of fear of alerting potential thieves to the value of their possessions and their vulnerability to theft. Antiquities collectors do not report thefts for fear of attracting the attention of the governments of the countries from which their pieces were originally smuggled. Collectors who have bought stolen art or who have purchased art legitimately with money that was dishonestly acquired or not reported on tax returns are also reluctant to report thefts. In France, private collectors often do not report thefts because they have failed to disclose the existence of the artworks in order to evade the French wealth tax.

Crimes other than theft also go unreported. Fraud by dealers and auction houses is kept secret in order to maintain the public confidence in the art market that is required for the continued sale of art at escalating prices. Dealers and auction houses try to convince the public that fakes and forgeries are rare, rather than frequently encountered phenomena that buyers must guard against, especially buyers who collect prints by Joan Miró, Marc Chagall, Pablo Picasso, or Salvador Dali.

Complete and reliable statistics on the extent of art crime do not exist. The sale of fakes and forgeries is occasionally reported in the press, but the frequency of that behavior has never been measured. The same is true for the various types of fraud engaged in by members of the art world. We also lack a complete accounting of crimes of vandalism; indeed, even defining art vandalism poses problems. Theft of art from museums, galleries, homes, and churches is reported with some frequency to the International Criminal Police Organization (Interpol), headquartered in Saint-Cloud, France; the Federal Bureau of Investigation (FBI), a branch of the United States Department of Justice in Washington, D.C.; and IFAR, a private foundation based in New York City.

Interpol has had limited success in developing a central registry of stolen art. Reports of art thefts are accepted only if the agency has reason to think that the stolen objects have been transported across national borders. The agency has been criticized for being slow in disseminating information about art thefts and for failing to update its records periodically by eliminating works that have been recovered. Because Interpol's statistics are incomplete, any trends they reveal might not reflect actual changes in art theft, but simply show changes in the willingness of victims to report such crimes to that agency. Trends in Interpol's data could also reflect a change from thefts in which art is kept within the country in which it was stolen to thefts in which stolen works are thought to have been smuggled across national boundaries. Interpol data do suggest an upsurge in art thefts; the number of notices of stolen paintings sent out tripled from 1965 to 1990.

In the late 1970s, the FBI began to focus more resources on thefts involving losses of great value, a category that includes many art thefts. The FBI's jurisdiction is limited to the investigation of interstate transportation of stolen goods valued at more than $5,000, theft from interstate shipments, and receiving stolen property that has crossed state lines. However, if a theft victim or the victim's agent, such as an insurance company, seeks the help of the FBI in investigating a loss of more than $50,000, the FBI routinely offers assistance. The FBI started its National Stolen Art File (NSAF) in the early 1980s, recording information about stolen art and updating its entries every six months to delete recovered property. The agency catalogues the stolen art in great detail, allowing agents to compare a suspicious work with one known to have been stolen by programming the shape, medium, and subject matter of the two works. According to the FBI, the NSAF system is underused, with few police departments other than those in New York and Los Angeles providing the FBI with much information on art theft. Only law-enforcement agencies have access to the file, although the owner of a stolen work can use it through the law-enforcement agency that is investigating the loss. The FBI restricts access to the system to protect the privacy of victims and to prevent forgers from learning what has been stolen, making a copy, and selling it as a stolen but authentic work. Currently limited to paintings, prints, and sculptures with a value of at least $2,000 that have been stolen in the United States, NSAF is a less complete file of stolen art than the IFAR file, which includes a greater variety of stolen objects and covers thefts committed throughout the world.

The International Foundation for Art Research has been acting as a clearinghouse for stolen art since 1976. Headquartered in New York, IFAR opened an office in Switzerland in 1983 and another in Rome in 1986 in order to collect reports of stolen art more quickly. IFAR's goals are to report and recover stolen art, prevent the sale of misattributed and forged art, and prevent art fraud. To achieve these goals, it offers a cataloguing service for collectors and accepts queries and reports of stolen art from businesses, museums, individuals, and law-enforcement agencies; modest fees are charged for publishing information about stolen art in IFAR's newsletter and for searching the agency's archive to see if works have been reported stolen. The foundation's newsletter, which includes black-and-white photographs of objects that have been reported stolen, was first called *Art Theft Archive* and then *Stolen Art Alert*; it is now published ten times a year as *IFAR Reports*. In 1987, the Art Dealers Association of America, which began gathering data on stolen art and antiquities in the 1960s, agreed to merge its files with IFAR's records, and in 1991 IFAR formed a partnership with England's Art Loss Register. In 1991, there were 40,000 stolen works in IFAR's image database, and that system began to be computerized. IFAR readily admits that its records are incomplete, because many victims do not report their losses to the foundation.

Organizations that collect reports of stolen art estimate that the recovery rate for all stolen art is only about 10 percent, although the rate for well-known and valuable works may be as high as 50 percent. However, the incompleteness of the data on stolen art and its recovery makes it difficult to assess the accuracy of those estimated rates of recovery, which are based on the number of stolen objects reported to IFAR, Interpol, and the FBI. Recoveries of stolen art may not be reported to those agencies for a variety of reasons: a desire to keep secret a payment by an insurance company to the thieves or their agent, the inconvenience of notifying the agency of the recovery, and the lack of any incentive to report the recovery. Because of these problems, we do not know precisely the rate at which stolen art is recovered.

Criminologists could study art theft more productively if, in addition to keeping files on stolen *artworks*, the FBI, IFAR, and Interpol also maintained accessible records on art *crimes*. Such data would permit more conclusive answers to questions such as: When and where are art thefts most likely to occur? Has the amount of violence used by art thieves increased over the years? Has the proportion of all art theft that victimizes museums declined over time as security measures have improved? How long does it take the police to respond to the report of an art theft? At present, scholars do not have the data to answer such questions.

Data on art crimes other than theft are even scarcer. For example, we have no accurate measure of the extent of art vandalism. Fine and Shatin (1985:137) suggest that neither museums nor insurance companies keep good records on art vandalism because most attacks involve little damage, there is not much that can be done once the vandalism has occurred, there is a fear of copycat vandals, and insurance companies do not want to publicize the infrequency with which art vandalism occurs because they profit handsomely from the policies they sell to protect museums against losses from such acts.

THE SOCIAL CONSTRUCTION OF VALUE

How would Westerners explain to a member of a preliterate tribe that an old piece of canvas with some oil paint daubed on it, Vincent van Gogh's *Portrait of Dr. Gachet,* is "worth" $82.5 million, the price that a Japanese collector paid for it in 1990? A fraction of that amount would feed the entire tribe for centuries.

The value of art is not intrinsic; instead, it is "socially constructed," to use the term employed by sociologist Charles W. Smith (1989) in his study of auctions. One indication that art has no intrinsic value is the large difference between the price that an object will fetch at public auction and the price it will fetch on the black market. A painting auctioned for $100,000 at Sotheby's or Christie's would probably bring no more than $10,000 if sold by a thief to a dealer.

Contrary to the idea that the value of a piece of art is a product of its aesthetic quality, some inner aspect of the work that is recognizable to connoisseurs, sociologists see the value of art as a product of the way that the art world is organized. Social organization, or social structure, is a recurring pattern of interaction among people who occupy certain positions in the art world and play specific roles associated with those positions. The network that is the social organization of the art world is made up of artists, collectors, museums, dealers, auction houses, and scholars (including critics, art historians, and archaeologists). Others who play roles in the art world, but are not generally acknowledged to be part of that world, include art and antiquities smugglers (who may also be dealers, museum personnel, or archaeologists), thieves and grave-robbers, and professional fences.

Recurring patterns of interaction among those people and institutions create values for works of art, values that in recent years have accelerated rapidly. Through that interaction, people and institutions respond to works of art in ways that determine their financial and aesthetic value. Gallery owners price paintings by new artists high enough to make them seem worthwhile to collectors, but not so high as to frighten off buyers who are wary of acquiring pictures by unknown artists. Museums appraise artworks for collectors, who in turn donate the works to the museum and take tax write-offs, a practice that has produced inflated appraisals. Collectors compete avidly with one another for highly esteemed paintings; sometimes they seem more interested in being publicly recognized as the buyer than they are in the piece itself. Auction houses routinely withdraw artworks from sale when the bidding does not reach a "reserve" or minimum selling price that has been agreed to in advance by the owner of the work; this practice maintains prices at high levels.

Collectors play an important role in the social construction of value through the way they perceive and respond to art. Their construction of the value of art is social in that they do not live in isolation; other people's responses interact with an individual collector's reactions to give meaning to artworks. Art that was once rejected—such as Jackson Pollock's drip paintings or Andy Warhol's paintings of Campbell soup cans—over time may be ascribed greater value through changes in the ways that people react to those works. Collectors' perceptions of the value of art are influenced by commentary by critics, acquisitions by museums, aggressive marketing by auction houses, sales tactics by dealers, and purchases by prominent collectors. What few collectors once had any interest in may, over time, become avidly sought after and dearly paid for. The social process through which value is constructed gives art a seductive appeal; collectors are drawn to an object, feel it "speaks to them," and believe their collections have a hole without such a work.

The value of art is not only a product of the social organization of the art world, but is also influenced by social forces external to that world. Prices for art have increased because of the general rate of inflation, the instability of some nations' monetary systems, a growth in the surplus wealth available for investment, and tax laws that encourage the purchase of art for investment purposes.

EXPLAINING ART CRIME

Given its high value, why is not more art stolen or forged? One factor inhibiting art crime is the awe most people feel toward art, an awe reinforced by the way that individuals and institutions in the art world treat works of art. Art is revered, mystified, and ascribed an otherworldly quality by dealers, museum curators, scholars, and collectors. Theft, forgery, and vandalism are made to seem almost sacrilegious. Art crime is also inhibited by the lack of any utilitarian function for most works of art. Thieves prefer to steal things that they can use—money, cars, or at least property that is readily convertible into cash. The uniqueness of most works of art makes them identifiable and thus difficult to dispose of, especially for thieves who lack contacts with fences or shady art dealers.

Despite such obstacles, art crime is common today. Opportunities for one type of art crime, theft, can be examined by using the routine-activities approach, a perspective that sees crime as developing in the social context of everyday activities. This perspective links crime to the presence of suitable targets and motivated offenders and the absence of guardianship. Many artworks are suitable targets for theft because they are small enough to conceal, easy to transport, and valuable. However, another trait makes art an unattractive target: it is not high in liquidity. Indeed, the more valuable the object, the less easy it is to convert into cash. Guardianship refers to the protection of property from thieves. That a thief could steal the *Mona Lisa* from the Louvre in 1911 is astonishing to us today, but security was lax then. Even today, works of art are not always well protected. In 1989, a fourteenth-century Chinese vase valued at more than $500,000 was taken from an acrylic case in Boston's Museum of Fine Arts while the museum was open and guards were on duty. The third component of the routine-activities approach is the motivated offender; even with a suitable target and the absence of guardianship, there must be a motivated thief before a crime will occur. This raises the question of *why* thieves steal art, a question that has several answers.

The Motives for Art Crime

Some thieves hope to sell stolen art to a dealer but have no clear idea about how they will do this before they commit the theft. Other thieves steal on commission, selecting particular works of art and delivering them to someone for a price that was agreed on before the crime. Thieves also steal art with the intention of ransoming it to the owner or the owner's insurance company. Occasionally, thieves steal art just to have it for themselves.

The motives for art theft have an important bearing on the question of what happens to stolen art that is never recovered. Thieves who cannot find an illicit outlet for a well-known work they have stolen may simply destroy it so as not to be caught with the incriminating evidence. Thieves also deposit stolen art in bank vaults until statutes of limitations have expired and they can sell the art without risk of prosecution. Collectors who commission thefts may be content to hang stolen art on their walls and enjoy it in privacy.

Art crimes other than theft also have various motives. Sociologist Jack Katz (1988) suggests that we look at the way that offenders themselves construct a social reality that produces the motive for their crimes. Trying to understand the meaning that art vandals give their acts can help make sense out of what at first seem to be the actions of mad people. Some vandals attack art as a symbol of the social order; others claim that voices commanded them to act. Katz suggests that offenders often impute to objects a power that seduces them into crime.

Fraud is another art crime with several motives. The usual one is profit, but revenge or a sense of gratification at outwitting an opponent can also lead to fraudulent behavior. Forgery is often done for profit, but some artists who have felt mistreated by the art establishment have executed and sold counterfeit works of art to show the world how easy it is to fool critics and dealers.

Justifying Rhetorics and Techniques of Neutralization

People who violate the law often use "justifying rhetorics" to present their actions favorably to others, asserting that their behavior is consistent with commonly accepted values and therefore morally acceptable (Fine, 1983:77). Forgers claim that they have created works as beautiful as those done by the masters, and that art historians who criticize them have repeatedly shown that they cannot tell the authentic from the counterfeit. Grave-looters criticize archaeologists for removing their nation's cultural patrimony to the basements of Western museums, where it often lies neglected for years. Throughout the book, we will see that members of the art world, both those generally considered legitimate and those seen as criminal, use such justifying rhetorics to explain their violations of the law. Often, too, we will find competing rhetorics, as people with different interests argue the correctness of their behavior and the impropriety of those who challenge them.

Justifying rhetorics are closely linked to "techniques of neutralization," culturally available explanations that allow potential offenders to render inoperative the restraining influence of the law (Sykes and Matza, 1957). Because everyone, to some extent, is socialized to regard the law as legitimate, before people can violate the law they must overcome the hold that the law has on them; only then can they avoid moral blame and maintain their self-esteem while committing crime. To do this, potential criminals use culturally available techniques of neutralization to argue that they have no criminal intent and that their behavior is justified in some way. Members of the art world sometimes deny responsibility for their violations of the law; dealers claim that the person from whom they purchased stolen art lied to them about its origin, auctioneers say that announcing that a painting has been sold when it has attracted no bids is common practice in all auction houses, and forgers assert that dealers passed off their "reconstructions" as authentic works. Antiquities dealers deny that their trade in illicit objects injures anyone when they claim that the citizens of source-countries do not appreciate their cultural heritage, and when they argue that the best way to preserve that property is to make sure that it is sold to the people who are most likely to appreciate it, usually well-to-do collectors and museums in the West. Those dealers also "condemn the condemners" when they point to the corruption and inefficiency of government officials who complain about the illegal exportation of objects from their countries. The claim that "everybody is doing it" is also used to make it easier for those in the art world to break the law, as is the frequently heard statement that the laws governing their behavior are ill advised or unnecessary.

The difference between techniques of neutralization and justifying rhetorics is that the techniques are used by potential law violators prior to breaking the law, whereas justifying rhetorics are rationalizations offered to others after the law has been violated. However, the two are closely associated, with justifying rhetorics that have been used in the past being available for use as techniques to neutralize the law in the present. If forgers who have been caught in the past have justified their actions by saying that no one was really hurt when they created aesthetically pleasing works in the style of an Old Master, then artists today who consider forgery can neutralize the law by telling themselves that they will not be hurting anybody if they create a counterfeit work.

THE ORGANIZATION OF ART CRIME

Mary McIntosh (1975) has suggested that criminologists should study the ways that crime is socially organized rather than focusing their attention on the individuals who break the law. Criminologists have repeatedly investigated the ways that criminals differ from noncriminals; they have less frequently examined the ways that social organization generates criminal behavior: how the structure of social relationships produces motives for crime, creates opportunities for crime, and thwarts law enforcement. In this book, we look at art crime as a collective activity rather than studying art thieves or unscrupulous dealers as deviants divorced from the social context of the art world.

Howard Becker has demonstrated that works of art are products of collective action by a network of people whose recurring cooperative activity makes it possible for art to be created. According to Becker (1982:370), "Collective actions and the events they produce are the basic unit of sociological investigation. Social organization consists of the special case in which the same people act together to produce a variety of different events in a recurring way." Becker uses this sociological perspective to examine the process by which artworks are produced through the interaction of artists, gallery owners, museum curators, critics, collectors, and support personnel. In Chapter 1, we use that perspective to look at the production of value for works of art, the way that the social organization of the art world results in some works being revered and valued at millions of dollars, while other works are defined as virtually without aesthetic or financial value. That sociological perspective is also used for another purpose in this book, to look at art crime as a product of the social organization of the art world. Like art itself and the value attached to that art, art crime is the product of collective action, an outcome of interactions and networks established in the art world for legitimate purposes.

Art can be produced by the network of people in the art world because those people share certain conventions, which are understandings embodied in common practice that make recurrent cooperative activity possible. Likewise, conventions in art world transactions—the way that dealers, auction houses, and museums operate, for example—are sometimes conducive to crime. For instance, most antiquities purchased by American museums in recent years have been bought in violation of the export laws of the nations from which the objects came. Nevertheless, museum curators continue to buy antiquities that they know, or should know, have been illegally exported. Conventional transactions between curators and dealers avoid raising questions about the legality of the sale of antiquities. In one interaction between a New York antiquities dealer and "a curator of Oriental antiquities from a major museum west of the Hudson River," the curator picked up a 4,000-year-old bull carved in serpentine that was "virtually unique." The dealer showed the curator photographs of a similar bull in the collection of New York's Metropolitan Museum of Art, a piece less graceful in execution and discolored and pitted because it had been through a fire. A reporter describes the interaction between the dealer and the curator as follows:

Then the curator asked the dealer where he had acquired the piece. From a French dealer, he replied, who had it in turn from a Pakistani. This excited the curator's interest. Pakistan. That might mean the piece came from an Indus Valley site. The

Metropolitan believes its bull came from southern Mesopotamia and is Sumerian. It is known that there was trade between the two cultures across the high central plateaus of what is now Iran.

In what direction had the two bulls gone? Were they from the same culture but carried far apart by trade? Or had the art of one influenced the other? If so, which one had been the source of influence? The discussion ended without any definite opinion being expressed. (Brandt, 1990:92–93)

Prior to leaving, the curator told the dealer that he was interested in the piece but needed to discuss the price with his director and board of trustees. The dealer suggested that the price was negotiable.

The reporter then remarks:

Now, consider the implications of this little scene. For one, the curator in question never once asked the dealer in question whether this marvelous, amazingly preserved, 4,000-year-old treasure had been legally exported from Pakistan. He never asked to know the circumstances of its appearance in the West; he never brought up the legality or even the propriety of acquiring it for his museum.

In fact, this piece *had* to have been smuggled out of Pakistan. That nation's Antiquities Act of 1975 requires an export license for all antiquities and grants them only for the purposes of temporary exhibition abroad, or in accordance with excavation licenses given to legitimate archaeologists, or in exchange for antiquities of a duplicate nature—nothing that pertained to this piece. It is inconceivable that the government of Pakistan would have allowed a piece of this extraordinary quality and rarity to leave the country legally. That was an issue the curator never raised. The only issue for him was price. (Brandt, 1990:93)

Conventions structure interactions between curators and antiquities dealers: price can be negotiated, but likely violations of export restrictions are not mentioned.

The process by which works of art are illegally acquired is socially organized; it involves recurrent patterns of interaction among legitimate and illegitimate members of the art world. The looting of antiquities requires an elaborate, multi-layered network of grave-robbers, middlemen, and dealers. Bands of thieves often commit a series of art thefts from museums, galleries, homes, or churches. The way that these gangs select their targets, organize their thefts, and dispose of their loot is structured systematically. Fraud involves the purchase or sale of art through deception, and deception usually requires organization. Some dealers who accept paintings on consignment fail to pay the owner when they sell the pictures. Those dealers often maintain a gallery as a front, manipulate invoices, and write bad checks to give the victim a sense that the transaction is legitimate. Forgery involves the production of art that is passed off as a work executed by someone else.

This crime typically requires a studio, materials to produce the counterfeit work, and interaction between the forger and a dealer who can sell the object.

An elaborate network is often used to distribute forged and stolen art. That network may be used to smuggle illegally exported antiquities or stolen art from one country to another. Organized crime gangs such as the Mafia and international drug cartels have reportedly engaged in such smuggling. Networks are also used to sell stolen or forged art; fences, shady dealers, and unscrupulous collectors are part of such networks.

Understanding the way that art crime is organized and the way it is related to the organization of the legitimate art world is important for developing policies to reduce art crime. Knowing that most dealers and museums avoid purchasing art that they know is stolen, both because they will not have title to such works and because they will be unable to resell or display it, IFAR in 1979 established a newsletter to publicize stolen art. The resulting publicity for stolen art, along with the publicity given to stolen art by Interpol, has probably deterred some thieves and has certainly led to the recovery of much stolen art. The last chapter of this book examines policies for curbing theft, fraud, forgery, and vandalism that can be derived from what we know about the social organization of art crime.

❧ *One* ❧

The Value of Art

Art critic Robert Hughes has observed that art theft and the high price of art are both "part of the general fetishization of works of art that has taken place in society, particularly in America. Art is no longer priceless, it is priceful. We overvalue art, and then we're surprised when the chalices are stolen" (cited in Golden, 1989:34). Only art that is valuable is worth stealing, smuggling, and forging. Fraud is committed only if it will yield a profit, and vandalism attracts attention only if the target is valuable. Art crime is thus closely associated with the price of art.

Art prices were relatively stable between the two world wars, but they began to rise in the 1950s. Prices for Pablo Picasso's works were thirty-seven times higher in 1969 than in 1951, and prices for Marc Chagall's works rose fiftyfold over that period (Myers, 1983). The increase in the price of art was especially dramatic after 1983, with prices peaking between 1987 and 1990 and then falling somewhat after 1990. Picasso's *Yo Picasso* sold at auction in 1989 for $47.9 million, twice the pre-auction estimate and eight times what it sold for in 1981. Jasper Johns's *False Start* sold in 1960 for $3,150; in 1988, it brought $17.5 million at auction. From 1975 until the late 1980s, works by the following artists recorded these price increases: Jackson Pollock, 750 percent; Pierre-Auguste Renoir, 490 percent; Claude Monet, 440 percent; Edgar Degas, 350 percent; Camille Pissarro, 220 percent; and Alfred Sisley, 220 percent (Duthy, 1988a, 1989b). Even works by more obscure painters have skyrocketed: from 1975 to 1988, prices for watercolors by English artist Thomas Girtin increased by 310 percent, prices for paintings by Swedish artist Bruno Liljefors rose by 340 percent, and prices for works by Scotland's J. D. Fergusson appreciated by 460 percent (Duthy, 1988b, 1989a, 1989c).

THE MEANING OF VALUE

Value typically refers to economic value, but art also has cultural value. This is nicely expressed by Paul M. Bator (1981:28) as follows:

[I]n a variety of complex ways, the art of a society is both a manifestation and a mirror of its culture, and . . . the existence and awareness of a common culture is intimately tied to the existence and awareness of a sense of community. The national artistic patrimony is therefore closely linked to the process of education: the study of a nation's art is part of the process through which citizens learn who they are. . . . A perception of a common culture and common past is one way of learning that we are part of a community, that we belong to one another in a special way.

In Mexico, relics of the past have served the important function of forging a nation out of people with European and Indian heritages. The theft of the fifteenth-century painting *Madonna of the Graces* from a church in Alanno, Italy, in the early 1980s had a devastating effect on the cultural identity of the 3,700 townspeople because of the painting's association with community rituals, miraculous cures, and local legends; that impact was far more important than the economic loss from the theft (Suro, 1987:48). The theft from a Thai temple of a lintel depicting the creation of the universe left only a sculpture showing the destruction of the universe; a spokesperson for the Thais remarked, "Symbolically, it's quite bad to have the destruction there and the creation gone" (cited in Wilkerson, 1988:14).

The cultural value of a work of art may be quite different from its financial value. Crimes such as the defacement of Stonehenge or the defilement of a Native American grave site harm cultural property of great significance, even if they result in little economic loss. An icon stolen from a Greek Orthodox church in Queens, New York, in 1991 was returned by the thieves after they had stripped from it adornments of gold, silver, and jewels valued at more than $800,000; despite that loss, the clergy and parishioners were overjoyed at getting back their precious icon of St. Irene, a unifying symbol for the congregation.

The financial value of art depends more on a shared belief in its value than on the law of supply and demand. If the public's belief in the value of art weakens, prices can plunge. Likewise, a drop in art prices can reduce public confidence in the art market. Because even small losses of value can set off a downward spiral in public confidence, auction houses and dealers have developed strategies to maintain confidence that prices will continue to increase.

Contrary to the basic principle of supply and demand, at a constant level of demand, increases in the supply of art do not seem to lower prices. In fact, flooding the market with "great art" is more likely to *raise* prices by triggering a highly publicized competition among collectors (Burnham, 1975:208). Paradoxically, at that same constant level of demand, a reduced supply of art might also increase prices by encouraging collectors to bid avidly for the few works that are offered for sale.

The economic value of a work of art is the price for which it can be sold at auction or to a gallery, collector, or museum; it might also be equated with its appraised value, an amount agreed to by an insurance company or art expert. Economic value reflects in part the historical and cultural importance of a work, but other factors that influence its value include the following: current fashions in art; perceptions of how good an investment art is at a particular time; dealers' and auction houses' promotional efforts; the artist's reputation; the scarcity of works of a similar type by the same artist; the work's provenance or "biography"; and the piece's size, medium, subject matter, age, and condition. The economic value of a work of art thus does not rest exclusively, or even primarily, on its intrinsic "quality," but is instead influenced by a multitude of factors extrinsic to the work itself.

The value of art is the product of a three-part social process. First, the artist, interacting with other members of the art world, produces an object. Cultural beliefs in the special creative abilities of the artist support the idea of artistic reputation, an important determinant of value. Second, individual and institutional collectors influence value by what they are willing to pay for art. The reasons that collectors buy art are thus important to understanding the process through which the value of art is socially constructed. Third, a distributional network joins artists and collectors. Dealers and auction houses play an obvious role in this network, but so too do such scholars as archaeologists, art critics, art historians, and biographers, for their work shapes perceptions of value held by both collectors and artists.

ARTISTS AND VALUE

Is it a Rembrandt? Or is it a Drost? Those questions about *The Polish Rider,* a seventeenth-century Dutch painting that hangs in New York's Frick Museum, have been hotly debated (Bailey, 1990). Is it not the same painting, regardless of who painted it? In a real sense, it is not, for aesthetic response and economic value are significantly influenced by the artist to whom a painting is attributed.

The Emergence of the Artist as Creative Genius

Before artists signed their works, art was valued more for what it was than for who created it. Since the Middle Ages, the rise of individualism in the West has given birth to the idea that the artist is a creative genius. The absence of an individual to whom to attribute a piece of art does not mean that it has no value; the high prices paid for Native American pottery, pre-Columbian statues, and ancient Greek sculptures indicate that great value is often attached to unattributed works. Nevertheless, the value of Western fine arts produced since the Middle Ages is significantly influenced by attribution to specific artists.

Out of the Renaissance came the idea that art, rather than being the product of skilled artisans, was the product of creative geniuses, individuals who somehow transcended tradition to produce unique works. During the fifteenth century, contracts between patrons and artists began to change from specifying the quality of the materials that artists would use to demanding that artists use their special skills to produce works of "unique character and invaluable quality" (Becker, 1982:15). Artists were increasingly seen as gifted people capable of creating works of great beauty that expressed profound human emotions and values. The idea of reputation implied that all of an artist's works, but none that the artist did not create, should be included in the body of work on which the artist's reputation was based, because that body of work revealed the artist's essential qualities and worth (Becker, 1982:352–353). Reputation thus became "free floating," or attached to anything produced by an artist; even slight works by major artists such as Picasso "are almost like minor relics of a saint" (Burnham, 1975:73). Picasso reportedly once signed a napkin in a restaurant and handed it to a young artist, telling her "Don't let it go too cheap."

Contrary to the view that socially isolated creative geniuses produce art is Becker's sociological insight that artistic production is very much a collective activity. Artists rely on the manufacturers of canvas and paint for their supplies. They depend on one another to develop and sustain traditions that give their own work meaning. Critics develop theories of art and criteria for identifying good art, thereby providing rationales for the artist's work. Artists also depend on galleries and museums for exhibition space, and on dealers, museums, collectors, and the government for financial support.

Authenticity, Reputation, and Value

Because scholars and critics evaluate artworks in the context of an artist's entire body of work, and because artists' reputations depend on creations that express their special gifts, the art world strives to establish what is and what is not the product of a particular artist. Attribution and authenticity are of great significance to collectors, dealers, museums, critics, and scholars, because their judgments are affected not only by the quality of a work but also by the identity of the person who produced it. Fakes that masquerade as the works of well-known artists are devalued, even if they have greater aesthetic merit than some pieces executed by the original artist. Not only are the fakes themselves denigrated, but sometimes even authentic pieces by the artist whose work they pretend to be are reduced in value. For example, prices for graphic works by Dali and Chagall have been depressed by the widespread faking of their art.

Critic John Berger claims that a painting's value is linked to its authenticity or proper attribution and to its provenance or documented "line of descent." The prevailing view in the art world is, "It is authentic and therefore it is beautiful" (Berger, 1972:21). Thus, the fourteen pages devoted to Leonardo da Vinci's *Virgin on the Rocks* in the catalogue of the National Gallery of Art in Washington, D.C., discuss not the aesthetics or meaning of the work, but rather questions about who commissioned it, legal disputes over its ownership, the date it was executed, and so on. The catalogue seems intent on showing that the picture is genuine and that a nearly identical work in the Louvre is a replica. *Both are originals. The church/patron rejected his first painting and he redid it.*

Fine arts are evaluated in terms of the artist who produced the work. If an artist with a first-rate reputation paints something as good as his or her best work but signs a pseudonym, that work will not command the same price nor even evoke the same emotional response as will works signed with the artist's real name. Museum visitors often look first at the card identifying the artist before stepping back to appreciate the work. Their appreciation is influenced by their knowledge of the artist and the prices the artist's works command in the marketplace. Vincent van Gogh's celebrity status as a tortured genius neglected by his contemporaries has pushed the prices for his paintings far above the aesthetic value most critics and scholars place on his works.

If, as has happened in recent years with some paintings once thought to be by Rembrandt, a work of art is reattributed to another artist, is the picture's aesthetic value any less than prior to reattribution? The work of art remains intrinsically the same, but its economic value will be less. The difference is due to the reputation of the artist said to have executed the work. For example, consider

Rubens's "Daniel in the Lions' Den," which was auctioned in 1882 for 1,680 pounds by Christie's London, then resold in 1885 for 2,520 pounds. In 1963, having been attributed in the meantime to Jacob Jordaens, it was auctioned for a mere 500 pounds; but in 1965, now acknowledged as a school piece by Rubens, it was acquired by the Metropolitan Museum of Art in New York for 178,600 pounds. (Frey and Pommerehne, 1989:398)

Because reattribution can have such a dramatic effect on market value, art historians and critics have sometimes been pressured not to reattribute works to less-renowned artists, and museums have occasionally rejected or ignored reattributions by even highly esteemed scholars.

Establishing and Maintaining Reputation

Just as art itself is the product of collective activity in the art world, so too are artists' reputations the result of collective activity. Art historians and critics try to determine which works were actually executed by an artist so that they can make judgments about the artist's reputation. Dealers make similar judgments about reputation, as well as ratifying decisions made by art historians and critics, when they decide what prices to ask for works attributed to an artist. The prices paid by collectors and museums reflect both their judgments about attribution and reputation and their acceptance of judgments by art historians, critics, dealers, and other collectors and museums.

In considering why some artists are popular and financially successful and others are not, dealer John Bernard Myers (1983:157) remarked that some artists simply do not learn to "play the game of being an artist." They may be indifferent to art critics, museum curators, and individual collectors, and they may not socialize easily with others in the art world. Unsuccessful artists often prefer to be left alone and let their art speak for itself. Successful artists typically have a flair for making themselves into celebrities who attract attention to themselves and their art. They actively participate in the social process that produces reputation.

In their study of British and American painter-etchers from 1880 to 1940, sociologists Gladys Engel Lang and Kurt Lang examine the building and survival of artistic reputation, which they define as a socially constructed expression of "a shared belief about the probity, generosity, ability, achievement, etc., of a known person" (Lang and Lang, 1990:xii). Claiming that there are more good and great artists than will be recognized as such over time, the Langs view an artist's reputation as the product of *recognition*, or the esteem in which the artist is held by others in the same art world, and *renown*, or the recognition of the artist's work beyond the limited art world of which he or she is a part. Once established, reputation feeds on itself, with high prices bringing attention that turns the artist into a persona; critics and dealers are essential to the development of that renown. Celebrity status further increases public interest and prices, which in turn attract investors and people who hope to become publicly known as astute collectors. The Langs show that the durability of an artist's reputation depends on four factors:

1. *Lifetime initiatives.* This involves an artist's efforts to produce and pre-serve enough work to attract dealers, collectors, curators, and art histori-ans. For a reputation to last, there must be a critical mass of work and a substantial clientele. Future identification of an artist's work is made easier if the artist maintains records of his or her output and the technical details involved in producing the works. Providing for the custodianship of the artist's output, as by donating impressions of prints to libraries or museums, also facilitates future identification of the work.

2. *Survivors.* Reputations are more likely to endure if the artists have relatives or acquaintances who have an emotional or financial stake in perpetuating that reputation. After the artist's death, those individuals can prepare a catalogue or exhibit or donate a collection to a museum.

3. *Linkages in memory.* Reputations are more likely to persist if an artist has an association with a school, period, region, important artistic or literary circle, or has proximity to a cultural or political elite that gives the artist visibility after death. An association with a major artist can create a "halo effect" that helps ensure an artist's reputation.

4. *Figures in a landscape.* Artists may stand out if their names are associated with a controversy, geographic position, historical coincidence, or ideology.

Artists' reputations do not, then, rest solely on the intrinsic quality of the works they produce, but are instead the outcome of social interaction among artists, others in the art world, and people in the larger society.

COLLECTORS OF ART

In addition to the artist, both individual and institutional collectors play important roles in determining the value of art. If no one wants to buy a work of art at any price, it has no market value. If there is much demand for artworks that are in short supply, market value will be high and apt to appreciate over time. An understanding of the value of art thus requires attention to the various reasons that institutions and individuals buy art.

Collecting as an Expressive Activity

Collecting can be understood as an expressive activity, one that is enjoyed as an end in itself. One group of behavioral scientists concluded from their research that collecting is a kind of addiction, a thrill-seeking behavior that produces exhilaration at finding new objects, craving and loss of control, release from other feelings, and reassurance through the repeated ritual of acquisition. Collectors enjoy competing with one another for desirable pieces and "winning" by acquiring things that others also want. The act of building a collection legitimates acquisitiveness by giving it a noble purpose such as the preservation of art or the development of knowledge. For the collector, this process transforms objects into "sacred icons," with the place where the collection is kept sometimes being imbued with a quasi-religious aura (Belk et al., 1988).

Collectors enjoy making fine distinctions among similar objects and acting as caretakers to their collections. They develop their own personal categories of what they want to collect, refine and expand those categories over time, and enjoy acquiring objects that fit those categories. They define what is worth having in a particular category in terms of quality and authenticity; weakly executed paintings or forgeries have no place in most collections (Alsop, 1982:71–76).

Part of the appeal of building a collection is the satisfaction of completing a gestalt, a unitary and cohesive set of items in which each forms a part of the whole. Collectors enjoy adding to their collections new items that "fit" with what they already have. In a sense, a collection has an aesthetic appeal as a collection, a beauty that is more than the sum of its parts. Millionaire Walter Annenberg expressed this when he tried to buy van Gogh's *Sunflowers* in 1987. The painting was eventually sold to a Japanese corporation for $39.9 million, with Annenberg stopping his bidding when the price reached $20 million. He later said he had wanted to add the painting to his collection, which included van Gogh's *La Berceuse,* because the artist had once written to his brother Theo that he hoped that someday *La Berceuse* would hang in a museum with one of his paintings of sunflowers on either side (Hoving, 1987:25).

Art collectors see their possessions as extensions of their selves, as a way to measure and present themselves to the world. In fact, most people, not just art collectors, see their possessions as material expressions of their ideal selves, as indicators of the kinds of people they want to be. The things they see as special form a "map of their self-image and personal history and of what they think is important in their lives" (Goleman, 1987:C6). Possessions become a way for people to differentiate themselves from others and assure themselves of their uniqueness. Not surprisingly, collectors often worry about what will happen to their collections when they die.

In a survey of eighty-two families, Csikszentmihalyi and Rochberg-Halton (1981) found that visual art was mentioned second most frequently after furniture as the kind of objects most significant in the lives of the respondents. Defining visual art as any two-dimensional representation other than a photograph, the researchers concluded that the bulk of significations carried by visual "works of art" is not connected to aesthetic values and experiences but refers to the immediate life history of their owners: reminding them of relatives and friends or of past events. People pay particular attention to pictures in their home because in doing so they relive memorable occasions and pleasing relationships. Of course, the interesting question is why pictures rather than appliances, let us say, or other things, serve this purpose so frequently. Perhaps something peculiar to a work of visual art enhances these experiences. The qualities invested by painters in their work, the order they bring to their paintings, presumably act as catalysts for attracting and directing the viewer's attention toward pleasant memories. Or, possibly, appropriate moods and sentiments are released because of the cultural conventions attributed to art. (Csikszentmihalyi and Rochberg-Halton, 1981:65)

The strength of art collectors' attachments to their collections is indicated by the grief they typically experience after the loss of a part of their collection through theft or arson. Their grief usually goes well beyond their financial losses, which are often covered by insurance, suggesting that their art has deep personal significance.

Collecting for Aesthetic Reasons

There are aesthetic reasons to collect art. Bonnie Burnham (1975) suggests that some collectors want to enjoy art freely, unimpeded by obstacles and distractions that reduce a museum-goer's enjoyment of art: crowds that obscure paintings, uncomfortable benches, guards who try to keep viewers away from the art, and security measures such as glass covering oil paintings and railings surrounding sculptures.

More fundamentally, the art itself is aesthetically appealing; people like what they collect, and they collect what they like. Walter Annenberg describes the aesthetic appeal of art, which he acknowledges also has investment value, as follows: "I sold stock to buy the Picasso and these other things because they're much better to look at than securities in a box" (cited in Glueck, 1990:C13). He also comments, "I must have quality. An interest in art grows in you and it takes over. My wife and I set out to get things that we genuinely loved and respected and wanted to live with" (cited in Glueck, 1990:C13). Japanese industrialist Ryoei Saito spent a total of $160.6 million for two paintings, Renoir's *At the Moulin de la Galette* and van Gogh's *Portrait of Dr. Gachet,* in a three-day period in 1990. Certainly, those purchases were partly for investment purposes, but Saito also had an aesthetic reason for buying the pictures. He said that he "fell in love" with the van Gogh when he saw it in a museum two years before, and when he learned it was to be sold, he told a dealer, "Make sure you get it. I must have that painting no matter what" (cited in Reif, 1990b:C28). In 1991, he expressed a desire to be buried with the paintings, but recanted following public outrage that the pictures would thus be lost to the world forever.

One eminent American art collector, Dr. Albert C. Barnes, described the aesthetic appeal of collecting as follows in a 1915 paper:

> What are some of the pleasures? The least is the mere possession, the best, the joy that one can feel but not express to others; between these two extremes are pleasures that may be compared to the notes of a piano, limited in what can be produced only by the performer's skill and knowledge. Good paintings are more satisfying companions than the best of books and infinitely more so than most very nice people. I can talk, without speaking, to Cézanne, Prendergast, Daumier, Renoir, and they talk to me in kind. I can criticize them and take, without offense, the refutation which comes silently but powerfully when I learn, months later, what they mean and not what I thought they meant. That is one of the joys of a collection, the elasticity with which paintings stretch to the beholder's personal vision which they progressively develop. And that is universal, for a painting is justly proportionate to what a man thinks he sees in it. As a substitute for other pursuits, collecting, living with, and studying good paintings—the enthusiast believes—offers greater interest, variety, and satisfaction than any other pleasure or work a man could select. (cited in Greenfeld, 1987:53–54)

Collecting as Conspicuous Consumption

John Berger (1972:139) has said that oil painting between 1500 and 1900 "before it was anything else, was a celebration of private property." Prior to 1900, oil paintings often depicted such possessions of the picture's owner as a house, land, and furnishings. Some paintings portrayed the owner's ancestors, a way of claiming high social standing by declaring one's lineage. The oil paintings themselves were unique objects that could be owned in a way that other art forms such as poems, music, or drama could not be. Paintings thus conveyed an owner's social status to others who viewed the works. When mechanical reproduction of original works of art became possible, the original pieces took on even greater social meaning, becoming important less for what they portrayed than for the fact that they were original (Berger, 1972).

An important factor in the birth of art collecting in the West was the rise of a wealthy merchant class interested in acquiring the trappings of the well-to-do and speculating in art. Those motives gave rise to a market for art during the Renaissance, were important again in the late eighteenth century, and were critical to the appreciating value of Impressionist works in the twentieth century. Impressionist art was at first rejected by the Royal

Academy of Paris because of its entrenched ideology about what constituted good art and because it did not have the capacity to cope with the big increase in the numbers of artists working in France during the late nineteenth century. The rise of a wealthy merchant class looking for art to buy and the large supply of paintings eventually led to a system that brought demand and supply together, a system that included dealers who sold the paintings and critics who legitimated the style of Impressionism (White and White, 1965; Wolff, 1981).

In *The Theory of the Leisure Class*, Thorstein Veblen (1934) argued that social standing can be enhanced through *conspicuous consumption*, the purchase of items that are publicly displayed so as to attract the attention and awe of others. Acquiring the material possessions associated with an upper-class cultural style can help the upwardly mobile establish that they belong in that higher social position (DiMaggio and Useem, 1978). Art is well suited to act as a symbol of status: it is often expensive, rare, and old, and it attracts the attention of high-status people (Csikszentmihalyi and Rochberg-Halton, 1981:30). One well-known collector acknowledges the status-striving motive for collecting art, saying "You bet I'm a social climber, and I'd rather use art to climb with than anything else" (Robert Scull, cited in Greenfeld, 1987:41). Abstract Expressionist artist Mark Rothko was hostile toward collectors for this very reason; he thought they had the instinct of vultures, took pleasure in mere possession rather than aesthetic appreciation of art, had a strong need to be *au courant*, were capricious, exploited artists to enrich themselves through the resale of works, and were too concerned with social climbing. Rothko also believed that many collectors saw themselves as superior to the artists whose works they bought, were self-satisfied because of their wealth, and knew little about art (Myers, 1983).

Because the price of art sold at auction is widely publicized, along with the name of the buyer if that person so desires, public attention and esteem can be gained by buying art at auction. After purchasing a Gauguin painting for $180,000 at a 1957 New York auction, Basil Goulandris told a Parisian auctioneer, "Having that picture knocked down to me has made my name known everywhere. . . . In terms of advertising, the articles the press has published about me are worth easily double the sum I spent that afternoon" (cited in Tomkins, 1988:46). Commenting on art auctions, one gallery owner remarked, "Where else can somebody spend ten million dollars and make it public without seeming totally vulgar?" (cited in Tomkins, 1988:60). That dealer also remarked that he knew people who had said they wanted to spend a million dollars on a painting, and it did not especially matter which one. An auctioneer once urged the audience to raise a bid up from just below $100,000 by saying, "Come on, make it a hundred thousand, it'll sound better when you tell your friends" (cited in McGill, 1986b:15). In 1989, Japanese real-estate magnate Tomonori Tsurumaki did something much like that, buying Picasso's *Pierette's Wedding* for $51.3 million with a telephone bid that he made in the middle of a party he was giving for five hundred guests at a Tokyo hotel. Two years earlier, Japan's Yasuda Fire and Marine Insurance Company paid $39.9 million for van Gogh's *Sunflowers* in order to attract world attention to the company's one-hundredth anniversary.

Auction sales receive much publicity, but most art is sold privately, and many buyers try to avoid publicity out of fear of attracting thieves. For those collectors, consumption is certainly not conspicuous. Once they own a work of art, visitors to their homes may be impressed, but it is questionable whether they spend hundreds of thousands of dollars on art solely to gain the esteem of that small, though significant, group.

Collecting as Investment

Many collectors hope to gain financially when they sell or donate their art. As one buyer remarked at a 1989 New York auction, "Art is just a very secure investment. I don't think anyone here is bidding because they have emotional or intellectual ties to the art. It's money making more money" (cited in Blowen, 1989:88). Indeed, one of the appealing aspects of investing in art is the challenge of making an astute acquisition. Collecting involves deal-making and gamesmanship, a competition with other collectors for increasingly scarce artworks and a satisfaction at winning that contest. Calvin Tomkins has described art collectors in the 1980s as

made up in large part of men and women who have struck it rich in real estate, public relations, corporate takeovers, and other high-risk sectors of the economy. These people are drawn to contemporary-art buying for many of the same reasons that they are drawn to real estate or corporate takeovers: they like to take chances, to play their hunches, to operate in the fast lane. (Tomkins, 1987:114)

The rapid acceleration in art prices during the 1980s was attributable in part to "the terror of the closing door," the then-common perception that great art, which would provide the most secure investment, was diminishing in availability. As a result, some collectors felt a sense of urgency in acquiring the few fine works that were offered at auction. In 1989, the purchases of an American eighteenth-century desk-bookcase for $12.1 million and a German teddy bear from the 1920s for $88,000 were attributed to "auction fever," a determination by buyers to acquire such items at any price; combined with competition from other bidders, that determination pushed prices far beyond pre-sale estimates for the pieces (Reif, 1990c). Such high prices, in turn, fueled the public's belief in the investment value of art.

An important factor in the upsurge of interest in investing in art during the 1980s was the 1983 purchase of Sotheby's auction house by A. Alfred Taubman, a real-estate magnate who aggressively recruited new art collectors. Rather than selling to dealers, as Sotheby's traditionally had done, Taubman aimed the house's sales directly at the public. The demonstrated ease with which art could be sold at auction convinced buyers that art could be resold at a profit after a short time, in contrast to the past when the owners of art might have to wait years to find a buyer.

Federal tax laws have had an enormous influence on the behavior of collectors, and consequently on the price of art. Between 1952 and 1986, Americans could donate art to museums or other nonprofit institutions such as universities and claim a federal tax deduction based on the market value of the art at the time they donated it, even if that amount was significantly more than they had originally paid. Museums provided appraisals of the value of the donated art, and collectors were allowed to hold on to their donations until they died. The law induced wealthy collectors to donate art they might have been holding on to because of appreciating values, and it encouraged more well-to-do people to collect art, which was given liquidity by the tax law. By drawing more collectors into the market, competition for art increased and so did prices.

About 85 percent of the objects in a typical American museum collection have been donated (Rasky, 1990). Until 1986, federal tax law encouraged the transfer of artistic property from the private collectors to public institutions, a policy that led curators to cultivate the tastes of the wealthy and then encourage them to donate their collections to the museum. By allowing less liberal deductions for donations to museums, the 1986 Tax Reform Act curtailed such giving. Because art prices had then reached a high level, auction houses offered collectors an outlet for their art that was more lucrative than the donation of that art to nonprofit institutions. Sellers had to pay capital gains taxes on the profits from the sale of art that had appreciated in value, but even then they made handsome profits. After the 1986 tax law revision, museums that had been counting on adding certain paintings to their permanent collections, in some cases because those works had long been on loan to the museum by the owner, were disappointed when the owner instead sold the paintings at auction.

Collector John Whitney Payson, who announced in 1987 that he was going to sell van Gogh's *Irises,* which had been on loan for ten years to Maine's Westbrook College, gives the following example of the implications of the 1986 tax law for donors. A painting bought for $10,000 that appreciated in value over time to $100,000 would have brought him a $50,000 tax savings had he donated it to a museum prior to the 1986 change, but that same donation would only have netted him a tax benefit of $2,100 after the tax law revision. Before the change in the law, donors could deduct the appreciated market value of a work of art; after the revision, they could only deduct the original purchase price. In addition, tax rates had been reduced over time, so the percentage of the lower value (the original purchase price) that could be deducted was also lower. For wealthy collectors, large donations were also subjected to an alternative minimum tax, requiring them to list the appreciated value of the work they donated as if they had sold it at auction, and then pay a minimum 21 percent tax on the market value of the gift. The 1986 law did not permit collectors to take substantial deductions for their donations until they died, causing some of them to delay their promised gifts to museums. Overall, the 1986 law provided strong disincentives to donate art to museums and made it more profitable for collectors to sell their art at auction, even after they paid the required tax on the difference between the sale price and the original purchase price. However, some observers claimed that the increased number of sales at auction was less a result of the new tax law than it was a result of the higher prices that collectors could realize at auction.

Donations to art museums did drop significantly after the 1986 federal tax code revision, falling by 63 percent from 1986 to 1988 (Glueck, 1989; Rasky, 1990). However, donors were aware of the impending tax law revision, and so they may have donated objects in 1986 that they otherwise would have donated a few years later. That would have inflated the number of donations in 1986 and reduced giving over the next few years, thereby exaggerating the impact of the law on donations. On the other hand, a spokesperson for New York's Metropolitan Museum of Art has suggested that matters might have been even worse than the statistics indicate, because most of the donations made to that museum after the 1986 tax law revision were the result of long-term commitments that collectors honored despite the reduced financial advantage to themselves. Over time, fewer such commitments to donate art might be made.

Because of the decline in donations due to the 1986 tax law, museum officials argued that only further tax revision that gave collectors an incentive to donate art could revive the flow of art to American museums and stop the flight of important works to foreign countries. Reacting to pressure from museums, universities, and some legislators, Congress enacted a one-year change for 1991, later extended for the first six months of 1992, that again allowed donors to take tax deductions based on current appraised market value for art they donated to nonprofit institutions. The effect of that change was a substantial increase in donations; for instance, in 1990 New York's Metropolitan Museum of Art received $9 million worth of art from 156 donors, but in 1991 it received $40 million worth of art from 285 donors (Vogel, 1992a). In 1993, President Clinton signed into law a tax code revision that once again allowed donors to deduct the full current market value of major gifts to nonprofit institutions.

Japanese tax laws discourage individual ownership of art. The top tax rate on personal income is 85 percent, estate taxes are high, there is a large tax on most donations to museums, and so there is no tax advantage to donating art. As a result, most collecting of expensive art in Japan is not by individuals but rather by corporations that buy art and either display it in their own museums or lend it to public institutions. Those corporations regard their art collections as valuable assets that will appreciate over time and that can be liquidated at a profit if necessary (Chira, 1987; Woodruff, 1988).

Economic trends in Japan, the United States, and elsewhere have produced new wealth that has been used to buy art. Corporate mergers and real-estate transactions have freed funds for the purchase of important works of art at unheard of prices. One art critic claims that the crucial people in the booming art market of the 1980s were

global investors in leisure: Japanese, Australian and German tycoons, entrepreneurs, middlemen and women of all kinds with a talent for manipulating that scene, promoting full-blown reputations overnight and dealing with the rise and fall of the art market in the commercial terms of any other market, say, soybeans or cotton. (Taylor, 1989b:86)

Recent increases in the standard of living of the well-to-do residents of industrial nations have outstripped the supply of desirable luxury goods such as great art, and so the price of those things has risen even faster than the cost of living (Burnham, 1975:228). One economist comments on rising art prices as follows: "In the 70's, you would have blamed this on inflation, saying people were buying art as a hedge against inflation. In the 80's, we haven't had any real inflation. I think you have to say it is all due to the remarkable creation of new wealth" (cited in Reif, 1987:C18). Between 1963 and 1989, wealth became increasingly concentrated at the top of the American class system, with the wealthiest 1 percent of households controlling 37 percent of the nation's wealth by 1989 (Magnusson, 1986; Nasar,

1992). In 1988, there were well over a million millionaires in the United States, although most of them did not spend large sums of money on art. Sotheby's director Alexander Gregory has observed, "The upper echelons of the art market consist of a few dozen people. They're not affected by the financial market in the way ordinary people are because they function on a totally different scale" (cited in Taylor, 1987:54).

The varying economic fortunes of nations influence the international flow of art, with art traditionally moving to prosperous nations that have generated the surplus wealth to purchase art and that believe that art is a good investment. Art moved to the United States between 1880 and 1914 and again in the 1920s and 1930s (Reif, 1990a). In the mid-1970s, when the price of oil was high and oil-producing countries were making great profits, Arabs were prominent at Western auction houses. In the late 1960s and early 1970s, the Japanese bought much Western art, but in 1974 the oil crisis slowed their buying activity significantly. With the success of the Japanese economy and the highly favorable position of the yen on the international currency market—it more than doubled relative to the dollar between 1985 and 1990—Japanese collectors returned to the art market in a big way in the 1980s (McGill, 1986c).

When investors believe that certain forms of investment, such as stocks and bonds, will yield low or unpredictable returns, they seek other ways to invest their money. During the 1980s they often turned to art, and the price of some types of art—particularly modern art (produced between 1900 and 1950), Impressionist art, and contemporary art (produced after 1945)—rose dramatically. Omitting art offered at auction that did not sell, Salomon Brothers (cited in Elsworth, 1990:F4) reports the following compound annual rates of return over the ten years ending June 1, 1990:

Modern art	24.1%
Impressionist art	23.7%
Contemporary art	21.6%
Stocks	17.3%
Bonds	12.6%
Old Masters	12.3%
Coins	7.3%
Diamonds	6.4%
Housing	4.7%
Gold	-4.3%

Despite this recent trend, experts have questioned the long-term investment value of art. According to Citibank vice-president Stewart Clifford, "For a person who isn't passionate about collecting art, we would say your return on investment would be better elsewhere" (cited in Bender, 1985:F27). A. Alfred Taubman, chairman of Sotheby's Holdings Inc., agrees: "I don't believe in reports that show how art is going up against some other investment. I don't believe you should collect on that basis" (cited in Bender, 1985:F27). Lawrence Malkin claims that even if a buyer gets into the art market when prices are low, long-term profitability is usually modest. Because of compound interest, he says that government bonds are actually a better investment than art, citing the following example:

In 1754 the king of Saxony paid 17,000 ducats (worth £8,500 pounds in the currency of the day) for Raphael's "Sistine Madonna," then the highest price ever paid for a picture. In the unlikely event that it came on the market today, the auctioneer would probably start bidding at about $50 million, where van Gogh's "Irises" left off. Even $100 million would be far below the yield on government bonds. . . . Buying and holding government securities would have left you about *thirty* times better off in real terms than would investing in art. (Malkin, 1989b:166, 168)

When the British Rail Pension Fund in 1989 sold twenty-five works of art in which it had invested between 1974 and 1981, it received about ten times what the works had originally cost, an annual return of 12 percent. Many of the works were Impressionist paintings, which had appreciated dramatically, but other pieces had increased little in value. In fact, the fund's manager said that once inflation, forgone dividends, and the costs of the transactions were calculated, the fund's entire art portfolio had increased in value by only 3 percent a year, a rate of return less than for stocks and little better than real estate (Malkin, 1989b:169).

Economists have demonstrated that art is not an especially good investment. One study of the price performance of fifteen hundred paintings between 1780 and 1970 concluded that older pictures had a long-term rate of return only half that of common stocks; the rate of return for more recent pictures was about the same as for common stocks (Anderson, 1974). A study of 1,198 transactions between 1635 and 1987 found that the median rate of return on paintings was 1.5 percent per year, half of the real rate of return for government securities over the same period. Thus, investing in paintings rather than securities would have produced a real annual opportunity loss of 1.5 percent. In neither the 1635–1949 period nor the 1950–1987 period did paintings yield a real annual rate of return as high as government securities. The profitability of investing in paintings was not significantly greater in the later period than in the earlier one, but the high rate of inflation after 1950 meant that the attractiveness of paintings relative to government securities was greater in the later period; that may account for the erroneous perception that paintings have been better investments than other financial assets over the past few decades. This study confirms the results of earlier research by economists: "Investments in paintings are not financially lucrative. They yield a smaller real rate of return and are exposed to higher financial risk than investments in financial assets" (Frey and Pommerehne, 1989:405). Economist William D. Grampp (1989) points out that not only is the average long-term return on art relatively small, but the vast majority of art that people buy—especially contemporary art—eventually becomes worthless, in the sense that it has no resale value at all.

Despite this evidence, the public continues to believe that art is a good investment. In part, this is because people ignore or underestimate the cost of buying and selling art; the effects of inflation and compound interest; the risk of having a work of art reattributed or declared a forgery; the chance that a work of art may be destroyed by fire, stolen, or vandalized; and the money they must spend to insure, maintain, and restore art. Popular faith in the investment value of art is strengthened by the extensive media coverage of the record prices paid for famous paintings sold at auction. Auction houses focus press attention on their sale of first-rate paintings by celebrated artists such as van Gogh and Picasso, neglecting to mention that they will not accept for sale some lesser works of art. They also ignore the relatively modest increases in value for certain schools of art. For instance, Old Masters paintings showed an average annual rate of increase in value of 9.1 percent from June 1, 1974, to June 1, 1984, compared to an average increase of 7.9 percent in the Consumer Price Index over that period. During that decade, both rare coins and United States stamps appreciated in value faster than Old Masters paintings (Bender, 1985).

Even though it is not accurate, the perception that art is a good investment has important consequences. It leads more people to pay attention to the art world and thus broadens the audience for art, bringing into the market more buyers who are able to invest relatively small amounts. As the cost of works by well-known artists escalates, the desire to invest in art causes less wealthy collectors to buy works by unknown artists in the hope that their works will also appreciate. The desire to invest can make potential collectors more discriminating, leading them to read about the art they are considering for purchase. A desire to get their money's worth can produce enthusiastic collectors who eventually build important collections, act as patrons of aspiring artists, and lobby for more government support of the arts. More-over, art that is regarded as an investment is likely to be well cared for over time (Passell, 1990).

The various motives for collecting art—as an expressive activity, for aesthetic reasons, as conspicuous consumption, and for investment purposes—are not mutually exclusive, but are probably all present to varying degrees in any given collector. People are most likely to buy art if they enjoy collecting it, respond to its beauty, relish showing it to others, and believe it will appreciate in value. Collectors may say different things about their motives for owning art to different audiences: business partners may be told what a good investment a painting is, but a museum curator may be told how much the collector loves the work of a particular artist.

MUSEUMS AND VALUE

Museums play an important role in creating value for art. The addition of an object to a museum's collection legitimates the artist's work and enhances his or her reputation. According to New York gallery owner Mary Boone, "Collectors . . . can make a market for a certain artist, but these feelings have to be corroborated by a noncommercial group, museums or critics. Without that, an artist's popularity won't continue" (cited in Temin, 1987:B4). Aware that exhibiting art in a museum will enhance its value, skeptics viewed a proposal by Nasser D. Khalili to loan and then donate his $1.5 billion collection of Islamic art to Great Britain as a way for him to sell the art at higher prices after the fifteen-year loan period expired. These skeptics regarded Khalili as a dealer out to maximize his profits rather than as a collector who intended to donate his art; he denied any intention to sell pieces from the collection in the future (Rockwell, 1993).

Museums also increase the value of the art in their collections by restoring, displaying, and publicizing it, and by carrying out scholarly investigations. The enhancement of market value through a museum's efforts is exemplified by the case of an Egyptian ornamental breastplate that was stolen from Lafayette College in the late 1970s and found in 1990 in the collection of Boston's Museum of Fine Arts. The breastplate had not drawn a bid above its reserve price when it was offered at a Sotheby's auction in 1980, but the Museum of Fine Arts bought it for $160,000 soon after the auction. When Lafayette College learned of the breastplate's whereabouts in 1990, the piece's market value was estimated to be between $600,000 and $2 million. One part of the museum's claim to ownership of the breastplate was that it had considerably enhanced its market value by restoring, studying, and publishing it, thereby demonstrating its importance and rarity. Lafayette College responded that the museum owed the college damages because the museum had been enriched by its possession of the breastplate and should have learned from its 1988 research on the object's provenance that it had been stolen. Lafayette did not dispute the museum's claim that its efforts had significantly enhanced the breastplate's market value. A 1992 agreement allowed the museum to take legal title to the breastplate after paying Lafayette an undisclosed sum.

Prices for art are pushed upward when museums compete with one another for scarce items in their efforts to build as complete a collection as possible. Such a collection, especially if it includes highly publicized items, enhances a museum's prestige and attracts crowds. Highly visible purchases also educate the public about the value of art. The Metropolitan Museum of Art's 1961 purchase of Rembrandt's *Aristotle Contemplating the Bust of Homer* for the unprecedented price of $2 million was a milestone in leading the public to see art in a new way, as a solid investment that would appreciate over time (Burnham, 1975:232).

After the 1982 inheritance of a $1.2 billion endowment by the J. Paul Getty Museum in Malibu, California, many people in the art world feared that the museum would use its resources to pursue works of art aggressively, pushing prices too high for other museums and collectors to afford. In fact, since 1982 the Getty has been just one of many wealthy buyers in the art market; others, notably wealthy Japanese business executives, have had an even greater impact on prices. The Getty has frequently limited the amounts that its curators can spend on new acquisitions; many individual and corporate collectors have no such limits and have thus been able to outbid the Getty at auction. However, the Getty has paid some high prices; in 1989, it spent $35.2 million for a portrait by Jacopo Pontormo and $26.4 million for a Manet painting, and the following year it paid a high but undisclosed price for van Gogh's *Irises,* which had been sold in 1989 for $53.9 million. The one segment of the art market that has been affected by the Getty's buying is Old Masters drawings, which the museum has pursued fervently and paid top dollar for. The Getty's purchases have pushed up the prices of those drawings, and the museum's interest in the field has attracted wealthy individual collectors, whose bidding for the drawings has reinforced that upward pressure on prices (McGill, 1987d).

Museums have generated a new appreciation of art among the public through blockbuster shows that attract large crowds. Museum visitors whose interest is sparked by those exhibitions and who have the resources may become collectors who then compete with museums for art, pushing higher the prices paid for the diminishing supply of top-quality works. Artworks that museums want to acquire then rise in price beyond their resources.

THE DISTRIBUTIONAL NETWORK

Dealers and auction houses bring together artists who create objects with institutional and individual buyers of art. Scholars also play an important role in this process by providing intellectual justification for the prices that collectors pay dealers and auction houses for artworks.

Art Dealers and Value

The transformation of artists from artisans who executed works according to a patron's specifications to independent creators of unique objects, a change that began in sixteenth-century Italy, led to the emergence of art dealers who could bring those artists together with collectors. Seventeenth-century Parisian artists signed exclusive contracts with dealers because the French academy prohibited its members from personally selling their own art. Dealers also provided important financial support for the artists, who were vulnerable after they gained their independence from wealthy patrons (Jones, 1984).

Although modern art dealers are engaged in a commercial enterprise, some of them define their role in the art world as more educational and archival than commercial. New York dealer Mary Boone says, "Galleries have to do with ideas. I probably wouldn't have chosen to show the artists I have if I wanted money. Most of them were unknown when I started to show them. It's not about mercantile interests" (cited in Temin, 1987:B4). Despite such claims, gallery owners and free-lance dealers try to maximize the price of the art they sell, for their livelihood and that of the artists they represent depend on it. Indeed, there were reports during the art boom of the 1980s that Boone, who denies the primacy of mercantile interests, kept her artists' prices artificially high by buying back their paintings at auctions at inflated prices (Servin, 1991). When dealers exhibit unknown artists whose works sell for low prices, it is apt to be because they lack the opportunity to represent renowned artists who command high prices.

One dealer describes his role as shaping people's tastes and leading them gently into an appreciation of art (Myers, 1983). Because many more people appreciate art than are willing to buy it, dealers must convert those who appreciate art into collectors. They do this by subtly teaching gallery visitors how to look at art, have confidence in their taste, and display art (Becker, 1982:113). In recent years, dealers have organized to present art fairs, which have attracted thousands of people who might be too intimidated to visit a gallery. Those fairs promote art and educate the public, allowing people to see a wide price range of offerings by many dealers in a setting in which there is no pressure to buy.

Symbolic interactionism illuminates the process by which dealers "educate" collectors. Dealers and potential buyers respond to a symbolic object, the work of art. Dealers talk about the way they see the work, pointing out its style, techniques, and materials. Sometimes they claim that they are not instructing collectors or cultivating clients but are simply sharing their enthusiasm; however, because of their authoritative role in the art world, dealers' expressions of enthusiasm, no matter how sincere, do influence potential buyers and are usually intended to do so. Potential buyers may respond verbally to dealers' statements about art, or they may simply come to perceive the art differently. Through such interaction, gallery visitors may learn to appreciate art enough to buy it. Dealers may also learn to respond differently to works of art by listening to their clients' reactions, but most dealers see themselves as connoisseurs who make independent and authoritative aesthetic judgments of the art they are offering for sale.

To be a successful dealer requires enthusiasm and verbal skill. Often dealers employ esoteric jargon to enhance the perceived value of artworks. Art is valued in part for the feelings that it evokes from viewers, and dealers try to translate those visual depictions and emotions into words. Never an easy task, this process is assisted by a vague, mystifying language that creates an aura around works of art. This enterprise has been described as follows:

Every dealer develops, over time, an artfully crafted spiel. Objects, even exquisite ones, do not sell themselves. In the art world, a hefty dose of pretension generally goes into the presentation. The dealer who can make his client feel slightly out of his depth is already one-up. If a sense of cultural obligation can be inculcated, so much the better. (Grimes, 1989:18)

One highly successful dealer in prints and old maps, W. Graham Arader III, frequently praises objects excessively, but, according to one report, he is able to make even his insincere flattery of artworks "seem definitive, even documentable." "When he says that something is 'the most fabulous thing I've ever seen' —on a hyperactive day, he might utter the phrase fifteen or twenty times—he means it. He spouts superlatives for all occasions" (Singer, 1987:50).

Through their interaction with potential customers, dealers try to create a personal bond and a sense of trust that convinces others to accept their aesthetic judgments. In doing so, they create value for works of art. According to Arader,

Things are valued how they're valued. And who's creating the value? I am. I sell the stuff, so I'm creating the value. So are auction houses, other dealers, collectors.

It's pretty shaky. It involves factors such as "Do you like me?" and "Do you enjoy buying from me?" and "How well do I serve you?" As a dealer, I try to do all the things that a good slave can do. I'll give you reference books. I'll frame your print nicely. I'll come to your home and hang it. I'll help your kids get into boarding school. (cited in Singer, 1987:80)

Dealers sometimes point out the investment value of art to potential customers, urging them to buy the work of new artists and hold onto it until it appreciates. However, relatively few contemporary works have appreci- ated enough for buyers to resell them at significant profit, and so many dealers in contemporary art do not emphasize investment as a reason to buy art (de Coppet and Jones, 1984).

Commitment to the development and improvement of their clients' collections is another goal of dealers, who say that because there is never enough good art to meet the demand, they try to find the best home for each piece. Earlier in this century, dealer Joseph Duveen became wealthy by selling Europe's art to rich Americans; his methods have been described as follows:

Duveen had to use new techniques of salesmanship: he persuaded a few American millionaires to pay fortunes for pictures which would ensure their immortality, first by associating them with an aristocratic past, and then, more permanently, by turning them into public benefactors celebrated for the collections they bequeathed to museums. It was the competition he engendered between his clients that set off the unprecedented upward spiral in picture prices. (Faith, 1985:26)

Some dealers claim that they employ their inspiration, taste, and schol- arship to invest in and guide particular artists so that audiences for their work will eventually be found (Myers, 1983). Other dealers say they are less "leaders of the pack" than lovers of art who experience it sooner and more intensely than other people. They note that they can succeed as dealers only if their connoisseurship and intuition allow them to predict trends before the public becomes aware of them. Dealers' statements often imply that it is less the art itself than their connoisseurship and salesmanship that bring success to an artist.

Dealers try to maximize the reputations of the artists they represent and the price of their work, because they often have a substantial amount invested in their artists. They support their artists while they are producing work, and they underwrite the costs of mounting exhibitions, sending announcements to potential buyers, and holding receptions for show open- ings. Because artists' reputations and the value of their work can be enhanced through scarcity, gallery owners also try to control their artists' output. Prices for Mark Rothko's pictures did not appreciate much after his 1970 suicide, apparently because of a plentiful supply of his works. The Rothko Foundation distributed some of his paintings to museums in accordance with his will, curtailing the demand for his paintings from that source. Later, following a trial in which the executors of Rothko's will were found to have engaged in self-dealing, artworks worth $40 million to $50 million were recovered by the artist's heirs and gradually sold on the open market, meeting the immediate demand for his art (Duthy, 1985).

Dealers try to set prices so that an artist will seem worthwhile but not too expensive. They raise prices if demand grows, sometimes hoarding an artist's works to limit supply and to have pieces to sell when prices reach higher levels. Prominent collectors often ask for or even demand discounts, knowing that dealers and artists benefit from having works included in their collections. Dealers frequently agree to such price reductions, sometimes even offering them first, because they know they will profit when they tell other potential buyers that one of the artist's pieces has been purchased by an esteemed collector. Price reductions for highly regarded collectors are thus a kind of advertising cost for dealers. Not only do such discounts benefit the dealer and the artist, but collectors gain additional respect for their connoisseurship and astuteness if other collectors later want to buy the artist's works and the prices for those works increase. Prominent collectors also have the power to damage an artist's reputation by selling off his or her works. The purchase of seven Sandro Chia paintings by British collector Charles Saatchi, an influential tastemaker who has one of the world's most important and most extensive art collections, helped push the price for Chia's works up from $10,000 to $60,000. When Saatchi sold all of his Chias in 1984 with no explanation, Chia's reputation was hurt and prices for his works dropped (Walker, 1987).

Auction Houses and Value

The staged and highly publicized sale of art by auction houses has played a crucial role in pushing art prices to unprecedented heights. According to Charles W. Smith's (1989) study of auctions, this method of selling merchandise assigns values and allocates objects through a competitive process that attaches prices to objects that previously were of uncertain value. Throughout the nineteenth century and the first half of the twentieth century, the prices paid for art at auction were relatively stable and, for the most part, lower than the prices paid to art dealers. Indeed, auction sales carried a stigma because many of them followed a death, divorce, or bankruptcy (Tomkins, 1988).

During the late 1950s and the 1960s, Peter C. Wilson of Sotheby's of London employed scholarship and promotional skills to increase the auction house's influence over the price of art. He used aggressive sales tactics to convince collectors that practically anything was worth buying. He optimistically viewed the value of art as endlessly increasing, due to a combination of limited supply and new wealth that would be spent on art if buyers could be assured that they were making a good investment (Burnham, 1975; Faith, 1985). Wilson successfully applied "the 100-pound rule" developed by Sotheby's Stanley Clark; this idea that there was a large unfulfilled demand for inexpensive items was based on Clark's finding that about 60 percent of the items sold at auction during the 1950s brought less than 100 pounds. To expand Sotheby's business, Wilson tried to attract middle-income collectors to the art market, in part by making the auction house less intimidating to potential clients. He also hired a public relations officer to build public confidence in the lasting value of art and convince people that they could afford to buy art (Burnham, 1975:191–207).

Sotheby's publicized a series of rags-to-riches stories that showed that anyone might have valuable items stored in an attic; this set off what has been described as a national treasure hunt in which people brought their possessions to auction houses for appraisal and sale (Burnham, 1975:195). In the process, they often became interested in buying other things for themselves. Efforts to get people to bring their treasures to auction houses for sale continue today; a 1988 advertisement in *Connoisseur* begins, "We know dozens of people who'd love to sit in your chair. They'll compete with each other in a very civilized way: by raising their paddles and bidding at Christie's. And competition like that can work wonders." The advertisement mentions an eighteenth-century chair, which the owner hoped to sell for $70,000, a figure based on the chair's quality and the fact that there was a similar one in New York's Metropolitan Museum of Art. The chair eventually sold for $275,000. In the advertisement, a Christie's senior vice-president sits in another chair soon to be auctioned for an estimated price of between $400,000 and $600,000 (*Connoisseur*, June 1988:61).

Since the 1950s, auction houses have expanded their market beyond what is traditionally regarded as art; the most prestigious houses now sell furniture, candlestick holders, wallpaper, ceramics, antiquities, antique toys, books, coins, stamps, and other objects. In 1991, for instance, the decorative arts categories accounted for about 55 percent of Sotheby's overall sales total, and fine arts for the rest. The expanded definition of what was salable at auction was necessitated by the scarcity of fine art of the highest quality. The reduced supply of great works of art pushed up prices for those pieces that were offered for sale, and the high prices paid for objects other than fine art helped to raise prices for fine art. After all, if a chair was worth $600,000, then what was the value of an oil painting by van Gogh, Renoir, or Picasso?

By describing a wide range of items as collectible, providing scholarly background on those items, and establishing prices they expected those items to fetch, auction houses "credentialized" objects that were not previously seen as collectible, leading buyers to compete for "hot" items before the supply dried up or prices got out of reach. That competition pushed prices higher. When objects sold quickly at high prices, buyers were reassured that the objects had intrinsic value and artistic merit. When Christie's of New York sold a colonial American desk in 1989 for $12.1 million, the highest auction price paid to date for something other than a painting, the dealer who purchased it for a client suggested that the high price might have a ripple effect in the antiques market, leading to higher prices for other furniture and bringing more fine furniture out of the homes of owners and into auction houses (Reif, 1989a).

As auction houses have expanded the kinds of things they sell, collectors have sought those objects from other sources such as art dealers and antiques shops. Prices charged by those sources have increased to keep pace with the prices paid at auction. Some dealers have even turned to auction houses as outlets for their wares, because they can reach more collectors that way than they could through a gallery or shop. Dealers have also used their own highly publicized purchases at auction to enhance their standing in the art world and push up prices for the kinds of art they sell. By paying $2.09 million for a Cycladic head at a 1988 Sotheby's auction, a record auction price for an antiquity, Edward Merrin, "already a major force in the market, could now claim to be the pre-eminent [antiquities] dealer in the United States" (Grimes, 1989:18). Pointing out that Sotheby's pre-sale estimate for the sculpture was only $400,000 to $600,000, Merrin's critics accused him of paying an unprecedented price in order to draw attention to himself and attract objects from private collections to sell at inflated prices. The possibility of an upward spiral in antiquities prices alarmed archaeologists, who feared that looters would be even more motivated to destroy ancient sites to find objects to sell to collectors, thereby making it harder than ever for scholars to study ancient civilizations. Museum curators feared that higher antiquities prices would attract more buyer-investors to the market, further depleting the supply of antiquities available to museums and forcing prices even higher, which would make it harder for museums with limited budgets to bid for such objects (Grimes, 1989).

Auction houses have adopted innovative promotional strategies to attract buyers and raise prices, though not every such effort has succeeded. In advance of a 1989 sale, Christie's sent a painting by Jacopo Pontormo on a tour to Japan, England, and Germany and published a lavish catalogue. It was not clear what the painting would sell for, but Christie's raised its initial estimate from $20 million to $35 million. When the painting sold for $35.2 million, no one was surprised, but there were only three bidders, an indication that Christie's had not achieved its goal of attracting more foreign buyers to the Old Masters field (Kimmelman, 1989a).

Sotheby's has marketed art aggressively in recent years, developing new fields for collectors, holding sales in different locations, and developing innovative and sometimes controversial financial arrangements for both consignors and purchasers. Sotheby's 1987 sale of van Gogh's *Irises* to Australian financier Alan Bond for $53.9 million was seen at the time as proof that art had retained its investment value after the October 1987 stock market plunge. When it was later revealed that the auction house had agreed in advance of the sale to lend Bond half of whatever he bid so that he could complete his purchase, critics claimed that this was a manipulation of prices aimed at buoying public confidence in the art market. Dealer Richard Feigen described that kind of sale as "exactly like buying on margin. The problem is, there are regulations in the securities market that are not in the art market. By extending credit you are further inflating prices, which are rapidly getting out of control" (cited in Reif, 1989c:C15). David Bathurst, a former official at Christie's, responded as follows: "Critics of auction house loans say they are a way of artificially pumping up prices. This is no more true than saying building societies pump up house prices when they grant mortgages" (cited in Reif, 1989c:C15). Dealers sometimes allow their customers to pay for art over weeks or months without charging them interest. However, banks rarely loan buyers the money with which to purchase art, even though they will loan money against art that people already own.

Two years after selling *Irises* to Bond, 10 to 25 percent of his loan had not been repaid. Sotheby's then took control of the painting, reselling it in 1990 to the Getty Museum for an undisclosed price; this allowed Bond to liquidate his debt. Had Sotheby's resold the painting at auction and had it brought less than $53.9 million, fear might have spread among the public that art prices were inflated, so a quiet sale at an unannounced price helped preserve the idea that art was still a good investment. Christie's, Sotheby's major rival, criticized the Bond loan, saying that it did not make such loans, even though it would help potential buyers find financing from other sources. Sotheby's loan violated no New York regulation on auction practices, but the auction house subsequently changed its policy so that buyers were no longer permitted to use art they planned to purchase as collateral for loans. A spokesperson for Sotheby's said that such loans had been made only six times for purchases of more than $1 million and that abandoning that policy would have little impact on its sales.

Auction houses have also been criticized for offering price guarantees to the consignors of art for sale at auction. Sotheby's initiated this practice, and Christie's reluctantly followed suit so as not to lose business to its rival. Under this policy, an auction house guarantees a consignor a minimum price for a single work of art or for a group of pieces, with the house sometimes charging a higher-than-usual commission if the art is sold. Guarantees attract art from dealers and probably induce some collectors to sell works they might otherwise have kept. If a work sells for more than the guaranteed minimum, the agreement between the auction house and the consignor determines what happens to the extra money: it may be divided between them, or it may go to the consignor. If the work does not sell, the auction house pays the consignor the agreed price and keeps the work. Auction houses are wary of the financial consequences of failing to sell works that have high guaranteed prices, but competition between houses has led to the occasional use of such guarantees to attract consignors.

Because price guarantees give auction houses a financial interest in the objects they are offering for sale, critics have suggested that such guarantees create a conflict of interest: the house is no longer acting as an impartial agent bringing seller and buyer together, but has instead allied itself with the seller. This gives the auction house an incentive to quote excessively high pre-sale estimates in order to encourage high bids, as well as an incentive to create as much pre-sale publicity as possible in order to generate more bidding. Competition among auction houses might also push prices up as each house tries to attract consignors by offering the highest possible guarantees. Recognizing the potential problems of price guarantees, Sotheby's in 1990 decided to mark in its sales catalogues those items for which it had guaranteed prices.

Auction houses have tried to stimulate art buying by investing their profits in projects aimed at expanding their clientele. They have established publishing houses, which print attractive monographs on "new discoveries" and thus legitimate higher prices for unknown artists. They have produced videocassettes to educate the public about art. They have commissioned original prints that are sold by mail order. Some houses have invested in travel agencies that sponsor tours to countries rich in art; when tourists return home, they find art from those countries available for sale at the auction house. In 1987, the head of Sotheby's of New York said, "We have 20,000 more private clients than we had four years ago. And it's changing the way we do business. We're becoming far more of a retail establishment, providing more services for our customers than was necessary years ago" (Diana Brooks, cited in Vogel, 1987:A26).

The auction process itself is designed to increase prices. Auctioneers describe items in exquisite and esoteric language, making objects more appealing than they might otherwise seem, and they create pressure on audiences to raise bids. Sotheby's chief auctioneer John Marion once remarked, "If a bidder looks like he's getting to the end of his string, I'll give him a break and look away and then—very quickly—look back and he'll think, 'Maybe I'd better bid again.' I play little mind games" (cited in Dullea, 1990:B4). In the heat of the bidding, people sometimes offer more than they would ever think of paying a dealer for the same object.

The practice of setting a secret reserve, the minimum price for which a consignor will allow a piece to be sold, keeps prices higher than they would be if objects were simply sold to the highest bidder. A collector who wants to sell a painting that he or she believes is worth $1 million may instruct the auction house not to sell it for less than that price. If the bidding only reaches $800,000, rather than acknowledge that the painting's market value may actually be less than $1 million, the consignor has the auction house withdraw the painting from the sale. This process of "buying in" sometimes involves an announcement that the painting was sold to a fictitious bidder in the audience, thereby maintaining the illusion that the painting was actually sold for $1 million. Sales are made only when the top bid at least maintains what the owner, in consultation with auction house experts, believes the object is worth.

Auction house audiences, including collectors and dealers, are "educated" about the value of art when they watch others offer money for art. That process may make dealers willing to pay more for artworks than they would have paid prior to the auction. Collectors who see other bidders willing to pay more than $100,000 for a particular painting may think that they would be foolish not to snap up a similarly priced picture being offered by a dealer. Collectors also become more willing to spend their money if they know that other buyers are willing to pay the same prices for similar works of art, because they are thus reassured that they will be able to resell their art in the future.

Scholars and Value

Scholars such as archaeologists, art historians, art critics, and biographers play an important role in creating and certifying the value of works of art. Their research and opinions are cited by dealers and auction houses to justify the prices that collectors are asked to pay, and collectors' tastes are shaped by the work of such scholars.

Archaeologists have been accused of contributing to the illicit trade in antiquities by sometimes being less concerned with reconstructing past cultures from the artifacts they uncover than they are with appreciating those objects as works of art stripped from their cultural context. Focusing on what was aesthetically best in past cultures contributes to a "cult of objects" that encourages collectors and museums to bid up the price of antiquities. Museums contribute to this cult of objects when they display ancient objects as works of art outside their cultural context (Giorgio Gullini, cited in Burnham, 1980c).

Art historians influence the value of art when they deattribute or reattribute works or confirm that a renowned artist did in fact execute a particular piece. They analyze an artist's style, the materials from which a work is made, and the provenance of the object to establish its authenticity. In so doing, they enhance, reinforce, or reduce the value of the object. They sometimes revise their aesthetic judgments and "rediscover" previously neglected artists, thereby enhancing the reputations of those artists. Their research enables art historians to carve out niches for themselves in the world of scholarship. It also affects the art market, because the rediscovery of artists provides dealers with works they can sell at higher prices. First, however, those dealers must "educate" potential buyers about the rediscovered artists and the higher prices their works now command. Dealers do this by referring to scholarly monographs, sometimes even underwriting the cost of the research and publications that they later cite to their customers.

Dealers and scholars have colluded on occasion, with dealers profiting from the sale of art that has had its value enhanced by the published work of scholars. Dealers and artists have curried favor with influential critics by giving them works of art; according to one art historian, during the mid-1960s the price of favorable attention to an artist by prominent critic Clement Greenberg was the gift of one or two major works (Marquis, 1991:132). Critics have built up the reputations of artists in whose work they have personally invested, and then profited from the sale of that art. Art historian Bernard Berenson sometimes overpraised artworks in which he had a financial stake, even vouching for paintings that he knew had undergone significant restoration so as to be made more appealing to buyers. He earned substantial commissions from the sale of paintings by dealer Joseph Duveen, collecting more than $8 million from Duveen during the twenty-six years of their partnership. There is no proof that Berenson ever knowingly gave a false attribution, but one biographer claims that Berenson and Duveen sometimes overestimated the quality of paintings. Moreover, Duveen financed much of Berenson's art criticism, which he then used to justify the prices he charged wealthy collectors (Simpson, 1986).

The response of critics to works of art, especially innovative ones, can legitimate controversial styles. Because they provide reasons for people to think that works are "good art," critics are important in creating and maintaining value. If critics develop a consensus that new works of art are important, museum curators and individual collectors will be more likely to believe that the value of such works will appreciate over time. Buyers are more confident of their own tastes when they are supported by the published opinions of critics.

Art magazines are important in establishing values and encouraging sales. Because of the importance of the "cult of the personality" in today's art world, those magazines are instrumental in the making of a contemporary artist's reputation. Magazines can get people talking about a new artist, consign artists to oblivion by suggesting they are passé, or draw attention to a gallery. One publisher who, not surprisingly, believes that art magazines are important to the health of the art world, remarks, "The most viable metaphor is an echo chamber. The sides of the box are gallery support, critical support from magazines, museum support, and support of collectors. If one of those walls is missing, the volume of interest in an artist doesn't build" (Knight Landesman, cited in Gerard, 1988:D10). Some observers have suggested that there is a connection between advertising and reviews, with dealers who advertise in art magazines more likely to get attention for their galleries and artists in the magazine's articles (Gerard, 1988).

CONCLUSION

The value of art is socially produced rather than intrinsic to objects. The Western conception of the artist as a creative genius gave rise to the idea that works of art are unique and hence valuable. By competing with one another for art, collectors and museums bid up prices, especially for top-quality works that are in diminishing supply. Museums enhance the value of art by displaying objects and creating public interest in art; ironically, this sometimes increases prices to levels that museums cannot afford. Dealers and auction houses have also pushed prices upward through aggressive promotion, and scholars have contributed to the value of art by providing intellectual justifications for the aesthetic importance of art.

The high prices that art now commands encourage a variety of art crimes. Thieves believe, often incorrectly, that a valuable work of art can be converted into a large amount of cash. When art is not easily traced, as is the case with recently unearthed antiquities, networks may form to smuggle objects from the country of origin to a country in which there are collectors and dealers willing to pay high prices for such objects. Artists and dealers have engaged in fraud by producing and marketing fakes and forgeries, and dealers have defrauded the owners of art by failing to pay them the money they were paid for art consigned to them by the owners. These and other crimes are inextricably linked to the social organization of the art world, which first socially constructs value for art and then provides opportunities to make illicit profits.

Fakes and Forgeries

The sale of faked and forged artworks is a worldwide problem, with tens of millions of dollars in counterfeit works being sold every year. Perhaps the biggest art forgery problem in the United States is the production and sale of counterfeit prints, a practice that has cost buyers hundreds of millions of dollars since 1980. Because people who buy art, even those not primarily concerned with art for investment purposes, expect that their acquisitions are worth what they pay, the discovery that they have bought worthless fakes will undermine their confidence in the art market and make them wary of buying art in the future. Forgery is also costly because it provides false information about the counterfeited artist's body of work, thus confusing art history and forcing scholars, dealers, and curators to spend time and money sorting out bogus works from authentic art.

The extent of the problem of forgery is often expressed in the assertion that of the 700 authentic works painted by Jean Baptiste Camille Corot, 8,000 of them are in the United States. Some of the fakes were produced by forgers, but others were done by Corot's students or other artists and then cavalierly signed by Corot himself (Mills and Mansfield, 1979:143–145). Thomas Hoving has said that in his sixteen years with New York's Metropolitan Museum of Art, he collected some 25,000 works and saw perhaps another 100,000. He remarks, "Fully 60 percent of what I examined was not what it was said to be," though not all of the misrepresented works were fakes (Hoving, 1986:41). Hoving calls most of the counterfeit art he examined "hilarious," including a silver plate that depicted Adam and Eve modestly covered by fig leaves, even though that convention did not develop until centuries after the plate was said to have been made. On one picture the craquelure, or fine cracking of the varnish that occurs over time on the surface of oil paintings, was actually black paint that had been applied with a single-haired brush.

Fakes are works of art made to resemble existing ones; forgeries are pieces that are passed off as original works by known artists. The mere production of a work that resembles an existing one is not a crime, but intentionally and deceptively passing it off as someone else's work is forgery, a type of fraud. Fakers and forgers may alter or add a signature, complete an unfinished work, misrepresent the work of a pupil as the work of a master, copy an existing painting, produce a pastiche out of bits from other sources, create an original composition similar in color and style to the work of a known artist, or duplicate an existing work (Becker, 1982:168). They go to extraordinary lengths to copy the materials used by the artists whose works they are counterfeiting, mixing paints from the same ingredients, using old canvas to paint on, and artificially aging their fakes and forgeries by cracking the surface varnish of oil paintings and "stressing" statues and pottery.

One tactic used by disreputable dealers and second-rate auction houses is to let inexperienced buyers purchase pieces they believe are by well-known artists for well below market prices, though considerably more than what they are really worth. The works will be appropriately aged and may include themes common to the work of the famous artist, perhaps even being signed with suggestive initials. The dealer does not claim that the work is by the famous artist, so if the buyer later complains about being tricked, the dealer can reply that if the picture had been by such a renowned artist, the price of course would have been much higher (Wraight, 1966:94–95). Apparently this tactic was used by Antonio Freppa, who marketed sculptures in the style of the Italian quattrocento that were created by Giovanni Bastianini during the latter half of the nineteenth century. Neither sculptor nor dealer claimed that the pieces were authentically ancient, but Freppa let his customers think they were duping him and buying an antiquity for the price of a contemporary reproduction.

Fakes and forgeries are defined according to the conventions of the art world, and those conventions have changed over time. In ancient Egypt and the Orient, copying another's work signified respect, even reverence. In Renaissance Italy, sculptors as renowned as Michelangelo tested their skills by trying to pass off their creations as ancient art. However, during the Renaissance the creative genius of the individual artist took on importance as a way to assess the value of art, and so passing off one's efforts as the work of another became an affront, a way of diminishing the other artist's reputation, a theft of that artist's ideas, and a way of deceiving the world (Jones, 1990; Steiner, 1990).

Deception in the production of art is an important problem in a market that places a premium on the artist as a unique creative genius. In Chapter 1, we saw that the value of art is based on much more than its intrinsic quality, with the reputation of the artist thought to have executed the work being a crucial element in determining value. Forgeries may thus have intrinsic beauty of their own and be appreciated by critics, collectors, and dealers until it is revealed that the artist thought to have executed the works did not do so. Then the objects usually become worthless, not because they are intrinsically any different, but because they are not what they were purported to be. A work that is reattributed to a lesser artist than the one originally thought to have executed it will usually suffer a loss of value but will not be tainted in the same way that deliberate fakes and forgeries are, because the artist who executed the work never intended to deceive anyone about the piece's creator.

Art evokes historical responses as well as aesthetic ones. Because of the culture's emphasis on the artist as a unique creative genius who worked in a particular historical context, people feel the need to have artworks properly attributed. Originality has been defined as "the artistic novelty and achievement not of one particular work of art but of the totality of artistic productions of one man or even one school" (Lessing, 1983:71). From this perspective, a forgery is not original because it is not actually a product of the style, period, or technique that represents a significant achievement when considered in the context of the time that the forgery was purportedly executed (Lessing, 1983:72). People see works of art as "historical documents as well as things of beauty," and if they know that a work is not authentic, their historical response will overwhelm their aesthetic response (Alsop, 1982:131). Original art can influence the course of art history and the work of future artists; forgeries merely imitate works that have been created in the past.

Art historians often disagree with Theodore Rousseau's statement, "We should all realize that we can only talk about the bad forgeries, the ones that have been detected; the good ones are still hanging on the walls" (cited in Goodrich, 1973:224). Scholars suggest that few if any undetected fakes will hang on museum walls for more than a generation because artists are of their own time, and works they create in the style of an earlier period will eventually be seen to be inconsistent with that earlier time. Forgers, argue such scholars, cannot help but inject some of themselves and the tastes of their time into the works they create.

Art historians and connoisseurs are probably not that skilled at uncovering fakes and forgeries, and some undetected counterfeit art must still exist. This is suggested by the fact that in several cases forgeries have been revealed only by those who created them. For instance, the frescoes painted on the blank walls of a German cathedral in the late 1930s by Lothar Malskat were widely accepted as restorations of authentic medieval paintings; the frescoes appeared on German postage stamps and were published in a book. That the pictures were modern forgeries was not revealed until Malskat, envious of the praise his supervisor was receiving for the "restorations" and angry at the small amount he was paid for his work, demanded that both he and his supervisor be arrested. They were both sentenced to prison in 1955. Had Malskat not admitted his deception, it is questionable whether the frescoes would ever have been found to be counterfeit, although the presence of turkeys in the frescoes might eventually have given them away, because turkeys were not introduced into Europe until more than two centuries after the frescoes were supposedly painted (Jeppson, 1970:196–208).

The appearance of fakes and forgeries on the art market fluctuates with cycles in taste and price. High prices for authentic art make it more worthwhile for artists and dealers to take the trouble to produce, document, and sell counterfeit pieces. To make a profit, counterfeit art must be sold for more than it costs to produce; it must also fetch more when sold as what it is purported to be than it would if it were sold as what it actually is (Taylor and Brooke, 1969:134). When R. A. Blakelock's paintings began to climb in price around 1916, many forgeries of his pictures were produced. In one year during the 1980s, the owner of Boston's Vose Galleries was asked to authenticate more than one hundred paintings thought to be by Blakelock; only one was authentic. When prices for art are high, even artists at the low end of the market can be worth counterfeiting. For years, American folk art was priced too low to be worth faking, but when prices increased—a weathervane selling for $203,500 and a sampler for $198,000 in 1987—more fakes began to appear on the market (Bohlin, 1988). Counterfeit works also become more common when the demand for art outstrips its supply, and when greedy or inexperienced collectors become indiscriminate in their purchases. The unearthing of an Egyptian cat cemetery in the 1950s increased the demand for cat sculptures; that demand was met with both authentic and fake pieces.

Because of the volume of art sold during boom periods, auction houses sometimes offer fakes and forgeries for sale, usually unwittingly. This is particularly a problem for types of art that are increasing rapidly in value but that lack documentation, such as Russian avant-garde art during the late 1980s. Scholars claimed that two outright fakes and one dubious picture were offered at Sotheby's 1989 London auction of Russian art. Doubts about those pictures were brought to the attention of Sotheby's officials prior to the auction, but they disagreed with the scholars' assessment and went ahead with the sale (Hughes, 1989).

THE PROBLEM OF ORIGINALITY

Conceptions of what is original art are socially constructed; that is, they depend on the social organization and conventions of the art world at any given time. Definitions of *original* are influenced by such social factors as the way that the production of art is organized (in workshops supervised by a master or in studios in which artists work by themselves), the way that artists are trained (to imitate a master's style or to develop a unique style), the nature of patronage (clients who want work done in a particular style or dealers and collectors who want something new and different), the practices of art dealers, the connections among artists, collectors' perceptions of the meaning of art, and the visual tradition in which artists work (Brenson, 1985).

There is much ambiguity about what constitutes original art, especially art that is produced in multiples. Experts differ in their views about what constitutes an original print, a category that includes etchings, lithographs, serigraphs, and other multiple-image works of visual art. Unscrupulous dealers have taken advantage of this disagreement in their marketing of counterfeit prints. A similar problem exists with surmoulages, which are casts of sculptures made from molds taken from an original cast. Art world conventions permit the marketing of multiple-edition sculptures and prints under certain conditions, and some states now have laws that regulate the marketing of multiples as original art.

Walter Benjamin (1968) observes that works of art have always been reproducible, but with industrialization it became possible to reproduce art mechanically. He argues that even the most perfect copy lacks the original's presence in time and space, but that improved mechanical means of reproduction have made it more difficult to distinguish well-done fake prints from the originals. Benjamin claims that the "presence" of the original is basic to the idea of authenticity, with the work's uniqueness being determined by the events to which it has been subjected over time, including changes in its physical condition and its ownership. Benjamin asserts that the "aura" of an original work is missing from mechanical reproductions, because the process of reproduction detaches fakes, clearly recognized reproductions, and even large-edition prints from the domain of tradition. Benjamin's views are contrary to the commonly accepted definition of multiple-edition prints as original art when they are produced according to certain conventions.

New York artist Michael Bidlo has raised the question of originality with his paintings, which are skewed copies of works by Picasso, Pollock,

Mondrian, and others. Bidlo sees his "appropriations" of others' art as extending the boundaries of what is accepted as art, claiming that his work is therefore an original contribution, a view disputed by some art critics. He acknowledges that he is attempting to devalue the original works of art, unlike forgers and fakers who seek to approximate original works as closely as possible. There is no question of fakery with Bidlo's art, because he clearly acknowledges what he is doing, signs the skewed works with his own name, and uses new stretcher bars and exposes the linen edges to show that his paintings are contemporary works. Copyright infringement has not yet been a problem because he has copied works that are in the public domain (Hayt-Atkins, 1988; McGill, 1988b).

In an unusual dispute over the question of originality, a collector sued artist Frank Stella when she learned that a painting of his that she intended to sell at auction had a near-twin with the same title, also painted by Stella. She said that she had not asked if there was a similar painting when she bought hers, because that question would not be likely to occur to the purchaser of an oil painting, which is supposed to be a unique work according to art world conventions. The court found Stella at fault, but did not award the collector any damages (Grant, 1987).

The question of originality arose again in 1992 in the auctioning by Sotheby's in Los Angeles of animation art from the Walt Disney Studios' film *Beauty and the Beast*. In the past, "cels," which are hand-painted gouaches on celluloid, have been used to make animated films, and a strong market has developed in recent years for vintage animation art. However, the 250 cels offered at the 1992 auction had not been used to make *Beauty and the Beast,* but instead were hand-painted copies of the computer-generated images that had been used to make the movie (Reif, 1992).

"Tourist art" produced on assembly lines in factories in Korea, Hong Kong, and Taiwan also raises the issue of what constitutes original art. In 1988, local artists in Rockport, Massachusetts, publicly objected to dealers' labeling such mass-produced works "original art." One artist defined an original as a piece that a person "creates from nothing, with energy, with sweat, your own ideas" (cited in Bickelhaupt, 1988:1). He argued that buyers should be warned that "schlock art" does not meet that definition of originality, because it is mass produced by groups of painters who do different parts of a painting and who may make thousands of copies of the same picture. That artist's objections to schlock art raise several problems. First, many Old Masters supervised apprentices in their workshops, with each apprentice completing a particular aspect of a painting; today no one questions the originality of those paintings, even though there may be a problem in attributing the pictures to a particular artist. Second, renowned contemporary artists might well question the originality of the works of the local artists who were critical of schlock art. Even though those paintings are executed by individual artists, they tend to feature the same unimaginative motifs—sea, rocks, sky, a seagull—and show little creativity in their conception.

In response to the Rockport Arts Council's objections to schlock art, Massachusetts in 1988 passed a law requiring any work of art that was not individually created, executed, and signed by the artist to be labeled as not an original work of art. Some of the artists whose complaints led to this law may sincerely have wanted to protect the art-buying public, but most of them were probably more interested in curbing the sale of schlock art because people were buying those cheap paintings rather than their own higher priced ones. The dealers who sell schlock art objected to the new law, saying that they tell their customers the paintings are done in Asia and that their customers know they are just getting a piece of decor art rather than an original work that will appreciate in value over time. That may also be exactly what customers think they are getting when they spend $150 to $500 for an original work by a local artist, and so they may prefer to spend less on decorative schlock art.

ATTRIBUTION AND AUTHENTICITY

A 1983 preview of a portion of an art collection later to be housed in a museum in Zagreb, Yugoslavia, was jeered by art historians because it included many forgeries and misattributed works. Some of them even thought that the show was a hoax, one describing it as "trash along with some good things. Ninety percent is junk" (cited in Decker, 1987:151). The collection's donor, Ante Topic Mimara, was responsible for the optimistic attributions, which apparently were to be retained by the new museum until his death allowed for more accurate attributions.

The question of whether a work of art is what it is supposed to be has become more important in recent years as more art has been bought and sold at higher and higher prices. High prices have made the issue of authenticity critical for museums, dealers, and collectors who are investing vast sums in art. For instance, a portrait of George Washington sold at Christie's in New York for $3,300 in 1987 was attributed five months later to Gilbert Stuart and resold for $495,000 at Sotheby's in London (Reif, 1988).

Old Masters paintings, defined as pictures executed between the thirteenth and the early nineteenth centuries, are ascribed to a particular artist when it is certain who executed the work; they are attributed to an artist when experts believe the work was probably by the artist. Works done by unknown artists under a master's tutelage are classified as belonging to the studio of the artist. The term *circle of the artist* is applied to works by unidentified but distinct artists closely associated with the named artist. Decreasing importance is given to works in the style of or by a follower of an artist, in the manner of an artist (that is, in the artist's style but painted at a different time), and after the artist (that is, a copy) (Patterson, 1991).

To professionals in the world of art, reattribution is not necessarily pejorative, even though it is often perceived that way by the general public. Reattribution can upgrade a work as well as downgrade it. Because of the subjectivity involved in reattribution, the decision to reassign a work to a different artist is often controversial. Most reattributed works are not forgeries or fakes, because neither the original artist nor the person offering the work for sale was trying to deceive anyone about the true authorship of the work. In the past, it was often accepted, even expected, for artists to copy a widely admired style or artist. The nineteenth-century German goldsmith Reinhold Vasters copied pieces at the request of churches and other clients; he also repaired originals and "enriched" them with new mounts or settings. Vasters assembled these pieces with a sense of artistry and harmony and was regarded as an artist in his own right. However, someone who was unaware of the derivative nature of his works might treat them as deliberate fakes (Glueck, 1986a).

Today it is standard practice for dealers to accept back from a client a work of art that has been found to be something other than what the dealer claimed it was. This warranty of authenticity—that is, that the artwork is what the dealer represented it to be—applies to fakes, forgeries, and works misattributed both erroneously and intentionally. Lawsuits by clients against dealers have resulted from disagreements over exactly what the dealer represented a work to be and whether it is authentic or counterfeit. Statutes of limitations require that claims of having been sold a fake or a forgery must be made within a certain period of time from the purchase of the work (Grant, 1987).

Defining Rembrandt's *Oeuvre*

As the belief that the individual artist is a creative genius grew over the centuries, the proper attribution of works of art came to be regarded as more important. In the seventeenth century, the distinction between pictures that Rembrandt executed by himself, those painted by him and his pupils together, and those done by his pupils under his supervision was relatively unimportant. Two centuries later, people felt that only a genius could create fine works of art, so any painting that seemed to be by Rembrandt must be his. However, twentieth-century scholars have shown that many of Rembrandt's less-esteemed contemporaries painted almost as well as he did. Using modern scientific techniques and carefully researching the social context within which artists such as Rembrandt worked, and taking advantage of modern means of travel and visual documentation, scholars have been able to attribute paintings more accurately (Glueck, 1986a).

Between 1968 and 1993, the Netherlands Organization for the Advancement of Pure Research funded a committee of art historians, originally seven in number, to scrutinize paintings attributed to Rembrandt. Using infrared lights, X-rays, microscopes, and other scientific tools, the experts of the Rembrandt Research Project analyzed paint, dated oak panels, studied the sketches underlying paintings, examined brushwork, investigated signatures, and studied all copies and reproductions made before 1800. Provenances were checked through all available pre-1800 sales catalogues. Even with all this evidence, the scholars were not always able to ascertain which works were original Rembrandts. Rembrandt often signed commissioned works that had been done largely by his pupils, for in his day it was the convention that the master of a workshop had the right to sign such paintings; the amount of work the master actually did on the painting depended on the price paid by the client. Rembrandt had about one hundred known pupils, whose job it was to make their painting look as much like his as possible. From one perspective those pictures can be seen as authentic Rembrandts, even though they do not fit a modern definition of originality.

One technique for attributing paintings is Morellianism, named after a nineteenth-century art critic who produced a systematic listing of the personal habits used by various painters in executing certain details in their pictures. This method may not be reliable for studying the works of painters whose styles changed radically or who were heavily influenced by their patrons' wishes. Inventive artists such as Rembrandt changed styles frequently, making it difficult to apply the techniques of Morellianism. Moreover, one of Rembrandt's assistants might repeat some of the master's stylistic habits for years after Rembrandt had abandoned the technique, later causing the assistant's paintings to be misattributed to Rembrandt. The Dutch commission found it difficult to apply Morellianism to Rembrandt's early paintings, but used the method to examine his later works. Over the course of its investigations, the commission accorded a greater role to traditional connoisseurship and less of a role to scientific testing, which was found to have its limitations.

Painstaking work by twentieth-century scholars has led to the reattribution of many pictures once thought to be by Rembrandt. In 1920 more than seven hundred paintings were attributed to him, but a 1935 catalogue ascribed only 630 pictures to him. A 1969 catalogue reattributed fifty-six works, expressed uncertainty about one hundred works, and said that only 430 works were undoubtedly by Rembrandt. Only about thirty of those 430 works had official documents proving that Rembrandt had executed them. The first three volumes of the six to be published by the Dutch commission evaluated 276 Rembrandts and assigned 144 to its A category (undoubtedly by Rembrandt), twelve to its B category (uncertain as to artist), and 120 to its C category (not by Rembrandt). Paintings in the C category were not recent forgeries, but instead had been executed by Rembrandt's pupils and by imitators who were his contemporaries. Experts expect that by the time all of the commission's volumes are published, the number of authenticated Rembrandts will be between 250 and 350, about half the number assigned to him in 1920 (Bailey, 1990; Koning, 1986).

The reattribution of Rembrandts to other artists by the Rembrandt Research Project provoked disappointment, irritation, and anger in the art world. Some of that reaction could have been avoided if the commission had told owners of Rembrandts that it was compiling a catalogue of the artist's works when it asked to inspect their paintings; the commission did not inform owners of the possible reattribution of their pictures. Moreover, in the earlier stages of the commission's work, some owners learned about the reattribution of their paintings from stories in the press rather that directly from the commission; later, the commission informed owners directly of reattributions before releasing that information to the press. The commission also provoked anger with what some critics argued were dogmatic attributions and reattributions, even in cases when members of the panel disagreed about whether a painting was by Rembrandt. Critics also complained that the commission reattributed more Rembrandts in American and British collections than in Dutch collections. With reattribution, owners found that their pictures had suddenly lost much of their market value, a matter of greater concern to individual collectors than to museums, because individuals are more likely to hope to realize a profit from the sale or donation of their art in the future. Despite the possible loss of market value if a painting is reattributed, no owner of a painting thought to be by Rembrandt refused to let the commission examine the picture, because doing so would have cast doubt on the picture's authenticity.

In 1993, all but one of the remaining members of the Rembrandt Research Project resigned. Those who left the committee were of retirement age, but there was speculation that they had resigned because of disagreement over the best way to evaluate works attributed to Rembrandt. Some of the panel members seemed to acknowledge the need for a new method to replace their connoisseurship by committee, an approach in which works were assigned to category A, B, or C by majority vote. In the future, outside experts were to be consulted, and when there was ambiguity and uncertainty about who executed a particular piece, that disagreement would be acknowledged.

RESTORATION AND ORIGINALITY

The restoration of deteriorated works of art sometimes raises questions about originality: How much restoration can be done before a piece becomes something other than the work executed by the original artist? Should artworks be allowed to age naturally, or should efforts be made to keep them looking as much as possible like they were when they were originally created, even if doing that requires the use of modern materials to convey the impression the original artist intended to create?

Debate over the restoration of Michelangelo's Sistine Chapel paintings in the late 1980s raised some of these questions. Critics argued that restorers had changed the appearance of Michelangelo's masterpieces to such a degree that the aesthetic response that recent generations had had to the paintings was no longer possible, even if the pictures looked more like they originally had. These critics contended that the restorers had used corrosive chemicals, made the colors too strong, not used due care, and removed some of the artist's final touches. However, in 1987 an international group of conservators issued a report that unanimously and strongly approved of the restoration as in keeping with the style of sixteenth-century painting and in the spirit of Michelangelo's original work. Several American artists refused to accept that conclusion. Robert Motherwell remarked, "The way artists stick together, I presume restorers stick together. And in the end, restorers have to make as subjective a judgment as an artist does" (cited in Russell, 1987:C17). *New York Times* art critic John Russell (1988:H1) responded, "One or two pseudo-controversies notwithstanding, the restoration of the Sistine ceiling has been received with virtually unanimous approval by those best qualified to talk about it." Russell did admit that the restoration might be a bit jarring to someone accustomed to looking at what centuries of dirt and poorly done conservation had done to Michelangelo's paintings.

In response to criticism from artists and art historians that restorers sometimes usurp an original artist's role, expert restorer John Brealey of New York's Metropolitan Museum of Art has said that just as musicians must interpret music written in the past rather than play it by rote, so too must restorers interpret an artist's intent when they restore artworks. Another restorer describes the process of restoration as "reviving the spirit of an object for the pleasure of those who contemplate it" (Dryansky, 1988:112). Restoration requires technical skills and scientific tools such as computers, microscopes, centrifuges, and spectrophotometers. It also requires an aesthetic sensitivity that has been described as follows: "A talented restorer . . . counts on the inspiration that comes when he has entered into a work deeply enough to recognize its inner music. He fills lost portions of the melody by intuition" (Dryansky, 1988:109).

The escalating value of art has increased conservation efforts and intensified the debate over what restorers can ethically do without destroying an original work of art. Conservation ethics require restorers to isolate restoration work from original work; this is usually done by covering a picture's original paint and varnish with new paint and varnish in a way that restored areas clearly show up under black light. This makes it possible to reverse and redo the restoration if that becomes necessary. In 1991, a Dutch government report questioned whether the restoration of a vandalized Barnett Newman canvas was reversible, concluding that the original paint had been covered with an alkyd coating that could not be removed. Irreversible restoration of a large area of a picture produces a work that is not authentic, because the original artist's painting is no longer visible on the canvas.

Just as artists are influenced by the conventions of the art world, so too are restorers affected, often unconsciously, by the conventions of that world. Restorers sometimes adjust their work to the tastes of the time and to institutional preferences; for example, they may restore a painting to meet the standard of the other pictures in a museum. Alterations that restorers working at one time feel are in the spirit of an original work may at a later time be seen by art historians as awkward additions that "can seem as offensive as graffiti" on a work of art (Dryansky, 1988:113). Some skilled restorers try to improve rather than respect works of art, even going so far as to regard the end products as their masterpieces. However, their failure to sign their own names to the works indicates that they realize that the pieces are not truly their own creations and that their market value depends on the perception that they were created by other artists.

Restorers' major customers are dealers and individual collectors rather than museums. Museum curators aim to stabilize the process of decay, bring out the original work, and perhaps suggest what has been lost due to deterioration, but they try to prevent restorations from being passed off as original works. Dealers and collectors often have a more tolerant attitude, using their taste and feeling for a work to decide what restoration is acceptable to them. Two types of clients of France's house of André, world renowned restorers of art, are "dreamers," who want their art restored to look like some ideal they have in mind, and "investors," who want "the most inconspicuous restoration possible so as to get the best sale" (Alain Milhau, cited in Dryansky, 1988:111). When filling in a missing piece of a damaged work of art so as to enhance its market value, the restorer must make an artist's decision about how the work should look; that decision can alter the original artist's intent.

The ethics of art restorers allow them to consider their clients' wishes when restoring works of art. Madame André has said, "We restore in a visible way for the museums, so there's no confusion. But for private customers, the work is invisible. We reassure the eye, save the aesthetic appeal. It is up to each customer to decide what he wants done" (cited in Dryansky, 1988:111). She denies that her house has ever done fakes in her lifetime, but she seems aware that dealers and collectors who are her clients may later sell their restored pieces as originals. In claiming that what a client says afterward about the restored work is not her affair, Madame André is on safe ground legally, but her house and other expert restorers are an essential part of the market in fakes and near-fakes.

Questions sometimes arise about the amount of restoration that has been done to a work of art. Some dealers are reluctant to disclose that information to clients; they may also minimize or justify any restoration work that has been done. Restorers at the house of André will answer queries from potential buyers about the work that has been done on a piece, but many buyers will not even ask because they are unaware that any restoration has been done. The Andrés will also give an opinion about the quality of a work of art and the extent to which damage has reduced its value, but they will not testify as to the authenticity of an object because "It's dangerous. It's a way of turning one customer against another" (Jean Michel André, cited in Dryansky, 1988:111). Perhaps more importantly, such testimony would require the Andrés to grapple with the difficult question of what is a fake and what is an original, and the answer to those questions could reduce the demand for their services.

A difficult question is how much of the original work must remain for a piece to be considered a restored original rather than a fake or forgery. One conservator claims that if more than 25 percent of a painting's surface is covered by overpaint, the painting no longer shows the artist's intent and should not be considered an original. The owner of a painting said to be by Albert Bierstadt sued the auction house from which he had purchased it when he learned that more than 50 percent of its surface had been repainted; the case was settled out of court, with the owner returning the painting to the auction house in exchange for a sum of money nearly twice what he had paid for the picture.

Some restorations contain enough elements foreign to the original work that they should be classified as fakes. The possibility that some such restorations will make their way into the marketplace as authentic pieces is suggested by one restorer's description of his work: "We restore invisibly. If it looks fake, that's deplorable. If it's a good job, nobody can detect it" (cited in Dryansky, 1988:113). One observer sums up the contribution of restorers to the market in fakes as follows:

Over and over again, restorers have engendered beauty where it had disappeared. If pedigrees have been secretly spoiled, departed life has been brought back. Moreover, ingenious restorers have often enough created entire masterpieces of pastiche that, if correctly identified, would be classed as fakes. How many Renaissance rock-crystal-and-gold bibelots were made in the nineteenth century? How much Louis XVI furniture, copied by the Faubourg Saint-Antoine at the height of its skill a century ago, has passed from expert to expert as original? How much Khmer and African art is being made in Europe today? Ask any dealer. The honest reply would be "Quite a lot." (Dryansky, 1988:109)

DETECTING FAKES AND FORGERIES

Experts often have a difficult time authenticating ancient objects. An Egyptian cat sculpture that had been on display for years in New York's Metropolitan Museum of Art was not examined closely until experts discovered that another piece from the same period was a fake. The Metropolitan's cat had not been excavated during a museum-sponsored archaeological expedition, but had instead been purchased from a reputable dealer, who could not supply a record of the sculpture's history. After learning that the other cat sculpture was counterfeit, the museum staff X-rayed its sculpture and found it to be made of a porous bronze rarely used in ancient times; this suggested that it might have been made recently. That conclusion was tentative, because there are no reliable scientific dating techniques for ancient metals, because the porous bronze might have been used by an ancient metalsmith unable to find other kinds of bronze, and because other pieces made of porous bronze might not have survived the centuries (McGill, 1987e).

The difficulty of detecting fakes has sometimes led museum experts to mislabel originals as fakes, making curators wary of destroying works they believe are counterfeit. In 1967, a curator at the Metropolitan Museum of Art discovered that a small Greek horse sculpture thought to date from the fifth century B.C. had seams that suggested it had been cast from a mold using a process not developed until years after the object was supposedly made. The horse also had an armature that might not have been characteristic of the period to which it was attributed. The museum staff declared the sculpture a fake and removed it from display. Later, X-ray analysis showed that the seams were not part of the original sculpture but instead were the result of the museum's having once made a plaster cast of the horse to use for manufacturing reproductions. Further research showed that the armature was indeed characteristic of the period to which the horse had been attributed. When a thermoluminescence test showed that the sculpture's clay and calcium core did indeed date from ancient Greece, the piece was declared authentic and returned to its display case.

According to Geraldine Norman and Thomas Hoving (1987a:99), California's Getty Museum and its former curator of antiquities have purchased "what many scholars consider to be some of the most conspicuous fakes ever to go on display in a museum." Most controversial was a Greek kouros, a statue of a male, which the museum bought for about $9 million. Many European dealers questioned the authenticity of the statue at the time of its purchase in 1985; few museum curators expressed doubts, apparently because convention dictates that curators refrain from criticizing the holdings of other museums. Some experts who examined the kouros declared it authentic; others thought it was an obvious fake. Skeptics pointed to the pristine condition of a statue that supposedly dated from about 530 B.C. They noted the lack of tool marks on the surface, although one expert claimed to have found evidence of such tool marks. Microscopic analysis found nothing inconsistent with ancient carving techniques, although knowledgeable and skillful forgers might have mimicked those techniques successfully. Critics said the kouros was a pastiche of details and could not be traced to a specific ancient Greek workshop. Carbon and oxygen isotope tests showed the statue to bear a specific "fingerprint" traceable to a particular quarry on the Greek island of Thasos, but no other kouros made of that stone had been identified. After the discovery in 1990 of an obviously fake torso similar to the kouros, one scholar claimed that both pieces had been made in a Roman workshop in the early 1980s from the same block of marble.

Those who defended the kouros as authentic said it was unlikely that a faker could have duplicated the changes in the chemical content of the statue's surface, changes that take place over the centuries. However, recent research has shown that the process of aging called de-dolomitization once thought producible only by the passage of time could be replicated in a laboratory. Defenders of the kouros said that it was unlikely that a forger would have discovered such a process or found it practical to use in aging a counterfeit statue, but a multimillion-dollar profit might have been incentive enough to take the trouble to do so. John Russell has said that although the kouros might be a modern fake,

[a]ll probabilities were against it, however, in that the faker would have had to be a person of great historical sensitivity and familiar with the sculptures produced in the Greek island workshops in the sixth century B.C. He would have to be a carver of genius. He would have had to be able to outwit forms of scientific analysis that have been developed only very recently. And he would have had to be a crook. (Russell, 1986:C18)

Contradicting Russell, Norman and Hoving (1987b) support their contention that the kouros is a fake with circumstantial evidence that Jiri Frel, the Getty Museum's antiquities curator who negotiated the purchase of the kouros, may have played a role in making the statue. Frel had earlier been employed in a workshop that produced other fakes and had once made a cast of a similar, but authentic, kouros owned by an Athens museum.

Methods of Detecting Fakes and Forgeries

Chemists can estimate the age of some objects by measuring the radioactive carbon content and chemical composition of the materials from which the objects are made. Information gathered by researchers on the materials available and in use during different historical periods allows them to authenticate or invalidate artworks. Meticulous counterfeiters try to use only the materials that were available to the artists whose works they are forging, but they often make mistakes. In 1988, Swiss authorities seized 193 questionable works of art said to be by Russian artist Mikhail Larionov, primarily on the basis of evidence that two pigments used in the pastels had not existed at the time the pictures were supposed to have been executed. The authenticity of the pastels was also questioned because the paper on which they were done was not the same kind that Larionov had used (Pancoast and Lowenthal, 1988).

An X-ray of a sketch or another picture beneath the surface of a painting can sometimes be used to authenticate the painting. In one case, the costumes in an underpainting were characteristic of a time later than the surface painting was supposed to have been done, indicating that the surface painting was a forgery. In one controversial case, van Gogh's *Self Portrait with Straw Hat* was authenticated by one expert when an X-ray found an underpainting that van Gogh had done two years earlier. The expert asked why a forger would bother to paint over an original van Gogh or forge the earlier one and then paint over it, because X-rays were rarely used to authenticate paintings until the 1930s, and the painting in question had been exhibited earlier than that. However, Swiss scholar and dealer Walter Feilchenfeldt questioned the painting's authenticity, because there was no information about the man who first sold it to the dealer Vollard and because van Gogh's family archives contained no documentation of the painting. Feilchenfeldt traced the painting back to Dusseldorf, the source of a group of thirty forged van Goghs exposed by his father in 1928. He suggested that the forger might have done the underpainting, found it not good enough to pass off as authentic, and then painted a second forgery over it. Those who defend the authenticity of the painting argue that van Gogh often failed to keep records of his output, sometimes paid for his food and drink with his paintings, and painted the same subjects repeatedly. They also claim that the picture was much better painted than the group of forgeries exposed in 1928, and that it had been exhibited too early to have been part of that group of forgeries (Collins, 1990).

Because scientific tests can prove a work of art counterfeit, but cannot prove it authentic, experts must also employ connoisseurship and scholarship to uncover fakes and forgeries. Connoisseurship and scholarship often raise initial doubts about the authenticity of a piece, which may then be subjected to scientific testing. If those tests conclude that the piece could be authentic, connoisseurship and scholarship are again used to reach a final judgment on the work's authenticity. Experts analyze stylistic elements such as the colors used, the way the paint is applied, the facial features and posture of figures, the use of light, the motifs, and the overall composition of the work. They study exhibition catalogues, books on the artist's work, photographs, and documentary evidence to determine whether a questionable work of art ever existed. Sometimes they recognize a piece as part of a set of counterfeit works uncovered in the past. They also compare the signature on a suspicious work with the signatures on authenticated works from the same period in the artist's career. One portrait was declared counterfeit because the forger had misspelled artist Peter Paul Rubens's name.

Jacques Dupin, the only person empowered by Joan Miró's family to authenticate his works, has said, "To tell a good fake is like solving a crime. A good fake is made with intelligence and sensitivity, by an artist himself. But no crime is ever perfect. There is always a clue" (McGill, 1985c:C15). Because Miró's forms are simple and his style seems easy to fake, he has been widely forged, especially since his death in 1983. However, his technique is not really simple, so he is much harder to copy than it would seem. According to Dupin, collectors and dealers around the world own at least several hundred counterfeit Miró paintings and several thousand forged Miró prints and lithographs. Most of the misattributed paintings are so badly done that they are easy to detect, but forged prints are harder to detect. Forged prints are so common that Christie's does not accept for auction any Miró print that lacks the print number and size of the edition; forgers have adapted by numbering their counterfeits.

Dupin once detected a forged Miró painting that had accompanying documents, had been authenticated by an auction house, and was being offered with a pre-sale estimated price of $50,000. One clue that the painting was forged was that it had been painted on a kind of board that Miró had never used. Moreover, Miró always wrote the title of a painting on its back, and no title appeared on the picture's back, even though accompanying documents gave it a title. Miró's signature on the painting's surface was well executed, but Dupin discerned that the handwriting style was one used by Miró during the 1920s, whereas the style of the painting was one he used during the 1970s. Most telling to Dupin was that "the work was plain, the colors were flat, the brushstrokes unsteady, and the composition feeble" (McGill, 1985c:C15). Dupin said that he knew immediately that the work was a forgery by his "physical reaction" to it, a reaction he said he had developed over more than three decades of looking at Miró's art. He describes forgeries as being made from the exterior, whereas original Mirós came from within the artist; forgeries show no feeling of creation or life. Dupin also thought the painting was a forgery because the documents seemed to be fraudulent and because he had never heard of the Parisian dealer listed as the painting's original seller, despite his wide knowledge of the French art world.

A spokesperson for Christie's said it had appraised the Miró at $50,000 from a photograph, and that such an appraisal is not the same as an authentication; appraisals are always introduced with the statement, "If the work is authentic, it would likely bring a price in the range of. . . ." The Milwaukee dealer who had put the picture up for auction on behalf of a private collector said that he would take it back and tell the owner it was a fake, even though the owner might wish to auction it anyway because some people collect fakes. Dupin responded that under French law, he would have been allowed to have the police confiscate the forgery; if he could then have demonstrated in court that it was a counterfeit, a judge would have permanently impounded the painting or had it destroyed.

Dupin relies primarily on his experience and knowledge of Miró's work to detect forgeries, but he sometimes uses scientific methods such as pigment analysis and dating techniques. Because those methods are costly, they are usually reserved for examining more expensive works such as Old Masters paintings. Thus, the market value of an artwork, if it were authentic, influences the decision to subject it to scientific testing for authenticity. Knowledgeable forgers will thus counterfeit less expensive artworks, aware that such pieces will be less meticulously scrutinized by experts. Their relatively modest cost is one reason that multiple-edition prints are widely forged.

THE SOCIAL ORGANIZATION OF FAKING AND FORGERY

Skilled and knowledgeable artists are needed to produce pieces that can convincingly be sold as legitimate. Unscrupulous dealers then market those fakes and forgeries to vulnerable victims, often providing the objects with false provenances. Some forgers mastermind the fraud, others claim to be naively exploited by disreputable dealers, and still others enlist acquaintances to consign their forgeries to dealers or auction houses for sale, thus obscuring the origin of the works. David Stein, a forger who was particularly adept at creating Chagalls and Picassos, peddled many of his pieces to dealers and collectors himself; he also used his wife and once even a pickpocket to sell his forgeries (Stein, 1973). Jean-Pierre Schecroum, who forged works attributed to Picasso, Miró, Léger, Braque, and other twentieth-century artists, marketed his works through a dishonest art dealer and three other accomplices, who also helped him concoct provenances for the pieces. Other counterfeiters, such as Alceo Dossena and Brigído Lara, have claimed that they sold their work to dealers as modern reproductions for small sums, only discovering later that the dealers were selling the pieces as authentic antiquities. Those assertions should be viewed somewhat skeptically, because both forgers took great pains to provide their works with patinas that suggested they were very old. As Otto Kurz (1967:316) has observed, "The artist who spends his life creating works of art in the style of a bygone epoch and remains immaculately unaware of the fact that wicked dealers may sell his creations as antiques, is a myth."

Profiting from Fakes and Forgeries

Profit is the primary motive of forgers and the dealers who sell their works. Their counterfeit art is worth producing and marketing because of the high price that authentic art commands. The potential profit from selling fakes and forgeries justifies the effort to make them, create false provenances, and find unsuspecting buyers. Today, even multiple-edition prints have reached price levels that make such efforts worthwhile.

Fakes in the Third World. In poverty-stricken Third World countries, the production of fake indigenous art can be an important way to supplement low incomes. For instance, in Thailand, where the annual per capita income is about $1,000, a counterfeiter was paid $12,000 by a dealer for one of his sculptures. The dealer then sold the forgery to a collector for $32,000, accompanying it with a statement that it was a genuine twelfth-century sculpture. Sculptures such as these are carefully made and aged, often being buried to acquire a patina that will convince buyers of their authenticity. Some observers believe that virtually all objects in Thai antiques stores should be viewed with suspicion because few authentic antiquities remain for sale. One collector remarks, "It isn't always a matter of deliberate deception. Many dealers just can't recognize the really good fakes, and when they tell you it's real they believe it." A sculptor is less charitable, remarking, "Perhaps they believe because they want to believe" (cited in Warren, 1988:XX12). Some collectors may even buy such fakes knowingly, hoping to profit by selling them to unsuspecting buyers or by taking tax deductions after donating them to museums.

The secrecy of the illicit trade in antiquities allows grave-robbers, middlemen, and dealers to pass off fakes and forgeries with few repercussions. Museums and dealers wary of buying looted or illegally exported objects do not inquire too closely about a piece's origin; when they do, they are usually given false information. To protect themselves, buyers must have sufficient knowledge to distinguish the authentic from the fake. In Asia, counterfeiters have made a new head for an ancient statue that is missing one, packed the completed statue in mud and buried it for a time, and then sold it as an ancient work of art. A buyer pays for the piece in advance, a common practice in the antiquities trade, and only when the statue is cleaned does the buyer learn of the deception. Duped museums usually house such fakes in their basements to avoid embarrassment.

Third World people find it easy to justify their production and sale of fake objects because the ultimate purchasers are usually wealthy Westerners who are seen as exploitative of the Third World. Support for this point of view was expressed in a letter by a New Yorker who was responding to a *New York Times* report on African art:

Consumers with more money than they need are being relieved of some of the surplus through their desire to buy into 'authentic' and deeply rooted cultures. . . . [I]n the case of 'fake' African art, . . . the money is flowing into a fractured economy that truly needs it, making at least a small step toward redressing the huge disparity in wealth between the former colonial powers and those cultures so rudely shattered by them. To the makers and sellers of 'fake' African art: Way to go. (Mittlemark, 1988:H22)

Although they are angry at foreign dealers and collectors who buy and smuggle authentic art from their country, most Africans are not troubled by the sale of fakes to foreigners. Indeed, that activity is looked on favorably as a source of income that can improve the standard of living in the villages where the counterfeiters work (Brooke, 1988). There fake masks and statues are produced and aged, sometimes by burying them in termite hills or kicking them around to "stress" them. They are then sold to Western tourists, dealers, and collectors or to indigenous traders who scour the villages on bicycles looking for pieces they can buy and sell to Westerners for profit. American tourists have sometimes contributed to the local economy by paying guides to help them distinguish the authentic from the fake. One local trader claims that French and German tourists are less apt to hire such guides and are thus easier prey. However, as Westerners have learned that indigenous carvers have become sophisticated at producing high-quality fakes, they have grown reluctant to buy any African art, curbing even the legitimate trade in authentic objects (Brooke, 1988).

Traders and dealers profit from the difference between African and Western definitions of authenticity (Burnham, 1975). For many Africans, a newly carved mask or statue is just as authentic as an old one, and so they willingly sell or trade old objects and replace them with new ones. However, Western dealers and collectors regard old objects as more authentic than new ones. For them, authentic objects must have a history of having been used in a ritual context; they must have been "made by a traditional African carver for a traditional use" (Christopher Steiner, cited in Brooke, 1988:H51). Recently made objects are usually treated as replicas intended to deceive buyers into thinking they once had a ritualistic function. To accommodate Western collectors, Africans sometimes "dance" modern objects in a special ceremony so that dealers can honestly claim that they have been used in a ritualistic context.

The Steele Forgeries. Even the relatively well-to-do have been enticed by the profits to be made from selling fakes and forgeries. In 1986, an Indiana couple whose gallery had been a major force behind the growth in popularity of artist T. C. Steele and the Hoosier School was charged with selling forgeries of Steele's oil paintings. The husband and wife were accused of trying to take advantage of the recent escalation of prices for Steele's work, an increase they had helped create through exhibitions, catalogues, and advertisements in national magazines. The best of Steele's oil paintings had risen in price from about $2,000 in 1976 to as much as $30,000 a decade later. The forged Steeles, most of which were sold for between $6,000 and $15,000, were not especially expensive paintings by contemporary standards, but even those prices were sufficiently high to make forgery profitable.

The limited attention given to Steele's work by the art world minimized the chance that the forgeries would be detected, an advantage for the counterfeiters because many of the paintings were obvious forgeries: they had been painted on new canvas and mounted on new stretchers, even though they were supposed to be a century old; the paint that was used dissolved instantly in solvents, even though it should have hardened over the years; and the canvases were stapled rather than tacked to the stretchers, even though there were no staple guns when Steele painted. In addition to the forgeries that were new pictures, some of the Steeles were old pictures that had been repainted or had had signatures added or altered (*The New York Times*, November 6, 1986).

The Artist as Counterfeiter

The production of forgeries and fakes requires a skilled and knowledgeable artist. Jack Hartert, a master forger who produced pastiches of European modern masters, knew enough about those artists' ideas "to manipulate the vocabulary of forms and motifs" they used and create convincing paintings in their styles (*Stolen Art Alert*, November 1982a:1). Another adept counterfeiter, Robert Lawrence Trotter, used his skills as an artist and restorer and his knowledge of art history to produce and market forgeries of American folk art. He created a pastiche of a John Haberle painting, knowing that Haberle was a good artist to counterfeit because only twenty-seven of his works were known, fifteen more were missing, and the prices for his pictures had appreciated in recent years, one selling for $517,000 in 1987. To produce his Haberle, Trotter stripped the paint from an old canvas, employed motifs from authentic Haberle pictures, artificially produced a cracking of the painting's surface varnish, used an antique frame, and fabricated a credible provenance.

Counterfeiters must use materials and conceive of compositions that will fool the experts. They may forge drawings on paper cut from old books, paint over a picture on an old canvas, or acquire marble that comes from the same quarry as that used by another sculptor. They must create a piece in the style of an artist whose works sell for prices high enough to justify the effort of counterfeiting, and they must execute it in a style that will convince connoisseurs. Often forgers copy a work from a different medium, perhaps doing a drawing that will appear to be a study for a known oil painting. Frequently, details give away a work as a forgery; for example, a particular kind of oriental carpet may not have yet been imported to Europe at the time a picture including it was supposedly done. Counterfeiters also have a difficult time re-creating the energy of the original artist; instead, they copy a style in a mechanical way that connoisseurs often recognize easily.

Artists age their creations to look the way buyers expect originals to appear. Counterfeit statues are given patinas that match as closely as possible those on authentically ancient objects; pieces are dirtied to make it seem that they have been underground for centuries, or they are chemically treated to make them seem old. Paintings have craquelure added artificially through heating or chemical treatment, or simply by pulling the canvas over the edge of a table and applying pressure with one's hands; painting over pictures on old canvases can also produce a convincing effect. Because buyers expect Old Masters paintings to have accumulated grime over the years, forgers dirty the surfaces of such forgeries. A clean surface on an Old Master picture may arouse suspicion that it is not authentic, or that it is authentic but has been cleaned and shown to prospective buyers who have rejected it.

Forgers employ justifying rhetorics to persuade others that they have done nothing wrong (Fine, 1983). They claim that their first forgery was intended as a practical joke or was a reproduction done for a legitimate purpose. They assert that they did not intend to pass their work off as someone else's until a collector or a middleman confidently claimed that the piece was an original work by a well-known artist. Forgers thus deny criminal intent in their initial counterfeiting activities, saying that they got more involved only when they realized how easy it was to fool the experts and how much money they could make.

Other counterfeiters have justified their deceptions as a protest against an art world that is intellectually corrupt and exploitative of artists. When his forgeries of drawings by English artist Samuel Palmer were exposed in 1976, Tom Keating remarked, "I flooded the market with the 'work' of Palmer and many others, not for gain (I hope I am no materialist) but simply as a protest against merchants who make capital out of those I am proud to call my brother artists, both living and dead" (cited in Haywood, 1987:119). Before engaging in the production of counterfeit art, many forgers had been unsuccessful as artists in their own right, later claiming that they had been rejected by the art establishment because of who they were; after all, they ask, have they not produced works as beautiful as those of the masters? What they omit, of course, is that those works were not their original creations.

When counterfeit art is traced back to the artist who produced it, he or she often says that the pieces were intended to be copies or reconstructions, not forgeries. Admitting that he or she made a facsimile of an existing work in the style of a well-known artist, even admitting that the work was signed with the name of another artist, may not be sufficient for a criminal conviction for forgery unless the prosecutor can prove beyond a reasonable doubt that the artist *intended* to defraud an unwary buyer. Two artists accused of forgery, Anthony Tetro and Christian Goller, both said in a 1991

"Nova" television documentary, "The Fine Art of Faking It," that they had made reconstructions of the works of famous painters, but both denied being forgers. Tetro claimed that he had painted his copies on commission for collectors who wanted to own one. Goller, who is both a talented painter and a skilled restorer, said, "Whoever calls me a forger is lying. I only paint in the style of the Old Masters. I add patina and crackle for decoration. You can't call that a forgery. . . . I think copies make art accessible. Everybody can afford to hang a Grünewald in his house." Goller also said that he does not forge the signature of the artist whose work he is imitating; neither, however, does he sign his facsimiles with his own signature. Both Goller and Tetro claimed that they had sold their pictures only as copies, not as original works by other artists. They blamed others for passing their work off as authentic and profiting more handsomely than they had. Goller admitted selling a Matthias Grünewald that he had painted to an admirer for only $2,000; later, the Cleveland Museum of Art purchased it for $1 million. Goller was proud that his creation had been mistaken for an original Grünewald, but wryly expressed dismay at yet another failure by the experts to distinguish the authentic from the counterfeit.

In contrast to the forger's rhetoric is that of the established art world. Dealers and collectors regard forgers as threatening the investment value of art by subverting the trust between buyer and seller that sustains the art market. Art historians worry that forgeries will confuse the world's under-standing of its artistic heritage; they claim that aesthetic appreciation relies on an understanding of the historical context in which art was produced and the whole body of work of the artist who created it, not merely on the physical appearance of art. Forgers, on the other hand, emphasize the object as a thing of beauty in and of itself, abstracted from any historical or biographical context. The established art world has typically responded to forgery by denigrating forgers as morally corrupt, egotistical, ambitious, and imitative, even when their creations had once been revered as works of genius (Fine, 1983).

The Dossena Sculptures. When Alceo Dossena died in 1937, experts estimated that Americans had paid between $1 million and $3 million for his forged sculptures; in today's dollars, the amount would be twenty times greater. Dossena did not think of himself as a forger, saying, "I am not a forger [or] a swindler. I never copied works. I simply reconstructed them" (Sox, 1988:176). Initially, Dossena may have unwittingly engaged in for-gery, with dealers selling his sculptures as ancient pieces without his knowledge, but when some of those pieces were later resold after being returned to dealers by museums that discovered they were not authentic,

Dossena must have learned that his works were being marketed as something other than what they really were.

Born into a family of artists and craftsmen, Dossena was expelled from school at twelve when he made fun of his teacher and classmates for believing that a sculpture of Venus that he had made, broken the arms off, and buried was an original work. That prank was precipitated by another teacher's showing little interest in the statue and by his classmates' derision as he carried the piece home. As a young man, Dossena was apprenticed to a Milanese stonemason and sculptor, from whom he learned ancient techniques of working with stone, aging statuary, and matching the individual styles of artists. Soon he was asked to create new copies of old statuary that was beyond repair.

Before making his fakes, Dossena would research the artist whose style he was going to imitate; he did not make exact copies of existing pieces. Over the years, Dossena developed a method of creating convincing patinas on works of stone; he dipped his sculptures into an acid bath about forty times, applied various chemicals to the stone, and then covered it with a black substance that he removed before polishing the piece. The resulting patina fooled experts into believing the stone had been weathered for centuries. Dossena also broke pieces off his completed statues and smashed them to make it appear that they had been damaged while being excavated. These elaborate efforts to make his creations seem ancient strongly suggest that Dossena knew the pieces were being marketed as authentic antiquities.

Dossena sometimes used old materials in creating his forgeries. In 1924, Boston's Museum of Fine Arts paid $100,000 for a marble sarcophagus that it thought had been executed by Mino da Fiesole. Steel heir Helen Clay Frick's agents had rejected the sarcophagus three years earlier because of doubts about its authenticity. In making this piece, Dossena had used some fifteenth-century fragments, but most of it he had created himself. Experts at the museum chose to define the tomb as a fifteenth-century original that had been rebuilt with nonoriginal additions and substitutions, raising the question of how much of an original work of art must remain for it to be authentic. In this case, most experts agreed that the sarcophagus was not an original Mino da Fiesole.

Two dealers and a middleman sold Dossena's sculptures to different outlets each time to avoid flooding the market and arousing the suspicions of dealers, curators, and collectors. Each piece was accompanied by a fabricated story of its origin. The dealers paid Dossena a very small portion of what they earned from selling his creations as original works, frequently complaining to him that they were not earning much for their efforts. Once Dossena was paid only 25,000 lire for a piece sold by a dealer for 6 million lire (about $360,000). Dossena's forgeries were revealed to the world when he demanded from one of the dealers $7,500 that he was owed for a piece the dealer had sold for $150,000. When the dealer refused, Dossena took photographs of his works to a Roman judge and sued for payment. His claim was dismissed for lack of sufficient proof. Eighteen years after Dossena's death, his son published a volume with fifty-one photographs of his father's sculptures, naming the museums that had bought and displayed them as authentic works of ancient art.

The van Meegeren Vermeers. Han van Meegeren, a Dutch artist who painted between the two world wars, never succeeded in producing work of his own that was recognized as worthy by the art establishment. He turned to faking and forging others' works as a way of gaining revenge on the critics who had slighted his work. Not every expert was fooled by van Meegeren's forgeries of oil paintings by the esteemed seventeenth-century Dutch artist Johannes Vermeer, but the influential Dutch art historian and critic Dr. Abraham Bredius, a special target of van Meegeren's hostility, declared van Meegeren's *Supper at Emmaus* to be an authentic Vermeer. Van Meegeren's poor imitations of Vermeer's work may have been widely accepted as authentic by Dutch experts because of their patriotic fervor, which took the form of an all-out effort to keep national treasures out of the hands of the Nazis, and because authentic Vermeers were in storage for safekeeping due to the war and therefore not available for comparison.

Van Meegeren's forgeries were cleverly done in the style of a single painting attributed to an early period in Vermeer's career; that uncharacteristic picture, which is not universally accepted as a Vermeer, portrayed a biblical scene and included large figures. In retrospect, it is surprising that no one considered the possibility of forgery when six additional paintings in that unusual style turned up between 1937 and 1943, none of them with a convincing provenance.

To produce his Vermeers, van Meegeren had to study the techniques of the Dutch master and then use his own skills to reproduce that style; he had first learned some of those techniques from one of his high school teachers. Van Meegeren executed his Vermeers on seventeenth-century canvases with paints that the master might have used, artificially aged the surfaces of the pictures, and mounted them in seventeenth-century frames. He had a paint supplier mix paints according to his detailed instructions; one piece of evidence to support van Meegeren's eventual claim that he had painted the canvases was a cobalt blue not available in Vermeer's time, a pigment provided by the supplier in violation of van Meegeren's instructions. Another piece of evidence was a modern form of resin that van Meegeren had used to age the paintings.

When van Meegeren's *Christ and the Woman Taken in Adultery,* with its forged Vermeer signature, was found in the possession of Nazi Reichsmarschall Hermann Goering, Dutch authorities traced the picture back to van Meegeren. Van Meegeren provided the authorities with a story to account for the picture's lack of provenance, saying that he had obtained it from an Italian aristocratic family that was down on its luck. Not believing his tale, Dutch officers arrested him for collaborating with the Nazis. Critics' regard for van Meegeren's skill as an artist was low enough that when he claimed that he had forged the painting, an admission he hoped would help him avoid the severe penalty for treason, no one believed that he could have produced such a beautiful picture. Materials were brought to him in his prison cell, and he demonstrated to the skeptics exactly how he had produced the Vermeer by painting another one. Two years after his arrest, he was convicted of forgery and fraud, but he died in a hospital before serving any of his one-year prison sentence.

Forgers often justify their counterfeiting in nonpecuniary terms, such as their enjoyment at fooling the experts or their demonstration that they are as skilled as the masters at creating beautiful art. However, the primary motive for most forgers is money. Van Meegeren was well paid for the six Vermeers and two de Hoochs he passed off as authentic, earning about $4 million for those pictures. Asserting during his trial that pecuniary motives had been unimportant to him, van Meegeren remarked that he had had to sell the pictures at high prices in order to avoid suspicion that they were forgeries.

The Stein Forgeries. A prolific forger best known as David Stein, but born in France as Henri Haddad, executed hundreds of forgeries that he sold as original works by Chagall, Picasso, and other modern masters (Stein, 1973). Stein moved from city to city in Europe and then to the United States, being wary of arousing suspicion by saturating the market with counterfeit art. When he arrived in a city, he would tour the local galleries to determine what they were buying, and then he set to work creating forgeries. He first tried to sell his creations to a prestigious gallery, knowing that word of his presence would quickly spread among local dealers.

Most of Stein's forgeries were drawings and watercolors; he avoided oil paintings because they took too long to complete and to dry, were too expensive for many galleries, and were most likely to arouse suspicion because they were the art form most commonly catalogued. Stein produced works in the manner of famous artists rather than making exact copies of their art; he created variations on themes that an artist had often used, assuming that few buyers would know every variation the artist had produced. Stein chose modern masters to forge because he could obtain materials indistinguishable from the ones they had used. He and his wife aged the paper on which he worked with tea. He had to practice the artist's signature and, equally as important, learn in what medium the artist signed pictures of the sort that Stein was counterfeiting. The cost of creating works on paper was small, the most expensive item always being the frame, which the Steins spent much time selecting.

Stein often sold his forgeries himself, a practice that is relatively uncommon for counterfeiters. He also used his wife to sell his works, sometimes having her pose as the owner, a role that allowed her to negotiate with a dealer and lower her asking price in a way that Stein, posing as a dealer, could not have done. A dealer who agrees to a lower price soon acquires a reputation as a soft touch among other dealers, and that would have cut into Stein's profits. On one occasion, Stein paid a pickpocket to sell his forgeries, but first he had to coach his accomplice to use proper diction and teach him something about the artists whose work he was selling. If Stein had used more accomplices to help him sell his forgeries, he could have sold more pieces before moving to another city, but using accomplices would have increased his risk of apprehension because more people would have known of his fraudulent activities.

Sometimes Stein fabricated documents to make his works seem authentic. He had a rubber stamp made that resembled that of a French gallery so that he could give his works the appearance of a provenance. When a New York dealer asked him for authenticating papers for three Chagalls, Stein said he would have to write to Paris for the papers. He then fabricated the papers himself and gave them to the dealer two days later, before realizing, as the dealer did, that the mail between Paris and New York could not have delivered the papers so quickly. The dealer notified the district attorney's office of his suspicions about the authenticity of the pictures, and Stein was eventually arrested, convicted, and sentenced to prison.

Lara's pre-Columbian Statues. Brigído Lara was arrested in Veracruz, Mexico, in 1974 for possessing what law-enforcement agents thought was a priceless pre-Columbian artifact that had been looted from a tomb. An archaeologist who examined the object declared it authentic, and Lara was convicted and imprisoned. Protesting that he was a forger rather than a looter, Lara finally persuaded prison officials to let his attorney bring clay and tools to his cell, where he made an exact duplicate of the piece that had led to his imprisonment. After his release, Lara went to work for the Mexican government as a restorer of ancient artifacts and a maker of replicas.

In the early 1980s, Lara announced that he had made several of the pre-Columbian figures purchased at Sotheby's in New York by the governor of Veracruz for the Jalapa Archaeological Museum. Eventually, Lara's statues were found in some of the world's best collections of pre-Columbian art; about a dozen had been shown in a 1971 Los Angeles show of 150 artifacts from Veracruz. Over a period of about twenty years, Lara had made hundreds, perhaps thousands, of sculptures in a pre-Columbian style, many of which entered the legitimate market and many of which are still regarded as authentic pre-Columbian pieces rather than as modern fakes (Crossley and Wagner, 1987).

Lara began by repairing and restoring artifacts brought to him by looters. Later, he made his own pre-Columbian look-alikes, claiming recently that he had intended those interpretations of ancient sculptures to be his own original works rather than forgeries of ancient works (Crossley and Wagner, 1987). Lara sold his statues to tourists, collectors, and middlemen who traveled from village to village seeking looted objects to sell to dealers. He asserts that he never sold a statue to anyone who was unaware that it was his own work, and that what happened after a statue left his hands was not his concern. When he learned that some of his customers had doctored his statues to make them seem old, he said that he never would have condoned that practice.

There are reasons to believe that Lara was more than an unwitting accomplice in the marketing of his statues as ancient works. He was once employed by a Mexico City atelier that specialized in the forgery of pre-Columbian art. He carefully studied authentic sculptures and ancient techniques of craftsmanship, and he took great care to make his statues conform to the conventions of pre-Columbian art. He used clay from regions where ancient sculptures had been discovered, and he kept in his workshop many kinds of powder for coloring his finished figures. He collected materials to give his statues patinas that would match those on the pieces he was imitating. He even invented his own wooden tools after studying the tools used by ancient people to make their sculptures. A charitable observer might conclude that Lara was simply a meticulous craftsman with high standards who wanted to provide collectors with reproductions as authentic as possible. Probably a more realistic assessment is that he made every effort he could to deceive potential customers into thinking that they were getting authentic pre-Columbian pieces (Crossley and Wagner, 1987).

Lara's sculptures began to appear in the United States in the late 1950s. In the 1980s, collectors and dealers recalled early doubts and rumors about the pieces, but for the most part their authenticity was not questioned when they first appeared on the market. According to one archaeologist, "These big figures came up all over. They appeared out of nowhere, resembling nothing previously excavated. I saw some in New York, Los Angeles, Paris. Museums bought them, big collectors bought them. But nobody asked,

'How come a big find like this?' " (Edmund Carpenter, cited in McGill, 1987g:C19). Many of the pieces were eventually reproduced in catalogues and textbooks as prime examples of the late classic period of the Veracruz region.

Pre-Columbian art has several advantages over other kinds of art for forgers. First, because most of it is not attributed to individual artists, it is easier to fake. That anonymity helped Lara avoid being accused of counterfeiting another artist's work; instead, he was copying a historical style. A second advantage is that the detection of pre-Columbian fakes is difficult, because scientific tests used on ceramics do not work for the kind of clay found in some of the regions from which the objects come, and because the cleaning of the pieces by museums often eliminates surface pigments and coatings to which thermoluminescence tests might be applied. A third advantage for forgers of pre-Columbian art is that because much of it has been destroyed or remains undiscovered, there is no complete catalogue of authentic pieces with which to compare newly discovered ones. There is still much that scholars do not know about the iconography of those ancient civilizations, and so it is difficult to determine if the markings on a newly discovered piece are inconsistent with authentic iconography. Indeed, Lara's fakes have actually been the source of some of what has been accepted as authentic pre-Columbian iconography, and he himself has had to explain why some of his statues could not be authentically pre-Columbian. For instance, he claims that no ancient piece depicting the wind god Ehecatl, whom scholars have written about for years, has ever been excavated, and that all works depicting that god are his own. So many of Lara's pieces have resided in museums and private collections for so long that his fakes have skewed scholars' knowledge of art from the late classic Veracruz period (Crossley and Wagner, 1987; McGill, 1987g).

Creating a False Provenance

The sale of fakes and forgeries requires the establishment of a false provenance. Fabricated invoices of earlier sales, fake labels from respected galleries, fictitious numbers from the catalogue of an artist's *oeuvre,* and concocted letters from dealers or collectors expressing an interest in buying a work of art will all give credibility to counterfeit works of art. Credibility can also be established by bribing an expert to declare a counterfeit work genuine; one renowned expert was offered $700,000 and then $1.5 million to declare a counterfeit Jackson Pollock genuine (Lowenthal, 1992). Fake art is sometimes marketed with authentic documents that have been stolen; papers have also been provided by a laboratory that has examined an original work of art, with photographs of the fake being substituted for those of the original and the laboratory's report being altered to fit the pictures of the fake (Goodrich, 1973:131). Pedigrees are also created by exhibiting fakes in reputable museums and galleries and by selling them at country auctions, where an accomplice is enlisted to buy the art.

The tactic of forging documents that testify to a work's past owners is most effective if the reputed past owners are eminent collectors who are deceased and unable to challenge the documentation. In describing the antiquities trade, a Swiss museum curator has claimed, "It's public knowledge that ninety percent of the certificates of origin accompanying such works of art are totally unreliable" (cited in Meyer, 1973:124). According to Norman and Hoving (1987b), the Swiss dealer who sold the Greek kouros to the Getty Museum concocted an elaborate provenance that included letters from five people—four deceased at the time of the purchase—who said they had seen the kouros in the collection of a Swiss physician. Experts determined that the letters were fabricated and that the statue had apparently never belonged to the doctor. A fabricated provenance does not necessarily mean that the object itself is counterfeit, because an authentic piece that is illicitly dug up and smuggled from a country might be given a concocted provenance in order to sell it.

Dealers in fakes and forgeries make up elaborate stories about how they obtained the works they are offering for sale. Their stories are most effective if they have a ring of credibility but are difficult to confirm. Stories often include an accident or disaster that destroyed documents that could have validated the works, as well as special circumstances that have forced the owner to sell the art. In trying to sell a collection of counterfeit drawings and paintings said to be by van Gogh, Rembrandt, Renoir, and other masters, Tony Barreiro claimed that he had paid an Arab sheik only $40,000 for the collection because the sheik had lacked proper documentation for the works. The reputed origin of a group of forged van Goghs uncovered in 1928 was an unnamed Russian collector who was said to have destroyed all documents that could have authenticated the paintings because he feared reprisals from his family if they learned that he had smuggled the paintings from the Soviet Union to Switzerland. In another case, Robert Lawrence Trotter enticed a dealer to pay $25,000 for a counterfeit painting by John Haberle with a convincing tale of how his wife disliked the picture that she had inherited from her aunt. Trotter told the dealer that he had established the price of $25,000 from an old appraisal and that he could provide the original bill of sale. Aware that an authentic Haberle might fetch more than $500,000, the dealer was delighted to buy the painting at such a low price.

A clever scam for marketing forgeries was developed by Eduardo de Valfierno and Yves Chaudron in the early part of this century. Operating at first in Buenos Aires, Valfierno would approach a woman whose wealthy husband had recently died and suggest that she buy a Murillo painting to donate to their church in her husband's name. The Murillos were painted by Chaudron. The two men later moved to Mexico City, where Chaudron continued to paint Murillos. Valfierno, who lived in a tourist hotel, would approach a well-to-do visitor and offer to steal a Murillo painting that was hanging in a local church, then ship the picture to the tourist's home. Valfierno would take the victim to the church to see the original Murillo; if the person agreed to the arrangement, Valfierno would turn the painting around and have the victim sign its back. Prior to the visit to the church, Valfierno or Chaudron had slipped one of Chaudron's forgeries into the back of the frame containing the original Murillo, so when the counterfeit picture was sent to the victim it had the signature on the back and seemed to be an authentic Murillo (Jeppson, 1970).

The Roman art dealers who marketed Alceo Dossena's forgeries provided them with false provenances that fit the style—Renaissance, Greek, Etruscan—in which Dossena had executed the piece. One dealer gave the origin of some of Dossena's sculptures as an abbey near Siena that had been buried in a seventeenth-century earthquake. He claimed that a priest had discovered the abbey and provided him with its floor plan, which showed the places from which several important sculptures had been removed. The dealer said that he could not reveal the abbey's location and had to dispose of the pieces in secrecy. Once a statue by Dossena was planted in a small chapel near Rome, and an agent for the Cleveland Museum of Art was taken there to discover it; the person who took the agent to the chapel was the friend of a prominent dealer, whose gallery just happened to be next door to Dossena's studio.

The strategy of salting tombs with fakes has also been employed to create believable provenances for counterfeit pre-Columbian pieces, with witnesses to staged excavations lending credibility to the objects' authenticity. A San Francisco dealer said that in 1957 he unearthed at a Veracruz jungle site three works now in highly respected American museums. His film of the dig shows the sculptures being taken from the ground, but some archaeologists believe that the dealer was the victim of a staged excavation. The dealer himself doubts it, saying that in 1957 the price of pre-Columbian art was so low that "you couldn't give it away" and that there would have been little to gain from such chicanery.

The revelation in 1991 that Priam's treasure, a hoard of gold and silver that had disappeared from Germany at the end of World War II, was stored in Moscow suggested the possibility of scientifically testing the authenticity of the pieces in the hoard, which has long been associated with the king of Troy. Questions have been raised for years as to whether Heinrich Schliemann, the German archaeologist who unearthed the treasure in 1871–1873, might have salted the site with artifacts he had bought from dealers and with forgeries made for him by a goldsmith. Schliemann was wealthy, so if he padded his discovery it was not for profit, but rather to support his theory that Homer's *The Iliad* was based on actual events that occurred in the Bronze Age (Burke, 1992).

Violating the Conventions for Multiple-Edition Artworks

Documentation of a work's provenance is one convention used in the art world to minimize the production and sale of fakes and forgeries. A similar function is served by conventions that evolved in the twentieth century to ensure the authenticity of multiple-edition images such as etchings, lithographs, and serigraphs. Prior to the twentieth century, artists identified their prints with a signature or sometimes a symbol such as Whistler's butterfly, but they did not number their prints and give the size of the total edition of the image. Today, in addition to being signed by the artist, authentic prints are expected to bear the number of the print and the size of the edition, such as 3/200, the third print in an edition of 200. Another convention is that the artist is supposed to have created the image on a stone, zinc plate, or silk screen, and then supervised or carried out the printing of the multiple copies, which rarely number more than 300. The original plate is then to be defaced or destroyed so as to prevent anyone from making additional copies.

Works not produced according to these conventions are defined as counterfeits, though some dealers argue that these criteria for authenticity are too strict. One bold counterfeiter simply cut out, framed, and sold as original works the frontispieces from art books. Worthless prints have also been made by someone other than the artist from the original plate but without the artist's authorization. Salvador Dali signed blank pieces of paper on which others printed images, then sold them as original Dali prints at high prices; those pictures are defined as counterfeits by art world conventions. Forgers have also photographed an original image produced by an artist, transferred the negative onto a lithographic plate or silk screen, and then produced thousands of copies. Counterfeits that are photo-offsets can often been seen, on close examination, to be composed of microscopic dots rather than continuous fields of color. However, improved technology now allows forgers to reproduce images in broad areas of color that simulate the appearance of original lithographs or serigraphs, without the telltale dots that would reveal the image to be an inexpensive reproduction (McGill, 1987b). Even with prints that are considered legitimate according to the conventions of the art world, the distinction between authentic and counterfeit is sometimes unclear. For example, some contemporary artists submit watercolors and oil paintings to lithographers, who make photographic mechanical lithographs of the image; the artists then sign and number the lithographs and sell them as original prints.

Counterfeited works by Dali, Chagall, Picasso, and Miró are often sold as original, hand-signed, limited-edition prints for between $1,000 and $8,000 each. In 1992, 75,000 allegedly counterfeit prints by those four artists were seized. Michael Ward Stout, a lawyer who has represented Dali in the United States, estimates that between $600 million and $1 billion of fraudulent or misrepresented works attributed to Dali were sold in the United States between 1980 and 1987 (Raab, 1987a). Many of the prints said to be by Dali, Chagall, Picasso, or Miró are actually high-quality poster reproductions of original oil paintings, watercolors, or works in other media that have forged or facsimile signatures and that have a true market value of less than $30 each. Today, there are so many counterfeit prints by those artists in circulation that auction houses refuse to sell prints said to have been done in recent years; for instance, Christie's will not sell any Dali prints published after 1949, because there is no catalogue raisonné for the artist's prints after that date. An artist's reputation often suffers when a large number of forged prints overexposes the public to the artist's style, makes it seem that any skilled artist can create works similar to the originals, and makes the public suspicious of all of the artist's prints.

A few states now have laws to protect the buyers of prints. Dealers are required to tell their customers if a print is part of a limited edition and, if so, the size of that edition. They are also required to tell their customers whether the plate from which the prints were made still exists and can be used to make additional impressions, or whether it was used to make earlier editions of the same image. Aware of public concern about counterfeit prints, an increasing number of print publishers are including a certificate of authenticity with each print. However, dishonest dealers who sell forged prints have learned to offer such certificates for what they sell, thereby guaranteeing the authenticity of one counterfeit piece of paper with another (Grant, 1987).

Sculptures are another art form sometimes produced in multiple editions, and, as with prints, questions have arisen about the authenticity of sculptures. Surmoulages, which are casts made from a mold taken from an original cast, are sometimes defined as counterfeit according to the conventions of the art world, but the meaning of authenticity with sculptures is unclear, because even original bronze sculptures are reproductions of other material and are not produced fully by the artist (Trustman, 1981). Compared to an original sculpture, a surmoulage is usually smaller, more crudely cast, made from different material, and has less crisp details, a different patina, and a forged signature.

The intent to deceive buyers is not always present in the manufacture of surmoulages. Legitimate foundries sometimes make surmoulages and stamp them as such, but even those pieces can be purchased by unsuspecting buyers as original works if the buyers are not knowledgeable about the identifying marks or if those marks are altered or obliterated by unscrupulous collectors or dealers. Moreover, when surmoulages are numbered and sold for high prices, the impression is conveyed that the buyer is purchasing a work of art that will appreciate in value rather than a mere reproduction; a similar deception occurs when photomechanical reproductions of paintings and prints are sold in limited editions (Trustman, 1981). Some foundries produce surmoulages at the request of the owner of an original sculpture; the owner then gives away or sells the copies, often giving one to the foundry owner for making the reproductions. If surmoulages or reproductions that cannot readily be distinguished from original sculptures flood the market, as has happened with Frederic Remington's sculptures, collectors will become wary and the value of the originals may fall. Dealers who intentionally misrepresent surmoulages or reproductions as original works often try to sell those copies in areas of the country where there are few original pieces in public collections, thereby making it difficult for buyers to discover that they have bought a counterfeit piece by comparing it to an original one (Pancoast, 1990b).

In 1991, New York implemented a law to protect future buyers of sculptures selling for more than $1,500. This law prohibited the sale of unauthorized casts without disclosing such information as the name of the artist and the title, dimensions, material, and number of casts made of the sculpture. The law was designed to deal with several abuses, including the sale of cheap replicas as valuable sculptures, the passing off of unauthorized copies as authentic pieces, and the representation of limited editions as more limited in number than they really were. Full disclosure of information about sculptures will help ensure that the price paid by a buyer is commensurate with the actual value of a piece.

The Marketing of Counterfeit Art

Honest dealers are sometimes fooled by the fakes and forgeries they are offered for sale, even after they try to authenticate them. Other dealers knowingly market fakes, and some of them refuse to buy back works they have sold that are later discovered to be counterfeit. In a few cases, dealers have systematically acted as conduits from counterfeiters to unsuspecting buyers; during the 1950s and 1960s, Joseph Hartert's New York gallery sold many forgeries produced by his son, Jack Hartert (*Stolen Art Alert*, November 1982a). Occasionally, forgers market their own creations, as did Robert Lawrence Trotter, who was described as "an incredibly slick and ruthless con man" by a dealer who bought a forgery from him (cited in Sill, 1990:98). Knowing that this dealer did not buy from strangers, Trotter cultivated her trust over time with a series of telephone calls, an offer to have her look at the paintings and furniture in his mother's estate, and forged documents that established provenances for the paintings. When legitimate dealers questioned the authenticity of his forgeries, Trotter offered them to other dealers or consigned them to auction houses for sale.

Described as a likeable and knowledgeable connoisseur, Henri Kuntz was a Toronto dealer whose gallery specialized in the sale of fakes and forgeries produced in France. Those works were sometimes copied from original art that had been stolen; other pieces were pastiches unlike any known work but that used elements from real paintings. The credibility of the counterfeits was enhanced by their expensive frames. Kuntz sold the fakes and forgeries to galleries in Toronto, New York, and Florida; he also consigned pieces to New York auction houses. In 1986, Kuntz was arrested and pleaded guilty to fraud, possession of stolen goods, and conspiracy to sell forgeries; he was sentenced to five years in prison (Pearson, 1986b). Following his release from prison, he was arrested again for similar activities in 1991.

In 1987, criminal charges for selling counterfeit prints were brought against New York's Carol Convertine Gallery, which had sold at least $1.2 million worth of fake prints over a two-year period. About ten salespeople who were known as qualifiers and who earned a 25 percent commission on their sales would screen potential buyers by telephone, mailing prospective customers price lists and brochures that claimed that a lot of money could be made by investing in art. In follow-up calls that employed high-pressure sales tactics, potential customers were offered prints by a famous artist who was said to have either prepared or supervised the production of the pictures. Fraudulent certificates of authenticity were provided with each print; the certificates lied in stating that the picture was part of a limited edition of 200 to 500 impressions and that the plate used to make the print had been destroyed or defaced. Both gallery director Carol Convertine and her husband Martin Fleischman were convicted of nine felony counts of fraud;

Fleischman was also convicted of eight misdemeanor counts of issuing false certificates (Raab, 1987b).

In another case, Center Art Galleries-Hawaii, Inc., was indicted on ninety-three counts of mail fraud, wire fraud, and securities fraud for selling forged Dali prints at $1,000 to $20,000 each, for an estimated total of $50 million in fraudulent sales. As with the Convertine-Fleischman case, the charge of securities fraud was a result of touting the investment potential of the forged prints to buyers. Center Art Galleries was also charged with forging Dali's signature on the prints and with lying about his participation in the production of the prints; in fact, he had played no role at all in making the prints. After a five-month trial in 1990, Center Art Galleries and its president and vice-president were found guilty. William D. Mett, the president, was fined $750,000 and sentenced to three years in prison; Marvin L. Wiseman, the vice-president, was fined $282,000 and sentenced to two and a half years in prison. They were also ordered to pay $368,000 in restitution to their victims (Pancoast, 1990a).

Because art collectors often spend large sums of money, dealers need a convincing front or persona to sell fakes and forgeries; they must appear to be honest, sincere, and knowledgeable about the art they are offering. Dishonest dealers are sometimes assisted by experts who vouch for the authenticity of the counterfeit works, either knowingly or through honest error. If dealers who want to sell fakes and forgeries can fool a respected appraiser or art critic, those experts will have unwittingly played a part in the marketing of the fakes and forgeries. When knowledgeable experts denounce artworks as counterfeit, they act as important obstacles to dealers who want to sell fakes and forgeries. However, some experts who have detected counterfeit works have kept that knowledge to themselves, because they fear that announcing how they learned that the art was counterfeit might alert forgers to the steps they need to take in the future to make their fakes and forgeries less easily detectable.

Elaborate networks of artists, dealers, appraisers, critics, and, in the case of multiple-edition prints, publishers sometimes make it difficult to determine who is responsible when a buyer is defrauded. Dealers who sell counterfeit prints often claim that they did not know they were not authentic. The dealer's source may claim to have been deceived about the authenticity of the prints by the publisher from whom they were purchased. The dealer's source or the publisher may say that the pictures were sold to the dealer as reproductions, and that he or she was unaware that the dealer was marketing them as original works. In one case, a wholesaler/publisher admitted to selling lithographic interpretations of original works by Salvador Dali. He said that he had bought the pictures from French publishers who had printed them under contract to Dali; those contracts purportedly gave the publishers the right to make editions of a thousand lithographic reproductions of original works by Dali. Even if those contracts were valid, however, they did not give anyone the right to sell the reproductions as original Dali prints. The wholesaler/publisher claimed that the reproductions were done on sheets of paper signed by Dali, but in fact most of the signatures were forgeries. He also claimed that the way the reproductions were represented to the buying public by the dealers who had bought them from him was beyond his control. However, one of those dealers said that she thought the pictures had been done by Dali himself because the wholesaler had provided her with certificates of authenticity (McGill, 1987b).

A recent development that may increase the amount of counterfeit art sold in the future is the emergence of companies that are producing and marketing works of art that they clearly identify as fake, but that are sometimes convincing enough to fool collectors and even connoisseurs. Forgery of the Month, Inc., of Chicago sells forged, signed drawings and prints attributed to well-known artists; for an additional fee, the company will provide a false provenance for the work. The company claims that it clearly identifies the works as counterfeit and is engaged in a practical joke rather than fraud. True Fakes Ltd., a New York gallery, sells original paintings in the style of twentieth-century masters, some with faked signatures, and puts a sticker on the back identifying the painting as counterfeit. Two Italian companies also produce clearly labeled forgeries of famous paintings, which are sold as counterfeits. These companies all mark their products as forgeries in some way: with a sticker on the back; by stamping the canvas, frame, and stretcher as fake; or with a certificate of falsity. However, some observers fear that those counterfeits—which are often carefully aged, creased, and torn to make them appear old, and which sometimes reproduce bright colors and even the texture of the original work with laser-transfer technology—will be sold as authentic works in the future. Buyers might remove or cover stickers and marks that identify the work as counterfeit, then sell it at a profit to an unsuspecting victim. The president of True Fakes Ltd. was told by her forgers that two of the company's paintings, done in the style of Matisse, had been authenticated and sold for large sums by a New York dealer.

Vulnerable Victims

The profitability of forgery depends on being able to find gullible buyers. Prices must be low enough to induce buyers to spend their money, but high enough to make it seem that the forgery is authentic. Buyers should ask themselves why they are getting a bargain price and why the object is not being sold at auction at its market value. Counterfeiters usually have a story to explain the bargain price, perhaps that the owner needs cash quickly or wants to avoid the embarrassment of a public sale.

The major factor responsible for the growth in the sale of counterfeit prints since the late 1970s is the rapid rise in art prices, which has made it impossible for many prosperous people to afford unique works of art such as oil paintings and watercolors. As a result, many of them have turned to multiple-edition prints, which are less expensive but are still original works, according to the conventions of the art world. Those multiple-edition prints also have investment value, a point emphasized by dealers and auction houses. For example, in 1960 the Museum of Modern Art bought one print in an edition of thirty-five lithographs by Jaspar Johns for $75; in 1987, Christie's sold another print in that series for $93,500.

Many of the busy professional people who are potential buyers have little knowledge of art and little time to verify the authenticity of what they buy. Dealers in fakes and forgeries purchase lists of the names and telephone numbers of prosperous but busy physicians, dentists, and architects who might be interested in investment opportunities; they then telephone them, trying to make quick sales that are charged to credit cards. This type of boiler-room fraud, commonly used in the sale of worthless stock, is related to the recent upsurge in telephone buying, which has been encouraged by telephone companies' advertising the benefits of doing business by telemarketing.

When victims realize they have been sold counterfeit prints, something that may not happen for years, they are often embarrassed and unwilling to testify in court. According to one law-enforcement official, "It's upscale fraud, directed at middle-class people who think they have some sophistication" (David Gilles, cited in Raab, 1987a:B2). Because victimized collectors often live some distance from the dealers from whom they bought the counterfeit art, they would have to commit considerable time and money to testifying in court in another jurisdiction. The modest cost of most prints makes many victims unwilling to take on the burden of a lawsuit, something that unscrupulous dealers take into account when they decide to market counterfeit prints. In one case, a physician who bought some prints over the telephone from a New York firm after being assured that they would appreciate in value discovered when he tried to sell the prints at a Sotheby's auction that all of the Chagall lithographs he had bought were fakes and that he had been vastly overcharged for prints by Dali and other artists. Overall, he lost $80,500. The gallery that had sold him the prints had gone out of business, and its owners could not be found. Rather than undertake the cost of a lawsuit, the doctor accepted his loss (McGill, 1987b).

Another victim of misrepresented artworks was an Indiana widow who paid $325,000 for fifty-four Russian pieces, nineteen of which were said to be by Fabergé; in fact, the pieces were worth only $36,000. Two New York dealers had warned Jacques Michel, a Denver dealer to whom they sold the pieces, that they were not by Fabergé. Michel researched the prices the objects would sell for if they were authentic Fabergé pieces and set prices accordingly so as not to arouse suspicion that they were not by Fabergé. Representing the pieces as by Fabergé, and saying that he had bought them from an immigrant family in dire need of money, Michel sold them to two dealers, Mary Jane and Robert Burton. The Burtons convinced the widow that the pieces were authentic by misinterpreting the false markings on the pieces for her. Warnings about fake works by Fabergé had surfaced by 1934, sixteen years after the Russian workshop had closed. Scholars began to document the workshop's markings in 1945, and today there is abundant literature on works produced by Fabergé. Careful buyers can consult that literature and learn to distinguish genuine pieces from imitations; dishonest dealers study that literature and, knowing more than many of their customers, are able to dupe them. Naive buyers such as the Indiana widow often rely on the honesty of dealers rather than take the effort to learn about what they are buying, and they sometimes find their trust misplaced. In this case, Michel made $160,000 from the sale of the pieces, but was ordered by the court to pay the widow $429,000 plus the more than $100,000 it had cost her to sue him (Lowenthal, 1988).

Buyers can demand from a dealer a written agreement that they can get their money back if their purchase is later discovered to be a forgery or something other than it was represented to be at the time of the sale. Lacking such a guarantee, one buyer of forged Dali prints was only allowed by the Hawaii gallery where he had bought them to exchange his counterfeits for two original Dali drawings, both of which also turned out to be forgeries.

Collectors who buy fakes and forgeries are victimized by an art world that is socially organized in a way that is conducive to such fraud. High prices for authentic art encourage some artists and dealers to try to profit from the production of counterfeit art. Through their use of false provenances and their violation of the conventions of multiple-edition artworks, those dishonest people cost buyers of art millions of dollars each year.

Fraud

Fraud is a criminal act by which an offender profits through intentional deceit, using trickery or misrepresentation to induce a victim to sell property or part with money. Fraudulent tricks, schemes, and devices involve representations and promises, express or implied, that are knowingly false or reckless (Schwartz, 1983). Art fraud, which includes, but is not limited to, the production and sale of counterfeit art, is made possible by the trust essential to art world transactions, a trust that is sometimes abused by collectors, dealers, auction houses, and museums. Naive art buyers, for instance, "are easily led astray by the 'tie-and-handshake' milieu of art dealings, which produces a warm climate for fraud" (Walder, 1980a:2).

Proving fraud in criminal court is difficult, because the prosecution is often unable to demonstrate beyond a reasonable doubt that the defendant intended to deceive the victim. Even a forger who deliberately produces a painting in the style of another artist and signs that artist's name might not be convicted of fraud if a jury or judge cannot be convinced that the forger intended to deceive an unwary buyer.

FRAUD BY COLLECTORS

Among the many forms of fraud engaged in by the buyers and owners of art are passing bad checks to dealers, making insurance claims that are based on intentional misrepresentation of the value of the art, taking unjustifiably high tax deductions, inflating the value of art that is being used as collateral for a loan, and using art to launder funds and avoid taxes and regulations.

Passing Bad Checks

Collectors have defrauded galleries and other owners of art by paying for their purchases with checks that are backed with insufficient funds. One technique is for a buyer to create a front as a wealthy collector, select a piece of art, and then tell the dealer that his chauffeur will return later to pay for it. The chauffeur presents a worthless check to the dealer at a time when the banks are closed, so the dealer cannot confirm if the check is good. In a variation on this scheme, a buyer suggests that as a reference the dealer call a telephone number said to be a bank's; in fact, the number is answered by an accomplice of the dishonest buyer (*IFAR Reports*, July/August 1986). The trust common to art world transactions, the eagerness of dealers to sell their wares, and the infrequency of such criminal activity make many dealers reluctant to challenge customers.

Insurance Fraud

Collectors who insure their art against theft or damage sometimes defraud their insurance companies through inflated appraisals, even insuring fakes and forgeries as authentic works of art. Insurance companies usually ask for the credentials of the appraiser who evaluates the art they are insuring, but often they take the appraisals themselves on faith, thereby creating an opportunity for fraud. Collectors may pay appraisers to inflate their valuations, or they may use forged invoices or other documents to deceive appraisers into believing that fake works are authentic and valuable. One insurance company paid a client $1 million after his art collection was stolen in a burglary. When the collection was eventually recovered, the company reappraised it, found it to be worth only $200,000, and sued for reimbursement of its overpayment. Another collector who had copies made of his authentic art was so pleased with the facsimiles that he commissioned their theft and then filed a claim to collect the amount that the originals had been insured for (Burnham, 1975:44).

Some collectors have even filed insurance claims when no theft has occurred. A Los Angeles physician was indicted for insurance fraud in 1981 for filing a false report of a theft of art that he claimed was worth $225,000. No theft had occurred, but the doctor collected from his insurance company and then tried to sell the art through a local auctioneer. The charge of insurance fraud was dropped when the physician pleaded guilty to art theft in another case. In 1987, a New York man was indicted for insurance fraud for collecting $1.8 million from his insurance company for thirty-seven pre-Columbian works that he falsely claimed had been stolen. When the objects were found in a Grand Central Station locker a short time later, the owner refused to buy them back from the insurance company for the amount it had paid him.

Tax Fraud

Museum curators have sometimes appraised at excessively high amounts art owned by collectors from whom they anticipate future donations. The collectors then use the curators' appraisals to support illegally high tax deductions for their donations. Such a scheme is called a "high-low," because collectors buy at a low price but claim deductions based on a high appraised value.

Federal tax reforms in 1981, 1984, and 1986 increased penalties for both donors and appraisers for what the Internal Revenue Service determined to be grossly faulty appraisals of donated art. Since 1984, the IRS has required independent appraisals and documentation for any donated pieces said to be worth more than $5,000; taxpayers taking excessive deductions face stiff fines. The IRS has also established an Art Advisory Panel of twenty-five art historians, museum curators, auction house officials, and dealers who determine the true market value of any donated art valued at $20,000 or more and who have the power to reduce the tax deductions allowed for such donations. Meeting privately for several days each year, the panel begins with the opinion of its member who is the expert on the market for that particular kind of art; the entire panel then discusses the quality of the work and decides whether the deduction that was claimed is justified. In 1987, the panel examined nineteen paintings valued at $1 million or more; they left the valuation of fifteen unchanged, reduced the valuation of three, and actually increased the valuation of one. The panel rarely makes an issue of differences in valuation of less than 15 percent, and it is reluctant to reduce valuations in cases in which there seems to be an honest disagreement. When it does reduce a valuation, the prestige of the panel's membership lends legitimacy to its decision (Malkin, 1989a).

Some donors who claim excessively high deductions do not seem to have intended to defraud the government; in other cases, their intent is unclear. Sometimes, however, the intent to defraud is apparent. For instance, a painting donated to a nursery school was valued at $200,000, a figure the panel reduced to $15. In another case, a collection of African primitive art donated to Duke University was appraised at $1.5 million, a figure reduced to $167,000 after the Art Advisory Panel concluded that most of the collection was tourist art that had been given the patina of age by counterfeiters.

To prevent museum directors from accepting worthless art, which they have sometimes done to ingratiate themselves with collectors who might donate more valuable works in the future, the federal government now requires directors to sign a form accepting all art donated to the museum. One former director has said that it is "amazing what museums are willing to accept. If the panel has had any influence, it is that collectors can't give junk away as easily as they used to." However, he adds, "If you have a big collection and a big lawyer, it's all taken care of" (cited in Malkin, 1989a:174).

Investment Fraud

Collectors have inflated the value of their art to use it as collateral in securing bank loans or as an asset for a company seeking to attract investors. The collection of James Paul Delaney, a retired Chicago probate lawyer, has been used for both purposes. Delaney once tried to get a museum built to house his collection, most of which reportedly consists of works that are optimistically attributed to Old Masters but that were actually painted by lesser artists. In exchange for the paintings, Delaney wanted the museum to pay him a substantial income and pay off an outstanding loan for several million dollars. When that scheme fell through, Delaney tried to use his art in other ways. He sought investors in his collection, but they shied away when they learned that experts had questioned the value of the art. Although his collection was appraised in 1981 at $150 million, by an appraiser who was later convicted of theft by fraud, Delaney once offered his collection to a dealer for only $5 million. In 1984, however, he claimed that it was worth $200 million; other estimates range from $7 million to $300,000 to a figure "in the tens of thousands" given by an auction house specialist (Decker, 1984).

Delaney was once arrested for conspiracy to defraud a bank by misrepresenting the value of his collection in an effort to obtain a $3.5 million loan; that charge was dropped because Delaney had not personally made any claims to the bank about the value of his art. In 1980, Delaney gave Robert Flaherty permission to use his collection as an asset for an art and antiques investment fund. Operating without a securities license, Flaherty sold stock in the company but never actually issued any stock. He was arrested for securities fraud and grand theft and sentenced to one year in jail. A short time later, another agent working for Delaney was arrested for attempted grand theft through misrepresentation of the paintings; he was sentenced to two years in prison. In 1984, there were eighteen lawsuits pending in Indiana and Illinois as a result of yet another effort by Delaney to unload his collection on unsuspecting buyers (Burnham, 1983; Decker, 1984; *Stolen Art Alert*, March/April 1983).

Delaney has explained the refusal of art experts to accept his collection as valuable, and his subsequent difficulty in selling it at what he believes is its true market value, as the result of an elaborate conspiracy against him. He believes that Sotheby's is angry that he was able to buy his treasures at very low prices. He accuses Christie's of treating his art shabbily when he tried unsuccessfully to have them sell it. He asserts that the Art Dealers Association of America is critical of his collection because he refused to let any of its members sell his paintings. He also claims that he has been drugged and beaten and then forced to sign contracts with others who have offered his paintings for sale (Decker, 1984).

Fraud by Corporate Collectors

In recent years, Japanese corporations and executives have paid record amounts for Western art; as of 1991, they had made five of the ten most expensive art purchases. There is evidence that some Japanese purchases of art have been made for such fraudulent purposes as concealing the transfer of large sums of cash, avoiding the payment of taxes, and circumventing government regulations. The chief curator of a Tokyo museum has said, "It was well known that art has commonly been used to hide money or secretly move it in the past few years" (Nobuo Abe, cited in Sterngold, 1991a:A1). In one case, the Mitsubishi Corporation said that it had paid $39 million for two Renoir paintings to two Frenchmen, but the Japanese government claimed that the two men do not exist and that fifteen of the thirty-six checks written in the transaction could not be accounted for. The press suggested that the missing money was siphoned off to secret political slush funds and that the art purchase was a way to avoid attracting the attention of auditors and regulators. In another case, Itoman & Company bought more than $500 million worth of art over a short period of time. The Japanese press suggested that the purchases may have been a way for Itoman, which was engaged in real-estate speculation, to give the sellers of property more money than allowed by government regulations by disguising payments as fees or profits from the sale of paintings. Because many art sales in Japan are completed privately rather than at public auction, those transactions are an easy way to hide money. As of 1991, no criminal charges had been brought against any Japanese corporation for its dealings in art (Riley, 1991; Sterngold, 1991a).

Japanese corporations have reportedly used art to launder money and thus avoid paying taxes. This can be done in several ways. One method is for a corporation to record the sale of a work of art for a certain amount, but agree with the purchaser that the real price is a lower figure; the difference between the two prices is then secretly returned to the corporation. A second tactic is to deposit the amount for which the work is ostensibly being sold in a bank in another country and agree that both the seller and the buyer can withdraw a certain sum from that account. A third scheme is for the seller and the buyer to agree on rapid deflation in the value of an artwork to allow for tax avoidance by claiming a loss, or to agree on rapid inflation in value if the work is to be used as collateral for a loan (Riley, 1991).

FRAUD BY DEALERS

Although most art dealers act honestly most of the time, some have used their positions in the art world to defraud artists, other dealers, auction houses, collectors, museums, and insurance companies.

Fraud against Artists

Artists sometimes complain that the dealers who represent them under-pay them for their efforts and make excessive profits from their creative output. Charges of outright fraud by artists against dealers are rare, but some artists have sued dealers, alleging that they have not paid them for works that have been sold. In the highly publicized Rothko case, the artist's heirs won a lawsuit involving fraud by the estate's executors.

Following the suicide of Abstract Expressionist Mark Rothko in 1970, his daughter Kate initiated a lawsuit against the estate's three executors—the artist's accountant Bernard Reis, anthropologist Morton Levine, and painter Theodore Stamos—and against Frank Lloyd and his Marlborough Gallery, one of the world's largest art-dealing firms. Kate Rothko contended that the executors, who were also the principals in the Rothko Foundation established by the artist's will, had colluded to defraud the estate and the foundation by making deals with the Marlborough Gallery that greatly undervalued her father's works. She claimed that those transactions were made out of self-interest on the part of the executors, Reis having been employed as an officer of the Marlborough Gallery and Stamos being represented by the gallery. She asked the court to remove control of the estate from the executors.

The major point of contention at the trial was the market value of Rothko's works. The executors and the gallery downplayed the value of the art to justify the low prices the gallery had paid the estate for it. Art dealer John Bernard Myers (1983), a witness for Lloyd and his gallery, questioned the value of the works left by Rothko, saying that many of them were in poor condition and in need of restoration and that some were of inferior quality. In contradiction, the petitioners claimed that many of the pieces would have sold on the open market for much more than the gallery had paid for them.

In his 1975 decision, Judge Millard Lesser Midonick agreed with the petitioners and removed control of the estate from the three executors. One of them, Stamos, was ordered to give his New York townhouse to the Rothko estate, though he retained lifetime tenancy. The judge ruled that the executors had acted in conflict of interest or negligently in selling one hundred of Rothko's works to the Marlborough Gallery at well below their market price and in consigning another 698 works to the gallery at the excessive commission rate of 50 percent. Concluding that the executors had shown a curious lack of hard bargaining and waste bordering on gross negligence in their transactions with the gallery, and finding that the prices that had been agreed to were too low and had unreasonably long pay-out terms, the judge canceled the contracts for the transfer of the paintings to the gallery and returned them to the estate. He also imposed damages and fines totaling $9,525,000 against Frank Lloyd and the Marlborough Gallery, but allowed for the mitigation of as much as $3.3 million of that amount if paintings that the gallery had already sold were retrieved and returned to the estate; eventually, Lloyd substantially reduced the fine by getting back many pictures that he had sold to European collectors. Judge Midonick also held Lloyd in contempt of court for some of the original sales, for which back-dated invoices had been faked in an effort to circumvent two restraining orders issued by the court (Glueck, 1986b; Seldes, 1979).

In 1982, seven years after the Art Dealers Association of America had expelled the Marlborough Gallery, charges of criminal malfeasance were brought against Lloyd for tampering with evidence in the Rothko case. He was convicted and given a community service sentence that required him to establish a scholarship fund and an art appreciation program for New York high school students. In 1986, he hinted that his handling of the Rothko estate might be justified, at least in part, by all that he had done to promote the artist's work during his lifetime:

From a perspective of experience and hindsight, I regret some of my actions, and if I had it to do over again, there are things I would do differently. However, I believe deeply that I contributed substantially to the successful careers of many European and American artists, in particular, Mark Rothko, and was instrumental in bringing to public attention the great talent that I saw in his work. (cited in Glueck, 1986b:C17)

Fraud against Other Dealers

Dealers trust one another to sell only what they have title to, pay for their purchases with checks that are backed by sufficient funds, and meet the terms of consignment agreements. That trust has been violated by dealers and by criminals posing as dealers. Those who engage in such fraud create fronts that will convince their victims of their reliability. They dress well, act in a refined manner, speak knowledgeably about art and the art market, drop the names of reputable dealers and clients they claim to know, and present fake documents vouching for their financial status and gallery affiliation. Perpetrators of fraud also work at developing rapport with their victims, who often remark later that they thought they knew the offenders well and cannot believe that they behaved so dishonestly.

In 1980, twenty-eight-year-old Massachusetts art dealer Steven Straw pleaded guilty to having conspired to defraud dealers and collectors of millions of dollars; one California gallery claimed to have lost about $7 million. Straw was a persuasive, charming, and knowledgeable confidence artist who created the impression of being successful and wealthy by using a personal jet, a computerized system to trace art, and his own commodities broker. Straw abused the trust common to art world transactions to exploit his customers, employing the classic confidence trick of using money from new investors to pay off prior investors, convincing them that they were making money and duping them into investing even more. He sold paintings he did not own, once selling to six different investors a Gauguin painting that had been acquired and displayed for two years by the National Gallery of Art in Washington, D.C., and that was not for sale. Another time he sold a Rembrandt painting that he did not own for more than $3 million to a Los Angeles dealer (Carter, 1980; Walder, 1980a).

Another form of fraud against other dealers is to use bad checks to pay for purchases. These check forgers might be seen as conventional criminals rather than as art dealers, but because they engage in the purchase and sale of art, sometimes legitimately, they can be regarded as dishonest dealers. One such dealer, Charles Heller, paid for his purchases with checks written on the account of a nonexistent Texas gallery, an account that once had a balance of $250 when he paid for a purchase with a check for $50,000. Heller preyed on the eagerness of dealers to make sales, presenting himself as an out-of-town dealer with a client who was anxious to buy paintings and decorative objects. Victims described Heller as a fast talker who was knowledgeable about art and the art world. Sometimes he deliberately confused dealers, once calling ahead to arrange a purchase and offering to show the dealer a letter of credit from a bank, then arriving unexpectedly on a Saturday when the bank was closed and could not be contacted to confirm the validity of the letter. The dealer let Heller take a painting in exchange for a check that turned out to be no good (*Stolen Art Alert*, October 1982).

In another fraudulent transaction, Robert Leads secured his purchase of two pictures by Renoir and Cassatt with stock supposedly worth $500,000, agreeing that he would pay the owner $560,000 in cash within thirty days or return the pictures. At the end of the month, the cash had not been paid, the paintings could not be found, the stock was discovered to be worthless, and Leads had disappeared. Eventually he was caught, pleaded guilty to theft, and was sentenced to two years in jail.

Another type of fraud committed by some dealers is consignment fraud. In this crime, a dealer accepts a work of art from the dealer, collector, or artist who owns it and promises to pay the owner a fixed amount after selling the work, keeping the difference between that amount and the selling price as a commission; after selling the work, however, the dealer does not pay the owner the amount on which they agreed. In 1984, Dennis Anderson was sentenced to three and one-third to ten years in prison for taking paintings on consignment, selling them, and then either failing to pay the owners or paying them with bad checks. Several galleries lost a total of as much as $2 million worth of paintings to Anderson. At the time of his criminal conviction, Anderson was also a defendant in eight civil lawsuits.

Consignment fraud was repeatedly committed by New Jersey dealer Claire Eatz, who has been described as a smooth con artist and a "habitual yet convincing liar" (cited in Ketchum, 1983:2). Eatz cultivated trust with her sweet grandmotherly image, by providing references from reputable dealers, and by acting honestly in some transactions. However, on several occasions she sold art that she had taken on consignment and then kept the full purchase price for herself, delaying and excusing her failure to pay the owner by saying that the buyer had sent her a miswritten check, was on vacation and unreachable, had had a death in the family, or was ill. She even mailed certified envelopes containing blank pieces of paper to some consignors and then expressed surprise that there were no checks in the envelopes. At least twice, Eatz sold a work that she had taken on consignment from a gallery, waited for her buyer to sell it to a second gallery, and then accepted the work from that second gallery to sell on consignment again; she failed to pay either gallery from which she had taken the painting on consignment. Eatz, who was sixty-four when she was convicted in 1985 of five counts of consignment fraud, was sentenced to six years in prison and ordered to make restitution to her victims to the extent made possible by her assets (Pearson, 1985a).

Fraud against Auction Houses

In contrast to fraudulent schemes in which one dealer victimizes another, dealers sometimes collude to defraud auction houses and those who consign their works for sale there. Auction rings are groups of dealers, frequently organized on the spot, that agree to keep bids low on a specific lot by designating one of their members to bid up to an agreed-upon maximum price. Prices are thus kept lower than would be the case if the bidding were truly competitive. If one member of the ring gets the piece, the group gathers somewhere else after the sale and holds a second auction among themselves, with bidding starting somewhat above the price paid at auction. The winning bidder in this second auction, called a "knockout" in England, pays each member of the ring an equal share of the difference between the winning bid in the knockout and the price the piece was bought for at auction. That winning bidder has managed to buy the piece for less than it would have cost at an open sale. Sometimes a few members of the original ring then bid among themselves in a second knockout, with the losing bidders receiving from the winner a share of the difference between the winning bid and the price paid for the piece at the first knockout (Wraight, 1966). A variation on this pattern was reported in London in 1985. A group of well-to-do dealers would collude to bid on one or two lots of Old Masters paintings, thereby keeping the prices low. Then, instead of holding a knockout auction on the spot, they would agree that they would later share the profits from the sale of the pictures (Wintersgill, 1985).

Auction rings violate regulations governing auction sales and have been illegal in Great Britain since 1927, but participants have rarely been subjected to criminal prosecution. Rings seem to be more common in smaller auction houses and estate sales than they are in large auction houses, which routinely protect themselves against such collusion through secret reserves that ensure that objects will not be sold for less than their actual market value. Rings thrive at out-of-the-way auctions where there are apt to be few bidders who know the real value of the pieces being offered. Auctioneers at those sales have even colluded with dealers by ignoring bids from members of the audience who do not belong to the ring. Dishonest auctioneers have also omitted pieces from catalogues or previews so that potential bidders not in collusion with them will not know everything that is being offered for sale (Wraight, 1966:106–16).

Fraud against Collectors

In addition to victimizing other dealers, art dealers have also defrauded collectors through consignment fraud. In one case, a California dealer agreed to sell a Grant Wood drawing and pay the family that owned it $400,000. He sold the drawing to a New York dealer for $100,000 and three works in trade that had a total value of $105,000. The New York dealer then sold a share in the drawing to a New York gallery. When the picture's owners were not paid the $400,000 that had been agreed to, they sued the California dealer, the New York dealer, and the New York gallery. Although the Uniform Commercial Code specifies that a consignor's dispute is only with the person to whom the property has been consigned, in this case the judge allowed the owners to sue all three parties because they "had reason to know that the ownership rights of the plaintiffs were being violated" (cited in Pennington, 1985:4). After hearing the case, the court ordered the defendants to return the drawing to the family or pay them the full $400,000. The family chose to receive the money, but the defendants persuaded the judge to allow them to return the picture to the family, which they did.

Because collectors are likely to sell art on consignment less often than dealers, and are thus apt to be less familiar with the risks involved in doing so, when they do consign their property to dealers they are advised to insure it for its market value and to have signed agreements that specify the amount they will be paid by the dealer and that obligate the dealer to pay for restoration if the property is damaged. If a percentage of the work's selling price is to be paid to the dealer as a commission, with the remainder to go to the owner, the owner should also reserve the right to see the dealer's bill of sale to ascertain the amount that the dealer was actually paid for the piece (Grant, 1987).

Another way that dealers have defrauded collectors is through misrepresentation of merchandise. Sometimes this involves the sale of fakes and forgeries that are produced explicitly for this purpose; that happened when four dealers lured investors to put up money for Mayan artifacts and then shipped modern pieces from Guatemala to the United States, where they tried to sell them as authentic objects. Misrepresentation can also take the form of deliberate deception about objects that are not what they are purported to be and that were never made to be passed off as original works. At a Los Angeles estate sale, a woman sold three cheap reproduction vases, which she had bought for $75 each, as authentic Ming vases; victims lost a total of $17,000. The woman pleaded no contest to three counts of grand theft through misrepresentation.

One case of deliberate misrepresentation occurred in England. Responding to an advertisement by a purported guardian of trustee funds who was interested in buying paintings, the owner of a valuable painting met with the trustee. The trustee, who was actually a confidence trickster posing as a dealer, then took the picture to an appraiser. Returning to the owner, the con man told him that the painting was not authentic, contrary to the appraiser's actual evaluation, and offered to pay the owner a small sum for it. The disappointed owner agreed to the sale, only later learning that the picture was sold at auction for forty times what he had been paid by the trustee (Wraight, 1966:103).

The question of legal liability for the misrepresentation of art is a complex one that depends on the claims that the seller makes, the degree to which the buyer has inspected the piece prior to purchasing it, and the expertise of the buyer and the seller. In a 1990 English case involving two dealers, the plaintiff, who had bought a Munter painting from the defendant, sued for the purchase price and damages when he learned that the painting was not by Munter. In negotiations prior to the purchase, the defendant had told the buyer that he did not know much about Munter's work and did not particularly care for it. The buyer said that he knew Munter's work well and paid the price the defendant was asking. Three months later, a collector who had bought the painting from the plaintiff learned that it was a forgery and demanded a refund; the plaintiff complied. Then the plaintiff sued the defendant from whom he had bought the picture. The defendant said that he had not represented the painting to be by Munter and that the buyer and he had agreed that the buyer knew more about Munter's work than he did. The court found in favor of the defendant (Feldman, 1990).

In the 1990 decision in *Balog and Balog* v. *Center Art Gallery*, a United States District Court ruled that the purchasers of counterfeit Dali prints could sue the dealers. The defendants claimed that the plaintiffs were barred from suing them under the Uniform Commercial Code, which requires that suits for breach of warranty be initiated within four years of a sale. However, the court ruled that the dealers' certificates of authenticity were express warranties of the prints' future performance, and that those warranties and other statements by the dealers that the prints were appreciating in value were reiterated to the buyers on several occasions after the actual sale. The court said that the plaintiffs could sue, ruling that the four-year period began at the time of the last warranty of authenticity rather than at the time of the original sale. The fraudulent conduct of the defendants was found to have prevented the plaintiffs from discovering that they had been victimized, thereby delaying their initiation of a lawsuit (Feldman, 1991).

Fraud against Museums

There are several reasons that fraud by dealers against museums is rare. Museum curators are knowledgeable about art and experienced in art world transactions and are thus less likely than private collectors to be victimized.

Dealers are reluctant to deal dishonestly with museums because they are valued customers, often being the first to be offered the dealer's best pieces. A dealer's prestige is enhanced by sales to museums, and until recently museums were the buyers most able to afford expensive art. Museums are visible institutions that are highly regarded in the art world, and dealers who antagonize them with fraudulent sales could jeopardize their careers.

In 1988, an esteemed London dealer was widely criticized for behaving unpatriotically and in a mercenary fashion in his purchase of a painting that was being sought by Great Britain's National Gallery. Phillips, a London auction house, had attributed the grime-covered German Renaissance painting to the workshop of Albrecht Altdorfer. Believing the painting to be by Altdorfer himself, rather than by his workshop, the editor of an art journal contacted the National Gallery; the museum agreed with the editor's opinion, which was later supported by the use of modern technology. The National Gallery's director then approached the head of Colnaghi's, a firm that had been dealing in art for more than two centuries, and asked him to help the museum buy the picture for any amount up to $100,000. They agreed that if the bidding exceeded that amount, the representative of Colnaghi's was free to buy the painting for his gallery. The painting was eventually bought by Colnaghi's for $120,000, more than the National Gallery had authorized it to pay. The director of the National Gallery then told Colnaghi's that the museum would pay considerably more than the $120,000 for the painting. Colnaghi's rejected the National Gallery's offer as well below the true value of the painting. The museum's director said, "The normal convention and the gentlemanly thing would be for a dealer to offer the picture to the gallery for a small markup" (cited in Yarrow, 1988:C21). Even though Colnaghi's actions seem to have violated an art world convention, no fraud was involved and no law was broken, and the dealer was cleared of any wrongdoing by the Society of London Art Dealers. Colnaghi's co-director said that his firm was a commercial enterprise and that most dealers would have acted as he had; he commented that he had not deliberately taken advantage of the National Gallery and that to do so would be "commercial suicide" (Yarrow, 1988:C30).

A libel case decided in 1989 also concerned the integrity of the relationship between a museum and an individual who was trying to sell it a work of art. An English court awarded £7,500 to a Renaissance scholar who had been attacked in a newspaper article for behaving recklessly and dishonestly in asserting that a plaster statue had been the model for Michelangelo's *David.* The court ruled that the newspaper's comments were neither justified nor fair. However, the court also said that it had reduced the damages to be paid to the scholar because he had behaved deceitfully, dishonorably, and in violation of professional ethics by offering the statue to Washington's National Gallery of Art without telling the museum of his financial interest in the sale of the piece, a commission of 5 percent of its selling price. This man was actually behaving as a dealer while presenting himself as a scholar with no commercial interest in the statue's sale (*The New York Times*, December 8, 1989).

Fraud against Insurance Companies

Because dealers must insure their merchandise to reduce their risks, they usually avoid alienating their insurance companies by defrauding them. When such fraud is committed, it sometimes involves large sums of money.

In one elaborate scheme, London antiquities dealer Houshang Mahboubian tried to convert into cash his collection of Persian antiquities, the mostly highly insured of which were counterfeit, by defrauding his insurance company. Unable to sell his collection of gold and silver vases, bowls, and jewelry on the legitimate market, Mahboubian insured it with Lloyd's of London for $23 million, $18.5 million of which he intended to collect following a burglary that he commissioned. Several times during 1985 Mahboubian flew to New York, where he contacted a dealer named Nedjatollah Sakhai, who helped him hire a gang of experienced burglars. Mahboubian returned to London and shipped to New York two crates that were carefully marked with his initials so the burglars could easily identify what they were to steal. The police learned of the scheme and arrested the three burglars just after they broke through the concrete walls of a Queens warehouse with sledgehammers and crowbars and removed the marked crates. After a six-week trial in which experts testified that most of the 105 pieces in the crates were forgeries, Mahboubian and Sakhai were convicted of conspiracy, burglary, attempted grand larceny, and attempted fraud (Johnson, 1987; Rohter, 1986).

FRAUD BY AUCTION HOUSES

Competition among auction houses is conducive to practices not always in the buyer's best interest. In their effort to attract attention, auction houses try to set new records: the highest price ever paid for any work of art, the highest price for a work by a particular artist, the highest price for an object other than a painting, the highest total annual sales. Pressure to set records leads to aggressive marketing and advertising strategies and to efforts to create and maintain the impression that the art market is booming and that buyers are wise to invest in art. Auction houses explain away their failure to sell certain pieces by pointing to a recession in the larger economy, the absence of big spenders from a particular sale, or other special circumstances. The failure to sell objects can hurt an auction house's reputation, because it suggests that the house did not gauge the market properly, gave an incorrect and inflated estimate to the consignor, or did not generate enough enthusiasm in the audience to bring bids up to where they should have been. In a sense, auction houses become their own victims, playing a major role in pushing prices up to unprecedented levels; owners then expect to get those high prices for their own art, even when the quality of that art or market conditions do not warrant such prices. When artworks fail to sell at those high prices, the public's faith in the investment value of art may be weakened.

The aggressive entrepreneurship of auction houses that has aimed to increase prices and expand the type and number of objects sold has, for the most part, been legitimate, but auction houses have also acted in ways that are deceptive and even border on the fraudulent. Those activities, like most white-collar crimes, are rarely dealt with in criminal courts. Occasionally they come to the attention of city and state agencies that are charged with the protection of consumers, but even then civil sanctions are applied rarely and reluctantly.

Auction houses sometimes engage in deception that stops short of fraud but that is designed to mislead buyers. For example, auction houses publicize dollar figures for annual sales and seasonal turnover in ways aimed at creating the impression of a bustling market that is rewarding investors handsomely, an impression that encourages more buying. Daily sales intakes are announced without subtracting from the totals those items that were not sold, usually because they failed to reach the reserve, or minimum price, established in advance by the consignor and the auction house (Burnham, 1975:209). Auction houses justify this practice by saying that dollar figures on unsold items must be kept secret to protect the consignors. They also claim that the last bid on a piece is a good indication of its actual value, even if that bid was below the reserve, because it indicates what someone was willing to pay.

By presenting *total* sales figures, auction houses conceal market trends for different kinds of items. Thus, an increase in total sales may hide a declining market for furniture of a certain period or for a particular type of ceramics. Even trends in the prices for one type of object may not be a good guide to the price that a specific item will fetch, so buyers must pay attention to the prices of specific items rather than to the overall sales figures emphasized by auction houses (Burnham, 1975). Presenting gross sales figures is certainly not fraudulent, but the practice is aimed more at producing public confidence in the art market than at offering useful information to the buying public.

In 1985, the New York Department of Consumer Affairs began an investigation of auction house practices, asking whether those practices deceived the public, withheld facts from the audience, and contributed to the inflation of prices. Department Commissioner Angelo Aponte said, "We are considering stronger regulations that will assure that the market becomes a free and competitive open market, which it is not at this point" (cited in McGill, 1985d:A1). After the investigation, which encountered considerable opposition from auction houses to any additional regulation, only a few minor changes were made. A lawyer for the department concluded, "We did a study of the industry, initially with a view of finding whether there was rampant abuse. We didn't find that. We found an industry that was going by some old rules. There were several areas that had become a regular part of industry practice that were unregulated, and that we felt needed to be addressed" (cited in McGill, 1986d:C17).

Bidding Practices

Naive outsiders come to an auction with a preconception about how it will proceed, in an open and above-board manner with the person making the highest offer getting the object. In fact, house auctions are conducted according to unwritten and complex rules that favor insiders. As growing numbers of the uninitiated have entered auction houses in recent years, more complaints about practices such as "bidding from the chandelier" and the "secret reserve" have been brought to the attention of consumer affairs agencies.

Auctions are like confidence games in that the auctioneer and the auction house create a front of respectability and credibility, use real or imagined shills to bid up prices, and then cool out dissatisfied bidders. Auctioneers use body language and a tone of voice that create excitement in the audience and encourage bidding, thus pushing prices higher. Houses seek to sell objects at the highest possible prices, because their commissions are a fixed percentage of the selling price and because higher prices attract more things to sell.

Bidding Off the Chandelier. One auction house practice that strikes some outsiders as unethical is bidding off the chandelier, also called bidding off the wall and pulling bids from the air. This is the auctioneer's practice of announcing bids in the early stages of a sale, even though no one from the audience is making those bids. Auctioneers claim they are bidding on behalf of the consignor of the object in an effort to spark the audience and push the price up to its secret reserve as quickly as possible. They claim that they only call in such bids once or twice to gets things started, and that if there are no real bids from the floor the bidding quickly stops. Auctioneers may also call out theoretical offers by order bidders who have told them prior to the sale the top price they will pay for an item (McGill, 1985e). Under New York regulations, calling in nonexistent bids is acceptable as long as they are below the reserve, but unacceptable after the reserve has been reached (McGill, 1987c).

Critics of the practice of bidding off the chandelier claim that it artificially boosts prices by deceiving unwitting bidders into thinking that they are actually competing with other potential buyers for a piece. A knowledgeable insider once challenged what he thought was an off-the-chandelier bid on a seventeenth-century atlas. Auctioneer David Redden began the bidding at $80,000, and print and map dealer W. Graham Arader III eventually raised the bid to $120,000. At that point,

the auctioneer acknowledged a bid of a hundred and thirty, and Arader, at peak volume, answered back, "Where's the bid, David? I don't see that bid. You're running it up on me, David! You're lying, David. There's no bid. You took that off the wall! I caught you, David! Where's the bid?" It was a dramatic moment, witnessed by about a hundred startled people. As Arader advanced toward the platform in a menacing manner, Redden abruptly halted the action, explaining that there seemed to be some confusion. When the bidding resumed—Redden agreed to start all over again—Arader bought the atlas for a hundred and twenty thousand dollars, plus ten per cent to Sotheby's. (Singer, 1987:85)

Secret Reserves. When owners consign works to auction houses, they usually negotiate minimum prices for which they will sell their property. The auctioneer starts the bidding on an object well below that reserve, and if the highest bid from the floor does not reach that price, the item is "bought in" (that is, not sold). Later, the owner is asked whether the house should reauction the item or return it. By one estimate, 10 to 20 percent of the items put up for auction are bought in because they fail to reach their reserves, although the percentage will vary with market conditions and with owners' willingness to reduce reserves when the market is in a slump (Taylor, 1989a).

Critics claim that the secret reserve violates the essential purpose of an auction, at least from the point of view of the naive outsider: to sell property to the highest bidder. In 1974, the Art Dealers Association of America campaigned against the secret reserve, arguing that the minimum price should be disclosed and that bidding should start at that price. Arguing that their customers would benefit from abolition of the secret reserve, many dealers expressed regret when, in its 1986 revision of auction sale regulations, New York's Department of Consumer Affairs failed to forbid the practice. One print dealer, who was also vice-president of the ADAA, observed, "The lack of a regulation about disclosing reserves is a sad result. It's a sham for the consumer, who comes away thinking there is real competition and real bidding for an object where there isn't" (cited in McGill, 1986d:C17).

The Department of Consumer Affairs did make a slight change in 1986, requiring auction houses to mark in their catalogues which items had a secret reserve, even though they did not have to reveal what the actual minimum price was. Auction house catalogues now briefly explain the concept of the secret reserve and carry a small mark next to *every* item offered for sale, so the new requirement has resulted in no additional information for prospective buyers. In explaining the department's failure to abolish the secret reserve, Commissioner Aponte said that doing so would have left New York at a competitive disadvantage with Europe, where the auction trade is less regulated. In effect, the department acceded to the threat by auction houses to withdraw their half-billion-dollar business from New York if they were overregulated. Aponte remarked, "I don't think it's unreasonable, given the clientele and players, to have that little bit of theater. We're trying to balance the fact of what New York City represents to the art world, and we still have to make this an attractive place to do business" (cited in McGill, 1986d:C17).

Auction houses defend their use of the secret reserve by claiming that dealers want minimum prices published so that they can engage in collusive bidding, forming alliances that agree not to compete in the bidding so as to keep prices down. Auction houses assert that their only defense against such a practice is the "little bit of mystery" involved in keeping the reserve secret. Stuart Greenspan (1985), editor-in-chief of *Art and Auction* magazine, has argued against the proposal made by some dealers that bidding should *start* at the reserve, saying that much of the success of auction sales depends on the excitement the auctioneer generates and the way the bidding is orchestrated. He says that the audience's uncertainty about the reserve lets the auctioneer draw in bidders. Greenspan believes that because auctions deal in luxury items, bidders are, or at least should be, sophisticated, and they are best protected not by regulations but by their own knowledge of the rules by which auctions are run. This implies that naive outsiders are not welcome in auction houses, or if they do attend and get hurt by practices of which they are unaware, that is too bad.

Another reason that auction houses and sellers want to keep reserves secret is that items that failed to sell at or above announced minimum prices would be stigmatized and difficult to sell in the future. Such a failure to sell at an announced minimum price would also call into question the expertise of the auction house in estimating the item's true market value. If a significant number of pieces did not sell at or above their announced reserves, public confidence in the art market could be eroded, possibly setting off a downward spiral in prices. Reserves thus help to maintain the current level of prices, because sales are not made at prices considered to be below market.

Announcing Sales. Auction houses have sometimes declared as sold items that have been bought in because they failed to reach their reserves during the bidding; on occasion, names of fictitious buyers have even been announced to the audience. Objects that have failed to sell at auction have been sold privately soon after the sale, with houses commonly recording those private transactions as auction sales. These practices are aimed at maintaining public confidence in art as an investment and at demonstrating that there is a ready market for art that collectors want to sell.

In 1977, Sotheby's of London hammered down a rare Guarnerius violin as sold for £115,000, a price reported in the British press as a record-breaking one. In fact, the violin was not sold at auction, but rather immediately after the conclusion of the auction, when the auctioneer approached the underbidder, the last person to bid on the violin before the auctioneer bought it in by announcing that it had been sold to a fictitious higher bidder. The auctioneer asked the underbidder if he wanted to buy the violin for £115,000, and the man agreed. Three weeks later the man hesitated to pay that price, and he and the auction house renegotiated a price of £99,000. At that point, Sotheby's had to tell the press that the sale had been private rather than completed at auction as previously announced, and that the price paid was lower than initially reported (McGill, 1985e). Both Sotheby's and Christie's have a practice of recording private sale prices agreed to soon after the end of an auction as auction prices if those private sale prices are at least equal to the price at which the item was hammered down during the auction. This creates the illusion that those sales were actually made during the auction.

In one notorious case, David Bathurst, chairman of Christie's London and New York operations, admitted that he had falsely reported that three paintings from a lot of eight had been sold for Dimitry Jodidio and his Swiss company Christallina at a 1981 auction. In fact, only one painting had been sold, a Degas for $2.2 million, but Bathurst had also reported that a Gauguin had sold for $1.3 million and a van Gogh for $2.1 million. Six of the eight paintings had actually received no bids at all from the audience, although Bathurst had announced fictitious bids from the chandelier in an effort to get the bidding up to the reserves. He later said that he had made the false report to help the paintings' owner, because it is hard to sell art privately after it has done poorly at auction. He also said that his false statements had been designed "to maintain stability in the art market which might have become depressed if the public immediately discovered that only one painting was sold" (cited in *The New York Times*, July 8, 1985:C13). When asked if he had lied to improve the position of the seller and the art market in general, Bathurst responded, "Improved is perhaps the wrong word. I mean less bad that way. The headlines weren't good anyhow, but they would have been worse if it had been seven out of eight as opposed to five out of eight" (cited in McGill, 1985a:C28).

Bathurst has described his misrepresentation as an "utterly unique" occurrence in his career, and some auctioneers, collectors, and dealers agreed that it was probably an isolated incident. A former Sotheby's official, certainly not a disinterested observer, remarked, "I think it is totally an exception from what happens at the major auction firms, and nobody knows that better than I do. The only thing an auctioneer owns is his good reputation—without it he is not credible in business" (cited in McGill, 1985b:9). Other observers, however, thought that Bathurst's lie was simply the most serious of a common pattern of abuses. One New York antiques dealer said, "Christie's is being singled out for practices which are prevalent by their competitors and throughout the whole industry. It is important that it be known that Christie's is not alone in the practices that this whole case refers to" (cited in McGill, 1985b:9).

In this case, Christie's settled with New York City's Department of Consumer Affairs, which licenses auction houses and auctioneers, by agreeing to pay a fine of $80,000, surrender Bathurst's license to conduct auctions for two years, and surrender for four months the license of Christopher Burge, who headed the house's Impressionist Department and had been aware of Bathurst's misrepresentation. Bathurst also resigned as chairman of Christie's, although that was not required by the settlement. In addition, the auction house agreed to cooperate with the agency in its ongoing investigation of auction house practices. Commissioner Aponte, the head of the agency, claimed that Christie's was culpable because it had taken no corrective measures after learning of Bathurst's misrepresentation. He said that his agency had sought the license of Christie's as well as those of Bathurst and Burge, but that it had agreed to the settlement out of consideration for Christie's role in the New York business world and the international market. Despite this relatively lenient treatment, Aponte voiced his hope that the settlement would send "a very clear signal to the art world that they are going to have to clean up their act" (cited in McGill, 1985b:9).

Insider Trading

In its investigation of auction house practices, New York's Department of Consumer Affairs found that members of the boards of directors of Sotheby's and Christie's had bid on and purchased art at their own auction houses, a practice a department official said could be seen as insider trading. Both houses said they had taken strong measures to prevent insiders from taking advantage of their positions to gain inside information on reserves or prearranged order bids that would give them an unfair advantage in bidding on items offered for sale. Auction house insiders are in a position to bid up prices, thereby forcing buyers to pay more and getting publicity for new record prices, but the Department of Consumer Affairs found no evidence of such abuses.

Erroneous Appraisals

Incorrect auction house appraisals, which can result in low pre-sale estimates, cost sellers money when they result in property being sold for less than its true market value. For instance, a painting bought by its owner in 1930 for $9 was given a pre-sale estimated price of $720 by Sotheby's in 1987. The price was low because the auction house failed to recognize the picture as a masterpiece and thought there would be little interest in religious art. The owner, believing that the picture was worth much more, took the painting to Phillips, another auction house, which at first estimated that it would sell for between $14,400 and $18,000. Further research by Phillips's director of fine paintings led to the reattribution of the painting to Annibale Carracci, and the picture's valuation rose dramatically. It sold at auction for more than $1.5 million (*The New York Times*, December 10, 1987). This case raises a question rarely ruled on by the courts: do acknowledged experts have any legal responsibility to consignors to identify and appraise objects correctly? Sotheby's certainly had a vested interest in correctly identifying the Carracci painting, because its commission would have been based on the selling price. Nevertheless, the owner would have lost about $1.5 million had the painting been sold at Sotheby's pre-sale estimate.

In 1977, an Iranian businessman bought a Fabergé egg from Christie's in Geneva, but refused to complete payment when he began to doubt the egg's authenticity. Christie's sued him, offering in court the testimony of an expert who stated that the egg was an authentic Imperial. The businessman lost the case and eventually paid Christie's $400,000, which included $150,000 in legal fees and interest. In 1985, he consigned the egg to Christie's in New York for sale. The same expert who had testified in court earlier reexamined the egg and took a different position, saying it was by Fabergé but was not an Imperial, because it had been doctored. Had it been an Imperial, it would have been worth about $1,750,000; instead, the expert appraised it at only $50,000. Christie's canceled the sale of the egg, and the businessman sued the auction house for $37 million. Christie's claimed that it had acted in good faith both times, saying that its expert had simply changed his mind (Burnham, 1987). There was no evidence of fraud, because there was no proof that either Christie's or its expert had intended to deceive the egg's owner. However, prospective customers might well question the objectivity of the expert who had offered two such different appraisals of the egg.

In 1985, Dimitry Jodidio filed a $10 million lawsuit against Christie's and David Bathurst for breach of contract, fraud, negligence, violation of fiduciary trust, and violation of New York's general business law. He alleged that they had misrepresented their ability to gauge accurately current conditions in the art market and to estimate correctly the value of the eight paintings he had consigned to them. He said that Bathurst's estimates were false and aimed at inducing him to engage Christie's to sell his paintings. Jodidio said that he had wanted to raise $10 million and had shown Bathurst eleven paintings, from which Bathurst selected eight that he said would bring $8 million if sold privately and up to $12.6 million if sold at auction. Only one painting sold at auction, and six of the eight pictures received no bids from the floor.

According to Bathurst and Christie's, Jodidio's lawsuit was self-serving. Christie's had agreed to charge him only a 4 percent seller's commission, less than the 10 percent typical for works in the price range of those being offered for sale. If the sale raised less than $9.4 million, Jodidio was to pay no commission at all, and Christie's would collect only the customary 10 percent of the purchase price from the buyer. Bathurst later said that he was baffled by the poor showing of the paintings at auction, attributing it to the "fickle mind of the modern art collector, which makes gauging a ripe market so difficult" (cited in McGill, 1985e:C20).

Finding that Bathurst had given his best-informed opinion of the paintings' value and had committed no fraud, a judge dismissed Jodidio's lawsuit in 1985. That ruling was reversed on appeal. In a trial beginning in January 1987, Jodidio claimed that Christie's failure to sell his paintings had reduced the prices that he could get for them in the future. He asked for $5.5 million in damages for his loss, an amount that included $2.2 million in interest. Lawyers for Christie's responded that auction houses cannot guarantee the results of a sale, because they cannot force people to buy. Eight days after the trial began, the parties reached an out-of-court settlement in which

Christie's paid an undisclosed sum to Jodidio and his company, and Jodidio and his company dropped their lawsuit. Christie's president claimed to be happy with the settlement, saying that it supported his firm's position that auctions were not predictable and estimates were not guarantees. He said that Christie's had made a cash settlement only because the trial had become "hypertechnical." Six jurors later said that had the trial ended at the time the settlement was reached, they would have found in Christie's favor (McGill, 1987f:C20).

In another lawsuit, Stuart Travis claimed that Sotheby's had falsified its appraisal of an Old Master painting he had purchased for $17,000 in 1977 at a Plaza Galleries sale in New York. The following year, he offered the picture to New York's Metropolitan Museum of Art as a gift, in exchange for which he planned to take a sizeable tax deduction. The museum suggested that Travis get the picture appraised by the Art Dealers Association of America, but he refused to do that when he learned that he would first have to commit himself to donating the picture to the museum. The museum then suggested that he get an appraisal from Sotheby's Old Masters department. The woman who headed that department appraised the painting at $30,000, attributing it to a minor artist rather than to Sir Joshua Reynolds, the artist to whom it had been attributed when Travis had bought it. Travis then sued Sotheby's for $12 million for falsely and negligently appraising his picture and for conspiring to damage his reputation. He said that his picture had been published in several scholarly works as by Reynolds, and that it had been appraised once and sold once with that attribution by Sotheby's. Travis claimed that "when Sotheby Parke Bernet had a monetary interest, either as auctioneer or as appraiser, in the subject painting, it is represented to be a work by Sir Joshua Reynolds, but when defendants had no such interest in the painting, it became the work of Tilly Kettle" (cited in *Stolen Art Alert*, December 1982:1). The judge eventually dismissed the lawsuit, saying that Travis had proved neither negligence, injurious falsehood, nor intended malice by the appraisers, nor had he demonstrated that the painting was authentic. The judge suggested that the plaintiff had planned to donate the painting to the museum only if he could secure a satisfactorily high appraisal.

The outcomes of this case, the Jodidio-Christie's dispute, and the disagreement over the authenticity of the Fabergé egg all support appraisers who make their judgments in good faith and on the best available evidence, even if their opinions turn out to be wrong or change over time (*Stolen Art Alert*, December 1982). Fraud requires the intent to deceive, and the courts found no such intent in these cases.

Selling Stolen and Counterfeit Art

Auction houses have sometimes unknowingly played a role in the disposition of stolen, smuggled, and counterfeit art. Robert Hughes (1989:63) comments as follows on the sale of fakes and forgeries by auction houses:

Because the auction houses trade in volume and compete intensively for material, they can sometimes be an unwitting conduit for fakes, particularly in ill-documented but now increasingly expensive areas of art. Few forgers would be dumb enough to try to send a fake Manet, let alone a forgery of a living artist like Jasper Johns, through Sotheby's or Christie's. But where fakes abound, some will inevitably turn up at auction; and where millions of dollars abound, fakes will breed.

In other cases, auction houses have sold property of which they should have been suspicious, such as American Indian pots that most likely were acquired in violation of federal and state laws. As chairman of Sotheby's, Peter C. Wilson sometimes proceeded with sales despite evidence that the objects he was auctioning were of questionable origin; one consignor was even under indictment for forgery and grand larceny.

In 1977, a teenager from a poor New York neighborhood told Sotheby's that he was the owner of a collection of nineteenth-century paintings that were eventually appraised for a total of $400,000. The auction house sold fourteen of the pictures in 1978 and had taken nineteen others on consignment, never publicly questioning their source. In fact, the paintings had been stolen from Pennsylvania's DeShong Museum. Eventually, the young man who claimed to own them was convicted and sentenced to a three-year prison term. The DeShong Museum sued Sotheby's to get the paintings back or be paid compensatory and punitive damages. In its defense, Sotheby's disingenuously claimed that the large volume of objects it dealt with made it impossible to check the titles to all items. Because this dispute was settled out of court, with the terms kept confidential, the legal responsibility of auction houses in circumstances of this sort was not clarified. In similar cases, the Art Dealers Association of America has filed *amicus curiae* briefs with the courts, arguing that if auction houses and dealers were legally required to verify that all consignors had clear title to the works they offered for sale, it would wreak havoc on the art trade (Burnham, 1987).

Sometimes auction houses and dealers know of outstanding claims on the works of art they are offering for sale, but fail to notify buyers of those claims. In 1983, Dutch art dealer Michel van Rijn paid New York's Wildenstein's gallery $2 million for a painting by El Greco. In his subsequent $30 million lawsuit against the gallery for misrepresentation, breach of warranty of title, breach of contract, damage to his reputation, and interference with his business relations, van Rijn alleged that the gallery had failed to notify him prior to the sale that a year and a half earlier the Rumanian government had claimed to own the picture; the government asserted that the picture had not belonged to the Rumanian royal family that had sold it to Wildenstein's. Only when he tried and failed to sell the El Greco to a Japanese museum in 1984 did van Rijn learn of the Rumanian government's claim, which was eventually dismissed because the government failed to present witnesses or documents to support its position (Burnham, 1987).

In 1984, the New York Attorney General charged Sotheby's with persistent fraud and illegality in the sale of fifty-six rare Hebrew books and manuscripts. The state claimed that the auction house had known that Dr. Alexander Guttmann, who had consigned the lot for sale, had smuggled the books and manuscripts out of Nazi Germany, did not have title to them, and therefore did not have the right to sell them. When it announced the sale of the books and manuscripts in 1984, Sotheby's told the *New York Times* that it did not know the identity of the seller of the most valuable item in the sale, because that item had been consigned through an agent. In fact, Sotheby's had dealt directly with Dr. Guttmann in preparing the auction, and he was the source of all of the books and manuscripts. Later, Sotheby's said that it had an obligation to protect the confidentiality of its consignors, apparently even to the extent of lying to the press. This dispute was settled in 1985 when Sotheby's agreed to recall the most valuable books and manuscripts from buyers, return their money, and redistribute the material to institutions where the public would have access to it. Sotheby's announced that the settlement indicated no wrongdoing on its part and therefore showed no need for it to change its practices. As is typical of disputes involving auction houses, the settlement failed to clarify the issue of the firm's legal responsibility and guilt (McGill, 1985d).

Traditionally, when auction houses were discovered to have sold property to which the consignor did not hold title, they claimed that they were merely acting as an agent for the consignor, as a middleman between the consignor and the buyer, and that any dispute about title was between the consignor and the buyer. Today, auction houses play a more active role in settling title disputes. In fact, American auction houses now guarantee the title; in England, title is still guaranteed by the seller (Vogel, 1992b).

Consignment Fraud

Major auction houses such as Sotheby's and Christie's honor their consignment agreements with sellers, but at least one auctioneer has apparently engaged in consignment fraud. Richard Esterhazy opened an auction gallery in Los Angeles in 1986, accepted hundreds of works on consignment, and held regular sales. Early in 1989, however, investigators found that he had closed his auction business and disappeared. Because he had not paid many of his consignors and had not returned their property, the missing property was considered stolen (O'Brien, 1989b).

FRAUD BY MUSEUMS

Because museums infrequently sell their art and because curators' standing among their peers depends on their ability to attribute and authenticate works of art accurately, there would seem to be little reason for museums to engage in fraud. However, in competing with collectors and with other museums for art, museums occasionally engage in deceptive practices bordering on fraud. Museum staff members have falsified export documents to smuggle art from its country of origin, bought art they suspect or should suspect is stolen or counterfeit, abused donors, colluded in tax fraud, and faked attendance figures.

Customs Violations

Museum personnel have fabricated documents to create the impression that objects purchased by their institutions were honestly acquired or legally exported. In 1970, a curator of Boston's Museum of Fine Arts made a false customs declaration when he failed to reveal that he was bringing into the United States from Italy a previously unknown painting attributed to Raphael, for which the museum had reportedly paid $600,000. Because no import duty would have been paid on the painting even if it had been properly declared, the curator was apparently trying to conceal the picture's origin, which he said was an old European family's collection. However, Rodolfo Siviero, head of the Italian Foreign Ministry's Delegation for the Retrieval of Works of Art, traced the portrait to a Genoese dealer who had sold it to the museum, whose curator then violated Italian law by exporting it without a license. The ensuing scandal led to the retirement of the curator and the museum's director, and the painting was returned to Italy. Later, experts questioned the picture's authenticity, and today art historians do not attribute it to Raphael.

Buying Stolen Art

In 1988, a curator of the Louvre was indicted for purchasing a Murillo painting that he knew, or should have known, was stolen. The prosecutor argued that documents shown to the curator by a woman who claimed to own the picture should have aroused his suspicion. That woman said that she had been left the painting in her grandmother's will in 1979. However, twice in 1981 the curator had tried to buy the painting from another woman, the picture's actual owner. The prosecutor argued that the curator should have been suspicious when someone else offered him the painting in 1985. The woman who claimed to have inherited the picture was charged with theft, falsification of a will, and sequestration of the elderly woman who actually owned the painting.

Curators around the world supported the curator, saying that they see so many paintings every year that there is no way for them to remember them all or keep track of them when they change hands. However, the Murillo was a picture that the Louvre's curator had been anxious to purchase, and it seems likely that he would have remembered it. French newspapers suggested that he might have suppressed any suspicions that he had about the painting because he was so anxious to acquire it (Greenhouse, 1988). When asked if it was not unusual for a museum to fail to investigate the provenance of a picture it was considering buying, the director of the Musées de France replied, "If we started rooting into matters of that sort, we'd never get to buy anything" (cited in Russell, 1989:H35). However, in many museums, including New York's Metropolitan Museum of Art, such "legal vetting" is standard policy.

Abuse of Collectors

The growing scarcity of great art and spiraling prices have made it increasingly difficult for curators to acquire first-rate works for their institutions. Competition among museums, which has always been fierce, has intensified in a market in which those few works of quality that are offered for sale stretch or exceed the resources that most museums have available for acquiring new pieces. This situation is conducive to the exploitation of those who own art and might be induced to donate it to a museum.

In 1968, a man consigned to an auction house a painting that an auctioneer and an art expert had told him was by the Carracci school. The highest bid on the picture at auction was only $366. Recognizing it as a painting by Poussin, the Louvre claimed the picture under French law and paid the amount of the highest bid for the work. The original owner then sued to reclaim the picture that the Louvre had bought for such a small sum. In 1987, a court finally ruled that the painting had to be returned to the widow of the man who had put it up for auction nearly two decades earlier. In 1988, she sold the painting for $1.4 million (*The New York Times*, December 14, 1988).

A similar dispute was resolved in 1989 when a French court concluded that the city of Strasbourg and its Museum of Decorative Arts had defrauded a seventy-three-year-old woman. In 1986, the widow, who was living on a small income, decided to sell a painting. An art consultant she hired told her that the picture was not by Simon Vouet, a seventeenth-century painter, but was instead by the Vouet school. After the curator of the Museum of Decorative Arts examined the painting and decided that it was actually by Vouet, he bought it from the widow for $55,000, a price he described to city officials prior to purchase as "very reasonable, and even decidedly advantageous, when one considers Vouet's fame" (cited in Greenhouse, 1989:H15, H20). At no point prior to signing the contract to sell the painting was the widow told that the curator believed the painting to be an original Vouet. When the curator and the city officials unwisely bragged about having bought an original Vouet, the woman sued, claiming that they had acted in bad faith by not sharing facts that indicated the picture was an original Vouet and by failing to tell her that the painting was worth much more than $55,000. The court ruled in the widow's favor and ordered the museum to return the painting to her, but the museum refused to comply. The museum's curator was then indicted for breach of trust. Museum officials claimed that the woman had assumed a risk in selling the painting, and that no one could be certain that it was indeed by Vouet. The indicted curator said that he had acted in the public's interest and not out of personal interest, which may be true if personal interest is narrowly construed to mean direct financial gain, but is not true if personal interest includes enhancement of one's reputation in the art world through astute acquisition of high-quality works of art.

Collusion in Tax Fraud

In order to attract gifts, museums have occasionally colluded with donors to defraud the federal government of tax revenue by overvaluing works of art. Perhaps the most egregious example of such collusion involved Jiri Frel, who was at the time curator of antiquities at the Getty Museum. Frel's scheme, which was uncovered by IRS investigators, involved the systematic overvaluation of thousands of objects so that donors could claim substantial tax deductions. An examination of the Getty's records by Geraldine Norman and Thomas Hoving found that the antiquities department was the only one in the museum that had attracted a significant number of donations. They thought it curious that a museum with $100 million to $140 million to spend on art each year would have such "a vigorous program of hustling gifts" (Norman and Hoving, 1987a:103). The donations came in large blocks, usually on the same dates that museum board meetings were held. Over a ten-year period, Frel acquired 6,453 pieces that he appraised at a total of $14.4 million, including $1.7 million for potsherds that one scholar described as being "almost as cheap as shells on the beach" (cited in Norman and Hoving, 1987a:103). Frel apparently told prospective donors that he would find appraisers to set high values on their donations; in fact, Frel and his staff did the appraisals themselves, in direct contravention of museum ethical codes. Independent appraisers later described the appraisals as two to five times higher than true market values. The only items appraised at their actual market values were those for which donors had appraisals done by two experts and those for which donors took no tax deductions.

Frel had established a system by which antiquities were sent to the Getty directly from dealers in Switzerland. He "would go to a dealer in Europe, pick out an object that he knew he could interest the board in purchasing, and urge the dealer to up the price from, say $20,000 to $80,000, with the proviso that the dealer add for free a host of fragments and study material—which Frel would make available to donors to give to the museum at, if they chose, inflated prices" (Norman and Hoving, 1987a:108). At first, the antiquities were shipped to a local gallery, which then "donated" them to the museum. Eventually, Frel had the objects sent directly to the museum. Some of the antiquities were then assigned to donors, who apparently never saw the objects, but who nonetheless were listed as donors on museum records submitted to the IRS. Some of those donors said that Frel never asked them to pay for the objects donated to the museum in their names.

In 1984, Frel was relieved of his position as antiquities curator for "serious violations of the museum's policy and rules regarding donations to the antiquities collection" (cited in Norman and Hoving, 1987a:107). However, he was then appointed senior research curator in France at full pay, presumably being retained because museum officials believed that he had had the museum's best interests rather than personal gain in mind when he had engaged in the tax fraud. Frel later admitted that he had made many mistakes while at the Getty and acknowledged that he had been lucky to have gotten off as leniently as he did, remarking "They don't realize the half of what I did" (cited in Norman and Hoving, 1987b:81).

Inflation of Attendance Figures

The Metropolitan Museum of Art's 1961 purchase of Rembrandt's *Aristotle Contemplating the Bust of Homer* for $2.3 million raised public awareness of art and attracted unprecedented numbers of visitors to museums. Bonnie Burnham (1975:232) sees this purchase as a turning point for museums, with the size of the crowds a museum attracts thereafter being used as a measure of its success. In their competition with other museums and other forms of entertainment for the public's leisure time and dollars, museums seek to increase their attendance to the highest levels possible.

Because museums depend for support on private foundations and government agencies, and because grants from those sources are often directly linked to attendance figures, some museums have overstated attendance, a practice that borders on fraud because it involves the intent to profit through deception. Following an audit by the New York Comptroller that found that the Metropolitan Museum of Art had inflated its attendance figures by 42 percent, a survey by the *New York Times* uncovered a more general pattern of museums inflating their attendance figures (Kleiman, 1987).

It is difficult to count accurately the number of people who visit a museum, but the fact that nearly all of the inaccuracies in such counts are overestimations strongly suggests that museums systematically try to make their attendance figures as high as possible. Some institutions count not only the people who enter the galleries to view art, but also those who come just to use the gift shop or the restaurant; some museums even count employees who are coming to work. At Washington's National Gallery of Art, visitors to one building are counted again when they enter the museum's other building.

If there were an incentive for museums to provide an accurate attendance count, they could count everyone who enters the museum just once and then deduct from the total the number of employees who are coming to work and the number of visitors who use the gift shop or restaurant but do not enter the galleries. However, there is no incentive for museums to do this. Instead, by exaggerating their attendance they can maximize both their funding and their prestige in the art world. If foundations and agencies that provide funds to museums would periodically conduct attendance surveys, the results could be used to fund museums according to the actual number of visitors they attract.

CONCLUSION

Some of the actions of collectors, dealers, auction houses, and museums are merely questionable, but others fit the definition of fraud as profiting through intentional misrepresentation. However, few disputes in the art world have produced criminal convictions for fraud. In part, this is because fraud is a notoriously difficult crime to prove, requiring the prosecutor to show that the defendant intended to defraud the victim. In the art world, criminal convictions for fraud are usually avoided by out-of-court settlements between the parties, with the terms of those agreements kept confidential so that no one will have to admit any wrongdoing. The settlement of disputes outside of court has advantages for the parties involved: a resolution is reached without undue delay, it is likely to be based more on fairness than on narrow legalistic criteria, lawyers' fees and court costs are minimized, no one risks a criminal conviction and sentence, both parties can maintain the semblance of having won, and commercial relationships are not irreparably damaged. However, such settlements also have disadvantages: parties can be coerced into agreeing to a deal, courts that intervene in similar cases in the future will have no legal precedents to rely on, and the legal responsibility of those who engage in deceptive practices is not clearly defined (Katsh, 1991:80–101).

❧ *Four* ❧

Art Theft:
Opportunities and Motives

A mong international crimes, only the cost of drug trafficking exceeds the estimated $1 billion dollars worth of art and antiquities that illicitly changes hands every year. More than 10 percent of that amount is art stolen from museums, churches, galleries, and collectors, but most of it is due to the plundering of ancient sites for objects that may not be masterpieces but that are easily sold to collectors and museums. Theft of cultural property is a particularly great problem in Italy, Greece, Turkey, Latin America, and the American Southwest.

OPPORTUNITIES FOR THEFT

Art and antiquities thefts result from the convergence of three factors: artworks that are suitable for stealing, the absence of effective security measures to protect those works, and the presence of people who are motivated to steal. In the terminology of the routine-activities perspective on crime, those components are referred to as target suitability, guardianship, and motivated offenders.

Target Suitability

Many works of art are suitable targets for thieves because they are relatively easy to remove from the museums, churches, or homes where they are displayed. Large sculptures present a problem for the thief because of their size and weight, and large oil paintings can be difficult to cut from their frames and remove from the premises. However, many valuable works of art are quite small and easy to steal. Most paintings on canvas can be cut from their frames, rolled, and concealed under a coat until the thief has escaped. Small sculptures, ancient jewelry, vases, and small pictures can be hidden under the thief's clothing or in a bag or briefcase. The ease with which a thief can carry away a work of art is an important factor in determining which pieces will be targeted; one small Picasso oil painting has been stolen three times from a Zürich gallery.

Target suitability is also influenced by the value and marketability of a work of art. This suggests that art theft might have increased in recent years with the enormous appreciation in the market value of art, although valuable art could now be less accessible to thieves because insurance companies require owners to protect it with security devices before they will insure it. The highly publicized escalation in the prices of renowned masterworks has had the effect of increasing the prices of works of art generally considered somewhat less meritorious, making even them attractive to thieves. Thieves might even prefer to steal works of moderate value because their relative obscurity makes them easier to dispose of. In addition, objects once not even considered works of art—such as antique furniture, religious relics, and Native American pots—now have a ready market. As a result, items that several decades ago thieves would not have considered worth the risk of stealing are now worth taking; if thieves can sell them for even 10 percent of their market value, they can net more money than they would from most more conventional thefts.

The 1987 burglary of the New York studio of the recently deceased artist Raphael Soyer illustrates the preference of thieves for artworks of relatively modest value. The thieves left behind many paintings and drawings that would have commanded higher prices on the legitimate market than the four hundred to five hundred prints and etchings they stole. Apparently, they made this choice because the paintings and drawings were unique works of art that could easily be identified, whereas the prints and etchings were parts of numbered series and thus not unique. Although the specific number of a print or etching in a series can be checked, thereby identifying it as stolen, those who buy art are less likely to do that than they are to check a unique work such as a painting or drawing. Because of that, the stolen etchings and prints were described as being like $1,000 bills, with the thieves able to make a substantial profit by disposing of them here and there over time (McGill, 1987a).

The suitability of art for theft is also influenced by its location. Thieves must adapt their modus operandi to the place where the art is kept: taking a painting from an alarmed and well-guarded museum poses different problems from those posed by a theft from an unguarded church or a vacant house. Although incomplete, the following statistics collected by the International Foundation for Art Research provide some evidence of where art theft occurs:

Reported Thefts of Art, 1983–1986

Place of theft	United States	Foreign
Church	1%	25%
Gallery	37%	11%
Museum	11%	11%
Private	32%	26%
Other	12%	3%
Unknown	8%	24%
Total number of thefts	717	1,690

Sources: Based on statistics from *Stolen Art Alert* (1983 cumulative issue, December 1984) and *IFAR Reports* (December 1985, December 1986).

Several tentative conclusions can be drawn from this table. Of the art thefts reported to IFAR, foreign thefts were much more likely than American ones to have occurred in churches. Those foreign thefts typically occurred in Roman Catholic churches in Europe, places that house much important art but usually have little security. There were 3,269 objects taken from 562 churches in Italy in 1990 alone (Stille, 1992). English churches have suffered the theft of monumental brasses, prior to the nineteenth century for their scrap value and more recently for their aesthetic value. Places of worship in the United States rarely house valuable art and thus are not targeted by art thieves.

A high proportion of art thefts in the United States is from galleries. This may be due to several factors. New York City is a major center of the art world, and the many galleries there attract thieves. Because IFAR is located in New York, knowledge of its theft-recording practices may be better there than elsewhere. As a result, a theft from a New York gallery might be more likely to be reported to IFAR than a theft that occurs elsewhere. Moreover, it is possible that there are as many gallery thefts relative to the number of American galleries as there are gallery thefts relative to the number of foreign galleries, but because there are so many valuable artworks in the highly vulnerable churches of Europe, the *proportion* of all foreign art thefts that is from galleries may be reduced by the frequent theft of art from churches.

The table also indicates that in both the United States and foreign nations, thefts from museums are a relatively small proportion of all thefts reported to IFAR; only one in every nine reported thefts is from a museum. This may be because museums are better protected than private homes, galleries, and churches; museums are more likely to hire guards and install sophisticated alarm systems. However, museums may also be less likely to report their thefts to IFAR than are private individuals or churches, perhaps because a museum's total holdings are less affected by any given theft. However, when thefts do occur from museums, the market value of what is taken is apt to be greater, on the average, that when art is stolen from churches, galleries, or homes. Thus, a single theft from a museum can produce a loss greater than several thefts from other locations.

The Looting of Antiquities. The theft of antiquities from grave sites, shrines, and ruins poses problems both similar to and different from the theft of fine art from museums, galleries, churches, and houses. With antiquities the question of ownership is usually less clear-cut; they usually do not belong to identifiable individuals or institutions. Instead, antiquities are often legally defined as part of a nation's patrimony and are thus not exportable without official approval. Problems arise when one country's definition of its patrimony is not accepted by archaeologists, collectors, dealers, museums, and the courts of other nations.

Not only is the question of who owns antiquities difficult to resolve when two or more nations' laws, interests, and citizens are involved, but that question can even arise within a single jurisdiction. A 1986 case in Ireland raised the issue of whether the individual who unearths an object, the owner of the land on which the object is found, or the national government owns the object. Dug up by Michael Webb and his sixteen-year-old son on another person's land, the Derrynaflan Chalice, an eighth-century artifact, was valued at up to $10 million. The day after its discovery, Dublin's National Museum offered $80,000 for the chalice, most of that amount to be paid to the owners of the land on which it was found; the landowners accepted the offer. The Webbs rejected the deal and sued to retain possession of the chalice. In December 1986, the High Court ruled that if the state wanted to keep the chalice and two other pieces found by the Webbs, it had to pay them £5.5 million. Because the museum's acquisitions budget was only £100,000, it would have taken it fifty-five years to pay for the pieces from its own budget. If the museum paid for the objects with specially allocated public funds, Irish taxpayers would be burdened with a debt of £5.5 million.

The National Museum's position, based on English law, was that the chalice belonged to the state as a treasure trove. Since the twelfth century, such discoveries have been considered the property of the Crown, under the theory that the objects had been deposited for its benefit. The museum's director said that this theory was supported by the burial of the artifacts beneath an upturned basin less than a foot underground, indicating that whoever had buried the objects had intended that they be found. However, the extent to which English law applies in Ireland is disputed among Irish legal scholars, and the High Court ruled that this legal principle was not a part of Irish law.

The director of the National Museum claimed that the Webbs had been trespassing when they found the chalice and that they had been illegally using a metal detector. One of the landowners, who had accepted a small payment from the museum, planned after the High Court's ruling to press a claim against the Webbs for trespass and larceny, asserting that ownership resided with the owner of the land on which the chalice was found. Without strict rules to protect the nation's patrimony, remarked the *Irish Press*, there would be "an undeclared treasure hunt with the consequent disturbance of important archaeological sites" (cited in O'Connor, 1986:2). The director of the National Museum expressed the same fear, saying that "up to a third of ancient monuments have been destroyed or are in severe danger" (cited in O'Connor, 1986:2).

Treasure-hunters often lose their claims to unearthed relics. In 1986, a Louisiana man had to give up two tons of artifacts he had excavated from Native American burial grounds to which he had been given access by the land's caretakers. He had kept his hoard secret for five years, until he learned that he did not have clear title to it. Confronting the land's caretakers, the state, tribal descendants, and the federal government, he argued in court that without his hours of digging, the Mississippi River would have destroyed the artifacts. Nevertheless, he lost his claim and the Tunica-Biloxi tribe assumed ownership of the hoard (*The New York Times*, December 31, 1986). Denying ownership or compensation to such treasure-hunters may mean that some artifacts will never be unearthed, but discouraging them can prevent damage to archaeological sites and preserve the relics of the past.

Guardianship

A second important factor in art theft is guardianship, the degree to which owners protect their art. When left unprotected, works of art are apt to be stolen; one small Rembrandt portrait has been stolen four times from the gallery at London's Dulwich College, which cannot afford electronic safeguards, and art is frequently stolen from delivery trucks left unattended outside galleries. As the market value of art has grown in recent years, concern about the protection of art has also grown, and that growing concern may have kept theft from increasing as much as might have been predicted from the rapid escalation in prices. In selecting which artworks to steal, thieves are attracted to objects that are poorly guarded or protected by devices they can circumvent. The use of more effective security measures by institutions that can afford such protection, such as large metropolitan museums, can displace art theft to less well-protected targets such as small museums, private houses, galleries, and churches. This may account for the relative rarity of museum thefts among all art thefts, despite the great value of museum collections.

Security in Museums. Bonnie Burnham (1975) has suggested that one unfortunate aspect of the escalation of art prices and the increased theft and vandalism of art is that museums, in order to protect their holdings, have made their art less accessible to the public. The aesthetic appeal of oil paintings is compromised by displaying them under glass, and railings or protective barriers erected around works of art to keep people at a distance also reduce museum-goers' appreciation of the art.

Museum officials are reluctant to speak publicly about the security measures they employ to protect their collections, believing that such information could attract criminals who would know what they needed to do to carry out a theft. Those officials are even unwilling to discuss security after a theft occurs, hoping that secrecy about their methods of guardianship will thwart potential thieves. Official reluctance to discuss security can even extend to an unwillingness to discuss or report thefts. Victims reason that publicizing a theft may attract thieves by revealing their vulnerability, and that it may be better to swallow their losses or recover what they can from an insurance company with as little public attention as possible. Museums also conceal their losses so as not to alienate potential donors, who might fear that lax security would threaten their gifts; this was a reason that Los Angeles's Southwest Museum failed to report promptly that Native American artifacts estimated to be worth $1.5 million were found to be missing after an inventory. The failure to report such thefts creates a problem for criminologists, making it impossible for them to measure accurately the extent of art theft and trends in that crime.

Museums employ a variety of security measures. They install special alarms to protect their most valuable pieces. Paintings are screwed to the wall. Breakable items are locked in Plexiglas cases, which are screwed down to heavy bases. Even these measures might be ineffective against clever thieves; in 1988, a Chinese vase worth at least $500,000 was stolen from a case in Boston's Museum of Fine Arts while guards patrolled nearby rooms. Museums use bars on windows and motion or perimeter detectors to monitor windows, doors, and display areas; those strategies are only practical for preventing break-ins when a museum is closed. Museums also protect their collections by rotating them, storing many of their objects in vaults at any given time.

One important line of defense for museums is the security guard. However, thefts sometimes occur during the hours when museums are open and guards are present, with thieves using an accomplice to distract guards or waiting until a gallery is unprotected. The limited budgets of many museums and the low wages that museum guards are paid sometimes make it difficult to fill positions, a problem cited as a cause of a recent upsurge in museum thefts in Greece. Because of an inadequate number of security guards, primarily due to absenteeism from work, Italian museums have closed down or shut off rooms; in 1991, about half of Italy's 1,673 museums were closed, and others had to be shut temporarily when no one showed up for work. To protect their nation's heritage, countries such as Egypt and Turkey have employed members of the armed forces to guard their museums. In most countries, being a museum guard is not a career position, but rather a minimum-wage job with high turnover. Most museum guards in the United States are college students and retired people; for the most part, they are hired and trained by museums rather than contracted for through outside security firms, the exception being when extra guards are hired for special exhibitions (Mason, 1979).

Museums have sometimes used volunteers in place of paid guards. At least one thief gained access to valuable artworks by posing as a well-meaning volunteer. Believing that privacy laws limited its right to check prior criminal histories to screen volunteer applicants, the Louisiana State Museum unwittingly used as a security guard a man who had been convicted of several art thefts in Massachusetts. He stole sixty Audubon bird prints valued at more than $1.5 million from the museum.

Even if honest security guards are hired and then trained well, they must act professionally in order to prevent theft. One burglary that was facilitated by unprofessional guard behavior occurred on Christmas Eve 1985 at the National Museum of Anthropology in Mexico City, where the eight security guards who were present got drunk and fell asleep. In another case, a security guard at a Philadelphia museum ignored several alarms on the night of a 1988 burglary because he thought they had been set off by workers doing round-the-clock renovation of the building. A report that the United States Interior Department was missing hundreds of artworks observed, "Although security guards were located at the main exits, we noted that they did not challenge people leaving the building with briefcases, handbags, large tote bags, gym bags, and other carrying cases, all of which were large enough to conceal artwork or artifacts" (cited in Shenon, 1990:10).

Thieves use various ruses to neutralize security guards: concealment, force, and trickery. One thief left a package in a Massachusetts museum, announcing that he would pick it up later. He returned after the museum had closed, but a guard let him in to get his package, only to be held at gunpoint while the thief and his accomplices stole a collection of rare coins (Mason, 1979:50). A 1990 theft at Boston's Isabella Stewart Gardner Museum, which produced an estimated loss of $200 million worth of art, was made possible by the unprofessional guard behavior of two young art school students who had been trained for only a week and were being paid $6.85 an hour. Disguised as Boston police officers, two thieves gained entry to the museum at 1:15 A.M. by luring one guard away from his desk, telling him they had a warrant for his arrest, and asking him for identification. The other guard violated procedure by returning to the museum's entrance rather than just staying in radio contact with the first guard.

Evaluating the impact that security measures will have on criminals is not always easy. A major museum exhibition of Cézanne's art in Aix-en-Provence, France, in 1961 was insured for $2 million. To protect the pictures, armed guards were hired, locks were checked and replaced, the grounds surrounding the museum were illuminated, and sensitive alarms were installed. After eight paintings were stolen in a burglary, the police suggested that the heavy shadows created by the floodlights might have helped the thieves conceal themselves and blinded any witnesses to the burglary. The police also suggested that the museum's strong windows and thick walls could have muffled any sounds the thieves made while removing the paintings from the walls (McLeave, 1981).

Guardianship can affect the kind of crime that is committed. If a museum is well protected against being broken into, thieves may commit an armed robbery rather than a burglary, thereby increasing the level of violence associated with the theft. A 1985 robbery at Paris's Marmottan Museum showed how difficult it is for a museum to protect itself against determined thieves. Two members of a gang of at least five armed men bought tickets and entered the museum as visitors, and then used firearms to force nine unarmed guards and about forty visitors into one room. Three other gang members removed nine Impressionist paintings from the museum's walls and placed them in the trunk of their double-parked car. All five thieves then rode away, a mere five minutes after the robbery began. One police official described the crime as unusual, saying that most art thefts are committed by burglars at night rather than by robbers during the day; only three other art robberies had been recorded in France since 1963.

In addition to functional displacement, the shifting of offenders from one kind of crime to another (e.g., from a burglary to a robbery), effective security measures can also displace thieves from one type of target to another (e.g., from museums to galleries or houses). This target displacement is suggested by the relatively small proportion of art thefts from well-protected museums, and the larger proportions from galleries, houses, and churches.

Security in Galleries. Art galleries typically take few precautions against theft, perhaps because owners believe that the small size of galleries makes the surveillance of visitors relatively easy. One dealer notes that his gallery has few problems with theft, although occasionally someone enters the inventory room during regular hours and steals a small piece (Charles Cowles, cited in de Coppet and Jones, 1984:247). Some dealers have tried to reduce the incentive to steal small, easily concealed pieces by not having those works signed by the artist prior to the show, thereby reducing the value of the pieces should they be stolen; the artist signs the works only after they are sold or after the show closes (de Coppet and Jones, 1984:248). Gallery owners sometimes try to improve the chance that any art that is stolen will be returned by photographing it and recording it with the FBI or the Art Dealers Association of America. Dealers may also hire security guards for their galleries, though doing so undermines the ambience of gentility and civility that dealers try to cultivate.

Thieves thwart gallery security by adapting their techniques to the requirements of a particular theft. If valuable paintings are kept in a gallery's vault, but the gallery itself is not well protected from invasion, thieves might break into the gallery at night and surprise the owner in an armed robbery the next morning. Thieves have also attacked alarm systems directly. In 1987, two paintings worth a total of $570,000 were stolen from a Zürich gallery by a thief who set off an alarm but escaped before being apprehended.

Security in Churches. Some European churches have more human traffic from lovers of art than from worshippers, the church's art being viewed more for its aesthetic appeal than for its religious significance. Some of those churches have diminished the awe-inspiring quality of their art by commercializing it, requiring visitors to deposit coins in boxes to illuminate paintings and selling souvenirs in gift shops (Burnham, 1975:77–78). Attracting visitors who see the art as commercially valuable property rather than as religiously meaningful pictures compromises the security of the artworks. Clergy face the same dilemma confronted by the directors of museums: limiting the access of potential thieves counteracts the institution's goal of remaining open to the public it wishes to serve.

Many European churches do not have the funds to provide effective security for their art, and insuring their property is usually prohibitively expensive. Because of inadequate resources, many paintings in European churches are in poor repair, allowing potential thieves to justify theft by saying that the owners have contributed to the paintings' deterioration through neglect. Security in Italian churches has been compromised in recent years by a reduction in the number of priests and by the closing of some churches after the 1980 earthquake (Stille, 1992). Occasionally, members of the clergy have even sold church property to dealers or collectors, usually to secure funds to pay for other church activities but occasionally for personal profit. One tactic is to sell an original painting to a dealer or middleman and hang a replica in its place in a dark corner of the church. In 1961, two Italian priests were accused of selling to eight antiques dealers $1.2 million worth of objects from their church and its art gallery; charges were dismissed because their motive had been to raise money to support the church and its work with the poor (McLeave, 1981:173–74).

Once an object is taken from a church, it is not likely to be recognized as stolen because of the enormous amount of religious property in existence and because of the frequency with which such things turn up in antiques shops. One way to undercut this illicit trade is to allow unwanted and surplus church property to be sold legally, thereby meeting the demand of dealers and collectors and raising funds for financially strapped churches. Doing that is now against the law in most countries where such an illicit trade flourishes. French law states that a church's movable property belongs to the state and cannot be sold or transferred. In Belgium, where church property has increasingly been lost through theft by outsiders and illegal sales by the clergy, the government ordered a photographic inventory of all movable objects in the country's churches so that items could be recognized if they turned up on the black market. Those photographs have been used to recover art that belongs to churches in Belgium (Burnham, 1975:82).

Security in Private Homes. The most obvious form of protection for an art collection in a private home is a sophisticated electronic alarm system connected to the office of a security firm. Perhaps equally as effective in preventing theft is the less obvious measure of not making it widely known to strangers that the house contains valuable art. Magazines that feature stories, with color photographs, of the interior of a home can be consulted by thieves who want to learn the layout of the home and what is available to steal. Public exhibitions and publications that give the name of a work's owner can also be used by thieves to locate art to steal. Large parties in the home can attract strangers who learn what they need to know to carry out a theft. Service and repair workers who enter the home are also in a position to gather information that they, or others to whom they convey the information, can use to steal works of art.

Motivated Offenders

There is little research on the thieves who steal art, in part because few such thieves are identified, arrested, convicted, and imprisoned. According to the FBI, in 1991 only 24 percent of all robberies, 14 percent of all burglaries, and 20 percent of all larcenies were cleared by the police. Because art thefts are probably better planned than the average theft, and probably executed by more experienced thieves as well, the clearance rates for art robberies, burglaries, and larcenies are probably even lower than the figures for all crimes of those types. Experts estimate that only 10 percent of all stolen art is recovered, although the rate may be as high as 50 percent for well-known works. Even when stolen art is recovered, the thieves are often not identified, prosecuted, and convicted; given a choice between recovering their art and bringing charges against the thieves, many owners choose to have their art safely returned to them. Art thieves who are convicted typically receive light sentences, rarely staying in prison for more than a few years. Consequently, at any given time there are few imprisoned art thieves available for interviewing, and those who are might well be unrepresentative of the much larger number of art thieves who have avoided imprisonment.

The degree to which criminals specialize in art theft is unclear. Recent research suggests that criminals as a group are less likely to specialize in one type of crime than to be versatile (that is, to commit a variety of crimes). Many art thieves are probably professional thieves of a general sort, willing to commit larceny, burglary, or robbery whenever lucrative opportunities arise, and open to stealing art or anything else of value. For instance, large losses have been inflicted on collectors and museums in France and Italy by gangsters whose usual activities are drug smuggling and extortion.

Former New York "art cop" Robert Volpe suggests that some thieves do specialize in stealing art (Adams, 1974). He claims that those thieves enjoy high prestige in the criminal underworld because of their skill, the "touch of culture" involved in their crimes, and the high social standing of the clients for whom they steal. One Massachusetts thief is widely known by law-enforcement officials to specialize in the theft of art; he is usually the first person to be questioned when art is stolen in New England.

The usual motive for the theft of art is pecuniary, but rewards other than profit are also important to thieves. A thief who stole silver candlesticks from the Brooklyn Museum said that he was motivated by a desire to embarrass one of the museum's directors. He claimed that the director was not caring for the pieces properly, and he hoped that the director would be dismissed for negligence when the theft was discovered. However, the thief was arrested trying to sell some of the silver, suggesting that profit was also a consideration for him (Adams, 1974:144–58). Another motive for theft was cited by an Italian tomb-robber; he profited from his crimes but also relished the fun of outwitting the police and the thrill of discovering hidden treasure: "You have worked so hard. Then you stand in front of the tomb and you are ready to open it. You do not know what is inside, and you must know. This is the moment. You would push away your father or your mother if they tried to stop you . . ." (Hamblin, 1970:84).

MOTIVES FOR ART THEFT

After a major art theft, experts usually speculate about the thieves' motives, usually in the absence of any concrete information about the thieves themselves. Following the 1985 theft of Impressionist paintings from Paris's Marmottan Museum, the curator remarked that the thieves "chose the museum's best works, the most expensive, without wasting any time. They knew exactly what they were looking for" (cited in Miller, 1985:C17). Because it would be nearly impossible to sell such well-known paintings, he suggested that the crime must have been "a special-order theft." An Interior Ministry official speculated that the pictures had probably been stolen for a private collector, or perhaps to blackmail the museum or the government. A police official said that such thefts are often for the purpose of extracting a ransom from an insurance company, although such efforts had usually failed in France. Interpol officials guessed that the paintings might have been taken by a political group intending to exchange them at some future time for the freedom of members of their group who were in custody.

There is no way to know thieves' motives unless and until they are apprehended and questioned. Based on cases in which thieves have been arrested, we can identify the following motives for art theft:

- for personal possession,
- on commission for collectors,
- for sale to dishonest dealers,
- for consignment to auction houses,
- on speculation,
- for investment,
- for ransom for personal gain, and
- for political purposes.

There is no way to know what proportions of all art thefts fall into each category, because most thieves are never identified.

Theft for Personal Possession

Bonnie Burnham (1975:69) has suggested that some art thieves justify their crimes by the indifference to artworks shown by the institutions that own them and by their frustration at trying to enjoy art in a museum setting. Art theft is caused by a "strange mixture of love for art, awe at its financial value, and the resentment that often comes from thwarted efforts to experience art in an intimate context" (Burnham, 1975:71). Lovers of art are frustrated by the way that museums display artworks: they cover them with glass to protect them from vandals, fail to illuminate them adequately, tolerate high noise levels in the galleries, and provide no benches for leisurely viewing. Burnham suggests a cycle in which theft and vandalism lead museums to take better security measures, with those measures then diminishing the quality of a visitor's viewing experience; frustration at the diminished viewing experience is then used to justify more theft and vandalism. In 1988, the night security supervisor in a Baltimore museum confessed to stealing eighty-one Asian porcelains, snuff boxes, and other pieces from the museum over a period of six weeks by jimmying open the Plexiglas cases containing the objects. He explained his theft by saying that he had loved to touch the objects, but when the museum's Conservation Department added locks to its doors, handling the pieces had become impossible, so he had to take the pieces so that he could hold them. By the time he was apprehended, he had melted down and sold for scrap several Egyptian gold rings, suggesting a pecuniary as well as aesthetic motive for his theft (O'Brien, 1988).

Some thieves tell themselves that taking a single painting from a museum's crowded walls will not deprive the museum or the public to any great degree, and that they will treasure the object and enjoy it in the privacy of their own home (Burnham, 1975:73–74). That perception is not common among museum visitors, but a few people who are otherwise predisposed to break the law can be impelled by such a belief to steal art. In such cases, it will be difficult to recover the art, because the thief simply wants to possess it rather than sell it. Some such thieves are, however, eventually driven by their consciences to return the art.

Burnham (1975) suggests that the increase in art theft between the late 1950s and the mid-1970s was due not to more people seeking to profit from the sale of stolen art, but rather to more collectors who wanted to keep the stolen art for themselves. Connoisseur-thieves, who are knowledgeable about art, steal or organize the theft of pieces that they want to possess. During the early 1960s, Dr. Xavier Richier organized a gang of burglars to steal designated medieval ecclesiastical artworks and eighteenth-century furniture from French cathedrals and chateaux in order to satisfy his passion for such objects; he kept the best pieces for himself, but 70 percent of the objects stolen in the burglaries, which numbered at least seventy-six, were sold for profit (Leitch, 1968). A man who stole three sculptures from a Boston church said that while praying he had been overcome with an urge to take some of the beautiful objects in the sanctuary; he used them in a votive altar he set up in his home. Another connoisseur-thief was an art student who used the opportunities provided by his work at unpaid jobs in various French museums to steal paintings that he liked; he did not try to sell any of them, remarking that he had "just wanted to admire them quietly at home" (cited in *The New York Times*, January 22, 1989:14). Etoh Mvondo, a twenty-year-old Parisian, snatched three paintings from the walls of three different French museums in July 1990. He announced to the court that sentenced him to a three-year prison term that he was simply building a private art collection: "I'm a lover of art. The idea of owning a Renoir at the age of twenty fascinated me" (cited in Riding, 1991:15). Louis Hillen, a commercial artist and painter, was a connoisseur-thief who pleaded guilty to the theft of nine artworks found in his New York apartment, where they were displayed with special mounts and lights. He told the police that the value of the pieces was unimportant, and that he had stolen them because he liked them and they had been easy to take from the Soho galleries where they were being shown.

Another connoisseur-thief was Dr. Frank Waxman, a Philadelphia osteopath who over an eight-year period stole 170 artworks valued at more than $1 million from at least twenty-five galleries in New York, Los Angeles, Chicago, Philadelphia, and Palm Beach. He took the pieces from dealers' desks, gallery stockrooms, and delivery trucks after signing into the galleries with fictitious and often pretentious names. Waxman had an unobtrusive appearance and was soft spoken and well dressed, so few dealers suspected him when they discovered their losses. Eventually, the artworks were recovered from Waxman's apartment, and he was incarcerated for several months and paid a substantial fine.

In 1978, two hundred Tibetan and Nepalese works of art were stolen in a burglary of Dr. Jane Werner's New York home. A short time before, she had been contacted by Craig Warner, who presented himself as a student of Tibetan Buddhism and a neophyte collector of Tibetan art. He befriended Dr. Werner and began to run errands for her. After the burglary, which occurred when she was away from home, Warner was questioned by the New York police. He refused to submit to a lie-detector test and disappeared a short time later. In 1989, the Los Angeles Police Department received a letter from a friend of Dr. Werner giving the details of the burglary and the Los Angeles address where Warner could be found. Confronted by the police in his home, Warner showed them his art collection, which included all of the pieces stolen from Dr. Werner more than a decade before (O'Brien, 1990b).

Perhaps the connoisseur-thief who has amassed the largest collection is Stephen Blumberg, a specialist in the theft of books and manuscripts from libraries; he also stole paintings, prints, stained glass windows, and antique furniture. When the FBI searched Blumberg's fourteen-room home in Iowa, they found a huge collection of stolen items estimated to be worth $40 million; two large trucks were needed to haul away the nineteen tons of material, which included about 21,000 rare books and 10,000 valuable documents. Blumberg had stolen the books and documents over a period of two decades from more than 140 libraries in the United States and Europe, often gaining access to valuable material with identification that belonged to a University of Minnesota professor of psychology. Blumberg owned an antiques shop in Texas, where he apparently sold some of his loot, but the enormous cache of stolen goods found in his home indicated that he took a collector's delight in amassing and living with the objects. Blumberg pleaded not guilty by reason of insanity, claiming that delusions had caused him to think that he was a guardian of the past who had to steal the books, documents, artworks, and antiques.

The Elgin Marbles. In 1801, Thomas Bruce, the seventh earl of Elgin, was British Ambassador to the Court of the Sultan of Turkey, which at the time ruled Greece. The architect of Elgin's new house in England suggested that Elgin hire artists, molders, and copyists to copy artwork in Athens for use in the new house. The primary site of interest to Elgin was the Parthenon, a temple built in 447–438 B.C., but he encountered official resistance to his proposed copying.

Three weeks after the British, who were allies of the Turks, won a victory over the French in Cairo, Lord Elgin got a permit to use the Parthenon's site. The permit specified that no one was to hinder him in his copying or in his removal of detached ornaments, stones, or figures that he found there. At that point, Elgin apparently did not believe that he had the right to loot the Parthenon, only the right to remove loose bits and pieces he found on the site, but his secretary urged him to take parts from the temple itself. An 1801 peace treaty meant that the French counsel would soon be returning to Athens, and he too was interested in collecting antiquities, so time seemed to be running out for Elgin. Consequently, he asked the British government to help him ship antiquities out of Greece, and it agreed. Elgin took marble panels, friezes, and statuary, some of which had been attached to the temple when he had arrived in the country. This dismantling of the Parthenon threatened its structural integrity; when the Greeks years later asked the

British for a copy of a marble statue needed to support the temple's structure, the British complied but billed the Greek government £30,000.

The British Museum, where the Elgin marbles now reside, has refused to accede to the Greeks' repeated demands for repatriation of the antiquities looted from a temple they regard as a symbol of their democracy and their cultural heritage. While not openly supporting Lord Elgin's actions, many museum directors oppose repatriation of the marbles out of fear that doing so would lead other nations to demand the return of property taken from them in the past.

Lord Elgin's defenders argue that what he took is now much better preserved than what was left behind (Hitchens, 1989). Peter Lacovara, an Egyptologist at Boston's Museum of Fine Arts, has remarked, "I think the British Museum has every right in the world to hang on to them. They wouldn't exist now if the British hadn't taken care of them" (cited in Temin, 1989:42). At the time that Lord Elgin was removing the marbles, Turkish occupation forces were extracting lime to use in the construction of houses and fortifications by burning Greek sculptures, and at one point they shelled the Parthenon. Material that Elgin left behind has been ravaged by the environment over the past two centuries. Today, air pollution in Athens could cause the disintegration of the marbles, according to Lacovara, though others point out that in recent years the Greeks have taken steps to preserve the Parthenon and would certainly take measures to preserve the marbles if they were returned. Lacovara even suggests that if the marbles were returned, the British government should charge Greece for nearly two centuries of storage and care; others note that the British have actually damaged the marbles in the process of cleaning them. Lord Elgin's defenders have also noted that antiquities were viewed differently when he took them than they are today, and that his actions were not defined as theft at the time.

Lord Elgin's critics see his behavior as looting that was made possible by Great Britain's power in the international arena. He took the marbles for personal use in his home and later profited by selling them to the British government when he experienced financial hardship, even though he received only half of what it had personally cost him to remove the pieces from Greece. One of his contemporaries, Edward Dodwell, said that Lord Elgin had despoiled the Parthenon of its finest sculpture, destroying some parts of the temple in order to remove other parts; to Elgin's theft for personal possession can be added the offense of vandalism.

Theft on Commission for Collectors

Some thieves steal on commission, taking artworks that a collector agrees in advance to buy for a prearranged amount. Collectors might place an order for a specific piece or simply make it known that they are interested in buying certain types of art. An informant who once posed as an art buyer for the FBI claimed that he could get nearly any object if he could meet a thief's price. Idi Amin, former ruler of Uganda, was a well-known collector of stolen art who commissioned thefts through connections in France, according to a former chief of security at New York's Metropolitan Museum of Art.

When thieves take only certain pieces from the collection of an individual or a museum, the police and the press often speculate that their selectivity indicates that the thieves were seeking specific works, perhaps to fill an order for a collector. However, thieves are forced by limitations of time and ability to choose only some works from large collections. Often their choices make little sense when examined in detail after the crime. For instance, the 1990 theft of thirteen pieces from Boston's Isabella Stewart Gardner Museum included a rare and valuable painting by Vermeer, but also a painting that was no longer attributed to Rembrandt; the thieves ignored the museum's strong collection of Italian Renaissance art and left behind Rembrandt's *Self Portrait* and Titian's *Rape of Europa,* once described as perhaps the greatest painting in the United States. A collector underwriting such a high-profile theft would seemingly have directed the thieves to be more selective in their choices. Perhaps, on the other hand, a collector commissioned the thieves to steal only the Vermeer, and on their own initiative they decided to take additional pieces and try to sell them on the black market. Without more information on the motives of the thieves, and their possible links to collectors or dealers, speculation about whether the theft was commissioned remains guesswork.

An article in *IFAR Reports* claims, with no supporting evidence, that it "is hard to imagine theft for hire in real life, and there are very few, if any, examples of this type of theft" (Pearson, 1986a:3). No one knows how many collectors have commissioned the theft of art, but there are certainly some. Evidence of the existence of such collectors does not often come to light, because they are apt to be circumspect in displaying the stolen art and do not try to sell it. If collectors were conspicuous consumers, they would not want to have a work of art unless they could display it to others, but collectors who can afford to commission the theft of a masterwork probably have sufficient resources and extensive enough collections to impress others without displaying the stolen art in their possession. Because most collectors derive pleasure from simply possessing and looking at their art, some of them will probably be happy to have a stolen work, even if they can never show it to anyone or sell it for a profit. A collector with a passion for Vermeer's art realizes that there is little chance of ever acquiring one of the artist's paintings legitimately, and so may settle for having a stolen one. Hugh McLeave (1981:8) refers to collectors who commission the theft of art as "wealthy fetishists who buy stolen art that only they can contemplate and appreciate"; they differ from legitimate collectors not in their aesthetic response to art but rather in the means by which they acquire it.

In 1981, the FBI uncovered a ten-member gang that had stolen about $1 million worth of prints and Western art from museums and galleries in the Midwest over a five-year period. A small antiques shop in Kansas City was the conduit of stolen art from the thieves to their elite clients, who were doctors and businesspersons from St. Louis and Kansas City. At first, those clients bought art from the shop, knowing it was stolen; later, they met with the thieves to order specific pieces to be stolen. One Kansas City surgeon was convicted of two counts of receiving stolen property.

Members of the New York Police Department have often uncovered thefts done on commission. They say that the extensive publicity given to art prices has stimulated a widespread demand for artworks, with collectors who cannot afford market prices sometimes commissioning thefts through brokers, who set prices, hire thieves, and ship the pieces to the collectors immediately after they are stolen. In a few cases, a fence has had a painting stolen, had a copy made, and sold the forgery to the collector who commissioned the theft. In a 1989 residential robbery in New York, one of the thieves remarked to the victim, an art restorer, that they were being paid $50,000 to steal his paintings. The victim, who had been handcuffed and covered with a sheet, offered to pay them even more, but the thief said that accepting that offer would endanger their families.

Theft for Sale to Dishonest Dealers

The problem of converting stolen property into liquid assets is faced by many thieves, but none face greater obstacles than art thieves who want to convert into cash objects that are often unique and therefore readily identifiable as stolen by art dealers and auction houses. One thief remarks, "The biggest thing about stealing a painting is having someone to sell it to. Unless you have it sold ahead of time, it's useless" (cited in Golden, 1989:35). Conventional wisdom holds that well-known stolen art cannot be easily disposed of because most dealers are knowledgeable enough to recognize such works and reputable enough to refuse to purchase them. However, in an experiment conducted for the television show "60 Minutes," the director of the Art Institute of Chicago was unable to recognize either a copy or a slide of a Cézanne painting that had been stolen from his museum less than a year before. With the passage of time, even the experts forget.

Prior to assuming the risk of a theft, thieves often have a buyer in mind, frequently someone who has purchased stolen art from them before. Some thieves work with dishonest dealers, who buy art they know is stolen and may even provide the thieves with "shopping lists" of the kinds of works they are most interested in purchasing.

In 1984, Boston art dealer Michael Filides was convicted of conspiracy, transporting, and receiving stolen property across state lines. A burglar testified for the prosecution that Filides had given him specific instructions about the kinds of stolen paintings in which he was interested: French and Dutch pictures of relatively small size, scenes with people rather than animals or portraits (which were too easy to identify), and no paintings with ships or American flags. The dealer told the thief to take the frame as well as the painting, saying that doing so would make it harder for the police to get the exact dimensions of the picture. The burglar said that Filides gave him a list of more than one hundred European artists in whose work he was interested. The Sunday morning after a Saturday night burglary, the thief would arrive at Filides's Newbury Street gallery dressed in jeans and sneakers. He made no effort to conceal the fact that what he was offering was stolen; in fact, he told Filides several times that the art was stolen. From the three hundred burglaries he committed, the thief was able to sell about forty paintings to Filides. Filides usually paid cash and offered no receipt, and few of the pictures were included in Filides's business records. Some of the purchases were of pictures that did not meet the criteria established in advance by the dealer. Filides denied ever ordering the burglar to steal for him and denied knowing that the art he bought from the burglar was stolen, despite the fact that the Art Dealers Association of America said that theft notices about the pictures Filides had bought had been sent to his gallery. The judge gave Filides a suspended sentence, five years on probation, and a $30,000 fine and required him to give one thousand hours of lectures on art to poor Bostonians.

In 1979, French dealer Paul Petrides, the acknowledged world expert on the works of Maurice Utrillo, was convicted of receiving nineteen paintings that had been stolen in four burglaries. During his trial, Petrides claimed not to have read the circulars he had received that listed the pictures as stolen. He changed the titles and dimensions of the paintings in his records and fabricated names for those from whom he had supposedly purchased the pictures. Then he shipped the paintings abroad for sale, encountering no obstacles from customs officials because of his eminence as an art dealer. Petrides was fined and sentenced to three years in prison, later lengthened to four; the judge remarked, "Specialist art thieves only act because they are assured of getting rid of their booty with the complicity of go-betweens and receivers of stolen property" (McLeave, 1981:258).

Another dealer who commissioned thefts was Henri Kuntz, who would visit galleries and carpet dealers in Toronto, select works he liked, and then order them stolen by thieves he hired through his contacts in the local criminal underworld. He told the thieves what to steal and where to find it. Prior to committing a burglary, the thieves would set off several false alarms at a targeted location to test police response time, and then break in and make off with the goods before the police returned.

One major theft has been attributed to a wealthy Greek olive oil manufacturer who reportedly hired members of the Italian Mafia to steal $35 million worth of Italian Renaissance art from the Budapest Museum of Fine Arts in 1983. The businessman's brother was a New York art dealer, suggesting that the paintings might eventually have been marketed through that outlet. In 1984, the Greek businessman was arrested and charged with theft and receiving stolen goods; he denied any wrongdoing, the charges against him were dropped, and the slightly damaged paintings were recovered in a Greek monastery. The outcome suggests that a deal might have been struck between the businessman, the Greek and Italian police, and the museum from which the art had been stolen.

Often a dealer and a thief will act symbiotically, rather than having a dealer specifically commission the thief to steal art. One antiques dealer describes this symbiosis as follows:

The process is always the same. Somebody comes into the shop and wants to sell something small. The next time, he buys something. He poses as either a collector or as a small-time broker. After a while you get to know the guy, and you see him around regularly. Once he has won your confidence, he starts selling you stolen things. He waits until he has the confidence of a dealer, and then he goes and robs a church or a small collection that he's had his eye on the whole time. He may even propose the merchandise before he has it—if you're not interested, he doesn't steal it. Half the time there is no way of knowing unless he shows up with something a little too good, or the police come around asking about him. And when they do find something stolen, whose pocket do you think the money to pay for this little caper comes from? The dealer's.

It enraged me. The small dealers like myself had a terrifically hard time—but there was easy money in dealing in black market *brocante*—that and fakes. And it's so easy, so easy for them. (cited in Burnham, 1975:54–55)

Sometimes brokers, independent middlemen who are not established dealers with their own galleries, play an important role in the theft of art. They might express a strong interest in a certain work, commission a shopowner or small-time dealer to get a particular piece, or even hire thieves to steal it. Rather than being concerned with the mechanics of the theft, these brokers research pieces worth stealing, using their scholarship to determine the value of a work and decide if it is worth stealing (Burnham, 1975). After such a theft, the thief immediately takes the work to the broker, thereby minimizing the chance of being caught with it. Sometimes the brokers, who are acting as fences, then hire a restorer to alter the piece so as to reduce the likelihood that it will be recognized, even though doing so can reduce the value of the piece.

According to one account, a few months before the 1985 theft of Impressionist paintings from Paris's Marmottan Museum, a known Japanese criminal, acting as a broker, circulated among Tokyo gallery owners a list of nine artworks that would soon be stolen. Those paintings were recovered in 1990 on Corsica, apparently as a result of a tip provided to a French commissioner while he was in Japan searching for paintings stolen in another theft.

Symbiotic relations between thieves and dealers also characterize the illicit antiquities trade. The profitability of treasure-hunting activity is evident in the illicit trade in Native American artifacts. A carefully chosen half-acre site can yield as many as four hundred ancient pots, many worth $5,000 to $7,000 on the art market, with some fetching $20,000. A masterpiece, such as a Northwest Coast mask, can sell for $70,000 to $100,000, and a nineteenth-century Navajo chief's blanket sold for $115,000 at a Sotheby's auction. The items looted from a single Anasazi cliff dwelling can sell for as much as $1 million. In addition to pots, looters take baskets, jewelry, textiles, and fur robes. Their most ghoulish activity is the theft of mummified bodies found in sacred burial chambers; prices for the remains of a Native American child start at about $5,000 (Goodwin, 1986). Not surprisingly, the tribes whose grave sites have been plundered see this as a sacrilege, as would anyone whose ancestors' remains were being unearthed and sold to collectors. In 1988, an amateur archaeologist who tried to sell a 1,350-year-old mummy of an Indian infant to an undercover federal agent for $35,000 was convicted and sentenced to sixty days in jail and three years on probation for trafficking in archaeological resources and possessing property stolen from federal land.

Local peasants in Third World countries unearth objects to sell to dealers or their agents who travel the countryside looking for ancient artifacts they can buy for a fraction of the prices they will command in large cities or abroad. The importance of this trade to peasant economies is exemplified by Costa Rica, where it was once estimated that amateur antiquities diggers outnumbered medical professionals by two to one, and where illicit archaeology supported as much as 1 percent of all economically active citizens (*Stolen Art Alert*, November 1982b). One Costa Rican landowner returned from Switzerland with $47,000 that he had been paid by looters as a "royalty" for allowing them to dig up antiquities on his land (Burnham, 1975).

Turkish peasants who unearth ancient treasures are paid but a small fraction of the objects' market value for their discoveries, although they are paid enough to make their work worthwhile. Those who are most successful may even be able to establish antiquities shops of their own. Money from the sale of the artifacts is diffused throughout the community and provides an important supplement to an otherwise weak economy. In addition to adding to the peasants' low incomes, the sale of looted antiquities also supports the local sponsor of the excavation, the owner of the land on which the pieces were found, those who transport the objects to dealers or their agents, and the local police who take bribes to ignore the illicit trade. This trade may support as much as 1 percent of Turkey's workforce (Burnham, 1975:113).

The 1986 theft of artifacts from Peru's Sipán tomb was motivated by the indigenous peasantry's low standard of living, the presence of perhaps 60,000 treasure-rich sites in the country, the high price collectors would pay for such artifacts, and the presence of dealers willing to mediate the flow of the looted objects from thief to collector. The arid atmosphere in the area of the Sipán tomb had preserved the buried treasures, providing suitable targets that could not properly be guarded by the police and the military, who were busy dealing with political unrest and the drug trade. Even though Peruvian law declares the state to be the owner of all pre-Columbian objects found underground, local peasants regarded the artifacts as theirs, as "a sort of bequest of riches from the past to help them get through the hard times today" (Plenge, 1990:76). A laminated gold mask that might sell in the United States for $120,000 could bring a grave-robber a small fraction of that amount, perhaps $4,000, but that is a vast sum to peasants whose average annual income is less than $1,000. The looters of the Sipán tomb justified their theft by the absence of available jobs, the back pay they were owed for work they had done, the hunger of their families, and the absence of any hope for improving their economic position after the cessation of land-reform projects a decade earlier. They denied the legitimacy of foreign archaeologists' claims to the artifacts, saying that those scholars had no ancestral ties to the objects. They also rationalized their grave-robbing with claims that the police sold the objects they impounded and that local museums duplicated original pieces, exhibited the fakes, and sold the originals for profit.

Theft for Consignment to Auction Houses

Thieves occasionally dispose of stolen art through auction houses, although house directors claim that pre-sale catalogues and the public nature of auction sales minimize the chance that stolen art will be consigned to them. Auction houses often fail to research the provenance and title of the pieces consigned to them, saying that to do so would be too expensive and time-consuming and asserting that they are merely middlemen who make no claims about title to the property they sell. In an experiment conducted for the television show "60 Minutes" in 1979, Sotheby Parke Bernet accepted for sale a Utrillo painting that was accompanied by a phony bill of sale.

Twin brothers who shoplifted prints from Los Angeles galleries took the pictures to a conservator to get rid of the fold and roll marks that had resulted from concealing the prints under their coats. They changed the print and edition numbers to make the pictures less identifiable and then consigned them to an auction house. One victim saw two of the prints in an auction catalogue and suspected that they were his; a close examination showed that the numbers had been tampered with. The arrest of the thieves made it possible for the police to clear fifteen thefts and recover $130,000 worth of art.

In another case, a tenant stole antique dolls from the owners of a house she had rented. She consigned the dolls to Christie's for sale, delivering them in a paper bag. Eventually, she confessed to the crime and returned some of the proceeds from the sale to the dolls' owners. After the owners threatened the auction house with a subpoena, and after the New York Police Department asked for its cooperation, Christie's wrote to the dolls' buyers and explained the problem. Some purchasers failed to reply, some returned the dolls, others had resold them, and one doll had been broken.

One thief who took advantage of the failure of auction houses to check provenance and title consigned for sale to New York's Parke Bernet auction house a group of paintings and decorative objects stolen from Pennsylvania's DeShong Museum during the late 1970s. Some might question the auction house's wisdom in accepting masterworks from the teenager who claimed to have inherited them, but he was delighted at the ease with which he was able to convert the stolen goods into cash through sale at auction, remarking, "They don't ask you any questions about who you are or where you got the paintings or anything. . . . You receive your receipt for your paintings and you make your exit. Months later they call you and tell you what was sold" (cited in Burnham, 1980b:2).

In another case, a man bought a painting, which had been stolen from an English church, in a sale at Christie's of London. The court ordered the picture returned to the church, and the man sued Christie's for the purchase price, the 10 percent buyer's premium he had paid, and the restoration costs he had incurred. Christie's refused to refund his money, saying that it was merely the seller's agent and did not have the "authority to make or give any representation or warranty" (cited in Pearson, 1984:5). The buyer claimed that Christie's was liable for negligence and misrepresentation and that the house's intervention between the seller and the buyer implied that it could pass good title. As is common in disputes of this sort, the disagreement was settled without admission of liability by the auction house, which refunded the purchase price and the buyer's premium to the man; it did not pay for his legal fees or restoration costs or for the increased value due to reattribution of the painting.

When auction houses sell stolen art, the original owner often sues to recover the piece. Because auction house policy usually prohibits disclosure of the names of buyers, the original owner often has to threaten legal action just to discover the whereabouts of the art. The person who purchased the stolen art through the auction house usually returns it to the original owner, but then sues the auction house and the consignor to recover the purchase price. Disputes of this sort are usually settled without a trial, so the legal responsibilities of auction houses in such cases remain unclear.

Theft on Speculation

Some thieves steal art on speculation, having no buyer in mind before the theft but hoping they will be able to find a collector, dealer, or fence to buy the stolen art. Most of these thieves know little about art, do not know what they have stolen, do not know how to sell stolen art most profitably, and are surprised at how little others will pay them for stolen art. Drug addicts who shoplifted solid bronze sculptures from New York galleries sold them for the scrap value of the bronze, destroying the pieces and netting less than they would have gotten by selling the sculptures as artworks on the black market.

The resale price for a stolen painting is rarely more than 10 to 20 percent of its value on the legitimate market; extensive publicity for the stolen art can lengthen the time that it takes a thief to find a buyer and reduce the black market price to 5 percent or less of true market value. Some thieves have drawn attention to themselves by asking a dealer to pay too low a price for a valuable work of art; others have caused a dealer to become suspicious by asking too much for what they have to offer. After one thief asked $1 million for a vase estimated to be worth only $35,000, the dealer reported his suspicions to the police and the thief was arrested. Naive thieves with little knowledge of art are often attracted to masterworks that have received much publicity for their high market value, not realizing that the fame of such pieces makes it impossible to sell them on the black market at any price. When stolen art cannot be sold, thieves hold onto it, hoping to sell it later when the police are no longer looking for it with the same diligence as they do immediately after the theft (Burnham, 1975:35–36). Eventually realizing the futility of selling well-known works, some thieves might destroy them rather than risk being caught with the stolen property.

Two thieves graduated from the theft of records and tapes from stores to art theft after reading that a man had stolen a valuable painting by Manet from a museum by simply lifting it off its hooks and walking out with it. To the thieves, that seemed like an easy way to steal something worth a lot more money than records and tapes. They traveled from city to city, dressed in workmen's clothing, took pieces of art from museums' vitrine cases during daylight hours, and shipped the objects home via Federal Express. Because they had no fence arranged in advance, they then had to find someone to buy their loot. They did this by looking in the windows of art galleries and antiques shops until they spotted objects similar to those they had to sell. Usually they made it clear to the dealer that the merchandise was stolen, but they were still able to find buyers. One dealer was sentenced to six months in jail and six months of home confinement for having conspired to possess stolen art; he knew that a vase he had bought from the thieves was stolen but made no effort to contact law-enforcement agents or the museum from which it had been taken (Lowenthal, 1991a).

Sophisticated thieves now realize that "less is more," that stealing less well-known and less valuable artworks can yield more profit because such pieces are easier to sell on the black market than famous masterworks. In a 1985 burglary of the Bennington (Vermont) Museum, thieves left behind a collection of Grandma Moses paintings and stole pictures that were less valuable, less identifiable, and more easily marketed. This pattern is increasingly common, suggesting that thieves might intentionally be stealing art that is easier and less risky to convert into cash. Another possible explanation is that as art has appreciated in value, more thieves have been drawn to art theft, including uninformed thieves who do not know what they are stealing and so leave behind more valuable pieces and ignorantly steal less valuable ones.

Theft for Investment

Sometimes art is stolen as an investment. In some countries, after the statute of limitations expires, not only can the thief no longer be punished for the theft, but title to the work passes to the person in possession of the work, as long as that person bought it in good faith and is not the thief. Some thieves and their accomplices store stolen art in vaults until the statute of limitations expires. During that time, if they have stolen wisely, the market value of the art will increase. They then concoct a provenance, often by buying the stolen art back at an out-of-the-way auction. The art may be resold several times in this way to obscure the chain of ownership and create a track record for the piece. The thieves then sell the art discreetly to a collector or dealer.

Until stolen art can safely be sold, it can be used as collateral for loans. In countries where good-faith buyers of art are protected by law, thieves have fabricated provenances to make themselves appear to be good-faith buyers, and then used the stolen art to borrow money from banks. Stolen art has reportedly been locked in vaults and repeatedly used as collateral for loans in Switzerland, Liechtenstein, and the Cayman Islands, among other places (Hennessee, 1990).

Theft for Ransom for Personal Gain

After the theft of valuable works of art, insurance companies often try to reduce their losses by offering rewards for the safe return of the art. Insurance companies that offer such rewards, typically a percentage of the work's market value, hope to get the property back first and worry later, if at all, about apprehending the thief. Rewards are especially likely to be offered for the return of fragile works or pieces that are especially vulnerable. For instance, the 1989 theft from a Houston museum of gold jewelry valued at $3.5 million led the insurers to offer $25,000 for the safe return of the pieces, a reward that the company announced was substantially more than the thieves would get for the gold if they melted it down and sold it as scrap. A museum security guard called to say he had the jewelry and wanted to collect the reward, claiming that he had been safeguarding the pieces after taking them from a woman he saw stealing them. No one believed his tale, and he soon confessed to the theft.

After the 1990 theft of $200 million worth of art from Boston's Gardner Museum, Sotheby's and Christie's offered a $1 million reward for the safe return of the art, even if the thieves claimed the reward. The FBI had urged the auction houses to offer the reward in order to draw out the thieves and perhaps keep them from taking the art out of the country, which would make it harder to recover. No one tried to return the stolen art and claim the reward during the first three-and-a-half years after the theft.

The willingness of some insurance companies to pay less to recover a work of art than they would have to pay the original owner gives thieves a motive to steal art. Indeed, before insurance for art was widely available, thieves had a harder time converting stolen art into cash. The relative infrequency with which art is stolen makes such insurance comparatively inexpensive, although the routine payment of rewards and ransoms could increase premiums to levels too high for many owners to afford. Ironically, if owners of art did not insure their collections, one motive for art theft would be undercut.

Offering rewards and ransoms has been criticized as a short-sighted approach that in the long run stimulates art theft and increases the cost of insuring art. That view is supported by the consequences of the payment of a ransom for the return of six paintings stolen from the Toronto Art Gallery in 1959; the artworks were valued at $1.5 million but insured for only $640,000. The thieves had verified the amount of the insurance prior to the theft, realizing that they could probably get a certain percentage of the insured amount as a ransom for returning the paintings. They threatened to burn the paintings if the ransom was not paid. When the paintings were eventually recovered, the police denied making a deal with the thieves, but they did not deny that the insurance company had paid for the return of the paintings. The thieves' success at extortion was followed by an epidemic of art thefts across Canada. Rewards led to the return of some of the stolen works, but others vanished, apparently into the hands of shady dealers and collectors who were willing to buy stolen art (McLeave, 1981). In a similar situation, a ransom was paid for the return of twenty-eight paintings stolen from Milan's Gallery of Modern Art in 1975; three months later, thieves stole thirty-eight pictures from the same gallery, including half of the ones taken in the first theft.

Some thieves steal art with the intention of extorting a ransom for its return, but others take art with no clear idea about how they will convert it into cash. Often they find that publicity about the theft makes it difficult for them to sell the stolen art. If they are unable to sell it, they may simply wait to see what happens. Sometimes the owner or the owner's insurance company offers a reward for the art, but if that does not happen, the thieves may demand a ransom. The more time that elapses between the theft and the collection of the reward, the greater the likelihood that the thieves had originally intended to sell the stolen art for profit but were unable to, and then turned to the insurance company or owner as a way to make some money from the crime. Thieves who cannot sell the stolen art to collectors or dealers and also fail to collect a reward or ransom sometimes return the art anonymously, though they may also destroy the art rather than risk being caught with it. In one unsuccessful ransom theft, eight works of art were abandoned in a vacant lot after the insurance company refused to meet the thieves' demand for a certain percentage of the works' market value. The thieves did not know that the owner had underinsured the art and that the insurance company could satisfy the owner's claim with a smaller payment than the thieves were demanding.

As with kidnapping for ransom, "art-napping" is difficult to pull off successfully, because thieves have a difficult time arranging for the collection of a ransom without exposing themselves to arrest. Constance Lowenthal of IFAR comments, "The problem is the people who steal are not any good at the second part of the game. That requires a whole different set of connections and skills" (cited in Butterfield, 1990:C20). A common tactic used by thieves is to have one member of their gang, or occasionally a hired outsider, approach the owner or the insurance company as a middleman who can negotiate the return of the artworks in exchange for a reward. After the transaction has been completed, neither law-enforcement officials, the insurance company, nor the owner will acknowledge publicly that the reward paid to the middleman was in fact a ransom extorted by the thieves, because doing so would encourage more theft. Law-enforcement agencies and insurance companies claim that ransoms are rarely paid to recover stolen art, but the actual extent of such transactions is unknown.

Sometimes it is difficult to distinguish between the payment of a ransom to the thieves or their middleman, and a reward paid to an honest person who is actually helping to recover the property. In one case, ten Impressionist works were stolen in a burglary from a Miami home. Several months later, a private investigator received a call from a man who said he had brought two of the works to Miami after buying them on a trip to Nicaragua. The caller said that he had been told the pictures were stolen when he took them to a local dealer for an appraisal. After the investigator paid the caller for the two paintings, the caller showed him photographs of the eight missing ones, which he said were still in Nicaragua. The investigator said he thought the man was telling the truth, so he paid him to retrieve the missing pictures, eventually giving him at least $100,000. The man who returned the art could have been a thief or an accomplice, but the story he told made it possible for the investigator to maintain the illusion that he was rewarding a helpful citizen rather than paying a ransom to a thief.

In 1961, a Pittsburgh millionaire with a valuable art collection equipped his home with an expensive alarm system, but when he left home one day without turning on the system, thieves forced open his front door and stole ten paintings. Against the advice of the police and his insurance company, he offered a no-questions-asked reward of $100,000, fearing that the thieves might destroy his paintings if they found they could not sell them. He enlisted a judge as a go-between after he was contacted by one of the thieves, but the FBI then entered the case, saying they had evidence that the gang that had stolen the paintings had crossed state lines, which made the theft a federal offense. Posing as the millionaire, an FBI agent negotiated with the thieves through a series of newspaper advertisements and telephone calls. He said he would not pay the reward until he saw that the paintings had not been harmed. One of the thieves told the FBI agent to go to a New York City hotel, where the FBI was able to trace a call from the thief. The thief returned one painting directly to the millionaire himself, then showed up at his home and demanded payment. The owner refused to pay anything until he had them all back. A month later the thief was arrested, because the FBI feared the paintings might be destroyed, even though the agents would have preferred to wait and arrest all four thieves in the gang. The FBI got a tip-off the next day and recovered the paintings. The thief who was arrested was convicted of interstate transportation of stolen property and sentenced to one and a half to five years in prison. The other three men were never apprehended. No ransom was actually paid for the return of the stolen paintings.

Another unsuccessful theft for ransom was planned over a period of three years by four men. The conspirators planned to hire armed robbers to steal ten Impressionist paintings valued at $25 million from a Connecticut museum, store the paintings in a warehouse, and then fly to Europe and demand a $2.5 million ransom. However, instead of hiring a real armed robber, the men hired an undercover FBI agent posing as a professional art thief. They were arrested shortly before the robbery was to occur. Because the paintings were all directly alarmed to the police, the robbery probably would have been interrupted anyway. The would-be thieves were sentenced to prison terms ranging from five to eight years.

Several thefts for ransom were committed in the south of France in 1960 and 1961. In one crime, twenty paintings were stolen from a restaurant. Because the paintings were uninsured, the thieves tried to extort a payment from the owners. When the paintings were returned, it was assumed that the owners had paid a small reward, perhaps $10,000, to the thieves. The following year fifty-seven important works valued at more than $1.5 million were stolen from a small, poorly protected museum in Saint Tropez. The thieves demanded a $100,000 ransom from the curator or they would destroy the paintings. Neither the curator nor the city, which owned the museum, had any way to raise that amount, and an appeal for public donations netted little money. The police opposed the payment of any ransom, believing that the art had been stolen by French gangsters, who would be unable to sell the paintings and eventually have to return the art in exchange for immunity from prosecution. The local crime boss had different ideas. Apparently with the help of a museum insider, a group of thieves then stole eight Cézanne paintings from a well-insured exhibition. The police, assisted by underworld informants, believed that the same gang had committed both thefts. Later, one person did offer to return all of the paintings from both thefts for a reward. The police rejected the offer, hoping to arrest all of the thieves. However, the company that had insured the Cézanne paintings was willing to negotiate with the thieves, and the French government took the position that the safe recovery of the paintings was the most important goal, so a deal was struck in which the gang was paid $60,000 and given immunity from prosecution. The Cézannes were returned immediately, but the other fifty-seven paintings were not recovered for sixteen months.

In 1974, a painting by Winslow Homer valued at $200,000 was stolen from the Malden (Massachusetts) Public Library. As is often the case, the owner and its insurance company were primarily interested in retrieving the painting, whereas law-enforcement officials were more concerned with arresting the thief. A private detective hired by the insurance company was approached by a representative of the thief, and the two settled on a reward of $21,500 for return of the painting. The cooperation of the prosecutor was needed, because either the detective or the thief's representative could have been charged with the crime of receiving stolen property. The thief who had actually stolen the painting got $10,000, and the remainder was kept by the representative. When the thief was asked if ransom-theft was risky, he replied that he did not think it was, saying "You have some paintings worth $1 million, and they give you $100,000. If they don't keep their word, they'll never get any more paintings back" (cited in Golden, 1989:42, 44).

One mysterious figure who has been rewarded for helping in the return of stolen art is referred to by law-enforcement agents simply as The Man. This individual has connections in the international drug trade, primarily in Colombia and Peru, and has been given immunity for any role he may have played in the theft or recovery of the stolen art because he is a key informant for the United States Drug Enforcement Administration. DEA agents permitted the New York Police Department to interview The Man about several art thefts that had led to losses of more than $13 million over a three-year period ending in 1991. As a result, art stolen in several important thefts, including a $10 million burglary of eighteen paintings from New York's Colnaghi's Gallery, was recovered, with The Man collecting hundreds of thousands of dollars from insurance companies. His exact role in the thefts is murky; he claims that he has acted only as a go-between with connections to the art thieves and that he played no part in the actual thefts, but he may have taken a more active role in planning and executing the thefts and in collecting rewards that were essentially ransoms for the return of stolen art (Sherman, 1991).

Most ransoms demanded by art thieves are for personal profit. A less common ploy is to use stolen art as a bargaining chip in negotiations with the criminal justice system. In 1876, Adam Worth and two accomplices stole Gainsborough's *Duchess of Devonshire* from a London art gallery in an effort to force the gallery's owners to put up bond for the release of Worth's recently arrested brother. His brother was released on a writ of habeas corpus before Worth could present his demand, but the painting was not returned to the dealer until 1901, in exchange for a modest ransom payment to Worth (Esterow, 1973:182–201). Another art thief pleaded guilty to the theft of some Andrew Wyeth paintings, but avoided a prison sentence for that crime by helping the police retrieve a stolen Rembrandt painting. That same individual reportedly organized from his prison cell the theft of an important historic state document to use if he were charged with other crimes in the future. A former prosecutor said that the things the thief had stolen "weren't necessarily taken to be resold. They were to be stored away, so maybe he could make a deal at a later time" (cited in Golden, 1989:45).

The demand for ransoms or favors for the return of stolen art is a form of extortion. Another unusual kind of extortion has developed in recent years in Moscow as Russian art has increasingly flowed to the West. Organized gangs have appeared in the studios of artists whose works are popular in the West and demanded that they sell them their paintings for nominal sums. In return, the criminals offer to protect the artists from other gangs and not to harm the artists' families. By paying something for the art, the criminals can prove that they bought the art; they count on the police to be ignorant enough of art prices not to know that what they paid the artists was much less than the market value of their paintings (Akinsha, 1990).

Theft for Political Purposes

Terrorists, revolutionaries, and others who steal for political reasons sometimes demand ransoms to finance their political activities; they have also demanded the release of prisoners who are members of their political group in exchange for the return of stolen art. Terrorists often realize that because art has sociocultural as well as economic value, stealing or vandalizing works that are important to a people's heritage can be demoralizing. Their acts of terrorism are designed to evoke emotional reactions in a population by striking at meaningful targets; art is well suited to that goal. Terrorism is calculated to show people that their leaders cannot protect even their culture's most revered objects, thereby suggesting that the leaders are also incapable of serving the citizenry in other ways.

Some thieves steal art to raise money for political causes. In 1971, a thief who stole a Vermeer painting demanded that a $4.8 million ransom be paid to assist Bengali refugees. A Picasso painting valued at $1.2 million was stolen in 1986 from Australia's National Gallery of Victoria by the Australian Cultural Terrorists, who threatened to destroy the picture unless the government increased its arts budget by 10 percent and established a $15,000 annual prize for young artists; the demands were rejected and the painting was recovered. In 1993, political factions in Cambodia were raising funds to support their fight for power by stealing treasures from ancient temples and warehouse repositories; they smuggled the objects into Thailand, where they sold them clandestinely.

In 1974, one woman and three men burst into a mansion near Dublin, Ireland, with pistols, denouncing the residents as capitalist pigs. The woman, who seemed knowledgeable about art, directed the men to steal specific paintings and told them how to handle the pictures. The gang stole nineteen paintings from the collection of sixty works; it also took checkbooks and papers, including certificates for the paintings. The paintings—nine of which were uninsured—were estimated to be worth at least $19 million at auction, and perhaps twice that amount. At the time, the crime was referred to as the biggest art theft of all time. A week later, a letter demanded the movement of several Irish prisoners serving life sentences in Great Britain to Ulster jails in exchange for five of the nineteen paintings. The others were to be returned for a payment of $1.2 million.

When the police eventually arrested the gang's leader, they found the missing paintings in her car and rented cottage. She was Dr. Bridget Rose Dugdale, an Oxford-educated economist and Irish Republican Army terrorist committed to uniting British-ruled Northern Ireland with the Irish Republic. She had hoped to finance the IRA's campaign with the ransom money. Dugdale, who came from a privileged background, had been wanted by the British and Irish police for months. She had once stolen some of her father's art collection to raise money for weapons, receiving a two-month suspended sentence for that crime, while her accomplice was sentenced to a four-year prison term. By the time of her 1974 theft, even the IRA had disowned Dugdale. Eventually she served six years in prison for the art theft and other crimes (McLeave, 1981).

After the police recovered the paintings stolen by Dugdale's gang, an elaborate alarm system was installed to connect the mansion to the local police station. Despite that measure, eighteen paintings valued at up to $45 million were stolen from the mansion in a 1986 burglary. That value was probably a conservative estimate, because one of the paintings was by Vermeer, one of only thirty-two existing works by the Dutch master; that picture, described as "one of the world's greatest paintings," might by itself have fetched $45 million at auction (*The New York Times*, May 22, 1986:C21). Seven of the eighteen stolen pictures were found near an abandoned van a few hours after the theft; two of them had been damaged. Eight other paintings had been recovered by 1993, but three were still missing.

In 1911, Leonardo da Vinci's *Mona Lisa* was stolen from the Louvre. The masterwork was not recovered for more than two years, and even then the motive of the thief, Vincenzo Perugia, remained obscure. Perugia, an Italian citizen, said that while working at the Louvre, he had become convinced that he was a soulmate of the great artists. He loved the great Italian masterpieces but resented their presence in France, saying he was bitter that Napoleon had "confiscated" Leonardo's painting from Italy, its rightful home. Perugia's knowledge of history was flawed, for the *Mona Lisa* had been painted by Leonardo under commission to a French citizen. After stealing the painting, Perugia said that he often locked himself in his room and stood "bewitched" before the picture. Fearing for his sanity, he eventually decided to sell the painting to a Florentine art dealer. There was some evidence that he had also tried to sell it to an English dealer earlier. The Italian police refused to believe Perugia's claim that his theft had been motivated by patriotism, preferring to think, as did most observers, that Perugia had been driven by a desire to profit from his theft; that would have been consistent with the fact that he had been arrested in France for attempted robbery. Eventually, Perugia was convicted and sentenced to just over a year in prison, a sentence that an appellate court reduced to seven months (McLeave, 1981).

In 1961, exactly fifty years to the day after the theft of the *Mona Lisa,* a thief stole Goya's *The Duke of Wellington* from London's National Gallery. A short time later, he demanded that £140,000 be paid to charity, claiming that he was trying to get money for people who deserved it more than those who loved art more than charity; specifically, he asked that the money be used to pay for television licenses for the elderly and the poor. He did not threaten to destroy the painting if his demand was rejected.

Scotland Yard decided to wait out the thief, and months passed without a word. A second note said that the painting was safe, and a third note made a new proposal: if the newspapers paid five shillings (60 cents) for every 1,000 copies of the paper sold, the thief would return the painting and the money could be given to charity. Fifteen months passed before the thief sent another note. He said that he had gone too far to turn back, even admitting that he was wrong, and he agreed to return the painting if it would be exhibited to the public for an admission charge to be donated to charity, after which it could be returned to the National Gallery. He also demanded immunity from prosecution. Following negotiations with a London newspaper, which told the thief it could not guarantee him immunity, the thief waited a month and then mailed a receipt for the painting, which was found wrapped in a package at New Street Station. The thief accused the newspaper of not living up to its agreement with him to make a charitable contribution, and he said that he had been snubbed when he tried to get the National Gallery to display the painting for charity.

Six weeks later, the thief, a sixty-one-year-old unemployed bookmaker's clerk, turned himself in, saying that after four years of silence he had confessed his crime to another man, and he feared that the man would turn him in for the £5,000 reward that had been offered for his arrest. However, he pleaded not guilty in court, saying that without criminal intent there could be no crime. The judge described him as an angry idealist, enraged at the British government for refusing to exempt old-age pensioners from the television license fee; the defendant had once been jailed for refusing to pay that fee. The judge instructed the jury that it must acquit him if it believed that he had intended to return the painting if his ransom attempt failed, but that it must find him guilty if it thought that he would hold on to the painting until he got the money. The jury found him innocent of stealing the painting but guilty of stealing the picture's frame, which was never found. The judge imposed a three-month prison term (McLeave, 1981).

There are various reasons to steal art, but we do not know how much art theft can be accounted for by each of the different motives. Much stolen art is never recovered, and that which is often is not traced to specific thieves; as a result, we do not have good information on art thieves and their motives. Each type of art theft differs in the way it is organized, especially in what the thieves do with the art once they have stolen it. In the following two chapters, we look at the organization of art theft and at the networks used to smuggle stolen art to its eventual destination.

The Social Organization
of Art Theft

A rt theft requires more than a motivated offender and an unguarded and suitable target. Various roles must be organized and several critical tasks completed. Thieves must acquire and apply techniques for stealing art, learn how to gain access to the target, and sometimes enlist the assistance of insiders and establish a convincing front. In addition to assembling an organization to carry out a specific theft, sometimes ongoing groups are involved in the systematic theft of art; organized crime gangs have committed numerous art thefts over the years in France, Italy, and elsewhere.

TECHNIQUES OF THEFT

Law-enforcement agents assess an art thief's skill from the modus operandi of the crime and the value of the stolen art. They assume that only the most skilled thieves will undertake thefts that require them to overcome significant obstacles. They also assume that if the most valuable works in a collection are stolen, the thieves must have had prior knowledge of the collection, perhaps because they cased the premises before the theft or were commissioned to steal certain pieces. Professional thieves are thought to have good connections with fences or collectors who are willing to buy valuable artworks, which would be easily recognized as stolen if the thieves tried to sell them to legitimate dealers or at public auctions. Law-enforcement agents thus conclude that careful planning and established networks are trademarks of professional thieves.

Thieves steal art in several ways, each requiring different skills and different degrees of planning. Some commit simple larceny, taking an object from a museum, church, gallery, or house without force and without illegal entry. Others engage in burglary, a theft that follows the breaking and entering of a building. Still others commit robbery, using force or the threat of force against people who own or guard works of art.

Special skills are required for some thefts. For example, frescoes have been removed from medieval churches with glue, a time-consuming process that requires ongoing access to the church and skill at carefully lifting the fresco from the wall on which it is painted. Thieves have learned this technique from legitimate jobs, such as salvaging art damaged in the floods in Florence, Italy. Because few thieves have such skills, the police can sometimes determine that several similar thefts were committed by the same offender; occasionally, they can even trace the thefts to one of the small number of people who have the requisite skills to commit the crimes (Burnham, 1975:79–80).

In 1986, thieves burglarized the Bennington (Vermont) Museum and stole three hundred paintings and other artworks valued at more than $1 million. The gang used its expertise in electronics to break into the museum through a metal door, shutting off two alarm systems and using police scanners to warn them of possible police interference during the crime. The gang, which had committed a series of art thefts on the East Coast, was broken up with a series of arrests for the interstate transportation of stolen goods. More than $1.5 million worth of art was recovered, most of it from the Bennington Museum but some that had been stolen from antiques shops in Massachusetts; law-enforcement officials estimated that the thieves had stolen more than $5 million worth of art and antiques. The gang seemed knowledgeable about antiques; one suspect was a Buffalo antiques dealer who allegedly fenced the merchandise for the thieves. According to a spokesperson for the FBI, "They did some very good casing of their jobs, a lot of painstaking homework ahead of time" (cited in *The Boston Globe*, February 24, 1986:44).

Robbery

The use of force or the threat of force to steal art is probably still the least common form of art theft, but art robberies have increased in recent years, probably because more effective security measures in museums and houses have produced functional displacement, the shifting of offenders from one kind of crime (burglary) to another (robbery).

Robbers sometimes case their targets in advance, determining the location and value of artworks and noting obstacles they must overcome to commit the theft. In 1989, a Houston gallery owner spent a long time showing two customers African and Tibetan art, though he remarked later that they did not seem to know much about such art. The following day, the men returned, browsed around, made a low offer on a sculpture, and then one of them pulled a pistol and ordered the dealer to the floor, binding and gagging him. The robbers packed up sixty-five Russian icons, and an accomplice drove them away with $500,000 worth of art. Eventually, an arrest was made of a Russian citizen who was carrying papers that indicated he was an American citizen.

In a robbery committed in Boston in 1989, two men kidnapped an art gallery owner from a subway station miles from his gallery, throwing a blanket over him, pushing him into the back of a van, and binding him with plastic cuffs on his hands and legs. They drove to his gallery and forced him to unlock it and turn off the alarm system. Because the thieves had apparently not cased the target, they had to ask the dealer what they should take; he responded by pointing out pieces that were well known and thus easy to trace. The robbers stole four paintings, including two by Grandma Moses that were valued at $100,000 each.

In another Boston theft, a casually dressed man, whom a gallery assistant thought might be an art student, entered a Newbury Street gallery in the afternoon. The visitor did not spend any time looking at the works on display, which immediately made the gallery worker suspicious. The man then held a gun to the head of the employee and tied him to a chair. Two customers who entered the gallery while the robbery was in progress were also tied up. The thief stole ten paintings; he also took a diamond ring and $25 in cash. The stolen art was valued at a total of $300,000, about fifteen times its value a decade and a half earlier. The robber loaded the paintings into a double-parked van, a common sight on Newbury Street and one unlikely to arouse suspicion. The thief's behavior during the holdup seemed amateurish; according to the gallery assistant, he "got more and more rattled, and he talked a blue streak" (cited in Golden, 1989:18). Eight months later, the thief was arrested in California when he tried to sell some stolen Oriental rugs, which a dealer recognized as belonging to a friend. The ten paintings stolen in Boston, as well as other objects, were recovered from the thief's home. No one had been injured by the pellet gun that he had carried during the dozen burglaries and several robberies he admitted to having committed in various cities (Gillette, 1989). The versatility of this thief in shifting between burglary and robbery is consistent with the finding from criminological research that most thieves do not specialize in a single type of crime.

In an unusually brutal art theft that occurred in Florida in 1984, two men posing as customers met with a married couple who were antiques dealers. After the dealers wrote three invoices for items the men were supposedly buying, the men robbed them of more than $500,000 worth of antiques, paintings, and jewelry, handcuffing them to a safe, gagging them, and then fatally shooting them.

In a 1975 museum robbery, two men entered Boston's Museum of Fine Arts about noon and stole a Rembrandt painting, then valued at almost $1 million but auctioned for $10.3 million in 1986. The robbers threatened one guard and pistol-whipped a second, and then ran from the museum and jumped into a car driven by an accomplice. From his jail cell a suspected art thief later negotiated the return of the painting in order to avoid a prison sentence for himself in another case. Nearly eight months after the theft, two investigators drove to a restaurant parking lot, where a man in a ski mask climbed into the back seat and asked them for identification. He then took from them the keys to the car's trunk, told them to go into the restaurant, and called them there ten minutes later and instructed them to check the trunk, where they found the slightly damaged painting (Ribadeneira, 1986).

Burglary

Probably the most common form of art theft is burglary, breaking and entering into a museum, church, gallery, or house to steal artworks. Most burglars try to avoid confrontations with security guards, homeowners, and other guardians of art, usually making sure that the premises are unoccupied before they enter. In one case, burglars stole paintings and prints from the home of a New York gallery owner after drawing him to a restaurant to meet with them as prospective buyers. After waiting there for two hours, the dealer returned to his burglarized home.

Burglars need information about where they can find valuable works of art in a building, and they need to do the physical work of removing the art from the building. They enter as unobtrusively as possible, usually through a door or a window that is concealed from the view of passersby. Targeted museums and houses are often on spacious grounds and surrounded by trees and shrubbery, thereby minimizing the chance that anyone will see the thieves enter the building at night.

Burglars sometimes use ingenious means of entry, some so unusual that the police are able to link burglaries to one another and to the same thieves. In one New York burglary, thieves entered the art studio of the recently deceased artist Raphael Soyer by tearing off the medicine chest in the apartment next door and punching through the medicine chest in Soyer's studio; they stole four to five hundred lithographs valued at up to $200,000. In another burglary in the same city, thieves lowered themselves into a building through a skylight by a rope that suspended them over a five-story stairwell, and then swung to the landing on the side. Eventually this burglary at Colnaghi's Gallery, which resulted in the loss of $6 million worth of art, and a burglary at the Perls Gallery, which produced a $2.5 million loss, as well as several other lucrative thefts were traced to a gang that entered galleries and apartments by way of the roof.

Larceny

Larceny, or simple theft without physical force or illegal entry, is not a common technique for thieves who target museums, because works of art are usually not left unattended. However, in 1988 one thief managed to walk out of a New York museum with a painting by Manet that was valued at $5 million, taking the picture from the wall while a video being shown on a monitor on the other side of the gallery diverted the attention of the dozen or so visitors in the museum. In 1989, thieves stole from Boston's Museum of Fine Arts a fourteenth-century Yuan Dynasty vase, valued at between $500,000 and $2 million. The thieves entered the museum when it was open, took off the top of an unalarmed display case, removed the vase, and left the museum. They had used this technique to steal from museums in Detroit, Albany, Syracuse, Boston, Baltimore, and Columbus, amassing an esti-mated $3.5 million worth of stolen art before being apprehended. Their thefts required planning and skill, because the top of the Plexiglas cases could not be easily removed with just a conventional screwdriver. Their thefts were committed in January and February from museums in cold climates, apparently a deliberate decision that allowed them to wear heavy overcoats under which they could conceal the stolen objects.

Shoplifters have often chosen galleries as easy targets where they can take advantage of the presence of a single employee and abuse the trust that gallery workers must show to cultivate customers. Shoplifters often work in pairs, one distracting the employee while the other grabs a small item or runs off with an object displayed near the front door. One well-dressed couple removed a Picasso etching from a gallery in a baby carriage. A series of thefts from Los Angeles galleries were committed by twin brothers, one distracting the employee's attention while the other stole prints from a folder or storage drawer and walked out with them under his coat.

In New York, a man and a woman committed a series of thefts at the end of the work day, choosing galleries in which a single employee was present. The woman detained or distracted the employee, sometimes by asking to make a telephone call to arrange the purchase of a piece. The man then walked around the shop and took something, often from a cabinet not visible to the employee. Sometimes he hid an object inside the gallery for later removal.

A similar strategy was employed by a well-dressed man who posed as an interior decorator. He would tell a gallery owner that he had come at the recommendation of another dealer and mention a famous actress he said had been his client. He carried a large satchel containing wallpaper and decorating samples to establish his credibility. After looking around, he would leave and then return later with an accomplice who posed as a client interested in buying antiques and decorative objects. The two men would distract the owner, sometimes by asking for photographs of an object, and then shoplift small items.

Another form of larceny from galleries is window vandalism. Thieves smash the window of a gallery with a brick or crowbar, grab objects on display, and flee. Sometimes they first have to use heavy wire cutters to break through outside metal gates before they can smash the windows. In one such theft from a New York gallery, the thieves stole a delivery truck, which they used to conceal the entrance to the gallery while they opened the gate, broke a window, and stole two antique lamps. Thieves often set off alarms in such crimes, but their speed and the slow response of the police give them time to escape.

Antiquities Looting

The looting of ancient sites has a long history. The tombs of Egyptian royalty were routinely plundered of gold, silver, jewels, and furniture soon after being sealed up; Tutankhamen's tomb was looted within fifteen years of his death. Looters, cemetery guards, priests, and political officials often collaborated to thwart efforts by Egyptian royalty to keep the locations of their tombs secret (Ceram, 1951:154–72). The Spanish began looting pre-Columbian treasures from Latin American grave sites in the sixteenth century. Indeed, the plundering of graves in Peru seems to predate the arrival of Europeans. The ancient Moche people apparently attempted to deter such looting by placing a poisonous mixture of herbs in their tombs; some modern treasure-hunters have reportedly died after inhaling the fumes, so it is now common practice to dig wide openings to the tombs for ventilation.

The looting of ancient sites has probably increased in recent years with the dramatic increase in the market value of antiquities. The rise in prices and the growth in nationalism have led many countries to pass cultural property or patrimony laws that define relics of the past as the property of the nation. When individuals uncover and sell such objects, they break the law, as do dealers and collectors who smuggle the objects out of the nation in violation of export regulations.

Treasure-hunters are usually poor peasants who regard their unearthing of antiquities as a way to supplement their meager incomes. To maximize profits, they often become quite knowledgeable about the value of the objects they dig up. A few have even managed to achieve a reasonable standard of living from their looting. The high prices paid by dealers, collectors, and museums for ancient artifacts have generated much treasure-hunting activity in the American Southwest, Turkey, Italy, Latin America, and elsewhere.

Plundering Native American Artifacts. The looting of Indian burial grounds and ruins increased dramatically after the first major auction of American Indian art at New York's Parke Bernet Galleries in 1971. Record prices at that sale shocked the art world, which until then had paid little attention to Native American artifacts. Demand for such pieces increased rapidly among collectors, who feared even higher prices. With high prices, a strong demand, and a limited legal supply, the situation was ripe for the development of an illicit trade.

The search for pots and other artifacts was once a recreational pastime for families who trekked into the wilderness to search for interesting objects with which to decorate their homes. Today, however, looting has become a highly organized, clandestine, and occasionally violent business with a complex network of diggers, buyers, and sellers. According to the FBI, one group of about seven hundred looters included everyone from construction workers to well-known politicians and entertainers. This network included employees of museums, art galleries, and auction houses who provided looters with information about what kinds of items would sell for high prices, as well as international art and antiquities smugglers who supplied objects for the overseas market, which thrives in Japan and Germany. In some cases, the leaders of looting gangs have hired college students to excavate sites and assume the risk of being caught. Scholars have also been involved in looting; one anthropologist is reported to have made more than a million dollars from the illicit trade in Native American artifacts. To make the looters' work easier, several specialty publications list newly discovered sites to plunder; in 1985, a magazine called *Lost Treasure* listed twenty places to find a fortune (Goodwin, 1986).

Bands of looters work at night in remote areas of Utah, Colorado, Arizona, and New Mexico, traveling to sites by helicopter and using heavy earth-moving equipment. Treasure-hunters carry rifles to protect themselves from competitors, landowners, and law-enforcement agents. After looting the sites, the ringleaders use pickup trucks to cart the artifacts away for sale to middlemen, who in turn sell them to museums, galleries, or private collectors who "frequently do not know, or question, how they were obtained" (Goodwin, 1986:66).

Because few looters of Indian artifacts are knowledgeable archaeologists concerned with understanding the cultures of the past, they often destroy the historic sites they plunder, making scholarly research impossible. Experts estimate that there are as many as 350,000 such sites in New Mexico alone, although only 55,000 have so far been identified. Of those that have been identified, as many as 90 percent have been disturbed or vandalized by treasure-hunters. The state's Historic Preservation Officer has said, "Because of [looting], New Mexico is losing its principal resource, its cultural heritage" (cited in Kane, 1986:F13).

Treasure-Hunting in Turkey. The Anatolian area of west central Turkey has historically been the crossroads of trade and the location of civilizations of grandeur, including that of the sixth-century B.C. ruler Croesus. Known in ancient times as Lydia, that region has long been the target of looters searching for ancient riches, including precious metals and jewels. The high prices paid for such antiquities in recent years have stimulated such looting. Also contributing to looting in that region is the absence of historical and ethnic links between the cultures that produced the buried artifacts and contemporary Turkish politicians and antiquities dealers. The extensiveness of the buried treasure and Turkey's large size make it difficult for law-enforcement agents to control looting. In addition, law-enforcement agencies' success in curbing the heroin trade has left a "glut of highly experienced and underemployed smugglers" and a large number of impoverished farmers who once grew poppies (Hoving, 1988:19).

Turkish peasants who supplement their low incomes by selling the antiquities they unearth have developed a sense of where they can find artifacts by looking at the geography of an area. They wait for the rains to uncover ancient tombs and valuable objects, and they dig at sites unearthed by archaeologists who have returned home after a summer of work. They hasten the process of discovery by using steel poles to probe rubble in order to locate subterranean spaces that contain artifacts. Some have bought or made metal detectors to help them search for buried artifacts. In 1984, three prospectors used a homemade metal detector to uncover what was then called "the greatest numismatic hoard ever," a collection of almost two thousand Greek coins dating from about 465 B.C. that were in mint condition and estimated to be worth as much as $10 million. One prospector knew an antiquities dealer in Istanbul who paid the treasure-hunters $692,000 for most of the coins (Acar and Kaylan, 1988).

Crews of looters are sometimes organized by powerful local residents. One Turkish religious leader sponsored an excavation to raise the funds with which to maintain his mosque; he paid the looters in goods rather than cash and sold the unearthed treasures to the agent of an Istanbul antiquities dealer.

The *imam* gave the agent first choice of the looted pieces, telling him at the same time of other recent discoveries in the area (Burnham, 1975:109–10).

Because they have little mobility and few contacts outside their village, local peasants and the leaders of looting crews usually sell their discoveries to dealers or their agents who are drawn to the area by rapidly circulated reports of newly found treasure. Some agents work out of local shops, where auction house catalogues are used as guides as to what is worth buying from looters and what they should pay for different pieces. Some dealers or their agents have even advanced money to peasants for additional excavations, and some have approached looters at the scene of an excavation, offering them a commission for valuable items in an effort to cut the crew chief out of a profit.

Agents and dealers who offer treasure-hunters less than the going rate are treated with disdain; knowledgeable peasants have thrown pepper dust in the eyes of those they believe are trying to take advantage of them. If treasure-hunters believe they have been treated unfairly, they might report their exploiters to the police or to customs agents. When members of a crew that helped unearth the lucrative Lydian Hoard in the late 1960s thought they had been unfairly cut out of some of the proceeds from the sale of the artifacts, they informed law-enforcement officials of the discovery of the treasure and the identity of those who had purchased it. Such disputes can turn violent; according to Turkish officials, more people have died as a result of competition in the illicit antiquities trade in their country than died at the height of the local heroin trade in the 1960s (Kaylan, 1987).

Grave-Robbing in Italy. Italian grave-robbers, known as *tombaroli*, compete with archaeologists for buried treasure, unfazed by the small likelihood of arrest and conviction and undeterred by the lenient penalties that would be imposed if they were convicted. The maximum penalty for looting antiquities is six months in jail, but most convicted *tombaroli* are incarcerated for less than a month. Under Italian law, the state owns all buried antiquities, but the enormous number of sites where such objects can be found means that full-scale enforcement of the law is neither feasible nor affordable. Moreover, other problems such as the Mafia and political terrorism compete for the scarce resources available to law-enforcement agencies.

Balanced against the small risks faced by the *tombaroli* are the great potential rewards: ancient coins can fetch $1,000 each, and lucky looters can improve their standard of living significantly. One Sicilian has observed, "You started seeing plain folks who built themselves nice houses and bought cars, and they had not won the lottery; they had found rich places" (cited in Suro, 1988b:C19). The superintendent of archaeology in one Sicilian city has said that Italian peasants loot graves for the same reasons that Bolivian peasants grow cocaine: because of the high price of the product on the international market, the activity pays better than anything else they can do. A Sicilian magistrate has described the *tombaroli* as "poor, uneducated men who want money for their families but who get very little for their efforts because they don't know the value of what they find" (cited in Suro, 1988b:C17).

The methods of the *tombarolo* have been described by Dora Jane Hamblin (1970:74) as follows:

He begins by looking carefully over his farmland, in daylight. He looks for humps in the earth. When he finds a hump he uses a primitive form of sounding device: he stamps his feet, hard, on the top of the hillock and listens for a faint hollow sound or a slight vibration. If he hears an echo or feels a vibration, he knows there is an empty space under the mound. It could be either a tomb or a natural cave. The next step is to examine the vegetation on and around the mound. If there is, at any point in its circumference, a patch of noticeably tall and lush grass, the *tombarolo* knows that he may have found the entrance to a tomb. He is trained to see, on the ground, the same phenomena which aerial photographers sight from the air: a thick layer of soil falls into the mouth of a tomb, and it supports a much lusher, taller growth of vegetation than does the thin soil which covers the arched roof of a tomb or of a natural cave.

Once he has completed this daytime reconnaissance, the *tombarolo* is ready to begin night work. For this he needs one or two friends. First, they find the mound in the dark, and then they thrust the probing tool into it. They push down as far as they can. When the tool hits something hard, it could be either the roof of a tomb or a layer of hard rock. The friends help push. If they break through into an open space, they reach for the pick and the spade and start digging to find out what they have come upon.

Another technique employed by some *tombaroli* is to construct a small hut above an underground chamber, allow some time to pass so that the hut becomes a part of the landscape, and then dig for the treasure from inside the hut, thereby concealing themselves from the authorities and from competitors for the loot. *Tombaroli* have also used electric saws and steel wires to cut frescoes away from the stone walls on which they are painted (Green, 1969).

The *tombaroli* justify their looting in several ways. They point out that although the state is required by law to pay finders a percentage of the value of any antiquities they uncover, in fact officials appraise pieces at well below market value. The *tombaroli* point out that the state of Italy is not Etruscan, and so it has no legitimate claim on the ancient Etruscan pieces they uncover. They argue that the cellars of Italy's museums are filled with antiquities that are never seen by the people of Italy, and that they are spreading appreciation of ancient culture when they sell objects to dealers who get them into the homes of collectors who will treasure them. *Tombaroli* do not see themselves as thieves, saying they would never steal works of art from a museum (Hamblin, 1970).

Latin American Huaqueros. In Latin America, *huaqueros* or grave-robbers have sometimes learned techniques of excavation while working on archaeological sites for scholars: they have learned how to make soundings, use steel rods to probe for burial sites, locate tombs and ruins from the geography of an area, determine the likely locations of intact vases, and remove buried ceramics without damaging them. Often archaeologists cannot describe their methods in words, but the indigenous people who work for them learn by example and later profit from their illicit use of those techniques. Unlike archaeologists, *huaqueros* conceal and lie about the locations of the sites where they discover treasure in order to protect their sources, making it difficult for scholars to study the cultures of the past (Burnham, 1975:113).

Iron probing rods, called *sondas*, sometimes damage ceramics that are underground, but that technique for discovering treasures is less time-consuming than traditional archaeological methods; one team of *huaqueros* located three grave sites in six hours. One digger says that he does not need rods or mechanical devices to find buried tombs, because he can recognize them by the way that grass grows on them, by the lie of the land, and by his knowledge of previous finds. Once this digger finds a pot, he says he can tell where others like it are apt to be. He has learned to dig to an object rather than having to excavate an entire site. The lore of such "bootleg archaeologists" in Costa Rica includes a belief that a layer of white sand about eighteen inches below the surface can be used to identify where artifacts will be found; they also believe that a stone altar is a sign of buried gold (Heath, 1971).

Because of their fear of the spirits that inhabit the tombs, *huaqueros* avoid certain sites or take measures to appease the spirits, such as offering them liquor or tobacco. One successful *huaquero* scared competitors away by spreading stories of killer dogs and giant bats and owls that mutilated anyone who tried to invade the sacred places. Those stories were given credence by actual instances of looters who had died when tunnels collapsed (Kirkpatrick, 1992).

A 1,500–year-old tomb in Sipán, Peru, which has been called the "the richest tomb ever excavated archaeologically in the Western Hemisphere," was taken control of by a government archaeologist shortly after looters had found the site in 1987 (cited in Leary, 1988:A18). At night, the *huaqueros* would sneak into the area to steal artifacts, forcing the government officials to post armed guards to keep the looters away. Local residents saw the archaeologists as merely a different class of tomb-plundering thieves, a group that was competing with local residents for the treasure. Their opinion changed somewhat when they realized that the archaeologists were interested in the objects as a way of appreciating and preserving the nation's cultural heritage rather than as a source of personal profit (Kirkpatrick, 1992; Leary, 1988; Saltus, 1988).

LOCATING ART TO STEAL

The first step in the theft of art and antiquities is to locate valuable pieces that are vulnerable to theft. Thieves who want to steal art from museums have an easy time locating it, but often a difficult time stealing it. Antiquities looters have a much harder time finding objects to take, but when they do the pieces are usually not well protected.

Professional art thieves sometimes try to do an inventory of the collections from which they hope to steal. They might determine who owns a painting on loan to a public exhibition and then learn where that person lives; this was done in a 1961 robbery of a California millionaire. In a theft from a London gallery, the thieves first learned that the owner had insured the works on the premises and then checked auction prices to determine how much the art was worth; they carried a catalogue with them when they removed the paintings from the walls. On rare occasions, thieves might even carry out a preliminary burglary in order to photograph the valuable art in a house and then discreetly circulate the pictures among collectors and dealers to find someone willing to commission a theft.

Shortly before the theft of a valuable scrimshaw collection from a historic house on Cape Cod that had recently received much publicity about its renovation, a well-dressed man took a tour of the house. Because he asked many questions, his tour took twice as long as usual:

They were not the usual questions, either. He wanted to know whether the paintings were signed and dated and how much the scrimshaw was worth. Apologizing to the guides for being inquisitive, he explained that he was an art student and his mother collected antiques. Once he stumbled into the range of the alarm system, and it flashed. "Do you have that throughout the house?" he asked. (Golden, 1989:48)

He left with a pamphlet describing the pieces in the house's collection. The following night, two men attacked the caretaker and stole the scrimshaw collection, six paintings, and several other items, using the pamphlet as a "shopping guide," according to the caretaker.

GAINING ACCESS TO THE ART

After locating art to steal, thieves must gain access to it. Accessibility will influence the kind of crime a thief will commit. Museum thefts sometimes involve stealth; thieves divert guards or hide inside the museum until after closing and then leave with objects concealed under their clothing. Thieves who do not know how to neutralize sophisticated alarm systems will not be able to burglarize museums that are electronically protected. Compared with museums, the security measures in houses and galleries are often easy to circumvent. Thieves who are wary of the risk of violence and identification that are associated with robbery will be careful to wait until the occupants of a house or gallery are away before committing a burglary. Larceny and burglary are probably the best strategies for stealing art from a church, because access to the building is usually easy, often no one is on the premises to protect the art, and electronic security devices are rarely present.

Art thieves often study their targets in advance of their crimes in order to assure themselves of easy access and exit, to assess their ability to remove the artworks, and to learn of obstacles they may encounter during the theft. Two burglars who looted Mexico City's National Museum of Anthropology in 1985 cased the museum for six months on fifty different visits before jumping a fence and entering through an air conditioning duct. Once inside the museum, the theft was easy, because the glass cases were not alarmed or even locked. The thieves took 124 gold, jade, and stone relics that were regarded by Mexicans as national treasures.

Two thieves dubbed "the Social Register burglars" committed a series of thefts from affluent homes in New York, New Jersey, and Connecticut between 1980 and 1982. They would check into a motel, select forty or fifty names of local residents from the Social Register, and call them. Of the ten or so who failed to answer, six or seven would still not answer when called back later in the day. The thieves would then drive by those empty homes and choose one to enter. Two men would be left at the home, and a third one would telephone the home again. Any alarm would be disconnected, and the thieves would then enter the home.

Sometimes thieves carry out a test-run to determine what obstacles they might encounter during the actual crime. Such a test-run was apparently carried out two weeks prior to the 1990 theft at Boston's Gardner Museum. Three people were involved in an early morning disturbance outside the museum. A man pounded on a side door, the same one used in the robbery two weeks later, and begged to be let in to escape two assailants. When the guard refused, the man drove off in a car with his two assailants. The incident may have been unrelated to the robbery, but the rapid and strange reconciliation of the three men suggests that it was a test-run to assess the guards' response to attempted intrusions into the museum.

Prior to a 1960 theft of twenty paintings from an expensive restaurant on the French Riviera, a couple who seemed to be of lower social standing than the other patrons dined at a table near a window through which burglars later entered the building. The couple seemed to be studying the layout of the restaurant and examining its paintings and the way they were hung. The theft was committed on a rainy day, apparently so that the thieves' footprints and their car's tire tracks would be erased. The thieves drugged a dog they apparently had noticed while casing the restaurant (McLeave, 1981).

The sixty-one-year-old man who stole Goya's *The Duke of Wellington* from London's National Gallery in 1961 took more than two months to plan his theft. He studied the layout of the museum. He learned from a casual conversation with a daytime guard that the night shift patrolled the corridors every twenty minutes and used keys at certain checkpoints. He found out that cleaning women arrived at 6 P.M., and that every corridor and exhibition room had electronic beams that would trigger alarms. When he asked the guard why the cleaning women did not set off the alarms, he was told that security was lax at that time. During the burglary, the thief wore a disguise so that from a distance he appeared to be a guard. He crouched down to avoid the electronic beams after he had climbed into the museum through a window, which he had earlier wedged open. After removing the painting from the wall, he lowered it out the window by rope and climbed down after it, leaving through an opening created by construction workers and driving away in a stolen car. The thief's careful planning suggests that a moderately intelligent person who is determined to steal a painting can find a way to do so (McLeave, 1981). As one suspected art thief observed, "If you work energetically at getting inside information, if you learn to deactivate the alarm system, and if you do your own surveillance, there is no work of art that cannot be taken" (cited in Golden, 1989:48).

TIMING THE THEFT

One critical factor in the theft of art is timing. Museum burglars often carry out their thefts on holidays or weekends, knowing that they will then have more time to commit the crime and that their theft will probably not be discovered for a day or two. The thieves who burglarized Mexico City's

National Museum of Anthropology in 1985 committed their crime on Christmas Eve; they encountered no resistance from the eight security guards who were present in the museum, because the guards had fallen asleep after a night of drinking. Several thieves overcame a lone night guard at the American School of Classical Studies in Athens two days before Easter 1990, a period during which many Greeks traditionally are traveling. The Bennington (Vermont) Museum was burglarized on New Year's Eve 1985, when it was closed for vacation.

Timing is also important in hit-and-run thefts in which offenders break into a gallery, house, or museum that has an alarm system, set off the alarm, grab a few pieces, and flee. Prior to committing such crimes, thieves may test the efficiency of the alarm system and the response time of the police by setting off the alarm and watching from a distance to see what happens.

Thieves sometimes employ tactics to delay an official investigation of the crime. Several have left cards in cases from which they have stolen objects; the cards indicate that the pieces have been removed by the museum's staff for conservation. A night security supervisor at a Baltimore museum stole objects from Plexiglas cases and carefully rearranged the remaining objects to create the impression that the display had not been disturbed; he also removed museum catalogue labels and made sure that no dustprints would reveal that objects had been taken from the case. Thieves who stole artworks from display cases in museums throughout the Northeast also tried to delay discovery of their crimes by rearranging the other objects in the cases.

One thief offered an explanation for his crime that was aimed at delaying a police investigation, thus giving him more time to find an outlet for his loot. He told a museum curator that he had borrowed carpets from the institution in order to make copies, something the museum would not otherwise have let him do. He promised to return the carpets soon if the curator did not report the loss to the police. Instead, the thief sold the carpets to dealers. It was his fifth museum theft (Burnham, 1975:70–71).

One technique for delaying discovery of a theft is to substitute a facsimile for an original work that is stolen. The thieves who stole objects from display cases in museums in the Northeast once replaced a valuable vase with a worthless one. In 1980, thieves substituted fake jewelry for the pieces they stole from auction houses in New York and London, delaying by days an investigation into their thefts. Paintings by Picasso and Magritte that belonged to a New York collector were secretly replaced with forgeries sometime between 1980 and 1985; they were not discovered to be missing until 1990, when the collector's estate was examined by experts.

In another theft, a native of Sweden who had worked as a butler for fifteen years in a wealthy Californian's home was accused of substituting a blown-up photograph for an original painting by a Swedish artist and smuggling the painting to Sweden, where he sold it for $500,000, probably more than it would have fetched elsewhere. That painting, which was part of a vast art collection, had hung in an out-of-the-way location in the home and was not discovered to be missing until five months after the theft, which was three months after the man had left the household. The jury acquitted the accused thief, believing that the prosecution had not proved its case beyond a reasonable doubt, but the painting's owner filed a $31 million lawsuit against the butler for theft, slander, invasion of privacy, and infliction of emotional distress.

Timing is also important in the disposal of stolen art. Thieves often hide their loot for months or years before trying to dispose of it, figuring that after some time passes investigators' efforts will be less intense and dealers and museums will be less apt to remember that a piece is stolen. When they eventually try to sell the stolen art, thieves often include it in larger lots of legitimately acquired pieces in the hope that each item will not be scrutinized individually by potential buyers.

THE USE OF INSIDERS

Art thieves sometimes use insiders for information or assistance in carrying out their crimes. Employees of the targeted victim may help thieves circumvent alarm systems or tell them when the art is least likely to be protected. Some insiders have taken more active roles in stealing works of art. In 1992, a former church organist admitted to stealing chalices, trays, and other religious artifacts from more than five hundred churches and synagogues in which he had played over the previous decade; he used his knowledge of where valuable pieces were stored, when he would be least apt to be detected, and where alarms were placed to steal as much as $2.5 million worth of material.

Theft from Museums

A security guard can help a thief learn about and overcome measures taken by a museum to protect its collection. In fact, law-enforcement agents often assume that an insider was involved if the thieves seem to have been familiar with the museum's security system or if they appeared to know where to find the most valuable works of art. That was the assumption in a burglary of a Detroit museum in which thieves entered a storage room where artworks were being kept temporarily; the burglars bypassed the room's door and gained access through a ventilator shaft and an unlocked closet. An aborted 1991 theft of twenty van Gogh paintings from Amsterdam's National Museum involved inside personnel; one of the two security guards on duty during the crime and a former security employee of the museum were arrested for aiding the four thieves by revealing details about the museum's security.

Workers involved in the renovation of museums are also in a position to gather information about building security that can be used to commit a theft. The 1911 theft of the *Mona Lisa* was carried out by a man who had worked in the museum, giving him the opportunity to learn how the painting was hung and what had to be done to remove it. He also had detailed knowledge of museum security and where the building was vulnerable. Wearing a worker's uniform, he hid in the museum until it closed and then cut the picture down and stole away with it. He left clues that the police overlooked, including fingerprints on the glass that had covered the painting. Because his name was on the police department's list of people who had inside information, officers questioned him soon after the theft, but they accepted his explanation that he had not been near the Louvre on the day of the crime.

Museum employees are in a strategic position to steal from their own institutions. Fred Drew, an American living in Lima who was involved in the smuggling of the Sipán treasures from Peru to the United States, claims that an employee of a Peruvian museum once offered to sell him ten fine pieces of the institution's pottery at bargain prices, telling Drew that he would write them off as having been destroyed in the last earthquake. The head of security at a museum in Santa Barbara, California, confessed that he had been commissioned to carry out a theft that occurred in 1978. In another crime in that same year, three paintings by Cézanne were stolen from the Art Institute of Chicago. Those pictures were recovered with the arrest of a shipping clerk who had worked for the museum and had helped store the paintings in the closet from which they were taken. Suspicions focused on him because he had been seen in the storage area carrying a large package. He resigned after being asked to take a lie-detector test. He was arrested when he tried to collect a reward for return of the paintings, and eventually he was sentenced to ten years in prison for receiving stolen property, extortion, and armed violence.

The 1989 theft of $250,000 worth of original comic strip art from a New York museum at first seemed likely to have been committed by an insider, because the art was taken from a storage area inaccessible to outsiders and because the thief had to have known where the strips were kept and had to have had the time to search the collection for the most valuable art. A former museum curator, who had started work there as a janitor seven years earlier, confessed to the theft, which he said was motivated by his need for money to pay off mounting debts. He agreed to help recover the art he had sold, and he was required by the court to pay $45,000 to the museum and do five hundred hours of community service.

While he was in charge of Brigham Young University's art collection, Wesley Burnside was involved in the loss of hundreds of items over a ten-year period. Burnside was responsible for appraising and handling the collection, but he frequently made questionable deals. He appraised at well below market value art that was to be traded or sold from the university's collection; he appraised at far above market value art that was to be traded, sold, or donated to the university by outsiders. He helped outsiders obtain art that had not been deaccessioned according to university policy. He returned works donated to the university to the original donors without the university's knowledge. He received commissions and other benefits for selling the university's art to prospective donors and other parties. He failed to monitor the quality of the works leaving the university's collection, and he failed to account for funds or artworks he received on behalf of the university. He mingled the university's collection with his own, and he made decisions he should have known were outside the scope of his employment and contrary to the university's best interests. Burnside admitted to all of these improprieties, which had been made possible only because of his position as a university employee (Day, 1988).

In 1991, John Quentin Feller pleaded guilty to the theft of more than one hundred porcelains from eight museums in the United States and England; he was sentenced to eighteen months in prison and fined $30,000. Feller, a professor at the University of Scranton and the author of five books and many scholarly papers, mostly about ceramics and glass, said that his first theft was in 1972, when he rescued from neglect some rare porcelains he found in the basement of the Wadsworth Atheneum in Hartford, Connecticut. Feller donated many of the pieces he stole to museums, keeping others for his personal collection; for his gifts, he was appointed trustee at the Peabody Museum in Salem, Massachusetts. As a recognized scholar and generous donor, Feller was given access to the material that he stole; he was rarely searched by museum guards. With one exception, he did not sell what he took, nor did he take tax deductions for his donations. Instead, he was motivated by the desire for the respect of others in the art world and the academic community, respect that could and did advance his own career as a scholar and art expert.

Thieves who work for the institution from which they steal have the best possible information about their employer's vulnerability to theft; if their thefts are done cleverly enough, they can avoid suspicion altogether. Directors, curators, and other staff members of Third World museums sometimes sell works from their institutions to dealers, middlemen, and collectors; they have also helped those buyers export the pieces in violation of national regulations. The director of an African organization that gives grants and assistance to museums comments on this problem as follows:

When people get such low salaries, and the salaries are not paid for two or three months and you have to feed yourself, the temptation to take things is a real problem. This isn't to justify the situation but to understand it. I don't know of anybody working in a museum who is getting rich by selling objects from the museums. (cited in Decker, 1990:111)

The sale of objects by museum employees can make it more difficult for Third World source-countries to enlist the help of Western art-importing nations in stopping the illicit international trade in art and antiquities. A European museum that returned to a museum in Zaire more than one hundred pieces taken during the colonial period learned that some of those objects were being offered for sale less than a year later. That European museum would probably be less likely to repatriate property in the future.

Theft of National Property

Government officials such as political leaders, military officers, and law-enforcement agents have sometimes exploited their positions to steal art. One leader who converted art that had been purchased with government funds into personal possessions was Ferdinand Marcos, who smuggled dozens of paintings out of the Philippines when he was deposed as President and fled the country in February 1986. That art, and other works in a townhouse and an apartment in New York that were owned by the Marcoses, had been purchased with Philippine treasury funds and belonged to the people of that nation rather than to the Marcoses personally. This theft is best seen as an elaborate money laundering scheme, according to documents used in a trial that led a New York jury to acquit Imelda Marcos of any violation of American law. During the early 1980s, Mrs. Marcos had regularly traveled to New York to buy art, often of dubious quality and excessive price. Bills were sent to a Philippine department store owned by friends of the Marcoses. Money was then sent to that store from the Marcoses' foreign bank accounts, into which they had deposited money from the national treasury and from bribes taken from contractors. Banks in the Philippines had been used to move money out of the country and into secret accounts in Hong Kong, Switzerland, and other nations (Barron, 1989; Shenon, 1988; Sherman, 1990).

In 1986, the Israel Museum exhibited a collection of antiquities it had bought for $1 million from the second wife of the recently deceased General Moshe Dayan. In response to criticism that the antiquities rightfully belonged to the state, Mrs. Dayan replied that her husband had invested all of their money in the collection and that he had seen it as an insurance policy for her. Dayan's defenders claimed that about 85 percent of the collection had either been purchased from dealers by Dayan with his own money or had privately been traded for with pieces in the collection. Mrs. Dayan claimed that the collection was worth twice what she was paid by the museum, but critics claimed that she could not legitimately sell what did not belong to her in the first place, suggesting that she should have donated the pieces that properly belonged to the state and sold the rest at market value. Critics also contended that Dayan never had to worry about the price he would pay for antiquities, especially when he dealt with local Arabs, because his stature as a national hero intimidated his sources, who wanted him to look on them with favor. In purchasing antiquities surreptitiously from landowners and contractors who accidentally unearthed them, Dayan ensured the survival of the objects and their continued presence in Israel, but he deprived the state of its patrimony and denied Israelis access to the antiquities until the state paid his widow $1 million.

Archaeologists are primarily interested in ancient objects for what they can contribute to a scholarly understanding of past cultures. To learn about the past, archaeologists need to study artifacts in their place of origin; the looting of ruins hinders or makes impossible such scholarly inquiry. To assemble his collection of antiquities, Dayan violated the basic tenets of Israeli archaeology as well as Israeli law. Archaeologists and government officials claimed that his actions made it difficult for them to educate the public about the proper preservation of ancient sites and the need to avoid looting. Though a general in the army, Dayan had no license to excavate, because he had no formal training as an archaeologist. He had not even applied for such a license, and the methods he used made it clear that had he done so, he would have been turned down. He did not excavate slowly and methodically, recording every detail of his work so as to be able to reconstruct the site later. Instead, he behaved more like a grave-robber, digging for pieces that he desired and using the wrong techniques and materials for reconstructing broken objects.

The discovery of the Sipán tomb in Peru raised questions about the symbiotic relationship between legitimate archaeologists and looters of cultural property that legally belongs to the nation. Archaeologists were tipped off to the location of the tomb by rumors that the area was the source of plundered gold and silver artifacts of high quality that were being sold on the black market in Lima. A long investigation culminated in several police raids on the homes of the looters of the artifacts. Archaeologists were led to the treasure-laden tomb by information extracted from the thieves. Some archaeologists deplore any interaction with looters, believing that it is even unethical to study objects that have been stripped from their original context. Other archaeologists are more pragmatic, including even looted objects in their inventories of a culture's artifacts. Some of the latter group have exchanged information with collectors who have illicitly excavated or exported pieces; the archaeologists do not report those collectors to the authorities.

Christopher Donnan, a leading authority on the Moche people whose treasures filled the Sipán tomb, was criticized for his role in the distribution of those looted artifacts. In the past, Donnan had hired *huaqueros* to help him find new grave sites, which he then excavated; he had also paid *huaqueros* for artifacts they had found in order to keep tombs intact until he could unearth them using appropriate archaeological methods. After the discovery of the Sipán tomb, Donnan contacted collectors and dealers around the world to photograph any Moche artifacts that turned up, even if they had been illegally excavated and smuggled from Peru. Donnan is intent on documenting the Moche civilization, even if it means dealing with grave-robbers and dishonest collectors and dealers; he believes that he cannot refuse to document artifacts simply because they have been looted or smuggled in violation of the nation's laws. Donnan contacted David Swetnam, the California dealer responsible for smuggling Moche treasures from Peru to the United States. Swetnam provided Donnan with photographs of the artifacts, which Donnan showed at a lecture he gave at the 1988 meeting of the Institute for Andean Studies at Berkeley. Because the audience included many collectors and dealers who were eager to buy the artifacts, scholars accused Donnan of acting as Swetnam's advance man, and the institute dropped all identifiable collectors and dealers from its mailing list (Nagin, 1990).

Theft from Private Collectors

Employees and acquaintances have sometimes taken advantage of their relationships with wealthy collectors to steal art. Other thieves have befriended or taken jobs with well-to-do collectors with the intention of stealing from them; that was apparently the case with Craig Warner, who befriended Dr. Jane Werner and then burglarized her home of two hundred pieces of Nepalese and Tibetan art while she was on vacation. When thieves seem to know exactly where in a house to go to steal artworks, or when a theft is committed when the victim is traveling, the police often assume that the thieves had inside information.

Domestics have exploited their access to the home and their employer's vulnerability to steal art. In 1985, a part-time nurse's aide to an eighty-five-year-old man was arrested for stealing two paintings from his apartment. In another case, a domestic employee replaced an original painting with a reproduction and sold the original; only when the owners were killed in an airplane accident was the substitution discovered.

In an unusual theft that occurred in France, a woman was accused of holding an elderly heir prisoner and stealing a painting by Murillo from her through fabrication of a will. The defendant, who had stepped into the role of nurse and confidante when the person who had been filling that role died, was charged with sequestration and failure to help a person in danger; she had allegedly held the heir captive and failed to feed her properly. When the defendant was asked to prove that she owned the painting, she produced a will purporting to show that she had inherited it in 1979 from her grand-mother, whom she said had been given it by the heir. According to an investigating magistrate, the will was fraudulent and had not even been filed until 1985; the defendant claimed that she had not discovered it until then. Evidence showed that the defendant's grandmother had died a pauper and had never known the heir (Greenhouse, 1988).

In another crime, forty Impressionist paintings were stolen from the home of an elderly French woman, who had left her villa in the care of a married couple while she was in the hospital. When she returned home, she found the pictures gone. Eventually, the police arrested the married couple, their daughter, her lover, and the elderly woman's nephew, who was found to have her paintings and furniture in his home. Also arrested were another woman, who was accused of selling some of the stolen paintings to a Paris art gallery, and the director of the gallery, who had sold the paintings to collectors and dealers in the United States, Germany, the Netherlands, Switzerland, and Japan. Six of the co-conspirators who had taken advantage of the elderly woman were eventually convicted and sentenced to prison.

In addition to domestics, other insiders have also used inside information to steal from collectors. One suspected member of an art theft gang that operated in the Midwest for nearly a decade was a security alarm salesman; he had both the expertise to circumvent security systems and inside knowledge about the art collections in houses in which he had installed alarms. An unusual form of theft that used inside information was uncovered in New York in 1988. The Public Administrator's office in Queens administers the estates of people who die without wills, have no heirs, or have named executors who refuse to serve. As a result of a sting operation, an employee of that office was arrested for stealing property from the apartment of a man who supposedly had died without a will. In fact, investigators from the state Attorney General's office had attached a fictitious name to a body in the morgue, made up a report of the man's death, and placed valuable property in an apartment rented in his name. When the employee of the Public Administrator's office filed a report on the property in the apartment, the Attorney General's investigators discovered that he had not listed several items that had been planted there. The employee was arrested for grand larceny and falsifying documents. At a news conference, the Attorney General displayed paintings, antique gold coins, silver chalices, and heirloom rings worth more than $100,000 that had allegedly been stolen by people associated with the Public Administrator's office (Reynolds, 1988).

Theft of Art in Transit and in Storage

Thieves have sometimes used inside knowledge to steal art in transit from one museum to another, from a dealer to a buyer, or from a collector to a warehouse. In November 1986, a painting by Delacroix was stolen by thieves who broke into a truck that had picked it up at New York's Kennedy International Airport. Only because the thieves had learned that the painting would be on that particular truck at that time were they able to steal the picture.

Collectors with holdings too extensive to display in their homes often keep some of their property in warehouses and other storage facilities; those places have been targeted by thieves. Because years sometimes pass before an owner discovers that the art is missing, tracking it down can be difficult. The extent of such crime is difficult to measure, because police departments do not keep statistics in a form that allows easy identification of the location of a theft as a warehouse or storage facility. The International Foundation for Art Research reports that it has received many complaints about thefts from such places.

One collector refused to sign for a delivery when she noted that two of the eight crates that had been shipped were missing. Checking the six that had been delivered, she found some of them empty and others to contain frames from which paintings had been removed. In another case, a collector watched as his art was packed in a New York warehouse for shipping to his new home. When he unpacked the crates in Texas, he found two paintings missing. Comments made to the collector as the crates were being packed led him to suspect one particular worker, a man who had joked about theft in the warehouse. The collector had given the worker permission slips to keep a few pieces that he no longer wanted, and he suspected that the worker used the slips to take the two paintings. The collector never recovered his art or received any compensation for the pictures from either the warehouse owner or the moving company. The moving company said that on delivery he had signed an inventory list verifying that everything had arrived safely; the collector said he had been told by the truckers that he had nine months to make a claim if anything was missing and so he simply signed the list without checking the crates.

Warehouse theft is sometimes systematic and organized rather than random behavior by a few dishonest workers. At one warehouse, valuable items were deliberately placed at the bottoms of boxes, which were subtly marked to indicate their contents. Employees would then slash the bottom flaps of the boxes, remove the valuable goods, fill the empty space with straw, and tape the boxes shut. That method meant that the same number of boxes would be present to be counted, that the contents would seem to be intact if checked from the top, and that owners would not learn of missing items until they fully unpacked the boxes, which might be years in the future.

Most warehouse theft is by insiders; one case involved the wife of a warehouse owner who consigned to Sotheby's a painting she said she had found lying around the warehouse. Other warehouse thefts are committed by burglars. One police informant reported hiding in a wooden box that was carried into a warehouse during the day; at night he broke out and stole several carpets, climbed back into the box with the carpets, and was carted out the next day by his accomplices.

Efforts to investigate warehouse theft have been thwarted by unions and by the owners of such facilities. IFAR reports a case in which undercover police officers infiltrated a warehouse and videotaped workers removing valuable items from crates. When the workers' union heard of the investigation, it threatened a national strike. In another case, when the owners of a warehouse learned that the FBI was investigating theft there, they tripled the rent for the office being used by the FBI, which coincidentally was in a building owned by the people who owned the warehouse. Another time, a man who arranged to store some equipment in a New York warehouse told workers on the loading dock that he had removed a piece from each machine so that it would not function. When he was refused rental space, he assumed it was because he would not be storing anything worth stealing. The head of the warehouse said that they had so much demand for their space that they did not need to rent to people who distrusted them (Ketchum, 1984).

Warehouse owners blame most losses of property on careless customers rather than on dishonest employees, saying that union workers do not steal because to do so would jeopardize their jobs. They claim that people who rent space often leave their belongings outside storage rooms and fail to lock their doors. They advise renters to check periodically on their goods and never to sign inventory lists until they fully check the contents of their boxes. One collector actually continued to pay the monthly rental fee for his storage space long after his possessions had been stolen, learning of the theft only when he tried to find his property after learning that the warehouse's address had changed.

USING A FRONT

Some art thieves employ fronts, ways of presenting themselves so that people who own or guard art will be deceived into thinking that the thieves are playing legitimate roles. Fronts have been used to acquire inside knowledge about art that can be stolen and to gain access to the art.

Gallery thieves often pose as potential customers, and even when they do not fit the image of a typical client, employees are usually unwilling to challenge them, a practice that thieves use to their advantage. That was the case in one New York gallery whose employees later said that a thief appeared from his shaky hands and rundown appearance to be a drug addict rather than a potential customer.

Thieves have also adopted disguises to gain entry to private homes. One man posed as a building construction inspector who needed to examine the ceilings in a New York apartment; once inside, he pulled a pistol, forced the housekeeper and building superintendent into a bathroom, tied them up, and stole thirty artworks, being assisted by an accomplice who had joined him. In another robbery in New York, two men posing as police officers handed an art restorer a package when he answered his door, asking him to identify the painting inside. As he began to open the package, the men attacked and handcuffed him and then stole valuable Old Masters paintings from his collection.

Other thieves have used disguises to get past museum security guards. The thief who stole the *Mona Lisa* dressed in a worker's outfit and posed as a member of the crew doing construction work in the Louvre. The two men who robbed Boston's Gardner Museum in 1990 gained access to the building at 1:15 A.M. by dressing as Boston police officers and telling the two guards that they had to call in a disturbance in the area; one of the thieves then asked one of the guards to see his identification because he thought he had a warrant for him. A similar ploy was used by six thieves in Brazil less than a year earlier; they gained admittance to the museum by showing police identification and telling the guards they had to search for thieves.

Thieves have posed as scholars to gain access to museums. One man pretending to be writing a book on Rembrandt stole two of the artist's etchings from an Ottawa museum and three more from a Syracuse museum, substituting photocopies that he had taken great care to make look as much like the originals as possible.

Dishonest art and antiques dealers have used fronts as apparently unprosperous junk or used furniture shops to conceal an active, profitable trade in stolen art and artifacts, charging relatively low prices for objects that are rarely insured, photographed, or given much publicity. In Europe, the shops of such dealers have a constant flow of objects stolen from churches and mansions (Burnham, 1975:39).

An elaborate form of fraud requiring a front involves brokers who try to dupe the innocent into buying stolen or fake art. One such confidence game is the European chateau sale, in which a broker approaches a well-to-do tourist who, after some conversation, is found to be not especially knowledgeable about art. The tourist is offered the unique opportunity of seeing some works of art that an out-of-luck aristocratic family has been forced to sell quickly and quietly, hoping to avoid the embarrassment of disposing of cherished family heirlooms at a public auction. The tourist is taken to an attractive but deteriorating chateau, which has been rented by the broker to convince the tourist that the art is actually being sold by an aristocrat. There the tourist is offered stolen or fake paintings at low prices. A condition of the sale is that the name of the seller and the exact price will not appear on the bill of sale. It is usually much later, often when trying to resell the art, that the collector learns that the paintings are stolen or fake (Burnham, 1975:49–50).

The Caravaggio Conspiracy

The importance of appearances in the art world is nicely demonstrated in Peter Watson's fascinating book and film of the same title, *The Caravaggio Conspiracy* (1984). Watson, a *London Times* journalist, went to elaborate lengths to investigate the stolen art market by presenting himself as an art dealer willing to buy stolen art. In 1979, the year that he began his investigation, 44,000 works of art had been reported stolen in Italy alone. Watson approached Rodolfo Siviero of the Italian Foreign Ministry, who told Watson of a stolen Caravaggio painting, *Nativity of Christ,* that he had been unable to recover. The picture had apparently been stolen by the Mafia in 1969 from a chapel in Palermo, Sicily, as part of a vendetta against Siviero, who for years had been aggressive in his efforts to recover stolen art. Siviero suggested that Watson, as an outsider, might be able to recover the picture, and he provided the journalist with two lists of names, one of suspected thieves and another of dealers who were rumored to have been contacted about purchasing the painting but had failed to contact the police about the thieves' offer.

To establish credibility as a dealer, Watson first had to learn about the art world in general and about Caravaggio's work in particular. To establish a new identity, he took the name A. John Blake from a gravestone and secured a birth certificate and passport in that name. He made contact with Sotheby's and Christie's in both New York and London. He carried letters from well-known people in the art world and stuffed his briefcase with photographs of paintings. He dressed expensively and flashily, and he limped and used a cane, all to draw attention to himself and establish his presence in the world of art dealers.

Watson employed two methods at auction house sales. He agreed in advance with auctioneers that they would announce his fictitious name as the purchaser of paintings that were bought in (that is, not sold by the auction house because they had failed to reach the minimum price or reserve agreed to ahead of time by the owner and the auction house). By announcing that items that had not reached their reserves had been sold to A. John Blake, the impression was created that Watson was a legitimate dealer who was actively buying paintings. A second method he used was to buy some paintings for New York art dealer Richard Feigen. Watson bid as instructed to beforehand on those works for which Feigen had clients. Feigen educated Watson about the intricacies of auctions, telling him that bidding was usually opened at about one-third of the lowest estimated market price for a work, although it might start higher if the house expected active bidding. Feigen told Watson to wait until the bidding seemed to slow down and then make bids by raising his pen. Watson wanted to act like an experienced art dealer but also attract attention as a big buyer. At a 1979 auction of Old Masters paintings at Christie's, he "bought" twenty-three works; several were purchased on behalf of Feigen, and the rest were marked down to him because they had not reached their reserves.

After Watson had established his credibility as a dealer, Feigen put him in touch with a New Yorker to whom two Italians had recently offered a painting they said was by Raphael, a painting that seemed likely to have been stolen. To maintain his front, Watson had to study the works of Raphael, an artist who had been widely forged in his own day. When Watson met with the two Italians in a rundown area of New York, they told him that they imported furniture and souvenirs from Italy; Watson assumed that their business was a front for smuggling stolen art into the United States. He was suspicious about the quality of the painting, of which they showed him only a photograph, and he told them he doubted it was actually by Raphael. When he asked if they had anything else to show him, they brought out a photograph of a painting allegedly by Tintoretto.

Watson took the photograph back to England to study, eventually matching the Tintoretto with a painting by Titian that had many versions. Still not sure if the painting was authentic or a forgery, Watson contacted art expert Christopher Wright, who told him about artists' studios of that era and how different pupils sometimes painted different parts of a single painting. Wright taught Watson about craquelure (the fine lines that appear over time in the varnish on a painting's surface), the yellowing of varnish with age, discoloration, and surface dirt. Watson also met with two expert art restorers who described themselves as "the eyes and ears of the London art trade." They told him that they sometimes heard rumors about stolen art and agreed to relay any such rumors to Watson and to mention to anyone offering information about stolen art that A. John Blake might be interested.

Watson learned from Siviero's list of a London art dealer who had been offered the stolen Caravaggio for which he was searching. He asked to be seated next to this dealer at a Sotheby's auction and made sure that the dealer noticed him by buying several works, including a painting by Delacroix. The dealer asked to meet with Watson after the sale and told him that he had heard of him. The dealer asked Watson if he could buy from him the Delacroix that he had just bought. Watson offered to sell him the painting for the price he had paid and for information about the stolen Caravaggio. After that dealer gave Watson the name of an art dealer in Naples, Watson never again contacted him about the Delacroix painting, which was not Watson's to sell.

Before contacting the Naples dealer, Watson devoted much time to the study of Caravaggio's life and art. Posing as A. John Blake, Watson met with the dealer from Naples and told him that he had a buyer in the United States for the Caravaggio. They settled on a price of 130,000,000 lire and arranged to meet in Naples in November 1980 to consummate the transaction. Watson went there but did not see the dealer, meeting instead with three men after being driven to a small café by a driver who tried to disorient him by taking a circuitous route. The men showed Watson a photograph of the Caravaggio painting, which appeared to be damaged; the photograph included a newspaper with a headline of the art theft to prove that the men had been in possession of the work after the theft. Watson and the men scheduled a meeting to exchange the money for the painting. However, a devastating earthquake then destroyed much of the town where the meeting was to take place, making it impossible for the parties to get together. That was a major letdown for Watson, given the amount of effort he had put into tracing the stolen masterpiece.

At that point, one of the two Italians in New York who had earlier offered Watson the painting by Raphael called to tell Watson that he had a different source of paintings. They met at a restorer's studio, and Watson was offered two stolen paintings, one of which he later found in Interpol's file of stolen art. Watson contacted the Fine Arts Squad of the New York Customs Office. The paintings were then smuggled into the United States, one covered with a water-soluble surface painting that was washed off before the final transfer to Watson. Watson was wired for the transaction, and his payment to the middleman was recorded by hidden cameras in a hotel lobby. Four men were arrested, including the Reverend Lorenzo Zorza, a high-ranking Vatican priest and diplomat to the United Nations who had been earning money by smuggling stolen paintings in his baggage. Zorza, whose share in the transaction was to be $8,000, was placed on probation for three years after pleading guilty to smuggling the two paintings.

The Caravaggio conspiracy demonstrates the importance of fronts in the illegal art trade. Watson was able to make contact with thieves and smugglers by establishing his credibility as an art dealer and by making it known that he was interested in buying stolen art. The two Italians in New York used their import business to conceal their smuggling of stolen art. Father Zorza used his roles as priest and diplomat to smuggle stolen art into the United States. In all three cases, the individuals were performing legitimate roles: Watson was buying art for Richard Feigen, the two Italians were presumably importing some goods legally, and Zorza was apparently attending to diplomatic and clerical duties in addition to his criminal activities. However, those legitimate roles were all used to facilitate and conceal illegal activity in the stolen art trade.

LAUNDERING STOLEN ART

The conversion of stolen art into money sometimes requires laundering, a process by which illegally acquired property is given the appearance of legitimacy. Sophisticated thieves may do this by stealing certificates of authenticity, bills of sale, and other documents that will establish the provenance of the art they are stealing, realizing that such papers will make it easier to sell the art to dealers and collectors. Other thieves disguise stolen art by altering it in some way; this is most often done with religious artifacts, antique furniture, or other objects that are not valued for their uniqueness. Thieves sometimes put stolen art up for sale at out-of-the-way country auctions, where they then buy it back, thereby acquiring a legitimate bill of sale that can be shown to dealers or collectors to whom they try to sell the art. Thieves or their brokers also try to sell stolen objects in nations such as Italy where good-faith buyers, even of stolen art, gain title to the property. The commander of the Italian police art squad says that antiquities stolen from archaeological sites often remain submerged for years, with dealers who buy valuable artifacts from grave-robbers holding on to the pieces until the official investigation abates and then selling the objects discreetly (Suro, 1988b).

After stolen art passes through several hands and acquires bills of sale, it gains the appearance of legitimacy and can rise to a higher level of the art market where a connoisseur, established dealer, or museum curator discovers it and purchases it for a good price. This sometimes happens at large auction houses, where thieves may present receipts as proof of ownership, even if they are not asked to do so. In 1989, a European dealer brought to Christie's in New York a Rembrandt drawing that had been stolen a decade earlier from an Amsterdam museum. An auction house employee traced the drawing to the museum that had last owned it and learned that it had been stolen. When the dealer who brought the drawing to the auction house for sale was informed of that, he immediately had it returned to the museum. It was not clear through whose hands the picture had passed in the decade since the theft, but the length of time that had elapsed suggested that thieves had held on to it before disposing of it (Reif, 1989b).

Thieves and middlemen sometimes try to give stolen art the appearance of legitimacy by exhibiting it in museums and other institutions. When a Turkish antiquities smuggler apparently encountered difficulty in selling an illegally excavated and illegally exported statue, he loaned it anonymously to the San Antonio Museum of Art, probably hoping that its legitimacy and value would be enhanced by being exhibited in that reputable institution.

ORGANIZED CRIME, THE DRUG TRADE, AND STOLEN ART

According to a detective who is a member of Italy's police art squad, organized crime gangs are deeply involved in art theft, both for profit and as a way to launder illegal profits from other sources. He is convinced that the Caravaggio painting that was sought by Peter Watson is in the hands of the Mafia, saying that it has not been recovered because gangsters are holding on to it to exchange someday for a political favor, or perhaps because the gangster who has it is in prison (Suro, 1987:50). In one raid, the police found the private bunker of a leader in the Neapolitan Camorra decorated with stolen art (Stille, 1992). Syndicates specializing in art theft have been uncovered, one financed by a group of antiques dealers in Turin, Italy. Until it was broken up, that group had stolen art and antiques worth about $17.5 million from two hundred French chateaux over a three-year period (Suro, 1987:52).

Organized crime has reportedly become more involved in art theft as the price of art has increased. Hugh McLeave (1981) proposes that a 1958 auction at Sotheby's was a watershed; what had previously been seen as priceless art then acquired specific price tags. As a consequence, leaders of organized crime began to consider the potentially great profits to be made from the resale of stolen art, even using museum catalogues and art magazines to find works worth stealing. Poor security in many museums, houses, galleries, and churches made art theft seem like a low-risk enterprise, and so gang bosses recruited thieves and petty criminals from other rackets to steal art.

Several art thefts in the South of France in the early 1960s were linked to organized crime. Crime bosses in that region controlled large gangs that were involved in prostitution, gambling, drugs, and violence. They were aware of all major crimes in the geographic area they controlled, and their relationship with local law-enforcement agencies was such that they sometimes provided the police with information about crimes of particular concern. Six suspects told the police that a 1961 art theft in Nice had been planned by a man who had recently been murdered, apparently because he was about to talk to the police. However, the police thought that a different gang boss might have arranged the art theft, set up the execution of that man, who belonged to a rival gang, and then told the arrested suspects to blame the murdered man for the theft. In another theft in that region in the same year, thieves who stole fifty-seven paintings were unable to sell them on the black market and unable to get a ransom for returning them. A crime boss in Marseilles then set up a second theft, this time of eight heavily insured Cézanne paintings, and offered the pictures from both thefts in exchange for a ransom from the insurance company. He was reportedly paid $60,000, and the thieves were granted immunity from prosecution. The absence of similar thefts in that region over the next fifteen years suggested that the local police and the crime bosses had struck a deal that organized crime would refrain from art theft (McLeave, 1981).

Another 1961 theft suggested the involvement of organized crime at the international level. A California millionaire was robbed at gunpoint in his home of the five best paintings in his collection. The thieves demanded payment of a $100,000 ransom, or they would destroy the paintings. The police used fingerprints found in the home to identify a convicted thief, who was arrested within a week and charged with grand larceny. Soon after, he disappeared. Following his flight, a gang broke into a mansion in Sicily and stole twelve Old Masters paintings, as well as other valuable objects. When FBI agents learned of that theft, they wondered if it might have been carried out by the thief who had recently fled from California. They wired the police in Palermo, and the man was arrested there. He admitted to the theft in Sicily and showed the police where to find the stolen objects. He was then extradited to the United States, where he received a two- to ten-year prison sentence for the California theft. He seemed to have been acting on orders from someone else, because he probably would not have been able to learn the whereabouts of the art in Sicily so soon after arriving there from the United States, nor would he have known how to dispose of the stolen art in Sicily. The FBI assumed that the Sicilian Mafia and its American counterpart were linked together in the art thefts and that they were employing professional thieves to commit robberies and burglaries. The thief would not discuss that possibility with law-enforcement agents, and the police could not verify their supposition through Mafia informants (McLeave, 1981).

According to law-enforcement officials, an increasing amount of art theft is connected with the international drug trade. One federal drug agent has observed that more drug lords, especially Colombians, have been showing up at art auctions or sending representatives there to buy art for them. Some of them may want the art for their own enjoyment or to elevate their social standing by presenting themselves as cultivated people of the world. Stolen art can also provide financial security; one cocaine producer who had bought gold pieces looted from the Sipán tomb reportedly sold them off whenever he had a shipment of cocaine confiscated by law-enforcement agents (Kirkpatrick, 1992). Other drug lords have apparently used their profits from the drug trade to pay for the expenses of art thefts and then used the stolen art as collateral for drug deals. Stolen art is less bulky and easier to transport across international boundaries than cash, and it is also more difficult for law-enforcement agents to trace than is the flow of money.

Law-enforcement officials report that stolen art is increasingly being found during drug raids. The discovery by federal drug agents of $227,000 worth of art in a Boston warehouse, which belonged to two suspected Boston drug traffickers, led one agent to comment, "We have recently discovered that major narcotics violators for some reason like to invest money in artwork. This is another indication of that" (cited in Neuffer, 1990:39). Stolen paintings were recovered in drug raids in Amsterdam in 1989 and in Scotland in 1990. Four seventeenth-century Dutch paintings stolen from the Detroit Institute of Art in 1982 evidently crossed state lines at least five times as collateral in a major shipment of cocaine from Miami to Detroit. In another case, Myles Connor, who was first charged with art theft in 1966, pleaded guilty in 1990 to the theft of two Dutch Masters paintings from Amherst College and to conspiracy to distribute cocaine; he had apparently planned to use the stolen art to establish a line of credit for a drug deal. The judge gave Connor a twenty-year prison sentence, more than twice what the prosecutor had recommended.

The burglary of Mexico City's National Museum of Anthropology on Christmas Eve 1985 was not solved until 1989, when 111 of the 124 works were recovered and two amateur thieves were arrested. The thieves had reportedly traded several of the stolen pieces for cocaine, and four suspects accused of complicity in the theft and distribution of the objects had ties to Mexican drug traffickers. The police solved the case with information provided by a recently arrested cocaine trafficker, who said he had been offered the stolen objects for $1 million (Bennett, 1989).

Reverend Lorenzo Zorza, the priest who smuggled two stolen paintings into the United States in his diplomatic baggage, was charged in 1987 with scalping $40,000 worth of tickets to a Broadway show. The following year, he was arrested for his role in a cocaine smuggling operation and charged with carrying money derived from illegal sources between the United States and Italy (*The Boston Globe*, April 2, 1988). Those arrests suggest that Zorza was part of a criminal organization, one that might use the same channels to smuggle stolen art that it uses to transport illegal drugs. There is also some evidence that Turkish smugglers of antiquities are involved in the trafficking of heroin. Consistent with the conclusion that art theft and smuggling are linked to the drug trade is the behavior of the Drug Enforcement Administration informant known as The Man, who has apparently used his connections in the international drug trade to help the New York Police Department recover art stolen in several major burglaries. Stolen art is most easily moved from one nation to another through established networks, suggesting that organized crime, or at least criminal organization, is involved in the international trade in stolen art. The following chapter examines the movement of stolen art and smuggled antiquities across international borders.

❧ *Six* ❧

The Distribution of Stolen Art

Because only 10 to 12 percent of stolen objects reported to the International Foundation for Art Research are recovered, we can only speculate about the eventual fate of most missing art. At any given time, much of it is probably still in the hands of thieves or their accomplices. Some of it is in the possession of collectors and dealers who have bought it from thieves or their fences. Other stolen art is returned to its owners after a ransom is paid, the police recover it, or the thieves abandon it.

After art is stolen, thieves often smuggle it out of the country as quickly as possible; sometimes they wait for a while so that customs agents will be less apt to be on the lookout for it. Art also moves across international boundaries in another way: during times of war, conquering nations have confiscated art from museums, homes, and churches in defeated nations. Probably at no time in history did more art change hands than the period during and after World War II. The Nazis stole art from its rightful owners throughout Europe, and later the Soviets systematically looted art from defeated Germany.

BUYERS OF ILLICIT ANTIQUITIES

The illicit trade in antiquities is multi-layered. At the top are collectors, dealers, museum curators, and scholars, all of whom hope to acquire the finest pieces available at the lowest prices possible. They buy illicit pieces from dealers and smugglers, who move stolen art and antiquities across international borders to the most lucrative market. In the source-countries, there are politicians, police officers, and customs agents who accept bribes or simply ignore the activities of dealers and smugglers. At the bottom of the system are grave-robbers, usually poor peasants trying to eke out an existence with the proceeds from their discoveries. They sell their treasures to local agents and middlemen, who then sell the pieces to dealers and smugglers who operate at the international level (Schaire, 1990).

Collectors, dealers, curators, and archaeologists who buy antiquities play an important role in the theft of the objects. In a few cases, their demand for precious objects has led them to participate actively in the theft and smuggling of objects, even sponsoring expeditions to acquire choice pieces. When they do that, they stimulate the local art market with the second-rate pieces they find, provide jobs for local workers, and sometimes donate objects to the national museum of the source-country. Those benefits come at a cost: the most important pieces are smuggled from the country (Burnham, 1975:174).

Most buyers of antiquities are not so directly involved in the illicit trade, but their demand for objects does stimulate theft, grave-looting, and illegal exportation. Buyers frequently fail to inquire about the origins of the pieces they are purchasing, even when it is obvious that laws must have been violated to get the objects from the source-country to them. Collectors justify their purchases of illicit antiquities by claiming that they will cherish and study those objects in a way that the source-country would not, because of negligence or corruption.

When the law of the nation from which an object comes prohibits an individual or institution from holding title to that object, the individual or institution may settle for merely having the object. At least until quite recently, collectors and museums in a nation other than the one that was the source of an ancient artifact could depend on the courts of their own nation to uphold their right to the object over the claims of a foreign government. Recently, the chance has increased that a foreign government will force a collector or museum to repatriate an object, either through a lawsuit or through an appeal to the government of the nation in which the object is being held. This change has increased the demand for antiquities obtained through strictly legal channels, but too few objects are available in this way to meet the demand of collectors, museums, dealers, and scholars. Prices have thus risen to unprecedented levels, leading to the enactment of stricter national patrimony laws in source-countries and encouraging those countries to take legal action to retrieve objects being held abroad.

National patrimony laws also affect collectors who live in source-countries. For example, since 1972 Mexican law has prohibited the establishment of a private collection of pre-Columbian art, required the registration of existing collections, and prohibited the export of such objects. A 1982 law in Costa Rica declared that all collectors could keep their antiquities if they registered them with the state, but that the state had certain rights of control over the antiquities, including the right to borrow them for exhibition and the right to take conservation measures. Any antiquities inherited after 1982 would pass to the state thirty years after they were inherited, and no antiquities could be sold or exported except by the National Museum. Collectors in Costa Rica, Mexico, and other nations with similar laws often want to take advantage of the high prices on the international market by selling their collections intact to foreign museums, but they are prohibited from doing so by their nation's cultural property laws. Knowing this, the national museum in their country usually offers them a price well below market value. Some of those collectors have then turned to antiquities dealers to negotiate a series of sales to foreign buyers, maximizing the total selling price but breaking up their collections and violating export laws (Burnham, 1975).

Private collectors and dealers in nations other than source-countries are not restricted by international agreements or professional ethics in the same way that museums and scholars often are. Those collectors and dealers are bound only by the laws of their own country, and often their own governments and courts do little to limit their collecting activity. Some of those collectors and dealers openly buy smuggled and even stolen art. Some try to convince the source-country that its art serves as an ambassador to improve international understanding of its culture when it leaves the country. Nasli Heeramaneck, a connoisseur and businessman, helped build the Indian art collections of many museums in the United States with illegally exported objects; he was both praised as a promoter of Indian culture and condemned as a profiteer who had depleted India's patrimony (Burnham, 1975:175–76).

Millionaire Norton Simon began to buy Asian art enthusiastically in the early 1970s. The demand for Asian art, and its prices, increased as a result, and some source-countries tightened their export controls. When Simon was asked if he knew that one important sculpture that he had bought, the Sivapuram Nataraja, was stolen, he replied that it was a matter of interpretation. He noted that there were several conflicting stories about the source of the piece and how it had left India. The Indian government protested its export, saying that it had been smuggled out of the country and had perhaps been stolen as well. Simon acknowledged that it had probably been smuggled, as were virtually all antiquities that left India, but that did not mean that it was stolen. He said he had been given a guarantee by the dealer that the sculpture had been legally imported into the United States and that he would hold legal title to it there, although that does not necessarily mean that it had been legally exported from India.

Simon's purchase of the sculpture was linked to a plan by New York's Metropolitan Museum of Art to mount an exhibition of his Asian art collection; both Simon and museum officials believed that the sculpture would be an important focus for the exhibition. After art scholars expressed concern about how the statue had left India, and the museum adopted an ethical acquisitions policy in response to two recent scandals, the museum asked Simon for proof of ownership for the pieces that were to be exhibited. Some antiquities dealers tried to stop the show, fearing that the controversy would ruin their business, which according to Simon relied heavily on the sale of smuggled goods. Simon agreed to return the statue to India if its government would take steps to ensure that no other such pieces would leave the country without export clearance and a permit. He claimed that he had behaved in the same way that other collectors, dealers, and museums had in purchasing antiquities and said that source-countries needed to take more effective measures to curb the trade in smuggled and stolen art, rather than relying on the impractical step of taking action once valuable pieces turned up abroad. He also said that the United States needed to tighten its controls on the importation of art stolen or smuggled from abroad. Simon asserted that all collectors and museums would gain from tighter controls, because seven-eighths of the cost of art purchased in the way he had bought the Sivapuram Nataraja was a result of its having been smuggled (Burnham, 1975:176–87).

The demand by collectors for pre-Columbian treasures stimulated the illicit trade in artifacts from Peru's Sipán tomb. One collector who purchased several dozen of the pieces was Nobel laureate scientist Murray Gell-Mann. He was praised by Peruvians when he eventually repatriated the pieces to Peru, but that action was not typical of other collectors and dealers, who justified their purchase of the smuggled Sipán artifacts as the best way to preserve the past and distribute beautiful objects to those most able to afford and appreciate them. Michael Kelly, a member of the smuggling operation who later assisted United States Customs agents in breaking it up, commented as follows about the collectors and dealers who were involved in the illegal exportation of the Sipán artifacts:

All these people around me were addictively exercising their egos, possessing artifacts at all costs. It's just like cocaine. It didn't matter if you broke a law, if you bribed somebody, or whether somebody dies in Peru. All that is irrelevant. They want their piece on the shelf with their name on it. And the fact that some poor *huaquero* is shot excavating these pieces for them—they don't care about that. There's no difference between cocaine dealers and antiquities dealers as far as I'm concerned. (cited in Nagin, 1990:145)

MUSEUMS AND THE ILLICIT ANTIQUITIES TRADE

Museums in Western countries are filled with objects gathered from Third World nations, sometimes in violation of cultural patrimony laws and export regulations. Following the Civil War, the first director of New York's Metropolitan Museum of Art removed 35,000 pieces from Cyprus while he was consul there, directly violating a Turkish ban on such exportation. Today, if a museum wishes to build or add to a collection of antiquities, it almost has to buy objects that are illegally exported and frequently stolen as well. A Cleveland Museum curator once remarked, "Even if I know it's hot, I can't be concerned about that. If the museums in this country began sending back all the smuggled material to their countries of origin, the museum walls would be bare" (cited in Hess, 1974:148). Once a museum begins to build a collection, momentum develops to acquire more objects and curators become reluctant to refuse pieces that will be important additions. Because museums are a major market for antiquities, purchasing objects of questionable origin stimulates the illicit trade in antiquities.

If a museum adopts an ethical acquisitions code, refusing to buy things unless their provenances are adequately documented and they were legally exported, choice items might not be offered to the museum. If a museum notifies the source-country that it intends to buy an object or if it requires a dealer to show an export certificate, the dealer offering the piece may lose money if it is found to have been stolen or illegally exported. Consequently, dealers avoid museums with ethical acquisitions policies, preferring to peddle their wares to less scrupulous museums or to private collectors; collectors ask fewer questions and are less apt to have their purchases closely examined by the press. Museums that apply their ethical acquisitions policy to donations risk alienating patrons who want to avoid too close scrutiny of their collections (Burnham, 1975).

Concern with building a museum's popularity in the community and enhancing its reputation among museum professionals makes some curators wary of the negative publicity that can result from controversial acquisitions. However, other curators agree with the position voiced by Thomas Hoving when he was director of New York's Metropolitan Museum of Art: scandals about unethical acquisitions will pass, but a museum's collection will endure. That attitude—taking pride in the size and quality of a museum's collection, and adding to it whenever possible—fuels the illegal trade in antiquities.

In his recent best-seller *Making the Mummies Dance*, Hoving (1993:69) describes curators as follows:

Aggressive collecting curators were more than a little larcenous. To land something great, they were perfectly willing to deal with shady characters. Though they wouldn't, they could tell you every smugglers' ploy ever concocted. In extralegal matters they could be sophisticated, but they were often naive about the subtleties of bargaining.

In *King of the Confessors* (1981), Hoving describes his own efforts in the early 1960s while he was an assistant curator at The Cloisters, a branch of the Metropolitan Museum, to buy a medieval carved ivory cross from one such "shady character." Ante Topic Mimara, described by a former close friend and partner as "an art dealer, a painting restorer, a forger, a thief, a genius at survival" (cited in Hoving, 1981:156–57), offered for sale many pieces that were so obviously forged or of very poor quality that other museums were unwilling to buy the cross from him, fearing that it too might be counterfeit. Hoving purchased the cross for a sum that was a record for his museum, even though Topic Mimara never revealed the piece's origin. Hoving's willingness to buy works of uncertain provenance is also evident in his account of the Metropolitan Museum's purchase in the early 1970s of a calyx krater, a painted Greek vase dating to about 510 B.C. The dealer from whom this "hot pot" was bought had been arrested in Italy and Turkey for trafficking in illegally excavated antiquities, and he communicated with his clients in an "espionage-style" code. Hoving (1993:310) described the attitude of the curator responsible for the vase's purchase as follows: "He didn't want to know anything [about the origin of the vase]. If he knew anything, he didn't want me to know what he knew. We established an unspoken understanding. We would consciously avoid knowledge of the history of the vase."

Some museums have adopted the position, though few admit it publicly, that building their collections takes precedence over questions of ethics. Their curators may publicly decry the destruction of archaeological sites and the loss of knowledge associated with that destruction, but they also claim that such pillage is beyond their control and that once a site is destroyed, they should buy the plundered objects for preservation and public display. They often seem to be more interested in the objects as art than as artifacts that can illuminate past cultures, and some have argued that once an object has been stripped from its original location, it is irrelevant where it is housed. Critics claim that this self-serving view encourages looting and that because museums are the primary purchasers of plundered antiquities, they are ultimately responsible for the actions of those who supply such objects.

Fear of alienating the public has probably reduced the illicit acquisition of antiquities by museums, but it might also have led museums to make questionable acquisitions in secrecy. Many museums keep questionable items in storage for years before displaying them to the public, or display them soon after acquisition but with little fanfare. When stolen or illegally exported objects are publicly displayed, source-countries sometimes respond by limiting museum workers' access to archaeological sites in the country. The museum could also have to spend a large sum of money on attorneys' fees if a source-country sues to recover illicitly acquired objects. Disputes of this sort have even damaged diplomatic relations between the source-country and the nation in which the museum making the controversial acquisition is located.

The Getty Museum and the Antiquities Market

The J. Paul Getty Museum of Malibu, California, has been involved in several controversial acquisitions of antiquities. Because the museum entered the market late, at a time when few antiquities were still available from unimpeachable sources, its aggressive efforts to build a great collection have sometimes resulted in the purchase of pieces stolen from archaeological sites, laundered by dishonest dealers, and documented with forged papers.

In 1988, the Italian government accused the Getty Museum of acting irresponsibly when it returned to an unnamed collector some pieces of ancient Greek sculpture that the museum had been loaned and that Italian authorities suspected had been illegally exported from Sicily. An Italian government official said, "Just as soon as the Getty Museum learned these pieces were the subject of an investigation, it got rid of them rather than help us determine whether the suspicions are valid or not" (cited in Suro, 1988a:11). The museum might have done that to protect the collector's identity, which it refused to divulge, and to conceal the collector's source of the antiquities. Museum officials saw such confidentiality as essential to continuing to attract loans in the future. They claimed that any question about the objects' provenance was between the collector and the Italian government; however, the government did not know who the collector was. An Italian official said, "I believe they acted imprudently because in effect these pieces have now disappeared again and could be sold or sent to another country" (cited in Suro, 1988a:11).

The Getty Museum was involved in another controversy in 1988, after it announced that it had purchased a ninety-inch-tall Greek statue. The museum refused to make public the name of the dealer from whom it had bought the statue, the price it paid, where it had been made, or its recent history. According to one report, the dealer was a Swiss citizen who had a record of violating Italian laws on the exportation of antiquities; apparently, he had been offering the statue for two years before selling it to the London dealer from whom the Getty Museum bought it. Aware of a rumor that a large statue had been illegally removed from a Sicilian excavation in 1979, and suspicious of the origin of the statue because there was no record of its having ever been part of any private or museum collection, the Italian government asked the museum how it had acquired the statue. Under Italian law, anything found underground in the country belongs to the government, so if the statue had come from Italy, the government would have initiated a lawsuit to recover it from the museum. The museum restated its policy of not revealing any details about its purchases, simply asserting that the statue had been purchased legally. The Los Angeles Police Department questioned museum officials and was satisfied that nothing improper had been done.

According to an article in *Connoisseur* magazine, "As a major collector of Greek and Roman antiquities, the Getty was fully aware that any major piece coming on the market—especially one that had never been seen before, like the monumental cult figure—might be 'hot'—stolen or smuggled" (Corbett et al., 1988:202). A spokesperson for the museum said that it was aware of that possibility, and that the museum purchases antiquities only after completing a three-stage investigation. First, it sends photographs and descriptions of a piece to government agencies in likely countries of origin, asking if there are any objections to the purchase of the piece or any claims against it. When the museum, prior to buying the statue, asked Italy for assurances that it was not stolen, the government was unable to reply because it had no knowledge that the statue had even existed prior to the Getty's request. The museum also contacted officials in Greece and Turkey before buying the statue. Because there was no documentation of the existence of the statue prior to its being unearthed, there was no way for any source-country to support a claim to the statue.

In the second step in its investigations prior to buying antiquities, the Getty requires the dealer selling the object to guarantee that there are no claims against it and to give appropriate indemnities to the museum. Finally, the museum provides information on the piece to agencies that keep records of stolen or missing works of art, although Interpol said that it had never received any notification from the museum of its proposed purchase of the statue. If the Getty buys a piece that later has a legally supportable claim made against it, the museum claims that it will return the piece to the country of origin without regard to any statutes of limitations.

DEALERS IN ILLICIT ART AND ANTIQUITIES

The black market in art has been described as "a tightly organized business operation which is all the more efficient for being excellently camouflaged within the honest trade" (Burnham, 1975:37). In the name of discretion, art dealers cultivate a mysterious aura around their activities, referring to their intelligence networks, keeping the sources of their merchandise secret, maintaining an aloofness, and tantalizing prospective buyers (Burnham, 1975:37–38). Dealers often have vague ideas about what constitutes ethical dealing; some even cultivate a reputation as ethically marginal.

Some stolen art is secretly distributed by brokers and private dealers, some of whom are aristocrats, scholars, archaeologists, and museum curators. Those brokers sometimes use their substantial financial resources, expertise, and taste to enter high society by selling to and advising rich collectors. A few amass considerable wealth by earning commissions when they sell art, but most of them earn modest incomes through buying art and reselling it to dealers at a profit (Burnham, 1975).

Legitimate dealers are angered by brokers and private dealers who trade in stolen art, because those brokers and private dealers both victimize legitimate dealers and hurt their reputations, making it difficult for them to win the trust of potential clients. However, Burnham (1975) suggests that most dealers, legitimate or otherwise, do not tell law-enforcement agents and the public everything that they know about the trade in stolen art. Their reluctance to reveal all they know, even to press charges against those who have sold them stolen art, is linked to their unwillingness to talk openly about the sources of the art they have for sale. Even when dealers become suspicious of a piece they are offered, they often do not check very closely into its origin. If the piece is later found to be stolen, they may say that they have known the source for years and that he or she could not have known that the work was stolen. Dealers also justify their purchases of stolen art by saying that if they refused to buy it, another dealer would buy it and profit from its resale. In sum, even legitimate art dealers contribute to the trade in stolen art by doing less than they could to curb it (Burnham, 1975).

In 1991, an English family filed suit in a New York court against Ariadne Galleries to recover sixteen Roman bronzes with inlaid silver that the family said had been illegally removed from its property a decade earlier. Five men had been arrested for the theft but had not been indicted because of lack of evidence. Torkom Demirjian of Ariadne Galleries claimed to have been a good-faith purchaser of the bronzes and to have seen no proof that they had been stolen, although the Getty Museum refused to buy the pieces because it was convinced they were stolen. Demirjian asserted that he did not know how the bronzes had been found or how they had left England or entered the United States, saying that his function when such objects turn up is simply to make "wonderful things happen to them" (cited in Beller, 1990:95). In another case, Demirjian returned a third-century mosaic head of Medusa that had been stolen from a Greek museum and then sold through Sotheby's in London; he expressed surprise that such a reputable auction house would have sold him a stolen work of art.

Reputable antiquities dealers claim that they will not sell objects that have been stolen in the source-country, whether from an institution, a shrine, or an individual, nor will they sell objects looted from monuments in the source-country. However, most dealers will sell pieces that have been in the possession of collectors or on the market for some time, even if those pieces were once part of known shrines or monuments. Many of those dealers will also sell imported antiquities that have been dug up, even if the excavations were unauthorized and even if the objects were illegally exported. They acknowledge that illegal excavations impede the development of scientific understanding of past civilizations, but they argue that the aesthetic importance of ancient artifacts is as great as or even greater than their scientific importance. They also assert that carrying out legal excavations would take centuries and result in the housing of all objects in museums rather than in the hands of private collectors, and they point out that many sites that archaeologists have excavated have never been documented in publications.

Dealers would like to be able to treat all antiquities simply as objects to be bought, exported, and resold at a profit, but they know that most antiquities are plundered and illegally exported. In India, obtaining a permit to export an artifact is a complex bureaucratic undertaking that can take years. Because Indian police officers and customs agents routinely accept bribes to allow objects to be exported illegally, and because there is little risk of arrest, dealers find it easy to justify breaking the law. They point out that because most source-countries allow little or no legal trade in antiquities, they are faced with a choice of breaking the law or going out of business. Dealers have even questioned the right of source-countries to declare unilaterally that they own all unearthed antiquities in their territory; prominent dealer André Emmerich has commented as follows:

Do the descendants of the Turks who drove out the Greeks from Asia Minor have a better right to the art made by the ancestors of the Greeks? Do the destroyers of the Maya civilization [have more right] to its remnants than we do? I propose that it's a basic moral question. I beg the obvious fact that the art of mankind—the art of ancient mankind—is part of mankind's cultural heritage, and does not belong exclusively to that particular geographic spot where ancient cultures flourished. I think that this country more than any other has a special claim to the arts of all mankind. . . . American institutions have bought the objects they have acquired, and have not only paid with money, but we have paid the debt with scholarly contributions. . . . I would say that probably the majority of work on pre-Columbian art has been done by American scholars. So I think we have paid our way. (cited in Meyer, 1973:28–29)

Although the laws of many source-countries give title to unearthed antiquities to the state and prohibit or restrict the export of such antiquities, few art-importing nations have laws against the importation of looted or illegally exported antiquities. Smugglers can be convicted of making false customs declarations and even required to forfeit falsely declared objects, but the courts in art-importing nations have been reluctant to define it as an offense to import artworks simply because they were exported in violation of another country's regulations. As a result, dealers often tell buyers that they will hold legal title to a piece once it enters their own country, an assertion that has been increasingly challenged by source-countries. However, those legal challenges have been expensive and time-consuming and have met with limited success. Courts in the United States have heard cases in which source-countries have claimed ownership of their cultural property, but those countries have had a difficult time proving that the property originated in their territory and that it was stolen or exported after passage of the law that gives title to such property to the state.

The Cypriot Mosaics Case

A 1989 trial in Indiana involved a dispute over the ownership of four sixth-century Byzantine mosaic fragments. A Cypriot clergyman claimed that the mosaics were part of his nation's religious and ethnic heritage. Dealer Peg L. Goldberg had purchased the mosaics for resale in 1988 after being shown photographs of them in Amsterdam by Michel van Rijn, a Dutch dealer who was once convicted of art forgery in France. Van Rijn said that he had been offered the antiquities by Aydin Dikmen, a Turkish dealer who claimed to be the official archaeologist for the region of Cyprus from which the mosaics came. Dikmen, who had previously been indicted but not convicted for smuggling antiquities, said that after finding the mosaics in the rubble of a church, he had legally exported them to Turkey. Goldberg borrowed $1.2 million from an Indiana bank to buy the mosaics. She kept $120,000 of that amount for herself, paid Dikmen $350,000, and gave $650,000 to Robert E. Fitzgerald, an Indianapolis art dealer who had brought the mosaics to Goldberg's attention in the first place. Fitzgerald, who had used three aliases at various times, had once been involved in a lawsuit that included van Rijn.

During her trial, Goldberg was characterized as naive and careless for accepting assurances from Fitzgerald and van Rijn, despite her knowledge of questionable deals in which they had been involved in the past, and for failing to demand proof for van Rijn's statement that Dikmen had been the official archaeologist for northern Cyprus. The Cypriot plaintiffs claimed that Goldberg should have been suspicious about the disparity between the $1.08 million she was paying for the mosaics and their true market value, estimated at about $20 million, the price she asked the Getty Museum to pay her for the mosaics. Goldberg's negotiations with Getty Museum officials were terminated when they came to suspect that the mosaics were stolen and suggested to her that she contact Cypriot authorities.

The trial revolved around the question of whether Goldberg had exercised due diligence in trying to learn whether the mosaics had been stolen or smuggled from Cyprus. Due diligence has been defined as "doing everything that a victim should do to find and recover a stolen work of art, and everything a reasonable and cautious buyer should do to be a good-faith purchaser and avoid buying stolen property" (Linda Pinkerton, cited in Honan, 1989a:E9). Due diligence is determined by looking at the value of the property in question and at the resources available to the victim of the theft or the prospective buyer of the property; more effort is required if the property is of greater value and if the victim or buyer has more resources with which to pursue information.

If there were any reason for Goldberg to have had doubts about the origin of the mosaics, she should have tried to remove those doubts before buying them, according to testimony offered during the trial. She said that she had contacted IFAR, the United Nations Educational, Scientific, and Cultural Organization (UNESCO) office in Geneva, and customs agents in West Germany, Switzerland, Turkey, and the United States. The plaintiffs questioned whether she had actually made those contacts, because she provided little evidence that she had done so. Goldberg admitted that she had not contacted the Republic of Cyprus, the Turkish Republic of Northern Cyprus, or the Autocephalous Greek Orthodox Church of Cyprus, the last known owner of the mosaics, saying that she had not known that the Church was almost universally recognized to be the owner of religious and cultural property in Cyprus. When the Greek Cypriots had been informed in 1979 of vandalism at the Church of the Kanakaria, the source of the mosaics, they had publicized the theft of the mosaics at conferences and in statements they circulated to scholars, museums, newspapers, and Greek-American organizations. At trial, Goldberg's attorney tried to show that this publicity had not resulted in widespread dissemination of information about the theft, claiming that Goldberg might not have learned about the theft even with more diligent efforts to relieve any doubts she might have had about the origin of the mosaics.

In August 1989, a federal judge found for the Cypriots on all counts and asserted that Goldberg had not been a good-faith purchaser and therefore must return the mosaics to the Autocephalous Greek Orthodox Church of Cyprus. The judge wrote as follows: "Because the mosaics were stolen from the rightful owner, the Church of Cyprus, Goldberg never obtained title to or right to possession of the mosaics" (cited in Honan, 1989b:A1). He said that Goldberg had not obtained clear title to the mosaics "because suspicious circumstances surrounded the sale of the mosaics which should have caused an honest and reasonably prudent purchaser in Goldberg's position to doubt whether the seller had the capacity to convey property rights and because she failed to conduct a reasonable inquiry to resolve that doubt" (cited in Honan, 1989b:C25). The lawyer for the plaintiffs reacted to the court's decision by saying, "Dealers who make a practice of asking as few questions as possible should take heed" (cited in Honan, 1989b:C25). The curator of medieval art at a Baltimore gallery remarked, "We are going to use this decision as the basis for formulating a policy on the purchase of antiquities. We will ask such questions as is the price appropriate? Was the work attached to a building? Was it removed in time of war? The more suspicious the circumstances the more circumspect the buyer must be" (cited in Honan, 1989b:A1).

The Trade in Native American Artifacts

Most gallery owners who specialize in Native American artifacts claim that they will turn in a seller if they have doubts about the legality of what is being offered for sale, but they then ask how they can be expected to tell whether a given artifact was unearthed legally or illegally. Dealers who present themselves as honest often claim that *other* dealers fail to question the source of the objects they are offered; they also accuse collectors of failing to inquire about the origins of pieces they want to add to their collections (Kane, 1986).

In fact, there is reason to believe that most dealers in Native American art behave unscrupulously, at least some of the time. At least three-fourths of the market in American Indian art is illicit, with such objects frequently being offered quietly to preferred customers rather than sold openly in galleries. In a sting operation in Phoenix, an undercover federal agent who offered stolen goods to thirty dealers was warned by only one of them that he should not be selling the pieces. The director of that sting operation said that dealers rarely ask where Native American objects come from, because they do not want to be culpable, nor do they want to have to refuse to buy objects that were illegally excavated (Barnett, 1990:104).

Dealers in Native American artifacts sometimes provide their customers with provenances that are fabricated by the dealer or by the middleman from whom the dealer bought the piece; often that information is not put in writing. One archaeologist claims that if dealers had to prove that the objects they were selling had not been stolen from public lands, the whole trade in Native American artifacts would shut down. This suggests that the looting of such artifacts could be curbed by requiring proof that the objects had been legally excavated.

In 1979, the Hopi found that three sacred tribal masks that had been stored in subterranean ceremonial chambers were missing. That loss threatened their way of life because of the power of the masks and their importance in Hopi rituals. Contrary to the claim by dealers that Indian artifacts without provenances will not find a legitimate market, photographs of the masks had been shown to reputable art dealers in Dallas, Los Angeles, Chicago, and Arizona. According to the FBI, those dealers should have questioned the origin of the masks and reported the people offering the masks to the authorities, but they did not do so.

A curator of the Art Institute of Chicago eventually accepted the Hopi masks as a donation from two Chicago businessmen. The FBI believes the curator was duped because he knew the person from whom the donors had bought the masks, Meryl Pinsoff Platt. Described as a minor player in the world of antiquities, Platt worked out of her home, offering her respected family name in lieu of documentation about the origin of the masks. It is not clear how she came into possession of the masks, but she apparently knew they were stolen; a letter from a Texas dealer informing her of that fact was retrieved from her garbage by FBI and IRS agents. Knowing that the stolen masks would be difficult to dispose of, Platt sold them to the two Chicago businessmen for only $11,700, although she certified in writing that their market value was $37,500. She then arranged for them to donate the masks to the Art Institute of Chicago, allowing them to claim the $37,500 as a tax deduction. In 1985, Platt pleaded guilty to dealing in stolen property and to aiding and abetting in a false document presented to the IRS. In a plea bargain, she agreed to help law-enforcement agents learn more about the black market in Native American artifacts. She was fined $6,000 and sentenced to thirty days in jail and an additional ten consecutive weekends of confinement (Goodwin, 1986).

After another sacred Hopi mask was seized by the FBI from a New York exhibition in 1989, Catherine Barnett (1990) set out to determine how it had traveled from the Arizona reservation to New York. Santa Fe dealer Joshua Baer had sold the mask for $75,000 to a Connecticut couple who had loaned the mask to the exhibition; he told them that it no longer had religious significance for the Hopi, which was not the case. Baer had apparently bought the piece from Don Stephenson, with whom he had dealt previously. Stephenson was a "runner" who regularly advertised, anonymously, in the *Navajo-Hopi Observer* that he wished to buy "anything that is old Indian made" (Barnett, 1990:142). He told Barnett that the mask had not been stolen and that he had bought it from one of the Hopi. In selling the mask, that person had violated the Hopi practice of treating its sacred material as collectively owned. According to Baer, Stephenson never told him the mask's provenance, and because such transactions are always in cash there was no documentation of Stephenson's purchase of the mask. Baer says that a common scam among Native Americans in the Southwest is for one of them to sell an object, which the tribe then reports as stolen or sold in violation of a tribal belief in communal ownership; when the piece is returned to the tribe, it is soon resold and then reclaimed.

Measures have been taken to curb the trade in Native American artifacts and to return pieces to the tribes that created them. A federal law enacted in 1990 created a category of communal property for objects of cultural and religious significance to Native Americans. The law restricts the future sale of such objects and requires all federal agencies and museums receiving federal monies to inventory such objects, notify tribes of what they have, and offer to return objects to the tribe that created them if the tribe so requests. Even without resorting to such legal measures, the Zuni have managed to curb a once-thriving trade in wooden statues of their war gods, which have sold for as much as $40,000 a piece. Since 1978, the Zuni have recovered more than fifty statues by educating museum curators and private collectors about the way the statues were created in a communal process for the whole tribe, meaning that no individual has any right to sell or trade the statues. Museums and collectors have been persuaded to turn the statues over to the Zuni, even though the religious beliefs of the tribe lead them to expose the statues to the weather so they will decay into dust as was intended by their creators (Suro, 1990).

THE SMUGGLING OF ART AND ANTIQUITIES

Moving art to another location, often another country, is often one of the first things that thieves will do after a theft. This makes recovery of the art and apprehension of the thieves much more difficult for law-enforcement agents, and it allows thieves to maximize their profits by moving the art to the place where they can get the best price for it. Even if the stolen art is found in another country, the government there will often protect its own citizens if they claim to have purchased it in good faith.

Thieves may also smuggle stolen art to another country when they find that they cannot collect a ransom or sell it to a disreputable dealer. The failure to collect a ransom for a Flemish tapestry stolen in 1977 from a castle in Italy led the thief to smuggle it into the United States; when the owner noticed an announcement of the tapestry's impending sale at auction, it was withdrawn from the sale.

Within the United States, thieves frequently operate across a broad geographic area, stealing art in one state, disposing of it in a different state, and living in yet another state. Two thieves arrested in Brooklyn in 1989 had carried out a series of museum thefts in Massachusetts, Ohio, and Maryland. Their mobility helped them thwart law-enforcement agents for several weeks, but eventually they were arrested when they tried to sell stolen goods to a New York City antiques dealer. Moving the stolen objects from one state to another gave them access to valuable art in museums around the country and made it easier for them to dispose of the stolen art. Less-than-famous artworks stolen in one city can be sold easily in other cities, whereas they might be recognized if they were offered for sale in the city where they were stolen.

In April 1989, three robbers stole twenty-one paintings from a Zürich gallery. About a week later, a New York dealer received a call from one of the thieves, who posed as a wealthy Swiss who wanted to sell his collection of Old Masters paintings. The thief offered to have his son bring some of the pictures to New York in a diplomatic pouch. Photographs of twelve of the paintings were left with the dealer, but he became suspicious and called IFAR and the FBI. The older thief, who was actually a Belgian citizen, was eventually arrested in New York with four of the stolen paintings, which he had smuggled into New York. He had previously been arrested for art theft and was using an alias and traveling on a false passport. He admitted to being one of the art thieves and to bringing the stolen paintings into the United States. The man posing as the son, who was another of the robbers, and a woman who had helped bring the paintings into the United States were also arrested (O'Brien, 1989a).

The paths used by smugglers are frequently circuitous. A Renoir painting stolen in Paris was smuggled to a New York gallery and then sent to Boston on consignment, after which it was shipped to Canada, back to Paris, and then again to New York; this process took six years and was not impeded by internationally circulated notices that the painting was stolen (Esterow, 1988). In another case, a man arrested for smuggling a statuette from India said that he was part of an international ring of thieves that smuggled artworks from India and Nepal to the United States, sometimes directly and sometimes through Switzerland. In a third case of smuggling, an Egyptian wall painting acquired by Boston's Museum of Fine Arts in 1978 was looted from a tomb in 1973, trucked to Libya, shipped to London, and then sent to the United States; the museum returned the painting to Egypt and got a full refund from the London dealer.

The origins of antiquities and the paths by which they make their way to auction houses, collectors, or museums are sometimes obscure. In 1990, fourteen ornate Roman silver vessels dating from the fourth and fifth centuries were to be auctioned at Sotheby's in New York at an estimated price of up to $70 million for the lot. This Sevso Treasure was accompanied by documents claiming that it had been excavated in Lebanon, but both Yugoslavia and Hungary asserted that the treasure had been unearthed in their territory and belonged to them. As a result of the dispute over the origin of the treasure, a New York court prohibited its sale until the various claims could be resolved. Scotland Yard investigated and found that the treasure had been consigned by Lord Northhampton, who had bought the pieces over a six-year period. In fact, Peter C. Wilson, former chairman of Sotheby's, had started to buy the silver pieces in 1980 and over the years had taken on partners in his venture, one of whom was Lord Northhampton. Wilson sought to acquire Lebanese export permits for the silver pieces even after they had been shipped to Switzerland; eventually, $800,000 was paid for falsified documents. A curator at the Getty Museum, a prospective purchaser of the treasure, questioned the authenticity of the documents after noticing that some Arabic handwriting on the documents that was supposedly by one person had been done by different hands. Investigators at Scotland Yard concluded that the owners of the treasure might have engaged in a conspiracy to defraud and taken money by false pretenses and suggested that criminal charges were likely; Lord Northhampton and Sotheby's were, however, not found to be parties to those offenses.

Smugglers often bribe poorly paid customs inspectors and border guards to ignore illegal exports and imports. When bribes are not effective in neutralizing customs agents or police officers, smugglers sometimes exert influence at higher levels. Dealer André Emmerich describes the importance of cooperation by well-placed officials to the antiquities trade as follows:

When I was active in pre-Columbian art, our export shipments from Peru were handled by the public relations head of an airline who happened to be the son-in-law of the president. . . . In Mexico, for a long time but no longer, the chief shipper was the head of Customs at the airport, whose sons made wonderful crates. And you'd best have the crates made by the sons. (cited in *Art & Auction*, 1990:131)

High government officials seem to have been influenced in a case in which several bribe offers were refused by a police chief who was investigating the looting of the nearly two thousand Greek coins from the Anatolian region of Turkey; one offer was a bribe that was three times his annual salary. After the prospectors who uncovered the hoard were convicted, that police chief was demoted to traffic officer, suggesting that those involved in the purchase and smuggling of the coins had influenced his superiors. Later, his replacement was transferred to a different post after seizing another collection of illicit antiquities (Acar and Kaylan, 1988).

Smugglers sometimes avoid the cost of a bribe by concealing the goods they are transporting. Paintings are cut from their frames and rolled up, or painted over with an easily removed water-based paint. Artifacts are broken into pieces and then reassembled when they reach their destination; the individual pieces appear to customs officials to have little value. Antiquities are covered with other material to make them appear to be modern reproductions. A unique method was used to smuggle Ecuadorian antiquities into the United States; they were left on an oil rig that was towed to New Orleans, but they were confiscated there by customs agents and returned to Ecuador.

The "60 Minutes" Experiment

The ease with which stolen art can be transported across international boundaries has been demonstrated several times by journalists. Following an art theft in England, a reporter from the London *Daily Mirror* was able to carry a full-scale copy of the stolen picture to Belgium, once by air and once by sea, without attracting the attention of customs officials (Green, 1969:254).

In an experiment carried out for the October 14, 1979 edition of the television show "60 Minutes," an artist painted a copy of one of three Cézanne pictures that had been stolen from the Art Institute of Chicago in December 1978. The director of the museum said that it would be difficult to move the stolen paintings out of the country because of their fame and the publicity given to the theft. Nevertheless, employees of "60 Minutes" were able to fly the copy of the painting to Canada, telling customs agents that it was worth $200,000 and presenting a fake bill of sale from a nonexistent Paris gallery as proof of ownership. Customs agents checked with Interpol, but the international police agency had no record that the painting had been reported stolen. The "60 Minutes" journalists then had no trouble flying the copy of the Cézanne painting back into the United States from Canada and then on to Paris. Sophisticated thieves can probably move stolen art across international boundaries even more easily; for instance, they might collude with a gallery owner to secure a more convincing fake bill of sale. If inexperienced journalists can smuggle stolen art with ease, imagine how simple it must be for criminal gangs involved in the international drug trade to move stolen art from one country to another.

The Smuggling of Italy's Patrimony

According to a Sicilian magistrate, the treasure-hunting *tombaroli* are not the most important part of the illicit antiquities trade in Italy, because "[t]hey have always been around and always will be," nor does he blame local collectors and antiquarians who purchase looted artifacts (Suro, 1988b:C17). Instead, he places major responsibility on international smugglers and dealers, often based in Switzerland, who illegally export artifacts from Italy for sale on the world market. This judge says that it is difficult to get evidence to prosecute the smugglers, because they are careful and clever. In addition to profiting from the destruction of historical sites and ravaging the countryside, the judge says that the smugglers are "the ones who stimulate the whole chain of criminal acts by putting money into it. All you need is for word to spread through Aidone that a man in Geneva paid thousands of dollars for something from Morgantina, and all kinds of people are out there with metal detectors" (cited in Suro, 1988b:C17).

Stolen art is smuggled from Italy in a variety of ways: by air or boat, packed in crates with other things or in suitcases with false bottoms. One way to ship stolen paintings was recounted to Peter Watson (1984:153) by a man who operated an import business in the United States. The canvas was wrapped around the support running between the legs of a table and then covered with cardboard for protection. The table was placed in the middle of a large shipping container holding other furniture to discourage examination by customs inspectors. Another method of smuggling is described as follows by a dealer in paintings and drawings:

One of my favorite techniques is to take a small station wagon, pile the back with mattresses, lay a work of art under them, and rent the services of a small child. On a very hot Sunday afternoon I drive from Venice to the border. So will thousands of other tourists. A few kilometers before customs I stop and buy a large ice-cream cone for the child. By the time I have reached the crowded border and the smartly dressed, white-gloved and harried customs officers, the child has smeared the *gelato* all over his face. The customs man always recoils in horror and orders me to drive through. (cited in Hoving, 1981:81)

Around 1990, Italians began to fear that their patrimony might be dispersed throughout Europe and the world when the European Community removed border controls in 1993. Since 1939, Italy has required government approval for the exportation of all works by artists who have been dead for at least fifty years, but that law has been ineffective. Italy is now the largest source of illicit art and antiquities in Europe; more than 250,000 paintings, statues, frescoes, coins, and other objects have been reported stolen since 1970, with the annual number increasing from 12,000 in the early 1980s to 28,000 in 1991 (Stille, 1992). With European integration, Italians feared that artworks not registered with the government by collectors might be treated like any other goods, free to circulate throughout Europe without restriction. Dealers throughout Europe and the governments of the art-importing nations of northern Europe favored such a laissez-faire approach; Italy, Greece, Spain, France, and other countries that wanted to protect their cultural property sought tighter restrictions on the movement of art and antiquities throughout Europe. In November 1992, a compromise was reached that required cultural property of a certain age and value to be returned to the country from which it had been illegally removed (Haberman, 1990; Riding, 1992).

Smuggling and the Demise of Communist Regimes

With the demise of Communist regimes in eastern Europe and the opening of the borders to the West, organized art theft has become epidemic. A Russian customs official estimates that only 10 percent of the art and antiques that people try to smuggle out of the country is confiscated by border guards; more than three times as many such objects were seized by Russian border guards in 1992 as were confiscated the previous year at the borders of the Soviet Union (Possehl, 1993).

The director of Czechoslovakia's Culture Ministry observes, "The problem is not only stealing but also wholesale looting, and it started the moment we opened our frontiers" (cited in Tagliabue, 1991:13). There were fifty church burglaries reported in that country in 1989, the last year of Communist rule, but ten times that number reported in 1990. With the end of Communist rule and the emergence of a free market, which brought high rates of inflation and unemployment and the devaluation of local currency, Czech residents desperate for cash began to sell family heirlooms for a fraction of their market value; they have also taken money for assisting

German and Austrian dealers in their removal of public shrines. Because decades of Communist rule weakened their pride in their culture and alienated them from their traditions, many Czechs now see folk art and antique furniture in terms of the hard cash those objects can fetch, rather than as a part of their heritage (Green, 1991).

Art and antiques stolen in Czechoslovakia turn up with regularity in western European nations. Four works by Picasso stolen from Prague's National Gallery in 1991 were recovered a few weeks later in Bayreuth, Germany. The thieves, who were habitual offenders from Czechoslovakia, had entered the museum by crossing a moat that had been closely guarded by police officers with dogs during the Communist regime; those guards were later removed as inconsistent with the new democratically elected government. Czech churches and synagogues have been looted by former members of the secret police, who ship stolen objects past overwhelmed or bribed customs agents and border guards. Smugglers have disguised antique furniture as modern reproductions and used false or doctored documents to elude customs officials. Smugglers prefer to work at the height of the tourist season, when the largest crowds are crossing the borders. In Austria and Germany, they sell the pieces privately to dealers and collectors for ten to twenty times what they would fetch in Czechoslovakia; smuggled objects rarely appear on the open market (Green, 1991).

What was formerly East Germany also experienced major losses of art during the last few years of Communist rule and the period immediately thereafter. Artworks were stolen from churches and museums and sold to dealers and collectors in the West. In 1990, East German police investigated art thefts that had resulted in losses of at least $18 million worth of property. German police have evidence that Western dealers seek out appealing objects in their country and then commission gangs of thieves to steal the pieces, which are often delivered to dealers in the Netherlands. In 1990, art thieves apprehended in Germany were found to be carrying lists of masterworks they said they had been commissioned to steal. Some of the thieves operating in Germany have been assisted by former agents for the Stasi, the East German State Security Ministry that had been charged with investigating art thefts. Those former agents had lost their jobs with the fall of the Communist party, and some of them were earning money by selling information to dealers who commissioned art thefts.

The central figure in the looting of East German art was Alexander Schalk-Golodkowski, former minister of Commercial Coordination and the Communist party's chief official for international trade. He used Stasi agents to approach the directors of small museums, telling them they had to trade works in their collections for pieces of equal value brought to them by the agents. Art was also taken from private collectors, who were told that it was being appropriated because of their failure to pay the required taxes; some were told that their art would be given to state museums, but those institutions never received the art.

To acquire foreign currency, the appropriated art was then sold through Art & Antiques Ltd., a government organization founded in 1973 that had a monopoly over the import and export of art and antiques. Schalk-Golodkowski used Art & Antiques Ltd. to take over the thriving export business of Siegfried Kath, who had amassed an extensive collection of art and antiques by traveling the countryside and buying up treasures. After Kath was charged with embezzlement and forced to leave the country, his 125 warehouses were used by the ministry of Commercial Coordination as collection points for adding to the already vast collection of paintings, porcelain, and other objects. Western dealers were invited to the warehouses to buy art and antiques; less expensive items were sold in hotels to Western visitors. Communist party officials skimmed profits from this trade and selected pieces for themselves. Art & Antiques Ltd. officially closed late in 1989, and Schalk-Golodkowski fled to the West just before a warrant for his arrest was issued, leaving behind a collection estimated to be worth $1.2 million (Norman, 1991).

The Smuggling of Turkish Treasures

Turkey is now the major source of illicit antiquities for collectors, museums, and dealers in the West. There are more ancient Roman towns in Turkey than in Italy, and more ancient Greek sites in Turkey than in Greece, so the majority of Greek and Roman pieces displayed in museums in the United States actually come from Turkey (Acar and Kaylan, 1990). Because Turkish law forbids the export of all antiquities, those acquisitions are illegal from the perspective of the Turkish government.

Organized criminal gangs based in Turkey employ middlemen to buy up artifacts from treasure-hunting peasants in the countryside and then move the objects to Istanbul. Some peasants bring their discoveries directly to dealers in that city. To assist in the search for antiquities, smugglers have purchased and distributed aerial surveys of ancient sites specially prepared for them by retired military officers. Until recently, American military bases were used as transit points to smuggle antiquities from Turkey, but the major smugglers now ship antiquities in officially sealed truck containers through Bulgaria to galleries they own in Munich, Germany. Bulgarian authorities apparently do not interfere with the smuggling, perhaps because they have been bribed. From their Munich shops, the smugglers sell the antiquities to dealers and collectors throughout the world.

The owners of the two major Munich galleries involved in this trade are members of families that have long been involved in smuggling. The most important smugglers, who belong to a cartel described as "a branch of the Turkish Mafia," are Kurds and Syriacs whose family roots are in the same town in Turkey, Mardin (Acar and Kaylan, 1988:76). There Syriac Turks have been renowned goldsmiths for generations, and local peasants have routinely brought them unearthed treasures for sale or trade, giving rise to a tradition among the Syriac goldsmiths of buying and smuggling antiquities. Kurdish Turks have a nomadic history and a tradition of moving goods across borders; they also have a feudal tradition of loyalty that is the basis of a tightly knit smuggling organization (Acar and Kaylan, 1990). These gangs were apparently involved in smuggling out of Turkey the valuable Lydian Hoard, the silver Byzantine treasure now at Dumbarton Oaks, and a rich hoard of nearly two thousand Greek coins. They have also been involved in the smuggling of heroin; French authorities recognized the names of some of those involved in smuggling the Greek coins as people also involved in drug trafficking.

One method used by these smugglers is to have export papers approved for other items and then alter the papers to use for transporting valuable antiquities that have been illegally excavated or are being exported without permission. On at least ten occasions, the smugglers have sought to maintain their control of the illicit antiquities trade by murdering competitors and members of their organization who have deserted to a rival gang or cooperated with law-enforcement agents (Acar and Kaylan, 1988).

The Decadrachm Hoard. In 1984, three Turkish treasure-hunters uncovered a hoard of 1,889 ancient Greek coins; some of them were decadrachms, a single one of which had sold at auction a decade earlier for $300,000. The Decadrachm Hoard was purchased by the Turkish smuggling cartel, which sold 1,680 of the coins to OKS Partners for $2.7 million. The three partners in that American company believed that because the coins had been legally exported from Germany, they would hold title to them, overlooking the fact that the coins had been illegally exported from Turkey to Germany and had been sold by a cartel that did not hold legal title to them. Later, the partners in OKS determined that the cartel had not sold them the entire hoard, contrary to their contract, which stated that at the time of the sale the cartel was unaware of any other coins in the hoard. Sellers of such hoards commonly hold back some pieces, assuming that buyers will later pay more to complete a collection. The cartel had held back six of the decadrachms, selling OKS only seven of them, meaning that OKS would have to buy the rest at even higher prices in order to control the market in that valuable coin. The Decadrachm Hoard contained as many of those coins as had existed aboveground prior to discovery of the hoard. The cartel offered OKS the remaining coins in the hoard for $1.5 million, prompting OKS to sue for breach of contract. Eventually the cartel sold OKS sixty-four additional coins for $800,000 but retained a financial interest in the coins that would allow it to profit from their resale.

OKS then loaned the collection to cultural institutions around the world in order to publicize the hoard and acquire the imprimatur of scholars and collectors, thereby enhancing the value of the coins. One partner, who was also a trustee of Boston's Museum of Fine Arts, loaned the hoard to the museum as a way of authenticating and promoting the coins. One observer has suggested that the museum did him this favor because a foundation he directed had loaned art to the museum in the past (Miller, 1988).

Some of the Greek coins were sold through dealers in 1987, but the following year when some of the coins were advertised as coming from Turkey, its government investigated. It seemed unlikely that all of the institutions and individuals involved in the sale and dissemination of the coins could be criminally prosecuted, even if the Turkish government could prove that the hoard had been stolen or illegally exported. Legal action of that sort would have required prosecutors to show that each party knowingly received, concealed, stored, bartered, sold, or disposed of the stolen coins, and it seemed doubtful that prior knowledge of the coins' provenance could be proved in court (Acar and Kaylan, 1990).

The Lydian Hoard. Trying to justify the controversial 1970 purchase of some gold artifacts by Boston's Museum of Fine Arts, a journalist revealed that New York's Metropolitan Museum of Art had a few years earlier bought a major collection of classical objects that it was hiding from the public. In 1984, that museum displayed a bowl much like one that a Turkish blacksmith had described as coming from an Anatolian grave excavated in 1966. The museum described the bowl's provenance as East Greek but failed to make clear how it had acquired that bowl and a second similar one. By referring to the bowl and other pieces as East Greek, the museum implied that their origin was somewhere in Greece or Turkey rather than the specific region of Turkey known as Lydia, where the Turkish government claimed the treasure had been unearthed in several excavations during the mid-1960s. Those who had dug up the treasure identified specific pieces in the Metropolitan Museum as ones they had unearthed; moreover, some of the pieces left behind in the tomb and some of those confiscated from the house of the leader of the looting gang matched pieces in the museum's possession (Kaylan, 1987).

According to the Turks, the bowl exhibited by the Metropolitan Museum of Art in 1984 was part of the Lydian Hoard or East Greek Treasure, a collection of 255 pieces, mostly of silver and gold, that are 2,600 years old. One of the greatest collections of antiquities ever unearthed, the Lydian Hoard was claimed as cultural patrimony by the Turkish government. The controversy over ownership of the treasure involved both state and national governments and precipitated a diplomatic crisis between Turkey and the United States. Officials of the Metropolitan Museum lobbied the New York state legislature to pass a law to protect its holdings. The Turkish government responded with threats to stop American archaeological excavations, and it hired a prestigious New York law firm to press its claim to the treasure in court.

The Turkish government claimed that after buying most of the Lydian Hoard from the treasure-hunters who had unearthed it, an antiquities dealer named Ali Bayirlar sold it to an international dealer named John Klejman, who then sold it to the museum for $1.7 million. Klejman ran his antiquities business from Switzerland, a country generally regarded as the world center for the smuggling and laundering of art and antiquities because of its lax customs laws. Klejman said that without knowing its origin, he had bought the treasure in 1966 from ignorant traders in Europe and that he had sold it to the Metropolitan in three lots, the last transaction occurring in 1968. Turkish officials disputed Klejman's story, claiming that they had evidence of a more direct path that the treasure had traveled from Turkey to the museum (Kaylan, 1987). In 1993, the museum agreed to return the Lydian Hoard to Turkey.

Museums are understandably reluctant to repatriate objects for which they have paid large sums, especially objects that have been in their possession for decades or even centuries. Nations that demand the return of their cultural property do not offer to compensate museums for what they had to pay to acquire the antiquities. On the other hand, countries such as Turkey have grown frustrated and angry at having their cultural patrimony shipped to Western museums and collectors. They object to the high cost of trying to keep that property in the country and the expense of finding and recovering it when it leaves the country. The pillage of ancient sites destroys historical information and with it the possibility that scholars will be able to learn about the customs, clothing, diet, and art of peoples of the past. Scholars know relatively little about the people of ancient Lydia, and the Metropolitan Museum's vagueness about the origin and nature of the objects in the Lydian Hoard made it difficult to learn about the people who made and used the artifacts and what those objects meant in the context of that ancient culture. The antiquities curator of the Metropolitan Museum was accused of selecting Greek-looking objects and displaying them alongside East Greek items purchased at other times from other regions, thereby confusing the cultural context and meaning of the objects. He defended that practice by saying that classical styles do not easily fall into distinct contexts.

Smuggling the Sipán Treasures

The objects looted from the Sipán tomb moved from the leader of the *huaqueros* through middlemen, sometimes called providers, to collectors and agents in Lima. *Huaqueros* did not send the providers their most important discoveries at first; instead, they tried to sell less significant pieces before offering the best ones. Collectors and agents who hoped to buy important pieces had to buy the first offerings, which sometimes included fakes. Negotiations between buyers and providers did not begin until they had spent some time in casual conversation about matters unrelated to the business at hand. Then potential buyers would try to minimize the significance of what was being offered so as to keep the price down, and dealers would exaggerate the quality of what they were offering to boost the price (Kirkpatrick, 1992).

California antiquities dealer David Swetnam, who masterminded the smuggling of the treasures from Peru's Sipán tomb to the United States, had previously been involved in smuggling ceramics from that country. He had sent the pieces to Bolivia, where they had been coated in clay and stamped in Spanish "Made in Bolivia." Then they had been shipped as modern folk art to Germany and from there to Canada, where Swetnam had picked them up and driven them to United States. There he had sold the pieces to collectors and dealers. When Canadian authorities intercepted two of his shipments in 1985, Swetnam abandoned that smuggling route.

When Swetnam learned of the discovery of the Sipán artifacts, he convinced several Americans to invest $80,000 to purchase some of the pre-Columbian artifacts, later repaying their investment with smuggled pieces. By not using his own money to buy the pieces, he reduced his risk in the venture. He contacted Fred Drew, a retired American diplomat living in Lima who had friends in positions of influence and who was part of a network of *huaqueros*, local dealers, and middlemen who traded in illicit antiquities. Drew, who used crutches because he had injured his knees when he fell into a shaft during a looting expedition, had set up illicit digs for ambassadors and military officers, bribing those who might try to prevent such excavations. Although Drew claimed that he had never personally taken a looted or illegally exported object out of Peru, he had often used airline personnel, runners, and once even a nun to do that for him. Drew justified his smuggling activity by pointing to the widespread corruption in Peru, the money he paid to economically needy peasants, and his scholarly commitment to the cultural property (Kirkpatrick, 1992).

Swetnam mailed Drew the investors' money in checks of less than $10,000 each to avoid having to file currency reports. To get the textiles, ceramics, and gold and silver pieces from the Sipán tomb out of Peru, Drew turned to Miguel de Osma Berckemeyer, an expediter with reported connections to the Medellín drug cartel. For 5 percent of the value of a shipment, Berckemeyer got the merchandise past customs officials in Lima; he paid half of his cut to airport personnel and kept the rest. Drew took 22.5 percent of the profits from the sale of the treasures, and he apparently underpaid Berckemeyer by deceiving him about the actual market value of the shipments (Kirkpatrick, 1992).

The treasures were shipped from Peru to England, which permits the importation of such artifacts. There they were stored, later to be sent to the United States in three shipments. To reduce the possibility of his own arrest, Swetnam paid an accomplice to smuggle the treasures into the United States. He was Michael Kelly, whose status as both a British citizen and a resident of the United States led Swetnam to believe that United States customs agents would pay little attention to any personal property Kelly brought into the country. Kelly's father had died recently, and Kelly wrote a letter explaining that the objects he was bringing into the United States had been collected by his father during his travels around the world in the 1920s; that would have been prior to passage of Peru's cultural property law in 1929, meaning that any artifacts in Kelly's possession had not been illegally exported from Peru.

Swetnam exploited the norm of secrecy about prices that prevails in the art market to defraud his investors. In raising money from them, he inflated the prices he said he had paid for the Sipán pieces, telling them that an artifact he had actually paid $5,000 for had cost him $10,000. When Swetnam sold a piece, he told investors that he had been paid less for it than he really had, for instance telling them that a piece that he had sold for $20,000 had only brought $15,000. Swetnam also told his investors that confidentiality prevented him from revealing to them who had purchased the pieces, making it impossible for them to verify the prices he said the artifacts had fetched.

Swetnam used a convincing front as a well-to-do dealer to develop a clientele for the Sipán treasures. He lived in a California mansion where his wife, formerly a maid there, was house-sitting for the owner, who was living elsewhere in the state. Swetnam entertained collectors and dealers at cocktail parties and luncheons, conveying the impression that he owned the house.

In 1987, Kelly brought over nineteen pieces, mostly ceramics and textiles, which were valued at $150,000. After a second shipment of similar pieces, Kelly reported the smuggling operation to United States Customs Service, apparently fearing that his role was becoming too well known to strangers, some of whom had called him to inquire about the Sipán artifacts. A third shipment included about $500,000 worth of gold and mosaics. Kelly helped customs agents record conversations involving Swetnam, and those tapes provided evidence for a raid on Swetnam's home and the residences of several investors and collectors. Nearly two thousand pieces were seized, most of them not from the Sipán tomb.

Although Swetnam and his wife were indicted on ten counts of conspiracy, smuggling, and customs violations, in the end only Swetnam himself was convicted. He was sentenced to six months in a federal prison camp but served only four months, the first person ever incarcerated for smuggling pre-Columbian antiquities. Swetnam relinquished his claim to eight of the pieces that had been seized from him; they were returned to Peru. The single most valuable of the 354 pieces returned to Swetnam was taken by his attorney as payment for legal services.

The Peruvian government then sued to recover the rest of the Sipán pieces, citing its 1929 cultural property law and a 1981 executive agreement committing the United States to help Peru in recovering illegally exported artifacts. However, the judge ruled that Peru's law was far from precise and was really only an export restriction, and one not even enforced consistently by the Peruvian government; moreover, said the judge, Peru had not proved that the artifacts had been stolen. As a result, a dealer who had bought Sipán artifacts from Swetnam was declared to have been a good-faith purchaser and allowed to keep the eighty-nine antiquities that had been seized from him (Nagin, 1990).

The International Trade in African Artifacts

Africa has a thriving trade in old statues, masks, and other artifacts that indigenous people trade or sell to the agents of Western dealers, who then violate cultural patrimony laws by shipping the objects to places where prices are much higher. Objects whose market value does not justify the risk of being arrested for smuggling and the cost of shipment to Europe or the United States are sold to tourists.

This illicit trade is rooted in a cultural difference in attitudes toward traditional objects. For Western collectors, pieces that are old are more authentic than objects that have been made recently. That attitude is based on a Western notion that originality is associated with the individual artist who first conceived and created a work of art. In contrast to this view, many of the objects of interest to Western collectors are considered important by Africans primarily for the functions they serve in rituals, and a new object can function as well as an old one. The differences in value that Africans attach to various ritual objects are based not on aesthetic merit but rather on the relative power of the objects to conjure strong magic and produce good effects (Burnham, 1975:123). Middlemen and dealers exploit the difference between Western and African perspectives by trading new objects for old ones and then selling the old pieces to Western collectors.

Smugglers, dealers, and their middlemen often maintain good relations with African museums. They rely on museum employees to inform them of the value of traditional objects, confirm the authenticity of artifacts, and tell them the history of pieces they do not recognize. Dealers and their middlemen know that resource-starved local museums cannot buy important pieces at market value, but to maintain good relations they occasionally donate less important pieces to them. Sometimes they profit from the sale of such pieces to museums; transactions of that sort provide a profit without the risk and expense of smuggling. Museum officials rationalize their relationship with dealers and their middlemen by saying that it allows them to learn about the activities of dealers and middlemen and to alert the government when important pieces are at risk of being shipped abroad (Burnham, 1975).

Many African artifacts legally belong to specific tribes, even though they are also protected by national patrimony laws and cannot legally be exported. When valuable or rare objects are smuggled out of the country, national antiquities officers contact the curators of European and American museums. Often those curators will then refuse, or at least be reluctant, to buy the illegally exported pieces. For this reason, antiquities dealers usually first try to sell their wares to private collectors, who do not have to worry about maintaining good relations with African antiquities officers.

Some smugglers of African artifacts have jobs conducive to that activity; others hire people with such jobs to transport the objects for them. Diplomats, airline pilots, and stewards are in strategic positions for smuggling artifacts, and some of them are paid to do so by dealers and their agents. For a fee they will carry objects through customs, where they do not have their belongings examined, and deliver the pieces to prearranged addresses. One steward even took art appreciation courses at a museum to learn what was worth smuggling and what prices he could command. Eventually, he began to buy and sell objects on his own rather than working for others. When he

could not afford to buy a piece, he would photograph it and get a collector
or dealer to advance him the money to purchase it. He would then return to
the country, buy the piece, and smuggle it out by small plane or by land
(Burnham, 1975:128).

The Illicit Trade in Chinese Antiquities

Following the 1949 Communist Revolution, Chinese peasants farming
new land began to uncover ancestral tombs that contained ceramics, jades,
and jewelry. Selling those objects could bring them more than they earned
from farming. This set the stage for the smuggling of those items to countries
where they would fetch high prices, but no trade developed then because
the government restricted travel by its citizens and allowed few foreigners
into China. Those restrictions were not lifted until the mid-1970s, and even
then there was no network in place to transport the antiquities the thousand
miles from the major finds in the north to the primary market for the objects
in the south, Hong Kong. Cooperation by government officials and customs
agents was needed before the objects could be moved freely to the south
and across the border into Hong Kong (Norman, 1988).

By the early 1980s, a network to transport antiquities from the north to
the south was in place. At the border, objects were moved by fishing boats
to Hong Kong or Macao under cover of dark, or by trucks that concealed
the contraband among legitimate goods such as produce. Illegally excavated
pieces began to appear on the Hong Kong art market with increasing
frequency after 1981.

Once they left China, the objects had a variety of destinations. Lesser
pieces ended up in small shops and market stalls in Hong Kong. Better
pieces were bought by dealers who kept the merchandise in the back rooms
of their shops, where they showed it only to special clients. Those major
dealers bought the Chinese antiquities from traders with whom they had
done business before, rather than directly from smugglers. The traders
scouted shops for important pieces, competing with foreign dealers and
auction houses who employed local agents to find pieces that could be sold
at a profit to Western collectors.

Collectors in Hong Kong, as well as in other Asian countries with cultural
ties to China, reportedly changed their collecting interests in response to the
illicit trade in Chinese antiquities. Collectors who had once bought Chinese
porcelains of recent vintage began purchasing older objects because of their
plentiful supply and relatively low price. Sotheby's helped to strengthen
interest in collecting such objects by holding local auctions that were
accompanied by sales catalogues describing the pieces honestly and accu-

rately, thereby instilling a confidence in buyers that was previously lacking because of the many fakes that were sold in Hong Kong (Norman, 1988).

A 1986 report on this trade that was published in a Hong Kong newspaper led the Chinese government to crack down on the smuggling; in that year, the government intercepted 5,200 items being smuggled out in 128 separate incidents. Smuggling seems to have abated thereafter; in 1988, a Hong Kong dealer reported, "Two years ago I was shown something good every day. Now it's only two or three times a week" (cited in Norman, 1988:176). Between 1989 and 1992, the Chinese government tripled its spending on the protection of cultural property, and smuggling seemed to diminish further. Despite such measures and the fact that smuggling cultural property is a capital offense in China, the trade continues. Some smugglers are even so bold as to show photographs or faxes of objects to Western collectors and then steal the pieces from poorly protected Chinese museums and ship them from China by boat (WuDunn, 1992).

ART THEFT AND THE STATE

In addition to the international movement of art and antiquities by smugglers hoping to reap a profit, artworks have also been moved from one country to another as a result of wartime conquest and the exploitation of colonial power. Sometimes an individual's desire to possess art is masked as an official act of the state; more often, confiscation is institutionalized as government policy. Nineteenth-century British expeditionary forces in Africa looted gold artifacts from the Ashanti and important masks and sculptures from Benin City. Napoleon's army appropriated art from conquered nations, the Nazis stole art from collectors and museums during World War II, and after that war the Soviets confiscated art from conquered Germany. Historian Hugh Trevor-Roper describes the reason for this form of art theft as follows:

[I]f art gives an aura of prestige to a city or dynasty, rival cities or dynasties, which set out to conquer or humble them, will also seek to destroy their "myth" by depriving them of this aura and appropriating it to themselves, like cannibals who, by devouring parts of their enemies, think thereby to acquire their *mana*, the intangible source of their strength. (cited in Failing, 1980:71)

Napoleon Bonaparte and the Plundering of Europe

Napoleon Bonaparte's unprecedented looting of Europe's art treasures began during his 1796–1797 campaign in Italy. Later, he ordered his director-general of museums, Baron Dominique Vivant Denon, to confiscate artworks from throughout Europe; Denon accompanied Napoleon on his campaigns and pointed out treasures that would enrich France. Prior to Napoleon, wartime looting had usually been carried out by soldiers on a random basis for personal gain or by armies for the personal pleasure of the head of state. What was different about Napoleon's campaign was that the looting was carried out in systematic fashion to make the nation-state of France the cultural center of the world. Nevertheless, well-placed individuals, most notably Josephine Bonaparte, did appropriate treasures for themselves (Chamberlin, 1983).

The French tried to justify Napoleon's plunder in legal terms, claiming that the ceding to France of the artworks was included in the peace treaties signed by defeated nations; of course, those treaties had been signed under duress. Leading French artists even issued a statement that the looting had been necessary to create a more favorable atmosphere for the arts in France and to educate the French people by providing them with models from antiquity.

Following France's defeat in 1814, the Allies seized the looted art. Stendahl protested that France had acquired the art by treaty but that the Allies had confiscated it without a treaty. Despite the resistance of the conquered French, most of the art was eventually returned to the countries from which it had been taken; that was a relatively easy task compared to the repatriation of Hitler's plunder because the French had housed most of the loot in museums and because the provenances of the works were usually known. However, hundreds of pieces had disappeared into personal collections or had been sold abroad to dealers or collectors who refused to return them (Chamberlin, 1983).

Art Theft and World War II

Before, during, and after World War II, there was an unprecedented amount of art theft, some by agents of the state and some by individual soldiers. In 1938, the Nazis enacted a law to allow the cleansing of museums of artworks that were considered "degenerate" or "too Jewish." Even before that law was passed, about 16,000 works of art had been removed from public view. In 1944, the Nazis compiled a list of about 22,000 pieces that they had confiscated since 1940, omitting from that list thousands of works that had earlier been destroyed or sold to French and Swiss dealers.

The Nazis' conquest of much of Europe was accompanied by the seizure of art to fulfill Hitler's plan to transform his boyhood home of Linz, Austria, into a pantheon of Aryan art. The looting was directed by Alfred Rosenberg and Dr. Hans Posse. Hermann Goering controlled Rosenberg and his

Einsatzstab-Reichsleiter Rosenberg and used that organization to amass an extensive personal collection of confiscated art. Unlike Hitler and Napoleon, who plundered art for the state, Goering's goal was personal; in 1943, he announced to Rosenberg, "I have now obtained, by means of purchase, presents, bequests, and barter, perhaps the greatest private collection in all Europe" (cited in Chamberlin, 1983:162). The art expert Posse, who was commissioned to build the Linz collection, used the Nazi party, the army, and the SS to plunder palaces, manor houses, churches, and museums. Posse justified the plunder in the name of better preservation of the world's cultural heritage and the relocation of the art to a place where it would be seen by more people. Until the Linz gallery could be opened, the stolen art was stored underground in an Austrian salt mine that had a constant year-round temperature and offered protection from Allied bombs.

The Nazis tried to justify their plunder in legal terms. Art could be appropriated if it belonged to the state's internal enemies or if it required protection from the state's external enemies. The confiscation of art from Jews throughout Europe was defined as appropriation from a state-designated internal enemy. Art that did not fit either category had to be bought from its owners, although the pressure exerted by the Nazis and the near-worthlessness of the reichsmarks with which the art was bought meant that such transactions were coerced and disadvantageous to the seller. Many of the pieces in Goering's collection were "presents" that were actually bribes to gain his favor (Chamberlin, 1983).

The German invasion of the Soviet Union was accompanied by the theft of art treasures housed in museums and czarist palaces. Not wanting to show the public how desperate the situation was, Soviet officials refused to evacuate artworks to save them from the invaders; they managed to save some metal objects to melt down for scrap value, but they left valuable Renaissance paintings behind for the Nazis. The Germans had planned their looting of Soviet museums and palaces from the beginning of the war, even designating an expert in the Leningrad collections to choose which pieces to steal after the invasion. The Soviets did not have a complete inventory of their art, but a government commission later estimated that the Nazis stole, destroyed, or damaged 564,723 museum pieces valued at about $1.25 billion.

Following the war, the Soviet government gave its soldiers permission to take anything they wanted from occupied Germany. As a result, thousands of paintings seized in Germany now hang in Russian homes. In 1990, one of those soldiers, Viktor Baldin, returned 362 master drawings he had safeguarded since rescuing them in 1945 from the damp basement of a ruined German castle. Over the years, he had refused lucrative offers from

Western dealers for the pictures in the hope that an eventual change in the political atmosphere would permit him to return the drawings to their rightful owners.

More significant than random thefts by individual soldiers was the systematic looting of art by the Soviets. The government established a Trophy Commission to commandeer whatever art could be found in Germany and return it to the Soviet Union in compensation for the Nazis' pillaging of their country. Brigades were organized that included art historians, artists, restorers, and other art specialists. Those civilians were disguised as Red Army officers to ensure compliance with their efforts to remove art from Germany. Members of the brigades reported that they were sometimes told by their superiors to steal works of less than museum quality for their superiors' personal collections.

In 1945 and 1946, millions of artworks were flown to the Soviet Union, where the Committee of Arts stored them in secret depositories. Many of those works were quietly returned to East Germany in the late 1940s and 1950s as a way of solidifying relations between the two countries, but thousands of works remained hidden in the depositories. Not until 1991 was the presence of those depositories officially acknowledged, a change made possible by *glasnost* and the ending of the Cold War. Though opposed by most Russian art historians, who saw the looted art as compensation for the losses inflicted by the Germans during the war, the Russian government agreed in 1991 to establish a special commission to explore the repatriation of the looted artworks. Many of those pieces will be difficult to return to their owners because they have been stolen more than once since leaving their owners' possession half a century ago.

An important collection of Old Masters drawings assembled by Dutch businessman Franz Koenigs before the war made its way to the Soviet Union by a circuitous path. In 1933, Koenigs used his collection as collateral for a large loan from some Dutch-Jewish bankers. In order to liquidate their assets just before the German invasion of the Netherlands, the bankers called in the loan, but Koenigs was unable to raise the cash to retrieve his drawings. Hans Posse had Hitler's permission to negotiate the purchase of the Koenigs collection, but neither Koenigs nor the director of the museum where the collection was housed wanted to sell it. Realizing that the Nazis could simply seize the drawings, they did sell some of the collection but managed to hold on to most of it. Later, 526 of the drawings that had been taken to Germany were seized by the invading Soviet army and shipped to the Soviet Union. One of the first acts of the Dutch Royal Government in Exile was to void all unauthorized dealings with the Nazis and to assert the claim of Dutch citizens to property illegally seized by the Nazis. When one of the

Koenigs drawings was submitted by a Soviet citizen to a British museum for evaluation in 1987, it was appropriated and returned to the Netherlands. Fearing that the more open atmosphere in the Soviet Union might lead to dispersal of the Koenigs drawings throughout the world, the Dutch government in 1989 circulated a catalogue of the missing drawings and announced that it would take legal action to retrieve them. In 1992, the Russian government announced that 360 drawings from the collection had been found and that it would help the Dutch recover the pictures.

After the war, the Art Looting Investigation Unit of the United States Office of Strategic Studies and the Monuments, Fine Arts, and Archives Unit of the United States Army compiled lists of artworks lost to the Nazis by collectors, museums, galleries, and governments. The Austrian salt mine, which had been booby-trapped by the Nazis to blow up and destroy its cache of more than 10,000 works of art, was saved by Austrian resistance fighters. Art was also found in more than two hundred official locations and many unofficial sites throughout Germany; other pieces had been dispersed around the world through sales to dealers and collectors. Thousands of the looted artworks are still missing, the most famous being the carved panels of the Amber Room of Tsarkoe Selo.

Between 1945 and 1952, American forces tried to restore the stolen art to its rightful owners. Individuals had to file claims through their governments, documenting their claims with photographs, invoices, inventory listings, or publications. According to Sol Chaneles (1987), more than 16 million objects were inventoried by the American forces in Germany, but most of the pieces were never returned to their owners because they had died in the war and in concentration camps or, if alive, had no way to prove that they owned the objects. Chaneles says that many of those artworks were "permanently borrowed" by American troops, often being mailed home for later sale through galleries. The reports of the Art Looting Investigation Unit remained secret for years, in part to prevent false claims for missing art, but also to cover up the extensive collaboration and profiteering by French, Dutch, and other art dealers, who had helped the invading Nazis negotiate the purchase of art that belonged to private collectors (Chamberlin, 1983).

Between 1952 and 1962, West Germany returned more than a million works of art to their rightful owners and heirs. Even today, claims for artworks are still considered by the German government, but proving ownership at this late date is difficult; between 1964 and 1979, only three claims were made, and two of them were settled quickly. Some of the nearly four thousand pieces still in the possession of the government now hang in German museums (Dornberg, 1988).

In 1973, the Austrian government declared that the art in its possession that it had been unable to return to the rightful owners and heirs would become state property, saying that there were no longer many claims being made. Art magazines and Jewish groups challenged that position and accused the Austrian government of trying to enrich itself at the expense of the art's legitimate owners. From then until 1985, the Austrian government and Jewish organizations worked together to find the owners of the unclaimed pieces. In 1985, the Austrian Parliament passed a law to return to their rightful owners and heirs more than eight thousand works of art that the Nazis had confiscated, some from museums but most from European Jews. The works were being held by the Austrian government in a monastery, although some had found their way into Viennese museums and Austrian embassies around the world. That law established a period until September 1986 for claims to be processed; unclaimed works were then to be auctioned off and the proceeds divided among Austrian Nazi resistance groups, the Jewish community in Vienna, and Jewish groups in the United States (Tagliabue, 1986; Tomforde, 1985).

Some Allied occupation troops stole art for themselves at the end of the war; as recently as 1984, IFAR was receiving a call every few months from a lawyer asking about the legal status of a work of art that a client had brought back from Europe after the war. In the period immediately following the war, dozens of soldiers were prosecuted, dishonorably discharged, or imprisoned for stealing property, some of it art. One such theft came to public attention in 1990, when the heirs of Joe Meador tried to sell several medieval German pieces known as the Quedlinburg treasures. The value of the pieces is difficult to estimate, because similar objects have never been sold on the open market. One piece was a tenth-century illuminated and illustrated manuscript of the Four Gospels in a jewel-encrusted gold and silver binding; another was a sixteenth-century illuminated manuscript. The treasures had been moved from a church in Quedlinburg, Germany, to a nearby mine for safekeeping at the end of the war. American troops were placed in control of the mine to safeguard the treasures, but that did not happen until several days after soldiers had arrived in the area, giving thieves an opportunity to enter the mine. Even after troops were assigned to guard the treasures, they allowed some soldiers into the mine to look at the priceless objects. Meador, who was stationed in the area at the time, apparently stole some of the treasures and shipped them home via the Army Post Office. Seven months after the treasures were found to be missing, he was court-martialed in another case that involved the theft of silverware and china from a French villa; he was fined and reprimanded for that crime, but apparently was not suspected of the Quedlinburg theft. There were reports in his battalion, however, of his cutting paintings from their frames else-where in Europe. Back in Texas, Meador displayed his loot to friends from time to time, telling them that he had collected it in Europe at the end of the war.

Several years after Meador died, his heirs sought to collect a finder's fee for the return of the stolen Quedlinburg treasures to Germany. Through intermediaries, in a transaction carried out in Switzerland, they first returned the tenth-century manuscript to Germany for a $3 million fee. Because that money was for the return of property that everyone acknowledged to have been stolen, the payment was described as ransom, extortion, and blackmail. That transaction would have been illegal in the United States, but Swiss law protects parties to the sale of an object that lacks a clear title. A transaction involving a second manuscript was aborted when it became public knowledge. The Quedlinburg church then sued Meador's heirs for the treasures. After a complex set of negotiations, in 1992 the treasures were returned to Germany by Meador's heirs, who received a total of $2.75 million in exchange for all of the treasures, including the first one that had already been returned. Critics feared that such a payment would open the way to future demands by thieves or their heirs, but others noted that there were no comparable treasures in the United States. The Germans claimed that the payment saved them substantial legal fees and an uncertain outcome in a Texas court and said that the finder's fee was consistent with a German principle of jurisprudence that permitted remuneration for finding lost objects. Willi Korte, who devotes his time to the recovery of cultural property lost during and after World War II, suggests that German institu-tions could be willing to make such payments because they "might not want to be perceived as crying over things they had had stolen when they themselves had been the most ruthless art thieves of the twentieth century" (cited in Swanstrom, 1993:6).

The Two Chinas

Between 1933 and 1949, a group of thirty museum experts moved around the Chinese countryside 19,500 large cases of artworks originally housed in Beijing's imperial palace. The Japanese invasion of Manchuria in 1931 was the impetus for the removal of the treasures from Beijing, but the termination of the war with Japan in 1945 was followed by internal strife between the Communists and the Nationalists. In 1949, eight of the thirty scholars and workers followed Chiang Kai-shek to Taiwan with three shiploads of crates, which included some 600,000 of China's most precious art treasures; the remaining 16,000 cases were returned to Beijing's Palace

Museum. Today the mainland Chinese Communists regard Chiang Kai-shek as a thief; contemporary Taiwanese Nationalists believe that they are safeguarding their people's cultural heritage (Sereny, 1983).

Korean Art in Japan

In 1990, a South Korean antiquities dealer broke into the home of a wealthy Japanese collector and robbed him of nine valuable porcelains that the dealer said had been taken by Japanese colonial authorities during their occupation of Korea following Japan's annexation of that country in 1910. During those years, the Japanese used their power to buy and appropriate some of Korea's best ceramics, paintings, and stone carvings.

As Korean nationalism has grown in recent years, the presence of its art in Japan has become a source of increasing irritation. Since Japan and Korea signed a treaty in 1965, Japan has returned more than a thousand works of art to Korea, but Koreans complain that Japan needs to do more about the large amount of Korean art still in the hands of private Japanese collectors. That art is regarded as especially important because of the destruction of many fine pieces during the Korean War, leaving some of the best surviving examples of Korean art in Japan (Sterngold, 1991b).

The War in the Persian Gulf

Following its August 1990 invasion of Kuwait, Iraq looted two Kuwaiti museums of their renowned collections of Islamic art. Dealers around the world were alerted to the possibility of trafficking in those objects, which were marked with museum registration numbers. After the 1991 War in the Persian Gulf, 17,000 pieces were repatriated to Kuwait by defeated Iraq.

A few months after the end of that war, Iraq claimed that priceless Islamic manuscripts, gold and silver coins, jewelry, statues, pottery, and carvings had been looted from its own museums by Shiite Muslim rebels, who unsuccessfully rebelled in southern Iraq, and by Kurdish rebels, who had looted museums in the North. Iraq warned auction houses and dealers around the world not to handle the stolen items, which the government had removed from Baghdad museums to more remote areas at the start of the war in order to protect them from Allied bombs. Iraq reported that the bombing had shaken loose some bas-reliefs and cracked some buildings and monuments but that no famous artworks, ruins, or buildings had been destroyed in the raids.

War has often resulted in the theft of art by conquering nations and by indigenous groups that take advantage of the breakdown of social order. Art is also damaged or destroyed during war by bombing raids and artillery fire. That harm is not usually defined as vandalism, but in the following chapter we will see that much art has been damaged and destroyed by the deliberate or negligent actions of people who do not fit the mold of the conventional vandal.

❧ *Seven* ❧

Vandalism

For centuries, the deliberate destruction of art has plagued its owners, especially museums, churches, and other institutions that want to maximize public access to their collections. Vandalism prevents those institutions from achieving one of their primary goals, the preservation of art for future generations. The threat that visitors will deface or destroy art also limits public access to art when owners refuse to loan their possessions to those institutions.

The term *vandalism* derives from the Vandals, an East German tribe that destroyed Roman art and civilization in the fifth century. The traditional image of a vandal is an ignorant, irrational barbarian lacking in taste and sensitivity. The term *vandalism* was associated primarily with the destruction of art until the nineteenth century, when it began to be used more generally to refer to any destruction of property (Cohen, 1973b).

DEFINING ART VANDALISM

Fine and Shatin (1985) define art vandalism as intentionally destructive and illegal damage to a work of art. They exclude from their definition damage that results from negligence, pollution, or harm inflicted by the person who created the work. Here we adopt a broader definition of art vandalism: the intentional or negligent destruction of a work of art. Following Fine and Shatin, we exclude destruction by the artist who created and still owns a work of art. Departing from their definition, we include a variety of acts that damage and destroy art in ways that are not deliberate: damage carelessly done by thieves in the course of stealing art, restoration that harms a work of art, deterioration of art that results from neglect by the owner or caretaker, the deliberate destruction of art by an owner or caretaker, and damage done to art during war or civil insurrection. Before examining deliberate vandalism, or conventional vandalism, we look at those destructive acts that are less commonly regarded as vandalism.

Felony Vandalism

Felony murder is a murder committed in the course of another felony, such as a burglary or rape. Even though the murderer did not begin the burglary or rape with the intention of taking a life, felony murder is usually treated as more serious than other kinds of murder. The commission of another felony at the time the offender kills someone is treated as an aggravating circumstance, one that warrants capital punishment in some states.

The law does not define a crime of felony vandalism analogous to felony murder, but the unintentional damaging of art by thieves in the course of stealing it might be seen as an aggravated form of vandalism. Stanley Cohen (1973b) calls this "acquisitive vandalism," damage done in the course of an effort to acquire money or property.

Thieves frequently damage art while trying to remove it from a museum, a home, or a church. They have broken statues from their bases and even removed parts of statues, figuring that if a whole statue is too big to take maybe they can find a buyer for its head. In a 1989 burglary in Wayne, Pennsylvania, thieves treated the goods they stole as if they had no idea of their value, damaging oil paintings, breaking antique chairs, and destroying a chandelier when they dumped it into their truck.

To ease their removal of oil paintings from a museum or a home, thieves often cut the canvas from the frame. If the painting is recovered, restorers may be unable to conceal the cut marks, leaving a permanent reminder of the theft. Even if thieves carefully remove a canvas from its stretchers, the change in tension often results in the cracking of the paint. When thieves roll or fold canvases to make their removal from the building less detectable, flakes of paint are often lost from the painting's surface. A Vermeer oil painting stolen from an Amsterdam museum was taken from its frame, rolled up, and sat on by the thief as he rode away in a taxi; the damage to the picture's surface could not be fully repaired after the painting was recovered. All twenty van Gogh paintings stolen by thieves from Amsterdam's National Museum in 1991 were scratched by careless handling, and three were seriously damaged.

In their haste to get antiquities, grave-looters do not use the careful methods of excavation employed by archaeologists, and so they frequently damage or destroy the ancient objects. According to the Italian police, about half of the objects discovered by the *tombaroli* are harmed in the process of digging them up (Hamblin, 1970:75). Pre-Columbian monuments in Guatemala and Mexico that weigh as much as five tons are thinned by hacking, sawing, or smashing them into smaller sections that can be removed more easily (Coggins, 1969).

Felony vandalism would also cover damage done to a stolen work of art while it is still in the thief's possession. Frequently, unknowledgeable thieves store art in conditions harmful to it, an environment that is hotter, colder, brighter, or more humid than the place from which it was stolen. Harm often results from the change in conditions and from extremes of heat, light, or humidity.

Restoration and Damage to Works of Art

Restorers sometimes make subtle changes in the appearance of a work of art, often to fit the standards of a particular time and culture; the use of dark varnishes to obscure the surface of oil paintings was once a common practice, and the addition of fig leaves to nudes of Adam and Eve is well known. Restorers also repaint pictures in ways that deceive viewers about the artist's original intent. Professional standards of restoration now mandate that any additions or changes be reversible, but those standards are sometimes violated.

People trying to clean or restore art have sometimes defaced and even destroyed it, though not deliberately. In the past, the cleaning of paintings with brooms has abraded the surfaces of pictures. In 1992, Veronese's *Marriage at Cana* was badly ripped when it fell on metal tubes being used by the Louvre to support the huge canvas while it was being restored. Since 1986, a team of Indian archaeologists and engineers has been cleaning Cambodia's Angkor Wat with hard brushes and harsh chemicals and filling in cracks in the temple with cement; their efforts have been criticized as temporary housekeeping rather than real restoration and for eroding details of the statuary and changing the temple's appearance (Shenon, 1992).

Recent restorations in Italy have led to charges that the chemicals and cleaning methods being used may do long-term damage to the works of art. The cleaning of the marble tomb of Ilaria del Carretto in Florence provoked American art history professor James Beck to accuse the restorer, Giovanni Caponi, of doing an unnecessary restoration that had caused irreversible damage to the sculpture. Beck said that the cleaned tomb looked "as if it had been treated with acid, cleaned with Spic and Span, and polished with Johnson's wax" (cited in Simons, 1991b:13). In response, Caponi brought a criminal charge of aggravated slander against Beck for damaging his honor and reputation. Caponi admitted to having no formal training as a restorer, but he said that he had been doing restorations for thirty years. He completed the restoration in only three weeks, a job that might have taken other restorers a year, by using a device that he had patented, a device that critics thought might abrade a sculpture's surface. After spending $20,000 in legal fees to defend himself, Beck was found innocent of aggravated slander in 1991.

Vandalism as Art, and Art as Vandalism

Just as restorers have sometimes been criticized for making alterations that obscure the artist's original intent, so have modern conceptual artists been attacked for deliberately changing others' art in order to create original pieces of their own. In 1989, conceptual artist Francesc Torres decorated a replica of a Greek statue of Zeus with a baseball bat and a television monitor in order to create what he and the Whitney Museum, where the statue was on loan, called an original work of art. Dietrich von Bothmer, head of the Greek and Roman art department at New York's Metropolitan Museum of Art, which owned the statue, protested the treatment of the statue and threatened to demand its return if Torres's additions were not removed. After the bat and monitor were removed, the statue was returned to the Metropolitan. An art collector then loaned the Whitney another replica of the same statue, to which Torres added his decorations.

A similar uproar was set off in Mexico a year earlier, when artist Rolando de la Rosa superimposed the face and bare breasts of Marilyn Monroe over the figure of the Virgin of Guadalupe, described by the president of a far-right Catholic group as "not only the mother of God and the mother of the Christian family, but the symbol of all of Mexican mothers" (cited in Rohter, 1988:4). The artist's alterations were seen as sacrilegious vandalism by outraged Mexicans of all classes and ethnic groups. Anger was so great that the artist, the director of the museum that displayed the work, and two government officials were charged with the crimes of having "offended, insulted, injured, stained, and dishonored" a national symbol and having disturbed the public peace.

These cases further blur the distinction between vandalism in the narrow legal sense of deliberate damage to others' property, and acts that intentionally or negligently harm such property. Here two conceptual artists altered original works of art and claimed that the results were original pieces of their own. The artists would probably not be convicted of the crime of vandalism, because their alterations were reversible and had been done with the permission of the caretakers of the art. For connoisseurs, however, conceptual art of this sort demeans and defaces the original work in much the same way that deliberate acts of vandalism do.

Negligence

Even though it is not deliberate, negligence by owners and caretakers of art can result in significant damage. Owners are often wary of loaning their art to museums because they fear theft, but lack of museum security poses less of a threat to their art than does carelessness in the shipping and handling of the art. Crates in transit are sometimes treated roughly and battered, and the art inside is damaged. In part because of the increased value of art, museums now go to extraordinary lengths to prevent damage to their art in transit, employing sophisticated crates and humidity-control measures and even dividing works among several planes so that not all of the art will be lost in the event of a crash (Kimmelman, 1993).

The conditions in which art is displayed and stored by museums and other institutions sometimes contribute to its deterioration. Paintings in Great Britain's Tate Gallery have been damaged by sunlight that comes in through the glass roof, by water leaking from the roof, and by high humidity (Rule, 1989). The collection of Boston's Isabella Stewart Gardner Museum has suffered over the years from high and variable humidity and heat, excessive levels of light, and dirt that comes in open windows during the summer and from a smoky boiler in the winter. Damage of this sort is not intentional, but such negligent treatment of artworks has done more harm over the years than deliberate acts of vandalism.

In 1988, the public learned that works of art stored in a warehouse by the New York Historical Society had deteriorated badly because of poor storage conditions. Some of the works were on long-term loan from the New York Public Library, which ironically had loaned the society the art because it could not afford to care for it. Some of the works were found covered with mold and mildew and splattered with what seemed to be paint or acid. Others had been torn, had pieces flaking off, or were separated from their frames. The paintings had been damaged by careless handling, high humidity, tar dripping from a roof, dirt, water, and variable temperatures. Bryant C. Tolles, an expert on museums who prepared a report on the artworks, concluded as follows:

Some particularly fine works of art and historical artifacts are being exposed to an injurious storage environment, and in fact appear to be beyond hope of restoration. Some items have lost all their value and may have to simply be thrown out. I can emphatically and succinctly state that the conditions at the rented warehouse space in Paterson are the most blatantly shocking that I have observed during my entire museum career. (cited in McGill, 1988c:23)

Even if some of the damage were reversible, the resources for such restoration were not available; in fact, the New York Historical Society had stored
the paintings in such conditions because it lacked the funds to pay for better
facilities.

Five murals donated by artist Mark Rothko to Harvard University in 1962
deteriorated in part because he had unknowingly used a kind of paint that
faded over time. However, the murals were also damaged by Harvard's
negligent treatment of them. To protect the paintings from the bright light
that flooded the room in which they hung, Rothko requested heavy curtains;
curtains were installed, but people regularly opened them to look at the view,
causing the murals to fade. The room was often used for cocktail parties and
dining, and the murals were soon defaced by pieces of food, dents caused
by people and their chairs, and even scratched initials. In 1979, the murals
were removed to storage.

Works of art are probably less likely to be damaged when they are indoors
under the control of museum curators or private owners than when they are
outdoors. In those more exposed settings, art is subject to deliberate vandalism, natural environmental forces such as moisture and sunlight, and
human-made forces such as acid rain and water pollution. When caretakers
ignore the ravaging effects of such environmental forces, their negligence
leads to the damage or destruction of art.

Italy, which has been called the world's largest outdoor museum, lacks
the resources to preserve its enormous volume of art and antiquities.
UNESCO officials estimate that four-fifths of all European art and architecture that needs to be preserved is in Italy. The Italian government has
started to inventory the works that need protection and repair, but the list is
incomplete, even though it now includes millions of items. Flooding, air
pollution, and neglect have ravaged Italy's patrimony to such an extent that
some observers have commented that art that is stolen and smuggled out of
Italy is at least more likely to survive than art that remains in the country
(Hofmann, 1989). Florence has been particularly hard hit by damage to
statues, reliefs, and fountains from acid air and polluted water. One controversial proposal is to bring works of art that are outdoors into climate-con-
trolled indoor environments and then replace the original works with
replicas. Critics fear this would change the city's appearance and make it
less attractive to tourists, who are essential to the local economy. Efforts to
cope with the pollution that has caused the damage have so far been
unsuccessful (Simons, 1991a).

In Egypt, antiquities that have not even been unearthed have been
damaged by natural and human-made environmental forces, contradicting
the belief that at least those relics would be preserved for future generations

to excavate, study, and appreciate. The increased use of irrigation canals has made the air more humid than it once was, and that humid air has seeped into underground chambers and damaged buried relics. Sewage, salts, and minerals have polluted the ground water, which has done additional harm to antiquities that are underground. Tour buses that vibrate the ground have also damaged unexcavated relics (Cowell, 1990).

Tourists also threaten the Buddhist art in the caves in a remote area of China. That art had been preserved for sixteen centuries by the dry desert air in the caves' interiors, but the moist carbon dioxide exhaled by tourists, mostly from other parts of China and from Japan, now poses a threat to the paintings. In an effort to preserve the art yet continue to attract the tourists who are so important to the local economy, the government is building eight cave replicas. A few of the original caves will remain open to the public, but access to the originals will be limited. Officials claim that the viewing conditions in the replica caves will be even better, but critics worry that tourists may not be willing to journey so far just to see reproductions (Kristof, 1989).

In 1992, a youth group using steel brushes to clean up graffiti negligently damaged some ancient wall drawings in a cave in southwestern France. Cultural officials announced that they would file a complaint against the group for their destruction of the prehistoric art. The head of the youth group, however, saw the negligence that led to the damage as that of the cultural officials who had failed to designate the cave a national treasure.

Lack of resources and public support often makes it difficult for museums, especially those in the Third World, to preserve the art entrusted to them. The public in many African nations regards museums as elitist Western institutions that display objects that have been stripped from the context in which they were created to function. The governments of poor nations earmark their scant resources for food, health care, and other purposes that have higher priority than the preservation of traditional art. Inadequate budgets—the 1989 budget for the National Museum in Mali was $2,000—do not allow museum directors to buy the conservation equipment and chemicals they need to preserve art, and little money is available to install climate-control equipment that would inhibit the natural deterioration of the objects. Because most of those pieces are made of organic materials, they are highly susceptible to heat, humidity, fungi, insects, and rodents. Given that resources are not adequate to preserving all traditional art, some experts have suggested that curators will have to choose which objects to preserve and which to allow to deteriorate (Decker, 1990).

Destruction of Art by Its Owners and Caretakers

Those who have purchased or inherited art and those who are the executors of the wills of deceased artists have sometimes deliberately destroyed works of art, assuming that their ownership or control of the art gives them the right to do so. Art has been altered, dismembered, and even destroyed because of changes of taste, a desire to maximize profits by selling pieces of a work of art, and the belief that art should be broken up and spread among as many appreciative owners as possible (Failing, 1980). Many regard such damage merely as disrespectful of the art and its creator, but do not call it vandalism because it is usually legal to destroy property that one owns or legally controls.

Others suggest that the law should require owners first to try to dispose of their art through sale or donation, and only allow them to destroy the art if no one is interested in acquiring it. They argue that artists try to speak to posterity through their work, and that the destruction of any of their work, even by a legal owner, infringes on artists' freedom of expression. Art is seen as having an intrinsic value to all of humanity, and owners are regarded merely as caretakers who have no moral right to destroy it. That belief was the basis of the public outrage that greeted the wish expressed by Japanese businessman Ryoei Saito in 1991 that he be buried with van Gogh's *Portrait of Dr. Gachet* and Renoir's *At the Moulin de la Galette*, paintings for which he had paid a total of $160.6 million the year before. Had Saito not recanted, many people would have seen his taking the two great pictures with him to his grave as little different from the acts of vandals, with both depriving the world of an important part of its artistic heritage.

The desire to alter the appearance of buildings and public places led to the destruction of many murals painted during the Great Depression by artists working for the Federal Art Project when those paintings were later defined as obstacles to the development of an area or when they no longer matched the public's taste (Berman, 1989:79). Another instance of the destruction of art by its legal owner occurred in 1980, when developer Donald Trump ordered workers to destroy with jackhammers several art deco architectural sculptures and some ornate grillwork on a building he was replacing. Trump had earlier promised the pieces to the Metropolitan Museum of Art if they could be removed at a modest cost, and the museum accepted the offer. Trump later decided that the friezes were "without artistic merit" and had a resale value of less than $9,000. He said that preservation of the pieces would delay by at least ten days the demolition of the building and cost his company $32,000 (on a project costing $100 million). Citing danger to passersby as another reason not to remove the pieces from the building, Trump had them destroyed (Berman, 1989:80).

Sometimes the owners of art seek to profit by damaging or destroying art. The wish to make more money led the sister-in-law of American artist Robert Henri to destroy thousands of his works after his death. She reasoned that if there were fewer of his works around, they would have greater value and be easier to sell. She slashed and burned paintings that offended her or that she judged to be of inferior quality. She even bought a rubber stamp marked "Destroyed" to save her the trouble of repeatedly writing that word in the artist's record book (Berman, 1989:78).

Auction houses and dealers have tried to maximize their profits by breaking up antiquarian books that contain drawings, prints, or maps in order to sell the freed pieces individually at a greater total price than they would fetch as intact books. No law in the United States prohibits this practice, because the damage is done by the owner of the book, but at least since 1900 some rare book dealers have regarded such behavior as reprehensible. At about that time, the 200 copies of the double-elephant-folio edition of Audubon's *Birds of America* began to be dismembered and sold piecemeal; today only fifty or sixty copies of that book are still in their original bindings (Singer, 1987:67).

In 1989, Sotheby's in London announced that it would break up one of two remaining sketchbooks by eighteenth-century French artist Hubert Robert, saying that it would be difficult to sell the book intact because few collectors would pay as much for an object they could not display on the wall as the auction house could fetch if it sold the drawings individually. A Sotheby's official said that the auction house was obligated to get as high a price as possible for the sketchbook's owner, and that the house was a commercial enterprise, not a museum devoted to the preservation of art. The decision to break up the sketchbook was criticized by art historians as a scandal and grotesque and led to the resignation of one consultant to the auction house. Those critics claimed that it was important to keep such books intact because they revealed the sources of artists' inspirations and the ways they worked and developed their ideas. In response, the auction house announced that it would first auction the sketchbook in sixty-eight individual lots, and then at the end of the bidding offer the sketchbook intact to anyone who would pay the total amount of the winning bids for the individual drawings. A Sotheby's official suggested that the critics form a consortium to buy the intact sketchbook, but the critics complained the auction house had not given them enough time to raise the funds to do that (Kimmelman, 1989b).

In defense of its decision to break up the Robert sketchbook, Sotheby's noted that in the past it had often failed to sell complete albums of drawings, and that when it did, the buyers were sometimes dealers who broke up the books anyway. One dealer renowned for freeing maps and prints from books, sometimes even in the auction house where he had just purchased them, is W. Graham Arader III. One dealer comments about Arader's practices as follows:

What bothers me about Graham is that he cuts up books. That is not the book trade. You can't collect *prints* that way. If you want to collect *prints*, then you must collect things that were made as prints in the first place, not plates removed from books that a dealer has destroyed. What offends me is such a dealer's failure to appreciate that a rare book has a numinous presence beyond the physical borders of the book itself. (cited in Singer, 1987:66–67)

Arader justifies this practice as "democratizing" art, making the prints or maps torn from books available to more collectors at prices lower than the intact book would cost. What is really involved is his desire to make money; the individual prints or maps can be sold for a sum far greater than what the intact book would bring. Critics suggest that if Arader's practice were carried to its extreme, dealers might cut up paintings or break up sculptures into smaller pieces that could be sold individually, obviously destroying the aesthetic value of the original, but allowing more collectors to have a fragment of an original work, say a piece of a painting by Brueghel or Bosch. One map dealer suggests that Arader's practices are not unique to him, but are instead common among dealers; he says, "If you can find a bookseller who has never broken a book, I'll be amazed. There's an awful lot of hypocrisy about that" (cited in Singer, 1987:67).

In recent years, laws have been passed to give artists the right to prevent those who own or control the art they have created from altering, damaging, or destroying it. Many European nations now distinguish works of art from other types of property, prohibiting the destruction or alteration of art without the artist's permission and guaranteeing artists the right to the integrity of their works, even after they have been sold. A Canadian law passed in 1988 gave artists the moral right to prevent the mutilation, destruction, modification, or commercial use of their art, even by someone who owns it. Canadian artists are allowed to secure an injunction, sue for damages, or get an accounting of the profits made from the offensive material. Those rights exist for the life of the artist and for the estate for fifty years after the artist's death.

In the United States, a 1949 court decision upheld the right of an owner of a mural to destroy it if he had legal title to it, but since the 1970s American artists have grown militant about protecting the integrity of their works. In 1973, when the executors of the estate of eminent American sculptor David Smith had paint stripped from several of his pieces, a practice he had vigorously protested, sculptors and painters objected strenuously. Since that time, artists have periodically complained about changes to their works, claiming that such changes destroy or alter the uniqueness of the art on which their reputations are based. Complaining that one of his murals had been changed by another artist who had been hired to make additions, artist William Smith asserted that the alterations had desecrated his work and that it was traumatic for him to look at the mural. His signature was still on the picture, which he said had become "an embarrassment to my name and reputation" (cited in Molotsky, 1987:C21).

In 1988, painters, sculptors, and film directors lobbied Congress to pass a law that would prevent alterations to their work after it left their possession, unless they first approved of the changes (Honan, 1988). They hoped to get the United States to sign the Berne Convention for the Protection of Literary and Artistic Works, an international agreement that emerged from an 1874 conference. The Berne Convention states:

Independently of the author's economic rights, and even after the transfer of said rights, the author shall have the right to claim authorship of the work and to object to any distortion, mutilation or other modification of, or other derogatory action in relation to, the said work, which shall be prejudicial to his honor or reputation. (cited in Mitgang, 1989:B7)

When Congress passed the Berne Convention Implementation Act of 1988, the United States joined seventy-seven other nations as members of the convention. However, because the act stated that the moral right clause would not be enforced in the courts of the United States, the actual meaning of the Berne Convention for American artists remains unclear and will emerge only as the courts apply it in specific cases.

The resolution of a highly publicized controversy a year later suggested that the law might do little to protect an artist's work from alteration or destruction after title to the work had passed to others. Sculptor Richard Serra had bitterly opposed an effort by the federal government to remove from a Manhattan plaza his 120-foot-long, 12-foot-high rusting steel sculpture, *Tilted Arc,* in order to make room for benches and chairs and make it possible to hold concerts there. Critics of the piece had said it was ugly, attracted graffiti, obstructed the flow of traffic, and destroyed what little open space there was in the area. The artist claimed that the sculpture, which had been commissioned by the government, had been created for the space that it occupied, and that removing it would effectively destroy it as well as violate his First Amendment right to freedom of expression. In 1988, a federal court declared that "the First Amendment has only limited application in a case like the present one where the artistic expression belongs to the Government" (cited in Dunlap, 1989b:32). Later, Serra argued that the removal of the sculpture would violate his moral right to the work under the Berne Convention. When his lawyers advised him that neither that treaty nor the federal law implementing it could prevent the federal government from removing the sculpture, Serra gave up his fight, proclaiming the Berne Convention a "meaningless piece of paper" (cited in Dunlap, 1989a:B2). The sculpture was removed, with federal officials saying that the government held full title to the sculpture but would treat it with respect and store it safely. Serra replied that the work was site specific and that he would never allow it to be shown again with either its title or his name attached. Interestingly, federal officials remarked that removal of the sculpture had returned the plaza to the original architect's conception of the space; the earlier addition of Serra's sculpture had apparently destroyed another artist's conception of the plaza.

The 1990 federal Visual Artists Rights Act gave artists the right to disavow a work of theirs that had been altered and the right to prevent owners from changing their works except for conservation. The way that this law will be implemented and its actual impact are not yet clear.

As of 1991, Massachusetts was one of eleven states with laws prohibiting the destruction of a work of art by anyone but the artist, with a few specified exceptions. One action brought under that law involved Elaine Yoneoka, an artist-in-residence during the 1985–1986 academic year at Concord-Carlisle High School. With her students, Yoneoka had created and signed a mural and donated it to the school. A few years later, the school disposed of the mural. Yoneoka sued the school, saying that she had to have large pieces available for potential clients to see in order to get commissions for other large works. She sought $65,000 in punitive damages and compensation for the destruction of the mural and the loss of a second commission because a potential client could not see the mural. School officials said they had not disposed of the mural maliciously, that the artist had been employed by the school, and that the school owed the artist no damages because the Massachusetts law specifically exempted art created by employees within the scope of their employment. As has been true of most cases brought by artists under such laws, the plaintiff and the defendant settled their differences out of court.

Damage during Wartime and Civil Insurrection

Nondeliberate damage to works of art sometimes occurs during wartime and civil insurrection, when harm is the by-product rather than the aim of the violence. For instance, the World War II bombing of Dresden, Germany, by Americans destroyed much important art and architecture.

Prior to the outbreak of the 1991 war in the Persian Gulf, scholars expressed concern over the possible destruction of ancient works of art and architecture in Iraq, a country described as containing the roots of Western culture. Iraq contains as many as half a million archaeological sites, including up to fifty thousand described as quite important and as many as two hundred that had been ancient capital cities. Scholars worried that unexcavated sites would be harder to dig up if they were bombed or overrun with tanks, and that such sites might be destroyed before they could be unearthed. Some scholars demanded that the war not be started so as to protect Iraqi museums and monuments, but others suggested that such an attitude was callous when so many lives were at stake. General Colin Powell, Chairman of the Joint Chiefs of Staff of the United States, said that every possible effort would be taken not to bomb cultural and religious sites, but critics feared that the bombing of military targets would inevitably damage nearby ancient sites. Despite the intensive bombing of Iraq during the war, damage to ancient sites and museums seemed to be minimal, according to reports from the Iraqi government. However, after the war the United Nations embargo led to changes in agriculture such as extensive irrigation canals and widespread plowing that do seem to have endangered archaeological sites.

The December 1989 uprising that led to the ousting of Rumanian President Nicolae Ceaucescu's Communist government devastated important works in the National Museum of Art. Ceaucescu's elite bodyguard troops used the museum as a fortress, firing on people outside with rifles, machine guns, and bazookas. Members of the Rumanian army joined the people in fighting against the troops inside the museum, shooting out the building's windows and making holes in its walls. Before retreating into underground tunnels, Ceaucescu's troops set fire to the museum, destroying the entire archives of the graphic arts and decorative arts departments and burning at least ten paintings beyond recognition (Binder, 1990).

DELIBERATE VANDALISM

Property can be damaged or destroyed in various ways, but the criminal law only defines an act as vandalism if it is deliberately committed by someone other than the owner of the property. That law is not enforced

equally against everyone who damages or destroys property, but is applied
only to certain behavior in specific circumstances. Acts of destruction that
threaten the interests or values of the powerful and wealthy are especially
likely to be punished as crimes of vandalism. Responses to acts of destruction are influenced by the symbolic importance of the property, both its
meaning in terms of a people's cultural heritage and the threat to the
institution of property posed by its destruction. Responses to vandalism are
also affected by the market value of the damaged property and the cost of
repairing or replacing it. Destructive acts seem to be more likely to be
defined as crimes of vandalism if they are committed by individuals rather
than by groups; group activities such as the wartime bombing of museums
and terrorist attacks on monuments are not generally regarded as vandalism
(Cohen, 1973a, 1973b).

The Social Context of Vandalism

In one sense, it is surprising that there is not more vandalism of art than
there is. The public has relatively free access to art in museums, churches,
and galleries, and few measures are taken to keep unruly or destructive
people out of such places. Moreover, art is usually displayed in ways that
leave it open to defacement or destruction. Curators prefer that museum
visitors be able to view artworks that are unencumbered by glass, barriers,
or devices designed to prevent vandalism, leaving the art vulnerable to
attack. Damage is rare enough and usually easy enough to repair that most
curators would rather risk vandalism than diminish the viewer's experience
of the art. Sometimes particularly valuable or popular works are given extra
protection, and guards and barriers are often added to artworks that have
recently been restored after vandalism in order to inhibit copycat attacks.

Most people who enter public places to look at art have not been explicitly
taught how to behave in the presence of art, but most of them treat the art
with respect and do not even consider damaging it. How is it possible to
provide an unscreened, unsupervised, and untrained public with such open
access to art and yet suffer so little vandalism?

To some degree, the audience that looks at art in public settings is
self-screened. People who go to museums differ from the general population
in ways that might lead us to expect that they would be less apt than the
average citizen to commit acts of vandalism: they are more educated, have
higher incomes and higher-prestige occupations, and are more likely to be
female (Hooper-Greenhill, 1988; Robinson et al., 1985:100, 102). All of
those variables are associated with relatively low rates of criminal behavior
in general, and probably with relatively low rates of vandalism as well.

Even though most museum-goers are not explicitly taught how to behave in museums, they are subtly socialized as to how to look at art. They approach works of art with a respect based on news reports about how valuable art is. The age of many works endows them with a degree of venerability. By interacting with and observing others in the museum, visitors learn to speak in hushed and reverential tones, stand back from a work of art while looking at it, and avoid touching the art. Visitors who do touch works of art will probably be told not to by a guard, letting them know that they are not as unsupervised as they had thought. Signs sometimes instruct visitors not to touch works of art.

Despite these formal and informal controls on the behavior of visitors to museums and other institutions, deliberate vandalism does occur. The deliberateness of vandals' actions is often clear from the tools they use to inflict damage on art: hammers, hatchets, knives, paint, acid, fire, even bombs.

Explaining Deliberate Vandalism

Theories of vandalism must explain the behavior of those who destroy or deface property. Often the accounts of their actions given by the vandals make some sense, but their explanations are often disputed by law-enforcement officials, the press, and the public. Theories of vandalism need to tell us why vandals choose to attack art rather than some other form of property and why they select a particular work of art to damage or destroy. Their selectivity often makes sense in terms of the accounts they offer for their actions, but may make little or no sense in terms of the explanations offered by the police or the press; a vandal who believes he is Jesus Christ might be able to explain why he attacked Michelangelo's *Pietà*, but an official explanation of the vandal as insane does not illuminate his choice of that sculpture rather than some other work of art.

Vandalism as Residual Deviance. Art vandalism is an example of what sociologist Thomas Scheff (1984) calls "residual deviance," rule-breaking behavior that does not fit into any other socially recognized category of deviant behavior. In twentieth-century Western societies, situationally inappropriate behavior that has no rational explanation is often attributed to mental illness. Vandalism often appears to be motiveless, because it produces no apparent reward for the offender, as would a theft. Because art is symbolic rather than functional in nature, art vandalism is even less likely than vandalism in general to have a rational explanation. Defacing a painting because a voice has told the vandal to attack the picture fits no generally acknowledged form of rule-breaking, and so it is frequently treated as a manifestation of mental illness.

Psychiatric explanations of art vandalism might strike many of us as correct interpretations of such seemingly irrational behavior, but such explanations are a twentieth-century creation, a product of the medicalization of deviance. Defining vandalism as the product of insanity helps society blame "sick" individuals rather than look at vandalism as a meaningful attack on the symbolic order by individuals who are fully aware of what they are doing. Fine and Shatin (1985) see two opposing forces involved in the symbolic drama of interpreting the meaning of art vandalism. Vandals try to portray their actions as legitimate, claiming that the work they attacked was chosen because it symbolizes the state or the community. On the other side, museum officials, the media, and the public try to transform acts of vandalism into meaningless behavior with no legitimacy, often labeling the vandal as insane. In this way, vandalism can be interpreted as an uncontrollable event, an inexplicable disruption of the social order, rather than as a challenge to that order.

The Seductive Appeal of Vandalism. In his innovative analysis of the "seductions of crime," Jack Katz (1988) suggests that shoplifters endow store merchandise with the power to seduce them to commit a theft; the objects are regarded as animate, as exerting a pull on the shopper. One shoplifter writes as follows:

There we were, in the most lucrative department Mervyn's had to offer two curious (but very mature) adolescent girls: the cosmetic and jewelry department. . . . We didn't enter the store planning to steal anything. In fact, I believe we had "given it up" a few weeks earlier; but once my eyes caught sight of the beautiful white and blue necklaces alongside the counter, a spark inside me was once again ignited. . . . Those exquisite puka necklaces were calling out to me, "Take me! Wear me! I can be yours!" All I needed to do was take them to make it a reality. (cited in Katz, 1988:54)

In Katz's perspective, criminals construct a social reality that draws them to law-violating behavior. In doing so, they are impelled by various emotions: boredom, despair, exasperation, resentment, failure, or frustration (Cohen, 1973b).

Vandals also endow works of art with a seductive power, claiming that the subject of the work or the artist who created it speaks to them in some mystical fashion. David Freedberg (1989) suggests that vandals attack art not only because it symbolizes the wealth, power, and religion of its owners, but also because vandals attribute life to the figure the work represents. He suggests that art historians should pay more attention to the way that people respond to art, the way that images appear, and the power those images are thought to possess by those who view them. When vandals attack works of art, they seem to target famous paintings and sculptures, suggesting that a work's notoriety makes the image more seductive to them. Even the security measures installed to protect famous works may attract a vandal's attention by suggesting that the work is a worthy target.

Art does seem to have a magical appeal, eliciting strong emotional and even behavioral responses from some people who look at it. According to the chief of psychiatry at a hospital in Florence, Italy, some people perspire heavily, hallucinate, fall into depression, faint, become euphoric, feel omnipotent, or feel persecuted when in the presence of great art. Those most likely to become disoriented have been characterized as impressionable, unmarried, between the ages of twenty-six and forty, traveling alone or in small groups, and without much experience away from home. People who live nearby, travel in large groups, or carefully plan their itineraries seem to be less apt to respond to art so emotionally. Critics of this psychiatrist's study minimize the role of art in causing such extreme reactions, claiming that travel itself is tiring and makes it more likely that psychiatric symptoms that are already present will manifest themselves. Indeed, more than half of the 107 patients said by the Florence psychiatrist to have become disoriented in the presence of art had previously seen a psychiatrist or psychologist (Haberman, 1989). What this study suggests is that people with certain predisposing psychological characteristics in particular social situations might experience strong emotional or behavioral responses to art. Learning more about the combination of factors most likely to elicit such reactions might illuminate the sources of vandalism, one extreme behavioral response to works of art.

Vandalism as Social Protest. Dario Gamboni (1983) has used the theories of Pierre Bourdieu to argue that art vandalism is a social protest by people who regard themselves as outsiders to an art world that foists on them objects they cannot understand. Because only a small elite participates in the production and distribution of art, most people do not understand the art and so feel socially inferior and educationally disadvantaged when those symbols are thrust at them, especially in public places. When classical works of art are attacked, it is usually because they symbolize the privileges of the ruling class or the power of the state. When contemporary art is vandalized, however, it is because people do not understand it or resent the high prices paid for objects that seem to require little skill to create. The general public thinks that it is being made fun of when an old bathtub is displayed as sculpture or when a canvas with a few streaks of paint is called art. Feelings of incomprehension and noncommunication engender frustration and resentment, which can then give rise to destructive attacks on art (Dornberg, 1987; Gamboni, 1983).

Gamboni has shown that some works of art are more susceptible to vandalism than others. Sculptures are less likely to be attacked if they are made of material that is more expensive and more traditionally used by artists; bronze pieces are more likely to be left alone than pieces made of plastic or iron. Objects that seem to have required more work by the artist are less apt to be targeted by vandals than those that suggest less craftsmanship. Modern art seems more susceptible to damage and destruction than classical art. Artworks displayed in more revered and better maintained settings such as museums are less likely to be vandalized than objects displayed in public places, where people who do not understand the art will feel that their space has been intruded on by incomprehensible objects that remind them that they are outsiders to the world of art. In 1980, forty-four of 107 artworks displayed outdoors at the Swiss Sculpture Exhibition in Bienne were vandalized; those works had all of the aforementioned characteristics that make artworks especially susceptible to vandalism. In addition, Bienne was an economically depressed town populated with unemployed metalworkers who resented the high prices commanded by sculptures that seemed to require little skill to produce (Dornberg, 1987; Gamboni, 1983).

The Justifying Rhetorics of Art Vandals

People do not usually offer justifications for their behavior, but they may do so if their actions convey no obvious meaning and if they think their behavior will be negatively evaluated by others. Because attacks on works of art appear to most people to be senseless, as they provide no material gain, art vandals often try to explain the meaning of their behavior (Fine and Shatin, 1985). Sometimes they proclaim a political or ideological purpose for attacking artworks that symbolize the dominant social order. They also profess to be morally offended by the content of the art. Other vandals express pleasure in the act of destruction, claim to be impelled by voices from outside the normal world, or say they destroyed the art for pragmatic reasons.

Political and Ideological Goals. Vandals sometimes have political or ideological goals, seeking through their acts of destruction to challenge established rules or beliefs. They may articulate moral justifications for their actions as they deface the work of art, or they might do so after they are apprehended. Vandals whose political or ideological goals threaten those in power might be punished more severely than vandals who damage and destroy art for other reasons (Cohen, 1973b).

Art vandalism was given political meaning during the French Revolution, when Parisian mobs pulled down statues of kings and burned paintings of royalty and nobility. Torn between a respect for the nation's artistic heritage and a recognition that art had been used as an instrument of social control, the revolutionaries generally supported the preservation of artworks until 1792, the year of the Paris Commune. After that uprising, a law was passed that decreed that feudal objects that had dangerous ideological content should be destroyed, and iconoclastic mobs deliberately set about the razing of monuments to the fallen monarchy (Idzerda, 1954).

For at least two centuries then, crimes against art have been a weapon of revolutionaries who recognize the symbolic value of art and attacks on it. Although art is most often defaced and destroyed as a protest against ruling class dominance, in some cases the ruling class itself has destroyed art that offends its political beliefs. As a result of an eighth-century edict by a Byzantine emperor, works of art depicting sacred figures were destroyed. A Diego Rivera mural at New York City's RCA Building was demolished in 1934 when the artist, an acknowledged Communist, refused to remove from the painting a portrait of Lenin, a symbol that the ruling class regarded as especially offensive and threatening because of the Great Depression. In 1943, the Nazis stockpiled and burned in a huge bonfire in the interior courtyard of Paris's Jeu de Paume Museum some five hundred paintings by Miró, Klee, Ernst, and other artists whose works the Nazis considered "degenerate" or "too Jewish." Thousands of such works were deliberately destroyed by the Nazis during the war.

Most vandals who give political reasons for their attacks on art claim that it represents a social order that unfairly favors the wealthy and powerful and oppresses the less fortunate. In 1990, two artists used knives to slash two paintings on display at an art fair in Paris, saying that they hoped by their actions to focus the world's attention on American imperialism and the inflated art prices that it engendered. The French press speculated that the financially unsuccessful artists may have been angered by a newspaper article the day before that quoted a price of more than $6 million for a painting on display at the show (Cremin, 1990).

Political terrorists damage or destroy art to show people that their rulers cannot protect even the most valued parts of their cultural heritage. Through such symbolic attacks, terrorists hope to weaken the resolve of the state and undermine its public support. Those attacks are a means of communication, a way to get free publicity for a cause. For terrorists who are well educated, art may be an especially important symbol of the social order they seek to destroy (Fine and Shatin, 1985).

During the second decade of the twentieth century, British suffragettes attacked works of art as symbols of an oppressive state that would not let women vote. One of them, Mary Wood, justified her destruction of a John Singer Sargent portrait as follows: "I have tried to destroy a valuable painting because I wish to show the public that they have no security for their property nor for their art treasures until women are given their political freedom" (cited in Fine and Shatin, 1985:138). The suffragettes, who attacked eleven works of art in a five-month period in 1914, opposed the taking of human life, but they were nonetheless engaging in terrorism. One activist described their vandalism as premeditated, rational, and under-standable, if not excusable. The suffragettes' vandalism was a way to oppose an oppressive social order, focus media attention on their struggle, build support, spread ideas, and destroy the security of their opponents. In contrast to the suffragettes' claim that their vandalism was a political act, wealthy and powerful groups insisted on seeing the vandals as mentally unbalanced. Admitting that their actions were aimed at getting women the vote would have acknowledged the goal being sought by the suffragettes, given their cause credibility, and perhaps encouraged other social movements to attack art to achieve their purposes. When confronted with art vandalism that has a political goal, the ruling class strategically tries to define such acts not as organized political behavior but rather as erratic, senseless behavior by deranged individuals (Fine and Shatin, 1985).

A more recent act of vandalism in which an expressed political motiva-tion was rejected by the authorities in favor of a definition of the attacker as mentally ill involved the 1987 defacement of a da Vinci drawing known as "the Leonardo Cartoon," which some experts valued at more than $35 million. Robert Cambridge entered the National Gallery in London with a concealed sawed-off shotgun and shot at the drawing from seven feet away. He later told the police that he had wanted to show his disgust with "political, social, and economic conditions in Britain"; he did not make it clear why he chose that picture as the target for his wrath (Rule, 1988:C15). His ideological explanation was not accepted by the authorities, and he was committed to an institution for the criminally ill.

Even vandalism that is obviously motivated by political beliefs is often interpreted as the act of a deranged person. In 1978, a bomb exploded at the Versailles Palace in France, damaging that architectural work of art and destroying several paintings that had been commissioned by Napoleon. Eventually, two members of the separatist Breton Liberation Front were arrested for the bombing. That group explained its attack on the widely recognized symbol of the nation's cultural heritage as a protest against the oppression of Bretons and the destruction of their culture by an imperialistic

French regime. Contrary to the group's political explanation of the bombing, the French public and press generally agreed that the bombing made no sense and was the product of unbalanced individuals. The attack might be seen as senseless in that it did not seem likely to help the Breton Liberation Front achieve its goals, but it did manage to communicate to the world the political goals of a group of which few people had previously heard (Fine and Shatin, 1985).

Another political act of art vandalism occurred in Guatemala in 1981, when a group of rebels scrawled graffiti on monuments and burned the laboratory and administrative wing of the museum at a Mayan site, destroying invaluable documents on the history of the site's excavation. The rebels also killed two people and stole nine jades from the museum. Apparently the insurgents intended to show the local people that their rulers were incapable of protecting their cultural heritage, although there were rumors that they were trying to raise money by ransoming the jades back to the government (*Stolen Art Alert*, September 1981).

In 1989, three Chinese men were charged with vandalizing a portrait of Mao Tse-tung that hung in Tiananmen Square, the scene of a pro-democracy revolt. The men had thrown black and red paint on the portrait, which was quickly removed by workers and replaced with a picture much like it. The vandals were seized on the spot by other demonstrators, who, after some discussion, turned them over to the police, saying that they opposed such acts of destruction. At the time, Mao was a somewhat ambiguous figure in China, revered as leader of the Communist Revolution but criticized for his role in the Cultural Revolution; nevertheless, he was still venerated by most Chinese, and the government interpreted the defacement of his portrait as a symbolic attack on the established order. The three vandals were found guilty of counterrevolutionary destruction and counterrevolutionary incitement and were sentenced to prison terms ranging from sixteen years to life. A 1992 report by Now Asia Watch said that the men had been tortured in prison, and two of them had been kept in solitary confinement in small dark cells that lacked heat and ventilation.

In 1989, a statue of Jefferson Davis, president of the Confederacy, was vandalized on the University of Texas campus at Austin, with the words "Roots (of KKK) fight racism now!" painted on the statue's base. The culprits were not immediately apprehended, but the defacement of the statue was linked to a protest against racism and for civil rights and to a campaign by black students to raise money to erect a statue of the Reverend Martin Luther King, Jr., on the campus. To black students, the defaced statue and three other statues that commemorated the Confederacy symbolized past and present policies of racial oppression. Students critical of the vandalism claimed that the memorials to the Confederacy had historical value.

A devastating act of art vandalism occurred in Florence, Italy, on May 27, 1993, when a car bomb exploded near the Uffizi Gallery, killing five people and wounding more than twenty. The bomb destroyed three paintings and damaged thirty-three other works; protective glass prevented even more harm. The authorities suspected that the bombing was the work of the Sicilian Mafia, which had recently been under aggressive attack by the government and which two weeks earlier had apparently aimed a similar bomb at a journalist critical of the Mafia. However, the Mafia did not claim credit for the Uffizi bombing, and some observers speculated that it might have been the act of political terrorists who were trying to destabilize the government. However, in Italy the line between political terrorism and Mafia violence is a thin one, with one former crime boss remarking that the Sicilian Mafia "is cultivating its old dream of being independent, of having a state of its own" (cited in Stille, 1993:2).

Offended Morality. The destruction of art is occasionally motivated by an offense to the vandal's sense of personal morality or standards of taste. In some cases, the culprit legally owns or is in control of the art. For example, a devout Catholic bought and destroyed an 1863 painting by Gustave Courbet that depicted a procession of drunken clerics, a picture the artist hoped would offend the church (Berman, 1989:75).

Art critic John Ruskin was made an executor of J.M.W. Turner's works after the artist died in 1851, leaving three hundred oil paintings and nineteen thousand drawings and watercolors to Great Britain. When Ruskin discovered that Turner's *oeuvre* included what he described as obscene drawings of prostitutes "in every posture of abandonment," he felt a "burden" had been thrust on him to protect Turner's reputation. He apparently urged the staff of London's National Gallery of Art to burn the drawings, which it did in 1858. According to Ruskin, "I am satisfied that you had no other course than to burn them, both for the sake of Turner's reputation (they having been assuredly drawn under a certain condition of insanity) and for your own peace" (cited in Berman, 1989:74–75).

A sense of offended morality also provoked an unknown vandal to deface glass photographic plates of works by E. J. Bellocq. Many of the pictures had been taken in the opium dens and red-light districts of New Orleans. Of the thousands of pictures that Bellocq took, only eighty-nine plates survive; on some of them, the faces of the New Orleans prostitutes have been scratched out, although the vandal might more easily have broken the glass plates.

Portraits that offend the subject, the subject's descendants, or others who revere the subject have frequently been destroyed. Thomas Eakins's portraits were often unflattering, leading to the destruction of at least eight and perhaps as many as twenty-three of the 246 known portraits that he painted; others were rejected outright by their subjects. British artist August John was once sent a package containing a portrait he had painted, with the subject's head cut off; the subject later told the artist that the painting had been too big for the place he had planned to hang it, so he had to make it smaller by taking off the head. The two parts of the painting were reunited after the subject died. In the 1920s, King George V commented to two officers of the Royal Academy of Art about a portrait of himself that he "would like to see the damned thing burnt"; they took him literally and destroyed the picture (cited in Berman, 1989:77). In 1955, Clementine Churchill burned a Graham Sutherland portrait of her husband Winston that neither of them thought flattering. Churchill had warned Sutherland to paint a flattering picture, saying, "Clemmie didn't like my portrait by Sickert, you know. She put her foot through it" (cited in Berman, 1989:79).

Most of these acts would not be prosecuted as crimes of vandalism, because they were committed by people who owned or had legal control of the works of art. However, recent changes in the law have given artists the right to prevent owners from destroying or altering works that the artist created, raising the possibility that civil suits, if not criminal charges, could be brought against those who destroy art they own or control.

Vandalism as Play. Much of the vandalism that occurs in museums is by groups of young people who are seeking relief from boredom through pranks, making fun of what others regard as serious, competing with friends for attention, or hoping to earn the respect of their peers for their courage or creativity. Often their play vandalism is not malicious, and they might not even regard it as criminal (Cohen, 1973b).

Vandals sometimes find it pleasurable or satisfying to destroy property. Those who break windows may enjoy watching the glass explode, observing the pattern of the broken glass, and listening to the tinkling shards. According to Allen and Greenberger (1978:313), the "enjoyment of a destructive act derives primarily from the visual, auditory, and tactual-kinesthetic stimuli that occur during the rapid transformation of material (destruction): this is the time when one experiences most intensely the 'fun' of destruction." They suggest that the "appearance of certain objects in the environment, a person's anticipation of the enjoyment during the vandalism, and perhaps also the anticipation of the postdestruction appearance of an object" can act as *eliciting cues* that produce vandalism or as *discriminative cues* that influence the selection of a particular target from the pool of potential targets (Allen and Greenberger, 1978:313). Even long after their acts of destruction, vandals remember with great clarity their feelings at the time of the act, the physical appearance of the property they damaged, and their reasons for choosing a particular target. This suggests that their behavior was not random and that they paid great attention to the consequences of their vandalism.

Vandalism can also be motivated by a sense of challenge. In the 1920s, a statue of Venus rising from the sea was placed in front of Venice (California) High School. The model for the statue was a sixteen-year-old student who later became Hollywood movie star Myrna Loy. Over the years, that statue has been repeatedly vandalized by students; they have dressed it in brassieres and hats, adorned it with flowers, painted it, even tarred and feathered it. In 1978, the vandalism became more violent, with the statue's head and one arm blown off by dynamite. After that attack, the school considered getting rid of the statue, but a local sculptor named William van Orden volunteered to restore it. Someone ripped off the statute's head the day after his restoration was unveiled. That was the first of about a dozen restorations he has done, each followed by vandalism. Van Orden remarks, "I think I'm inspiring some youngsters out there to counteract what I do. I don't think they're attacking Myrna. I think they're attacking me." While van Orden was working on the statue one day, "a student walked up, and he had the most malevolent look on his face, and I said, 'What's the matter, young man?' and he said, 'Don't bother fixing it, you old fool. I'll destroy it again.' " One student said her peers would continue to vandalize the statue "because they think it's funny"; they tell each other, " 'He's going to fix it again.' " After the 1989 restoration, which van Orden said would be his last because he was dying of cancer, the statue was housed in an iron cage. He commented, "They're going to need blowtorches to get in" (all citations from Mydans, 1989:A14). Given the vandals' creative efforts to date, the use of blowtorches would not have surprised anyone.

Religious Motives. Some art vandals claim that their actions are caused or inspired by forces outside the everyday world in which people live. Their explanations, which are often couched in religious terms, make sense to them but are usually not accepted at face value by others, who often regard them as mentally ill.

A 1972 attack on Michelangelo's marble sculpture of the Pietà was committed by Laszlo Toth, who was quoted as saying:

Today is my thirty-third birthday, the age when Christ died. For that reason I smashed the Pietà today. I did it because the mother of God does not exist. I am Christ. I am Michelangelo. I have reached the age of Christ and now I can die. . . .

Certainly you can kill me; go ahead and kill me; but I am Jesus Christ and if you kill me I am going straight to heaven. (cited in Fine and Shatin, 1985:143)

Toth did substantial damage to the great marble figure with a hammer, although the sculpture was restored to nearly perfect condition in eight months. Toth never clearly related his delusions to his act of vandalism, but he seemed to know that he had to offer some explanation for his attack. Religiously inspired vandalism is often justified in terms that have some internal consistency; Toth might be seen as delusional in thinking that he was Jesus Christ, but if he truly thought that, then his belief that he had the right to destroy a statue of himself makes some sense. Religiously motivated vandals typically refer to the specific target of their attack; they do not choose targets randomly, but rather in a purposive way to achieve some particular goal.

The press, the public, and the legal system defined Toth as mentally unbalanced, a label based not on available psychiatric evidence but rather on the apparent pointlessness of his attack and on his claim to being two long-deceased historical figures. Rather than focusing on Toth's regular church attendance and his calm demeanor as he was questioned by the police, the press emphasized past and current behavior that was consistent with labeling him as insane. Instead of treating vandalism such as Toth's as a serious threat to the social order that warrants harsh punishment, a response that would acknowledge the meaningfulness of the act, the courts typically label vandals as insane, institutionalize them for short periods, and thus define them as outsiders to the community (Fine and Shatin, 1985).

In 1975, a Dutchman named Wilhelmus de Rijk used a bread knife to inflict significant damage on Rembrandt's *Night Watch,* one of the world's most highly regarded paintings. During the attack, he said, "I have been sent by the Lord. I have been forced to do this by forces out of this earth" (cited in Fine and Shatin, 1985:143). According to one report, de Rijk said that God had ordered him to begin remaking the world by destroying the world, both the good and the bad things in it. He said he began with Rembrandt's painting because it embodied forces of both light and dark. In attributing responsibility for his destructive act to the Lord, de Rijk couched his explanation of his vandalism in a historical and religious context; by following God's dictates, he was behaving in the way that saints such as Joan of Arc had. In modern times, however, acting at the command of voices that only one person hears is more often defined as mental illness than as grounds for beatification. The press treated de Rijk as a lunatic, and indeed he had a history of serious mental disturbance. On the morning of his attack, he had caused a commotion by taking a seat in the pulpit of the church where

Rembrandt was buried, claiming to be the artist's son. Eventually, he was declared mentally ill and committed to an institution; a year later, he committed suicide (Fine and Shatin, 1985).

Pragmatic Motives. Some vandals have pragmatic reasons for damaging or destroying art, reasons that can readily be understood even by people who condemn their actions. Thieves who steal artifacts containing precious metals and jewels engage in vandalism when they melt down the metal and strip the stones, selling the raw material for its market value. From the time of Henry VIII until the nineteenth century, English churches were stripped of their monumental brasses, which were melted down to bolster the nation's treasury. In the early nineteenth century, Lord Elgin observed Turkish occupational forces in Greece burning ancient sculptures for the lime in the marble; they used the lime to build houses and fortifications. At the end of World War II, the Soviet Red Army's brigades that had been sent into Germany to loot artworks melted down numerous bronze and copper objects. In 1979, a security guard at Boston's Museum of Fine Arts stole a quarter of a million dollars' worth of ancient jewelry from the museum and had it melted down to sell for its scrap value. Drug-addict thieves have stolen bronze sculptures from New York galleries and sold them for the scrap value of the metal. Rising prices for gold, silver, and other metals can increase the destruction of works of art that are stolen for their scrap value.

Antiquities looters sometimes break up the objects they unearth to make it easier to sell or smuggle them; they have also destroyed or discarded material they cannot sell, perhaps because the origin of the pieces would be apparent to experts. Vandals have broken pre-Columbian objects unearthed in Mexico into small pieces that were easier to get past customs officials as uninteresting potsherds; the objects were then reconstructed when they reached their destination, although that left them in worse condition than they had been immediately after excavation. John L. Hess (1974:161) has suggested that an ancient Greek vase purchased for $1 million by the Metropolitan Museum of Art in 1972 had probably been expertly broken into pieces for illegal export and then reassembled after leaving Italy. His circumstantial evidence is that none of the many breaks in the vase cross any of the ten human faces painted on the surface, something highly unlikely to have occurred by chance.

Efforts to curb the illicit trade in antiquities can have the unanticipated consequence of encouraging vandalism. In 1972, Congress adopted the Pre-Columbian Monumental Sculpture and Murals Statute, which prohibited the importation into the United States of large stone pieces such as murals, pieces of temples, and steles (inscribed stone slabs). Intended to curb the destruction of temples and monuments in Latin America, this law actually made things worse, because looters began to break into tombs in search of smaller items not covered by the law.

One pragmatic reason for art vandalism is for thieves to minimize their risk of arrest and punishment by destroying art that they cannot sell for a profit and do not want to be caught with. The *huaqueros* who looted the Sipán tomb in Peru knew they could sell objects of silver and gold, but they destroyed hundreds of ceramics, ornaments, and textiles that they did not think were marketable. Bonnie Burnham (1980a:3) has noted, "Perhaps the most disconcerting aspect of the growth of art theft is the way in which each incident seems to add credence to the idea that paintings are stolen for some highly lucrative turnover. More often, in reality, the objects remain in the hands of casual thieves who are unable to negotiate them. In these hands, their greatest risk is destruction." Even experienced thieves sometimes have difficulty converting stolen art into cash. A burglar who regularly sold stolen art to a Boston art dealer said that over the course of his criminal career he had destroyed about ten paintings that he was unable to sell. Another thief claimed that during his criminal career he had burned or cut up more than fifty paintings that his fence would not buy (Golden, 1989:35).

The reasons for the defacement and destruction of art are many; some vandals act deliberately, and others damage art through neglect or ignorance. The impact of their behavior, intentional or not, is a significant loss of humanity's cultural heritage. Some damaged works of art can be restored, often not to their original beauty, but others are destroyed forever. How much damage and destruction has occurred is difficult to determine; harm to art still in the possession of its owners can be measured, but how many stolen works that have not been recovered have been destroyed by thieves unable to sell them and unwilling to risk being caught with them?

Curbing Art Crime

Because theft, smuggling, vandalism, forgery, and fraud are inextricably linked to the social organization of the art world, efforts to curb art crime must be grounded in an understanding of the way that world contributes to crime. The manner in which museums, dealers, and collectors house and display art can be changed to reduce the risk of theft and vandalism. Illicit transactions can be minimized by publicizing stolen and illegally exported artworks and by buyers investigating the origin of all pieces they consider for purchase. Public regulation and professional self-policing of dealers and auction houses can protect buyers from fraud and from deceptive behavior that artificially raises prices and thereby increases the motivation to steal and defraud. Giving the victims of theft longer to recover their art and lengthening the time after the theft during which thieves can be prosecuted would make art crime more risky and deter some offenders. Educating law-enforcement agencies about the importance of art crime and providing them with more resources to combat such crime might lead to more arrests and more recovery of stolen art. The trade in illicit antiquities could be curbed by international efforts to impede looting and smuggling.

IMPROVING SECURITY FOR ART

Better security for works of art will not always thwart sophisticated and determined criminals, but it can dissuade amateurs and opportunists from engaging in vandalism, theft, and smuggling.

Inhibiting Vandalism

Security measures can reduce art vandalism, though at a cost. As one critic remarks, "In their eagerness to protect and conserve the monuments entrusted to them, more and more curators and conservators are erecting barriers around them that violate the open, anti-institutional spirit that is almost the essence of modernist art" (Brenson, 1988:29). Berlin's New National Gallery, which experienced a disastrous attack on a Barnett Newman painting in 1982, now has an electronic surveillance system that rings shrill bells if anyone gets closer than eighteen inches to a work of art. At the 1964 New York World's Fair, Michelangelo's *Pietà* was exhibited behind a bulletproof glass barrier with a guard on duty around the clock; the public was shuttled past the sculpture on three levels of moving platforms. New York's Metropolitan Museum of Art covered with glass its $2 million acquisition, Rembrandt's *Aristotle Contemplating the Bust of Homer,* making it difficult to appreciate the surface texture of the oil painting. Measures such as these protect art but diminish the museum visitor's aesthetic experience of the work; one observer notes,

What we see is less a great painting than a picture of the way a museum believes a great painting now has to be treated. It is becoming a fact of life in museums that the more revered the art, and the greater the public desire to make pilgrimages to art's ever more holy body, the more it has to be protected from public contamination, and the more the holy body begins to suggest relics in a crypt. (Brenson, 1988:29)

Nevertheless, security measures such as guards and barriers have undoubtedly protected some unknown number of artworks from the depredations of vandals. In one case, a vandal who sprayed paint on Picasso's *Guernica* in New York's Museum of Modern Art did no lasting damage to the oil painting because it had been protected with a coat of varnish.

Damage to art in transit by careless airport workers, truckers, and customs officers is probably more common and more costly than the damage done by deliberate vandals. Especially at a time when prices for art are high, insurance expensive, and requests for loans frequent, owners must carefully evaluate the fitness of their artworks for travel and minimize the impact of shock, vibration, and variations in temperature and humidity on works in transit (Cassidy, 1991).

Public monuments are especially vulnerable to damage from the effects of the environment and from deliberate vandalism. The World Monuments Fund, an organization concerned with the preservation and care of monument art, has educated local residents about the importance of art, especially its potential for boosting the local economy by attracting tourists. Jobs have been created in those communities by training people in the skills needed to preserve monuments. Another approach is New York's Adopt-a-Monument program, which enlists foundations, corporations, and individuals to contribute funds to the restoration and maintenance of a particular monument that has been damaged by vandalism, the effects of the environment, and neglect. By getting patrons to care for public art, the city government admits that it cannot maintain the monuments by itself, but it creates a proprietary interest on the part of the patrons in preventing or undoing the ravages of vandalism, pollution, or deterioration with age. Vandalism in public museums might also be curbed by creating a greater proprietary interest by the public in an institution's art, perhaps by emphasizing the way that admissions fees are used to buy art for the museum's collection and deemphasizing donations of art by wealthy patrons.

Dario Gamboni (1983) has argued that what is needed to curb art vandalism is more art education. Improved museum security deals only with the symptoms of the problem by erecting barriers between the art-viewing public and the works of art. Instead, Gamboni claims, from the earliest years in school the masses need to be educated about art so as to minimize the resentment that stems from their incomprehension of such symbolic representations. To make people feel less excluded from the world of art, they need to be taught how to look at and appreciate art and how to understand what artists are trying to communicate (Dornberg, 1987).

Securing Art against Theft

Just as a determined vandal can thwart the best efforts to protect a work of art, so too can sophisticated thieves usually find a way to steal art. If electronic alarm systems effectively prevent a nighttime burglary, thieves will turn to armed robbery or larceny by stealth when the museum is open. Guards can be overcome by surprise or trickery at night and by force during the day. Even electronically alarmed paintings can be snatched from the wall if the thieves are able to get away before the police respond.

Despite the variety of criminal tactics available to art thieves, some theft can be thwarted by security measures. Because major museums seem to be at risk more from weak internal security than from weak external security, potential employees—especially security guards—need to be carefully screened, well trained, and well paid. Museums should avoid displaying objects in cases that can easily be smashed or pried open; cases that are used should be individually alarmed. Viewing areas should be designed to maximize surveillance by security guards, and guards should make sure that all pieces on a list of the works for which they are responsible are in place at the start and at the end of their shifts (Mason, 1979).

Most major museums in the West are now well protected from entry during the hours they are closed; in fact, their electronic external security has been cited as a reason for the apparent decline in burglaries of those institutions over the past two decades. However, effective external security seems to have displaced crime in three ways: thieves now steal more often by stealth during the hours that museums are open to visitors, they are more likely to use force or the threat of force to steal when museums are open, and they are more apt to seek out less well-protected targets such as small museums, houses, galleries, and churches. If all buildings that housed valuable art were alarmed with the most advanced security systems available, some thieves might give up art crime altogether rather than shift from burglaries to robberies and larcenies. However, the limited resources available to most owners of art other than large museums makes that unlikely. Given the continued existence of less well-protected targets, the theft of art will probably continue to be displaced from large museums to buildings from which it is easier to steal art. In sum, better security can reduce a particular institution's risk of suffering a theft, but that will not necessarily reduce the overall amount of such theft.

Security can be improved in art galleries by strategic placement of employees' desks to maximize surveillance, by limiting the number of visitors if the gallery becomes too crowded to maintain adequate surveillance, by frequently checking all rooms, and by displaying vulnerable pieces some distance from exits. A network among gallery owners can share information on suspicious visitors and commonly used techniques of theft, thereby alerting all dealers to possible threats to their art (Pearson, 1985b). When thieves are apprehended, dealers should press criminal charges rather than simply be satisfied with recovering their art; otherwise, thieves will see little risk in such crime.

Preventing the Looting and Smuggling of Antiquities

Curators, dealers, and collectors often assert that stopping the illicit trade in antiquities depends less on their efforts than on measures that the countries of origin should undertake. They argue that the governments of those nations should not only pass cultural patrimony laws but also must allocate the resources to enforce such laws, police ancient sites to prevent looting, and ensure that customs agents are honest and diligent in their efforts to prevent illegal exportation. The illicit antiquities trade might also be curbed by marking objects so that they can be identified by customs agents in other countries. In 1988, customs agents in Miami discovered fifty-one pre-Columbian artifacts that had been smuggled out of Peru; the objects were identified by stamps affixed by the Peruvian government when they had been registered under the country's cultural property law.

For relatively poor nations such as Turkey and Peru to police the extensive regions that hide troves of buried antiquities is a prohibitively expensive undertaking; even the wealthy United States cannot effectively patrol the areas of the Southwest that conceal unexcavated Native American sites. The governments of source-countries often do not even learn about major discoveries of antiquities until the objects turn up abroad. Then they must begin expensive and time-consuming litigation in foreign courts to recover that property, a process that risks a diplomatic crisis. In such lawsuits, the government must establish the source of the object in question, a difficult problem if it is not unique and if the government does not know precisely when and where it was unearthed.

Westerners often claim that if source-countries are sincere in their desire to prevent cultural property from leaving their countries, they should implement better export controls. In many source-countries the legal export of antiquities is very difficult, but bribing customs agents to allow such objects to leave the country is easy. One museum director comments as follows:

Do you know that more than half of what we pay for a fine African object is paid in bribes to government officials? We pay, in spite of the fact that in these countries the antiquities protection laws would often not stand up in court. We pay because everyone pays. This is the accepted way to obtain an object. Everybody within the country is making so much money that nobody is anxious to see strictly legal channels employed. (cited in Burnham, 1975:140)

India is one nation that has a vast supply of antiquities but no effective policy for curbing their illegal export. The failure of India's policy can be seen in the case of the Siva Nataraja of Sivapuram, a sculpture unearthed in India in 1952 and eventually purchased by American millionaire Norton Simon (Burnham, 1975). The Indian government had declared that the sculpture must remain in a local shrine rather than be placed in a museum, where security would be better but public access more limited. Because religious artifacts in India are controlled by cults rather than by the state, local priests have the right to sell them, although the state can refuse buyers permission to export pieces they have legally purchased. When the Nataraja turned up in New York in the early 1970s, India demanded its return, claiming that it had been exported without a permit. At the time the piece left India, it took at least two years to get an export license, the chance of being caught illegally exporting such an object was small, and the government rarely contested the illegal export of pieces on which it placed a low priority. Referring to the Nataraja and other Indian antiquities in Western museums, Norton Simon remarked, "Of course, they were probably smuggled. Nothing that comes out of India really isn't smuggled" (cited in Burnham, 1975:179).

After achieving their independence from colonial powers, many African nations became more interested in their cultural heritages. Realizing that their cultural property was rapidly being depleted by wealthy dealers, museums, and collectors in the United States and Europe, those countries passed cultural patrimony laws and began to collect indigenous art in national museums. Cultural property first had to be offered to the national museum, which usually had meager resources with which to purchase such objects; only if the museum rejected an object could the finder apply for an export license, which might be refused anyway. Antiquities officers in those nations often paid little attention to the international antiquities market, focusing instead on matters that they could control, such as the issuing of export licenses and the maintenance of national museums. Government officials often seemed to be concerned about the illegal export of cultural property more because it represented lost revenue for the state, which could sell the property or at least tax its sale, than because they deplored the loss of their cultural heritage (Burnham, 1975:131).

Western dealers, curators, and collectors have suggested that the illicit trade in antiquities might abate if source-countries with strict but unenforced export laws loosened them and made it easier to buy and export antiquities that are less valuable and more common. They point out that in some countries virtually every pot that is unearthed is defined as patrimony, until and unless the finder can convince bureaucrats to issue an export license. When there are thousands of virtually identical pieces, each one adds little or nothing to a nation's cultural heritage. Westerners thus argue that there is plenty of material to satisfy everyone's interests and that source-countries could protect and retain important pieces while permitting more common objects to circulate freely in the international market. They point to Japan and Great Britain as nations that distinguish between treasures that must stay in the country and less important objects that can be traded freely. However, neither Japan nor Great Britain is now a major source of antiquities that are being unearthed from previously unknown locations, and both are stable and highly organized societies that can devote considerable resources to law enforcement (Bator, 1981). Even if major source-countries such as Turkey and Peru loosened their cultural property laws, competition for the most prized pieces would continue to be intense; dealers, curators, and collectors would still try to export those pieces illegally if they could not be acquired through legal channels.

PUBLICIZING ART CRIME

Because thieves have a difficult time selling stolen and smuggled art that is easily recognized, the immediate circulation of photographs and other information to dealers, auction houses, newspapers, and magazines can reduce the incentive for art crime. Even if thieves can sell such highly publicized art, they will probably have to accept a lower price for it, which might weaken their motivation to steal again.

Museums, galleries, churches, and collectors need complete inventories of their holdings so that they can quickly determine what is missing after a theft occurs. Once they determine what has been stolen, publicity will be most effective if they have color photographs, invoices, and other documentation about the stolen art's provenance. That information can help the police know precisely what they are looking for and allow them to describe more accurately the objects that dealers, curators, and collectors might unwittingly buy. The Italian police report that they recover about 70 percent of stolen objects that have been photographed but rarely locate objects that are undocumented (Stille, 1992). Similarly, the FBI reports that only 5 percent of all stolen art and other valuables in its files is ever recovered, but that 90 percent of that property that is recovered has been clearly photographed. Not only do photographs make recovery more likely, but they make it easier for victims to verify that they are the rightful owners once the stolen art is recovered. The FBI encourages owners to store color photographs, videotapes, notes on the dimensions of the pieces, invoices, and other documentation in a location separate from the place where the artworks are kept (Robinson, 1990).

Some victims of art theft are reluctant to report and publicize their losses. They worry that publicity might impede the recovery of their art by encouraging the thieves to smuggle it out of the country or hide it in a vault for years; without publicity, reason those victims, their art is more likely to turn up soon after the theft. An oriental carpet dealer in New York who did not report the 1981 theft of five of his rugs found four of them in the local wholesale rug market a few days later. Private collectors sometimes do not report their losses because they do not want it generally known what they have in their collections. Collectors, museums, and dealers are also concerned that publicity about their victimization might draw attention to their vulnerability and make future thefts more likely. In a more general way, publicity about art theft can backfire by educating potential thieves about the high prices that art commands on the legitimate market, the difficulty the police often encounter in recovering stolen art, and the low risk of arrest and conviction for art thieves.

Despite the possible negative effects of publicity, on balance the reporting of art theft and the circulation of information about stolen art help in the apprehension of thieves, the recovery of stolen art, and the prevention of crime. Reporting crime helps law-enforcement agents establish patterns of theft and alert potential victims to their vulnerability. In New York, several shopliftings and thefts from smashed windows were not reported to the police by gallery owners, making it difficult for the police to discern the pattern and extent of such crimes. The failure to report crime also makes it difficult for the police to determine the rightful owner of art that is recovered when a thief is arrested.

IFAR has made a major contribution to the recovery of stolen art by publishing photographs and information on missing objects in its newsletter. The newsletter both disseminates information about what has been stolen and strengthens the owner's claim to the property if it is recovered. After it publicized the theft of three pre-Columbian bowls from Tulane University in 1980, a Los Angeles dealer who was offered the bowls recognized them as stolen and called IFAR and the FBI; the bowls were recovered and returned to the university. In 1986, a New York real-estate developer bought an ancient Roman sculpture from a Swiss dealer, who shipped it to the developer's Manhattan office. The developer then noticed a photograph of the statue in *IFAR Reports*, which stated that the piece had been stolen from an Italian amphitheater. The developer returned the sculpture, saying that he was pleased that it had been brought to his attention that it had been stolen. The dealer refunded the purchase price on the condition that his name not be mentioned. The developer said that he understood that the Swiss dealer had bought the statue from an Italian dealer, who apparently had purchased it from a peasant who had found it on his land (McGill, 1986a).

What is now needed is a complete international stolen art registry that is readily accessible to all individuals and institutions that own art, including nations with cultural patrimony laws that define antiquities as state property. IFAR's Art Theft Archive is the closest there is to such a system, but it could be improved with more funding and more cooperation from law-enforcement agencies, national governments, insurance companies, museums, dealers, and collectors. An ideal system would be fully computerized and have the capability of rapidly transmitting faxed color photographs of stolen art throughout the world. It would also incorporate information on stolen art from existing national registries, such as Canada's Repository of Stolen Artifacts (ROSA). As of 1991, IFAR's files were being put into a system that allows the matching of color on-screen images; this system includes data from Sotheby's, Christie's, the Society of Fine Art Auctioneers, Lloyd's of London, and the Art Loss Register. If information from other nations, especially Third World countries, is eventually incorporated into this system, it would help in the recovery of stolen art and antiquities by allowing any individual or institution considering a purchase to check that a piece had not been reported stolen or illegally exported. An increased rate of recovery would undercut the motivation to steal and smuggle art.

EDUCATING THE PUBLIC

Art crime might be reduced if the public were better informed about the problem. Public pressure can force museums to return stolen and illegally exported antiquities to their source-countries. Informed tourists and collectors might refuse to buy antiquities of doubtful origin if they knew the consequences of the illicit trade in those objects. Visitors informed about theft and vandalism could point out to museum guards the vulnerability of works that are being exhibited (Burnham, 1975:242–43).

Given the strong demand for good art, collectors should be wary of bargains or their good luck in finding pieces priced significantly below market value. Today there is a greater risk associated with buying art, especially for the purpose of investment, than was true in the 1960s, when fakes were less common and prices lower. Experts now tell collectors to spend years looking at art before making major purchases, and then buy only what they like and pay only what they can afford to lose should they decide to sell and find no interested buyer.

Collectors can help stem the tide in counterfeit prints by learning more about art and checking more carefully on the techniques used to produce the prints they are considering buying. Customers who suspect that dealers are selling counterfeit art should put them on notice by telling them that the art is questionable. Those who purchase fakes or forgeries should report the seller to the authorities rather than keep quiet for fear of embarrassment at being duped.

Gallery and museum exhibitions of counterfeit art have helped educate the public, art historians, collectors, and museum staff about the existence of fakes and forgeries, alerted them to the methods used by counterfeiters, and trained them to look more carefully at art. In 1986, the McIntosh-Drysdale Gallery in Washington, D.C., mounted an exhibition of fakes and forgeries in the possession of the FBI. The following year, Baltimore's Walters Art Gallery had a similar show of sculpture, jewelry, porcelains, and medieval and Byzantine art. The gallery juxtaposed the real with the fake to show art forgers' strategies, such as borrowing a motif from one medium to use in another and adding forged parts to otherwise authentic works. The exhibition demonstrated that most forgeries and fakes are discovered because of faulty iconogaphy, inexact workmanship, and by being "too much, too good" (Cohen, 1987:58). In 1988, the Museum of American Folk Art co-sponsored a similar show, displaying counterfeit folk art alongside authentic pieces. That exhibition divided fakes and forgeries into three categories: objects that had been made to deceive, objects that had been "improved" to enhance their market value, and modern objects that had been made innocently but had been "resold until they became pricey enough to have to be old" (Bohlin, 1988:A15).

Buyers should have artworks authenticated before buying them, because money-back guarantees from unscrupulous dealers are worthless. Art appraisers are not regulated by federal or state law, but the better ones are certified by the International Society of Appraisers or the American Society of Appraisers. Even though those professional organizations require their members to complete courses and pass tests, membership does not guarantee competence and so references should be asked for before hiring an appraiser. Because appraisers who charge fees based on the total value of the art might be tempted to overvalue it, those professional organizations have ethical guidelines that prohibit appraisers from working on commission, and the IRS disallows such appraisals; instead, appraisers should charge hourly or daily fees.

Art that is definitively identified as counterfeit should be stamped as such; a law such as France's, which requires fakes and forgeries to be confiscated and destroyed by the authorities, would reduce the chance that counterfeit art will make its way back to the art market in the future (Goodrich, 1973; Menn, 1987). In the United States, even if a counterfeiter is found guilty and punished, and even if the work of art is declared inauthentic, the work is usually returned to the owner, raising the possibility that it will eventually be offered for sale again. Asserting that fakes and forgeries should be confiscated by the state and destroyed, John Henry Merryman of Stanford Law School says that not doing so is "like allowing a batch of counterfeit money after it's been shown to be counterfeit to go out there and be recirculated again" (cited in Cornell, 1986:2). To prevent counterfeit art from showing up again, one Boston insurance appraiser has been systematically recording every forged or faked work of art she can learn about, as well as the names of the buyers of those works (Menn, 1987). In the absence of a law requiring the destruction of fakes and forgeries, a national registry of such counterfeit art might reduce its recirculation.

ETHICAL ACQUISITIONS POLICIES

One way to reduce the illicit trade in antiquities and preserve ancient sites from the depredations of looters is for museums to adopt ethical acquisitions policies. Such a policy was adopted in 1970 by the museum at the University of Pennsylvania: no piece would be purchased unless it had a pedigree certifying that it had been legally exported from its source-country. The following year, the International Council of Museums adopted a similar policy, and in 1986 it adopted a code of ethics prohibiting members from acquiring looted artifacts. In 1989, a museum director claimed that slightly more than half of museums "would never acquire a piece of another country's culture" (cited in Temin, 1989:42). Nevertheless, some museums continue to purchase questionable objects, justifying such action by the lack of interest that source-countries have shown in preserving their own heritage and citing the failure of those nations' ministries of culture to answer letters from museums inquiring whether specific pieces were stolen or illegally exported.

Bonnie Burnham (1975) has questioned the impact of ethical acquisition policies. Although the purchase of stolen and illegally exported antiquities by museums does stimulate looting, she claims that it does not follow that a refusal by museums to buy those objects will significantly reduce the illicit trade. Museums that refuse to buy antiquities often find that competing museums will buy those objects, perhaps storing them in vaults for many years to allow any controversy to subside. Even more likely is the purchase of those illicit objects by private collectors, who have fewer scruples about provenance and are less influenced than museums by ideas about what constitutes an ethical acquisition. Collectors are not pressured by other collectors to make ethical acquisitions in the way that museum curators are pressured by their professional peers to conform to such standards. Questionable purchases by private collectors might have limited investment value; the pieces could be sold privately, but the museums that refused to buy them in the first place would probably not accept them as donations either, making it impossible for the collector to claim a tax deduction.

Today, museums are more likely than they once were to check the sources of antiquities carefully and to repatriate objects that were stolen or illegally exported from the country of origin. That cooperation seems to have resulted more from curators' desire to avoid public embarrassment to their institutions than from the enforcement of international agreements. In some cases, governments have pressured museums or private collectors in their country to return questionable objects to source-countries in order to avoid the disruption of international relations that could result from a legal dispute over the antiquities.

In 1988, the Thai press accused the United States of using a helicopter to airlift a millennium-old carved sandstone lintel from a temple during the Vietnam War and demanded that the piece be returned so that the temple could be fully restored. Another part of that temple had been returned to Thailand after being discovered in California. The United States Department of State asked for a quick resolution of the dispute but denied that the lintel had been stolen, claiming that it had been "purchased by someone in the open antiquities market in Bangkok" and that it "was shipped to New York somehow. Who in Thai customs let it out? Why was no one interested then? How was it allowed out of the country?" (cited in Wilkerson, 1988:14). The United States government took the position that the Art Institute of Chicago held legal title to the lintel and that it was Thailand's responsibility to stop the illegal exportation of its antiquities. However, in late 1988 the museum agreed to return the lintel to Thailand in exchange for a piece of equal merit to be donated to the museum by a Chicago philanthropic organization.

In 1988, Boston's Museum of Fine Arts agreed to return to Egypt fragments of tomb paintings that had been in its possession for a decade, although they had never been displayed. The museum's director said that in light of evidence that the fragments had been stolen, repatriation was the right thing to do. He also noted that returning the fragments would maintain Egypt's cooperation in museum-sponsored digs in that country. When asked what the museum would have done had the antiquities been of greater value, either economically or in terms of the museum's collection, the director responded that in that case he would have tried to negotiate a long-term loan that acknowledged Egypt's ownership of the antiquities, or he would have returned the pieces and tried to negotiate a loan of objects of similar significance (Temin, 1989).

One international dispute that was amicably resolved involved some thirteenth-century Byzantine frescoes said to have come from a defunct chapel in the Anatolian region of Turkey. The foundation to which the frescoes had been offered for sale was suspicious, because the pictures looked non-Turkish and because they were said to belong to an anonymous Turkish gentleman. The foundation's directors sent a clearly worded letter, accompanied by photographs, to the cultural ministries and Washington embassies of the nine countries from which the frescoes might have come. It took two months to get a reply, during which time the directors worried that the Turkish gentleman might learn of their inquiries and sell the frescoes elsewhere. Finally, the Washington embassy for Cyprus replied that the frescoes had been stolen in 1974 from a Cypriot church shortly after the Turkish occupation, perhaps with the knowledge of the Turkish military. The foundation's directors then had to figure out how they could maintain the safety of the frescoes without alerting their owner, who might destroy them if he feared legal action. Through a Cypriot patron of the arts, an arrangement was worked out with the Cypriot Department of Antiquities and the Greek Orthodox Church of Cyprus, the rightful owner of the frescoes, that permitted the foundation to buy and restore the frescoes and place them in a chapel to be built on the foundation's grounds in Houston. The frescoes were to be on view there for fifteen years, with the arrangement subject to review thereafter (Hoving, 1988).

Bonnie Burnham (1975) has suggested that the illicit trade in antiquities might be curbed if museums could work out official exchanges or loans with the governments of source-countries rather than seeking to acquire such objects for themselves. Such a change would not, however, reduce the demand by private collectors for antiquities. Burnham's proposal also minimizes the desire of museum curators to build important collections for their museums, and building such collections means owning objects rather than simply displaying them. In addition, displaying the loaned cultural property of other nations might increase the interest of collectors in the heritage of those cultures; this could stimulate demand for such artworks, raise their price, and give thieves and looters a greater incentive to supply such objects to the dealers and middlemen in the illicit antiquities trade.

REGULATING DEALERS

Crime in the art world is controlled to some degree by professional associations. For example, the Art Dealers Association of America has established guidelines to curb fraud. However, membership in that organization is limited to dealers who have been in business for at least five years, and, according to one dealer, 95 percent of galleries go out of business in less than five years (cited in de Coppet and Jones, 1984:246). Membership in the ADAA is also voluntary, so disreputable dealers might not choose to join or be allowed to join. Moreover, the power of the ADAA over its members is limited; it can expel dishonest dealers but cannot take legal action to punish them.

In 1988, the New York City Department of Consumer Affairs announced that it would begin enforcing a city ordinance requiring galleries to post in a conspicuous place a list of the prices of all paintings and sculptures that were on display and for sale. The agency hoped that enforcement of the ordinance would combat the "price manipulations" that are "endemic" to the New York art world and reduce the "vagaries of mystery, theater, and snobbery" encountered by visitors to galleries (cited in McGill, 1988a:C17). This enforcement effort followed a 1987 investigation by the department's undercover agents, who presented themselves as potential customers but had a difficult time getting firm answers about the prices for various works of art.

Gallery owners protested the enforcement of the ordinance, arguing that it would lead to the unseemly commercialization of the atmosphere in galleries, perhaps eliciting rude comments and jokes about prices. They claimed that galleries are like museums, providing free exhibitions to the public. According to dealers, most visitors to galleries are just looking and are not potential customers in any real sense, and anyone who is interested can ask for a price list; in reality, price lists were not available in some galleries. Dealers asserted that posting prices would interfere with the public's enjoyment of the art, because people would react to the prices rather than to the art itself. Those who favored the posting of prices rejected the idea that galleries are like museums, seeing them instead as commercial establishments engaged in the business of selling art for profit. This point of view was articulated in a letter to the *New York Times*:

Art galleries are stores. Their proprietors, the art dealers, are merchants. Their primary purpose is to sell art in order to make a profit. They are not houses of worship. They are not museums. They are not schools. They are not eleemosynary institutions. The dealer is not an altruist dedicated to educate and elevate the public. He is a pragmatic businessman. . . . The art merchant should not take on the aura of the gifted artist and think that he is different from those who sell Tiffany jewelry, Halston clothes, Bergdorf furs, or used cars. (Alvin S. Lane, cited in Lyons, 1988:32)

Dealers argued that the ordinance requiring retail establishments to post prices was designed to allow customers to compare the prices of different items, but the unique nature of artworks makes such price comparisons meaningless in art galleries. This raises the question of how dealers manage to set prices for different pieces of art if comparisons among works are meaningless.

According to some dealers, the absence of a price list encourages interaction between gallery staff and the public. However, some visitors might prefer to browse and consider prices without engaging the gallery owner in conversation. Moreover, some visitors might be too intimidated to ask about prices, and the secrecy of prices could thus impede rather than stimulate interaction between the public and dealers. Dealers do employ a variety of strategies to intimidate visitors, allowing them into the gallery only after pushing a buzzer and passing a receptionist's inspection, marking off areas with velvet ropes, telling them they will have to be added to a waiting list for an artist's works, and instructing employees to be aloof rather than friendly (Gardner, 1991).

Some dealers worried that posting prices would threaten gallery security by informing potential thieves of the value of the art. The Executive Director of the International Foundation for Art Research agreed, "The recent decision to enforce truth in pricing at art galleries introduces a serious new security risk. Providing thieves and vandals with a shopping list will only add to the growing number of art crimes in New York" (cited in *The New York Times*, May 1, 1988:H40). Whether posted price lists will actually increase art theft is unclear, but they might well guide thieves to particular works within a gallery.

Some dealers responded to the enforcement of the ordinance by posting prices in inconspicuous places. In the six months following the announcement of the enforcement effort, nineteen violations of the ordinance were discovered during investigations of sixty-five galleries. All but one of the $200 fines were promptly paid (*The New York Times*, September 18, 1988).

REGULATING AUCTION HOUSES

The deception of auction house audiences, which has at times approached the fraudulent, was the subject of regulations implemented by the New York City Department of Consumer Affairs in 1986. Works offered with a secret reserve had to be so noted, even though the amount of the reserve did not have to be specified. Because auction houses reacted by marking all lots as having a reserve, this regulation resulted in no additional information for potential bidders. Auction houses were also required to announce immediately after completion of the bidding if a piece had failed to sell because it had not reached its reserve; previously, audiences had sometimes been led to believe that a piece had sold when it had actually been withdrawn for failing to attract a bid above its reserve. These and other changes were less sweeping than the reforms for which some critics of auction house practices had hoped.

Both auction houses and dealers need to be held more strictly accountable for accepting works of art under suspicious circumstances. Newsletters and flyers publicizing stolen art that are sent to auction houses and dealers should obligate them not to accept the stolen objects. Paintings that have been cut or torn from a frame, are presented unframed or wrapped in towels, are offered at far below market value, or are in the possession of someone who refuses to give a permanent address or demands cash as payment should make auction houses and dealers suspicious. Under such circumstances, they should be expected to contact the police.

Concerned with such auction house practices as the secret reserve, bidding from the chandelier, financing purchases by bidders, and guaranteeing prices to consignors, New York Assemblyman Richard L. Brodsky suggested at a combative 1991 hearing that perhaps art transactions should be covered by the same state regulations that govern securities investments. The situation most often cited as showing the need for such regulation was the $27 million loan by Sotheby's to Alan Bond to purchase van Gogh's *Irises* for $53.9 million in 1987; Bond used the painting itself as collateral for the loan, on which he later defaulted. Sotheby's has discontinued this practice, but as of 1991 it was still legal under New York auction rules. Because such practices can cause art prices to be "overestimated, overpublicized, and/or inflationary," Brodsky suggested that auction houses should be required to disclose information in the same way that companies were required to when they issued stock (Glueck, 1991:C14).

REGULATING THE INSURANCE INDUSTRY

In Great Britain, it is an offense to advertise to pay thieves directly for the recovery of stolen property on a no-questions-asked basis. In the United States, where such unconditional rewards are legal, insurance companies sometimes pay, usually 10 percent of the insured value of the property, for the recovery of stolen property (Fine, 1992). Those rewards are often paid to agents or middlemen who are hired by the thieves to exchange the property for the reward, which is then divided among the thieves. Sometimes the agents and middlemen are actually the thieves themselves. The payment of such rewards usually leads to the recovery of the stolen property but not to the arrest, prosecution, and conviction of the thieves. Insurance companies are less interested in the apprehension and punishment of the thieves than they are in the recovery of the stolen property, which means that they do not have to compensate their policyholders for their losses.

Prohibiting insurance companies from paying rewards even to the thieves' representatives might reduce art theft for ransom. Great Britain's Theft Act was passed in 1968 to curb theft for ransom by defining the dishonest handling of stolen property as a crime; a trial a short time later indicated to the insurance industry, art thieves, and middlemen that theft for ransom would no longer be tolerated by law-enforcement agencies. Art theft for ransom might be curtailed by requiring a conviction before any reward is paid, although such a law would probably have little impact on the overall problem of art theft, because relatively few such crimes are committed for ransom. Such a law might also inhibit the reporting of the location of stolen art by people who have no knowledge of who committed the crime. Such a law would be difficult to enforce in the United States, where the insurance industry is regulated more at the state than national level, and where even state regulation is sometimes ineffective. Unless the regulation of insurance companies becomes both uniform and stricter, they will probably continue to pay for the return of the art when they believe that doing so is in their best interest.

REFORMING THE LAW

Legal reforms might reduce art crime, but their impact will be muted by the international nature of the traffic in stolen art and the absence of any effective international law-enforcement agency.

Statutes of Limitations and Title Disputes

Following a theft, art is sometimes smuggled to a nation where the legal power to prosecute thieves expires quickly. There it is held in a vault or other hiding place until the statute of limitations expires. Thieves in France cannot be arrested after five years has passed from the time of a theft; in Great Britain and the United States the period is seven years, and in Italy and Germany it is ten years. After they can no longer be prosecuted, thieves sometimes offer to sell the stolen art back to the original owner, usually for less than its market value but more than it would fetch on the black market. If the original owner is not interested, the thieves turn to the black market, where the art might be sold to a dealer or collector (Burnham, 1975:47).

In addition to impeding the criminal prosecution of thieves, statutes of limitations in some countries protect good-faith or bona fide purchasers of stolen art. In common law nations such as the United States and Great Britain, a buyer cannot usually acquire good title from a thief, but in nations such as France, Switzerland, and Japan whose laws derive from the Roman civil code, good-faith purchasers are favored over original owners (Lowenthal, 1991b). In France, a bona fide purchaser acquires title to a stolen work three years after purchase, if the art was bought from an established dealer or in an open marketplace such as an auction or flea market. In Switzerland, title to stolen property is passed when it has been in the country for five years and is sold to a good-faith buyer, a term interpreted with some latitude in that country. A Japanese buyer becomes a good-faith buyer automatically by purchasing art in a shop or at an auction and acquires title to even stolen art after two years; prior to that time, an original owner can recover stolen art only by reimbursing the buyer for the amount that he or she paid for it. The laws of civil code countries stimulate markets in stolen and smuggled art, whereas the common law tradition encourages buyers to exercise due diligence before purchasing art (Lowenthal, 1991b).

Even when stolen art is recovered before title passes to another person, owners often encounter obstacles to getting it back. Recovery is facilitated if the victim has bills of sale, photographs, or other documentation of ownership. If the statute of limitations has not expired, the art might be held to be used as evidence in a criminal proceeding against a defendant accused of theft or receiving stolen property. Recovered art might also belong to an insurance company that has already compensated the owner for his or her loss. The company usually tries to sell the art as quickly as possible, typically offering it first to the original owner in exchange for the money that was paid for the claim. However, the insurance company might also put the work up for auction, where it could fetch more than the amount paid to the owner if its value has appreciated since the theft. To protect themselves from this contingency, some owners have policies that spell out exactly what will happen if one of their works of art is stolen and later recovered. Most owners want the right of first refusal on a recovered piece but do not want to be required to buy it back, especially if it has been damaged (Grant, 1986). If the original owner is reluctant to accept back the recovered art in exchange for the money paid by the insurance company to satisfy a claim, the company's investigators might suspect that the owner colluded in the theft or fraudulently claimed that the art had been stolen. That occurred in New York in 1987, when the owner's refusal to buy back thirty-seven recovered pre-Columbian pieces, valued at $1.8 million, led to his indictment for insurance fraud.

A complicated case that in the end failed to clarify how the statute of limitations should be applied to title disputes began in 1946, when artist Georgia O'Keeffe failed to report to the police or advertise the theft of three of her paintings. She circulated the story of the theft in the art community, but she was unwilling to confront the acquaintance she suspected of taking the pictures. In 1972, she finally reported the theft. When an art dealer said that he had bought and then sold the paintings in 1975, O'Keeffe demanded that the paintings be returned to her. The dealer refused, claiming that New Jersey's six-year statute of limitations had long since expired.

In the United States, a thief cannot pass good title to stolen property, and a buyer cannot acquire good title, unless the statute of limitations has expired. Statutes of limitations for title disputes are based on the legal principle of repose, the idea that good-faith buyers who currently possess property that was stolen in the past should at some time be free from the fear that the property they have paid for, cared for, and believe is theirs might be taken from them. Critical to the application of statutes of limitations is the discovery rule, which specifies at what point the period during which a rightful owner must bring a lawsuit begins. The original owners of stolen and illegally exported artworks want that statutory period to start only when they learn the whereabouts of their property and know whom to sue, but those in possession of that art want the period to begin from the time the owner incurs the loss. Museum officials, in particular, have argued that delay in a source-country's assertion of ownership means that they have often spent much money restoring, conserving, studying, and publishing a work of art by the time a lawsuit is initiated. Museums say they would not have incurred those costs had the original owner exercised due diligence in publicizing the theft and searching for the stolen art. Though good-faith buyers can suffer such losses when they are required to return artworks to their original owners, in a sense they are voluntary victims because they knowingly entered into the transaction to buy the art, and experienced buyers know that such transactions can involve title problems. Many such buyers do not really buy in good faith, because they ask few questions that might cast doubt on a piece's origin, require little documentation of its provenance, and buy from dealers with shady reputations (Weil, 1987).

In the dispute over Georgia O'Keeffe's three stolen paintings, the artist stated that she could not have begun a lawsuit against the dealer who bought them until she knew their whereabouts. A lower court decided that the six-year period specified in New Jersey's statute of limitations began to run from the time the paintings were stolen in 1946, that O'Keeffe had not reported her loss or made a timely assertion of ownership, and that the paintings belonged to the dealer and his client. However, an appellate court disagreed, holding that the six-year period should not have started until O'Keeffe knew where the stolen paintings were; the artist was thus awarded possession of the pictures. That appellate court held that the dealer, his client, and O'Keeffe were all innocent parties, but that the owner's rights should be favored over those of the dealer and his client because the law should make it hard to acquire title to stolen property. The court held that a buyer should insist on proof of title and that the dealer had bought the paintings without documentation of provenance, even though he could have checked with O'Keeffe as to whether his purchase was legitimate. In 1980, the parties finally settled their dispute out of court; one painting was to be auctioned and the proceeds divided between O'Keeffe and the dealer, and O'Keeffe and the dealer were each to get one of the other pictures (Feldman, 1979; Walder, 1980b).

In another long-running dispute, the Metropolitan Museum of Art's purchase of the Lydian Hoard between 1966 and 1968 was challenged in a lawsuit by Turkey. The museum asserted that Turkey was barred by New York's statute of limitations from recovering the treasure, saying that Turkey had essentially claimed ownership in 1970 when it learned that the museum had the hoard; the museum also claimed that Turkey had not exercised due diligence in searching for the treasure. Turkey responded that its first written demand for return of the treasure was in 1986, because it did not have certain knowledge that the museum had the hoard until that time; the lawsuit was initiated in 1987, well within the three-year period it had under New York's statute of limitations. Turkey asserted that it had been unable to locate the treasure sooner because of deceptive labeling and the withholding of information by the museum, because the museum had delayed exhibiting the pieces, and because the antiquities had been illegally excavated and exported and never seen by Turkish officials. In 1990, a judge opened the way for a trial by ruling that the dispute involved important issues of material fact, such as whether the museum had been harmed by Turkey's delay in suing and whether the museum had acted in good faith, but in 1993 the museum agreed to return the hoard to Turkey.

Courts have disagreed with one another in settling disputes between the victims of art theft and good-faith purchasers of stolen and illegally exported artworks. Some judges have been reluctant to support the claims of victims who have not reported their losses or undertaken diligent efforts to recover their art, especially when their lack of due diligence has been costly to good-faith buyers. In conflicts between the rights of good-faith buyers and rightful owners, the latter have prevailed more often than not in recent court cases in the United States, but such an outcome is by no means certain; prevailing can be expensive and time-consuming and often results only from an appellate court's reversal of a lower court's decision favorable to a good-faith buyer. Frequently, such disputes are resolved out of court between the parties and so no legal precedent is set that is favorable to either party; this encourages future litigation over the ownership of stolen art.

Victims of art theft should be expected to publicize their losses in order to prevent the unwitting purchase of their art by museums, dealers, or collectors. However, victims should not be required to undertake arduous searches of auction houses' catalogues or museums' acquisitions listings to discover if others have bought their property. Statutory periods for the assertion of ownership claims should begin to run not from the time of the theft, but rather from the time that the victim, the victim's insurance company, or a law-enforcement agency learns the whereabouts of the stolen art. The Uniform Commercial Code gives an owner three years after discovering stolen property in another person's possession to sue for the return of that property; owners are given an unlimited amount of time to learn the whereabouts of the stolen property. Under Indiana's six-year statute of limitations, the Cypriot claim to the Byzantine mosaics purchased by dealer Peg L. Goldberg was held to be timely because legal action was initiated within six years of the date that the plaintiff had learned where the mosaics were.

Buyers who fear a lawsuit by a party with a legitimate claim to a work of art should protect themselves by demanding documentation of the piece's provenance and by doing their own title search, including getting verification that the piece was legally exported and not stolen from the country of origin and that it entered the United States legally. Buyers should demand warranties from dealers that allow them to recover the purchase price if a title dispute arises.

Because statutes of limitations vary significantly from one country to another, and because it is difficult to prevent the international movement of stolen art, any single nation's effort to lengthen its statute of limitations would probably have little impact on art crime. If all nations standardized and lengthened their statutes of limitations, thieves might be dissuaded from smuggling and hiding stolen art because they would know that the risk would be the same wherever and whenever they tried to dispose of it.

Deterring Art Crime

More severe penalties might have a deterrent effect on art crime, especially if those penalties were imposed with more certainty than they now are. Greater recognition of the sociocultural importance of art might make legislators and judges more supportive of harsher penalties for art thieves, smugglers, and others involved in the illicit trade. On the other hand, more severe and more certain penalties could increase vandalism if thieves who believe they are about to be arrested destroy the artworks in their possession in order to avoid being caught with them.

In the United States, penalties for grand larceny, which encompasses the snatching of paintings from museum walls and shoplifting from galleries, are rarely severe; penalties for first-time offenders often do not include imprisonment. Burglaries are rarely cleared by arrest, and when they are, penalties for thefts in which art is stolen are probably no more severe than penalties for burglaries in which other forms of property are stolen.

The penalties meted out to those who damage and destroy art are usually insignificant. Vandalism of an important painting by the British suffragettes in 1914 could only be punished by a maximum jail sentence of six months; the penalty could have been three times greater had a window been broken. Laszlo Toth, who attacked Michelangelo's *Pietà*, was not charged with damaging a work of art; instead, he was convicted of damaging a place of religion and insulting a state religion. Wilhelmus de Rijk, who attacked Rembrandt's *Night Watch*, was prosecuted for carrying a concealed weapon rather than for art vandalism. Fine and Shatin (1985) suggest that because most laws punishing art vandalism are weak, inflated rhetoric is often used to discredit the vandals' behavior. However, lenient treatment that fails to recognize the sociocultural significance of art will not deter vandals and may actually encourage acts of destruction by communicating to the general population that art vandalism is a trivial offense.

INVESTIGATING ART THEFT

In their investigations of art crimes, police departments have goals that often conflict with those of insurance companies. Insurance companies are less interested in having thieves incarcerated than in recovering everything that was stolen so that they do not have to pay their policyholders' claims. The police, on the other hand, are usually satisfied with finding a single stolen work of art in a thief's possession, because that is enough for a conviction (Burnham, 1975).

Art Squads

A few law-enforcement agencies have squads or detectives who specialize in the investigation of art crimes. The FBI and the United States Customs Service have about a dozen agents who work on art crime; for two decades, customs agent Charles Koczka specialized in cases of art theft and smuggling, though only on a part-time basis. The New York Police Department has several detectives in a workforce of 26,000 who work part time on art crimes, and two officers on the 8,000-member Los Angeles Police Department are assigned to art crimes (Tye, 1990). A department in the French Ministry of the Interior has about thirty officers who specialize in art theft.

In 1968, Scotland Yard formed an Art and Antiquities Squad that at one time had thirteen members. It was disbanded in 1983 because of its cost, the growing importance of drug trafficking and armed robbery, and the constant need to train new members as others were promoted. In the late 1980s, that squad was rejuvenated as a result of the growing use of violence in art thefts.

During World War II, Rodolfo Siviero collected information on works of art that had been looted from Italy by the Nazis. Later, he used his position as a diplomat to retrieve many of those objects, an undertaking that required him to convince Allied officials that Italy's role as an enemy during the war should not preclude repatriation of its art. For many years the chief of the Italian Foreign Ministry's Delegation for the Retrieval of Works of Art,

Siviero tracked down and repatriated thousands of stolen and smuggled artworks from museums, dealers, and collectors around the world, using his persuasive skills more often than the legal system to accomplish his goals.

In 1968, the Italian government created the Comando Carabinieri Tutela Patrimonio Artistico to investigate art crimes; in 1992, this police squad had 120 members and a computerized database of 200,000 stolen objects (Stille, 1992). The squad arrested only 2,500 suspects between 1970 and 1987, but it recovered 112,000 works of art during that time (Suro, 1987). As its name indicates, the squad's aim is to protect Italy's patrimony, and it recognizes that thieves can eventually be caught but that artworks that are destroyed can never be replaced. An annual bulletin of stolen art published by the Italian art squad is circulated to galleries, dealers, museums, brokers, and auction houses in Italy and abroad, helping to negate any purchaser's claim that a piece was bought in good faith. According to one detective, "When works of art are changing hands, especially when they are moving from a gray state of quasi-illegality towards a cleaner condition, that's when they are most vulnerable and that's when they are easiest to get" (cited in Suro, 1987:52).

The Italian art squad has been given much leeway by the courts, being allowed to use telephone taps, sting operations, informants, and bank records in their investigations. It has also cooperated with Interpol in its investigations. A major theft from a Budapest museum in 1983 was solved when a screwdriver left behind by the thieves was traced to Italy by Interpol. After the international policy agency provided Italian investigators with the names of all people who were visiting Budapest from Italy on the day of the theft, the Italian police were able to determine that one man who was in Budapest on that date later traveled to Greece. Eventually, five Italians and three Hungarians were apprehended and the stolen art was recovered from a Greek monastery, apparently having been left there at the instruction of the Greek industrialist who had commissioned the theft.

Art squads are most effective when they work closely with dealers, auction houses, museums, collectors, and agencies such as the International Foundation for Art Research. Detectives can learn investigative skills from those in the art world that they cannot acquire through standard police training. They must then cultivate and maintain close relationships with members of the art community to enable them to track down stolen art and apprehend suspects. Often this requires detectives to exercise discretion in their investigations, because victimized dealers and museums fear publicity that would cast doubt on their expertise and honesty. Art crime investigators can organize networks of dealers to be on the lookout for thieves, and immediately after a theft they can circulate information on stolen art to the dealers most likely to be approached to buy it (Adams, 1974).

Robert Volpe, a former art crime investigator on the New York Police Department, sometimes provided misinformation to the press about the value of stolen art in order to disrupt negotiations between the thief and a fence. He describes his reasoning as follows:

It means nothing to the public whether the loot was worth six million or eight million dollars. The thief gets information from the press. When I was a detective and a painting worth a hundred thousand dollars was stolen, I'd say it was worth a hundred and fifty thousand dollars when I announced the theft. When the thief goes to the fence, he's saying to himself, "The fence is not going to outsmart me. I know what it's worth." The fence, however, knows it's worth only a hundred thousand dollars. So the thief takes it someplace else. For every additional person that the thief speaks to, it raises the possibility that a mistake will be made along the line and an informant will call the police. (cited in Esterow, 1988:135)

Informants and Undercover Work

In their investigations, the police often rely on members of the criminal underworld for information. After a successful theft, offenders often brag about their exploits. Sometimes those who learn of the theft in this way will exchange that information for cash or for more lenient treatment by the criminal justice system. One confidential informant gave the New York Police Department the names of the thieves involved in more than thirty unsolved art thefts (O'Brien, 1990a). Some informants are members of drug trafficking networks, because both drugs and stolen art are often moved through the same international networks.

The investigation of art crime often requires undercover work. Detectives establish fronts in order to gain entry into a network of thieves and smugglers; for example, Italian art squad detectives have adopted disguises as a collector looking for a bargain, a dishonest art dealer, a middleman willing to broker the sale of a stolen painting, and an art historian hoping to buy stolen objects at bargain prices for rich collectors. Stolen art is often recovered through "buy-bust" or sting operations in which law-enforcement agents pose as fences who want to buy the art, and then arrest the thieves. FBI agents employed such an operation to recover two stolen artworks in the Abscam case, and they have used a similar method to recover art that is being ransomed.

A French dealer who later became a private investigator frequently used disguises in his work; in doing so, he often encountered dealers who were also using false identities in their illicit transactions. In one case, he used money supplied by an insurance company to establish a false identity as a private art dealer, telling a suspected thief that he was buying art for wealthy American collectors. The thief then produced a list of eleven stolen works and discussed price and means of delivery with the investigator, who offered to buy four of the paintings and perhaps the other seven if everything went well. The police wanted to arrest the thief at that point, but the insurance company wanted all eleven paintings back, necessitating another meeting with the thief. Eventually, the police made an arrest and recovered nine of the eleven pictures (Burnham, 1975:57–64).

Law-Enforcement Resources

Most police departments do not have even a single specialist in art crime, much less an art squad. The paucity of law-enforcement resources devoted to the investigation of art crime reflects, in part, an attitude that art is just another kind of property, even if it has a high market value. That attitude minimizes the uniqueness of artworks and their importance to a people's cultural heritage, factors that warrant the devotion of greater law-enforcement resources to the problem of art crime.

In 1979, Congress passed the Archaeological Resources Protection Act to stop the plunder of Native American grave sites and ruins. The fact that the law permits fines of up to $100,000 and imprisonment for up to ten years is less important than the fact that the law has rarely been enforced because insufficient funds and personnel have been allocated to patrol effectively the millions of acres of federal land where looting occurs. In New Mexico, two agents cover 11 million acres of Bureau of Land Management territory; in Arizona and New Mexico, six agents cover 22 million acres of Forest Service land. Enforcement of this law is also made difficult by the requirement that prosecutors must prove that the artifacts were taken from federal lands and that the looter knew beyond a reasonable doubt that the objects were on federal land, points that are difficult to demonstrate conclusively in court. The Forest Service arrested forty people between 1979 and 1986, but only one was incarcerated. The law has been credited with scaring away some weekend hobbyists from looting, but it does not seem to have reduced the activity of organized bands of looters because the certainty of apprehension, conviction, and punishment is too low (Goodwin, 1986; Kane, 1986).

In 1984, a man was caught in Utah with more than $2 million worth of Native American artifacts that he had allegedly stolen from federal land. He was charged with excavating and removing about thirty-two rare baskets, a collection described as one of the most exceptional finds of its kind ever, likened by one observer to the uncovering of an ancient king's tomb. The alleged thief claimed that he did not know that he was on federal land when he stole the baskets and that he had simply stumbled onto a cache hidden a century earlier by other looters. After twenty months of investigation and nearly two years in the courts, the defendant pleaded guilty and was placed on probation. His professed ignorance of having been on federal land was the apparent reason for the lenient penalty (Goodwin, 1986).

Legal measures are too late to save the many Native American sites that have been destroyed by shovels, plows, and bulldozers, but hundreds of thousands of sites have yet to be unearthed, and greater resources for federal law-enforcement agencies, if reinforced by a broader recognition of the seriousness of the problem, could curb this plunder. A national strike force modeled on those that proved effective in dealing with organized crime might be able to infiltrate the criminal networks of looters and better protect sites that have not yet been excavated (Goodwin, 1986).

IMPEDING THE INTERNATIONAL MOVEMENT OF STOLEN ART

Because the illicit trade in art and antiquities is international in scope, control of that trade is beyond the power of any one government or law-enforcement agency. Recognizing the international nature of the problem, in 1970 UNESCO adopted the Convention on the Means of Prohibiting and Preventing the Illicit Import, Export, and Transfer of Ownership of Cultural Property. As of 1989, sixty-five nations—most of them Third World source-countries—had signed the convention. The agreement requires source-countries to

- compile inventories of their important artworks, monuments, and sites;
- develop export licensing systems;
- appropriate funds for scientific excavations;
- publicize losses of important objects; and
- make known their restrictions on antiquities trading.

Recipient nations must

- require dealers to record their transactions;
- prohibit unauthorized imports; and
- help repatriate illicit objects. (Burnham, 1975:166)

Some source-countries did not ratify the convention because they lacked the resources to implement its required policies. Western European nations refused to sign because the convention was incompatible with Common Market regulations, they objected to the repatriation of pieces in their museums, and they were able to protect their own archaeological sites from looting. Nations that refused to sign the agreement also said that they would not ratify it until export certification made it possible to determine if an object had been exported legally or illegally, but UNESCO refused to develop a universal export certificate, saying that the burden of applying the convention was on the signatory nations.

Among the major importers of art and antiquities, only the United States has signed the convention. In 1983, Congress passed the Cultural Property Implementation Act, which permits a foreign government to ask the federal government to restrict the import of precisely defined categories of archaeological objects that are part of its patrimony and in danger of pillage. This law does not prohibit the importation of all antiquities, nor does it apply retroactively to cultural property already in the United States. Instead, it aims to control the destruction of ancient monuments, the commercial exploitation of ethnographic material important to a people's cultural heritage, the looting of archaeological sites, and the importation of stolen cultural property. The law also places the burden of preventing looting and illegal exportation on the source-countries, and it requires the participation of other major art-importing nations before the president is compelled to act.

A request by a foreign government for a ban on the importation of specific material into the United States is made through diplomatic channels to the President's Cultural Property Advisory Committee, which then makes a recommendation to the director of the United States Information Agency; that agency has the power under an Executive Order to decide whether to grant the request. If the request is approved, the Customs Service develops a list of the specific materials that will be denied entry to the United States unless accompanied by appropriate documents. An exception to this process is a crisis situation, such as the looting of a major new site, the discovery of a new type of material, the destruction of a monument, a threat to the vestiges of a civilization, guerrilla activity, or civil turmoil. In those cases, the president can declare a temporary embargo in response to a request from the source-country (Pearson, 1985c; *Stolen Art Alert*, January/February 1983).

As of late 1992, only six requests to ban the importation of cultural material to the United States had been filed; four had been approved and two were pending. Factors inhibiting source-countries from making such requests include the difficulty of creating priorities among types of cultural property, the problem of listing the specific property to be protected, and the relatively low priority assigned by political leaders to the protection of such property (Squassi, 1992). One request, approved in 1989, was to ban the importation of antique textiles from Coroma, Bolivia, because the Aymara culture there had been jeopardized by the illegal exportation of about half of its textiles to the United States. Forty-eight of those textiles were returned to Bolivia in 1992.

The effectiveness of the UNESCO Convention is questionable. Because most art-importing nations have shown little concern with the ethical implications of acquiring illicit antiquities, efforts to curb their importation have not done much to curb the looting of ancient sites; a ready market for such objects still exists in Europe and Japan. Dealer André Emmerich has commented on the effectiveness of bilateral agreements that have curbed the importation of pre-Columbian artifacts from Latin America into the United States as follows: "It all goes to Geneva now. Don't kid yourself. The market continues, but not here" (cited in Grimes, 1989:24).

The UNESCO Convention has changed the international antiquities trade in subtle ways. Because recipient-nations would rather not alienate the political leadership of source-countries by becoming embroiled in international incidents, which can lead to bad publicity portraying the recipient-nation as a bully, recipient-nations have increasingly returned stolen and illegally exported objects to the countries from which they came, often publicizing the repatriation of those objects to maximize good will. In 1987, the United States Customs Service returned to Ecuador 153 ancient artifacts that had a market value of between $60,000 and $100,000 but that were considered priceless by Ecuador. The objects, which an Ecuadorian ambassador said "represent the very basis of our culture," had been confiscated in Florida after an attempt to smuggle them into the country to trade for weapons (cited in *The New York Times*, August 15, 1987).

Bilateral agreements between the United States and Latin American nations have relied on enforcement of the 1934 National Stolen Property Act. That law was the basis for the 1979 decision in *United States* v. *McClain*, in which pre-Columbian art from Mexico was seized from dealer Patty McClain and four others after they tried to sell it to an undercover FBI agent. All five defendants were convicted, but their convictions were reversed on appeal. They were tried again under a different interpretation of the 1934 law and were again convicted. Their convictions for theft were reversed on appeal, with the court ruling that it was impossible to determine if the antiquities had been exported from Mexico before or after enactment of its 1972 law that defined unearthed pre-Columbian objects to be national property. However, that same decision affirmed their convictions for conspiracy because after 1972 they had engaged in the smuggling of artifacts they knew to have been illegally exported from Mexico.

Prior to the *McClain* decision, international law had generally held that one nation did not have to enforce another's criminal laws; the *McClain* decision meant that a foreign government's claim to ownership of its cultural property could be the basis for the criminal prosecution of anyone who imported such property into the United States without a legitimate export license from the source-country, even if the material had been properly declared at customs. Since 1979, the controversial *McClain* decision has not been consistently applied or cited as precedent by the courts; instead, the dominant view has been that the legal system of the United States does not have to enforce the export regulations of foreign nations. Thus, in the Swetnam case involving the smuggling of the Sipán artifacts, the court questioned whether the objects had actually come from Peru and asked why Peru had made so little effort to enforce its own laws against the exportation of cultural property (Grimes, 1989). The court was also skeptical of Peru's claim to own all cultural property, because Peruvians are permitted to own, sell, buy, and inherit antiquities. The court saw the dispute as being over export control rather than over ownership in the usual sense of that term. In the United States, ownership is more often seen in terms of individual rights rather than in the collective or national terms in which Peru presented its claim to the Sipán treasures (*Art & Auction*, 1990).

The element of time is important in the enforcement of the UNESCO Convention and bilateral treaties. Source-countries must prove exactly when the cultural property left their territory, a difficult undertaking when government officials do not even know when the property was unearthed. Only if they can prove that the property was exported after passage of a national patrimony law can source-countries hope to enlist the support of the art-importing country in retrieving their antiquities. This issue came up in the Swetnam case; Michael Kelly's letter claimed that his father had collected the Sipán treasures during the 1920s, prior to passage of Peru's national patrimony law in 1929. In addition to proving when the disputed property actually left their territory, source-countries must also show that it entered the receiving country after that nation had signed the UNESCO Convention. The secrecy of the international trade in illicit antiquities often makes it impossible to prove exactly when cultural property left one country and arrived in another.

International agreements and the high price of antiquities have increased the likelihood that source-countries will exert pressure or take legal action to recover stolen and smuggled material. To avoid public embarrassment and substantial legal fees, buyers of art have grown more wary about their acquisitions (Honan, 1993). Some museums now require sellers to sign warranties that the objects are being sold legally, and they demand to know a work's provenance at least back to World War II. Museums also routinely write to the appropriate ministries in possible source-countries if they lack adequate information about an object's provenance; if the seller hesitates at such an inquiry, the museum will not buy the piece. In 1991, IFAR compiled a directory of the names and addresses of the appropriate government officials in more than ninety nations to whom inquiries about the origin of artworks should be directed. Although stolen and illegally exported goods are still acquired, often because too few questions are asked about an object's provenance, the increased care with which antiquities are now purchased demonstrates that international agreements such as the UNESCO Convention can have an impact on the illicit trade in art and antiquities.

Bibliography

Acar, Ozgen, and Melik Kaylan. "Part I: The Hoard of the Century," *Connoisseur* 218 (July 1988), 74–83.

————. "The Turkish Connection," *Connoisseur* 220 (October 1990), 130–37.

Adams, Laurie. *Art Cop: Robert Volpe: Art Crime Detective*. New York: Dodd, Mead, 1974.

Akinsha, Konstantin. "The Mafia Moves in Moscow," *Art News* 89 (December 1990), 142–43.

Allen, Vernon L., and David B. Greenberger. "An Aesthetic Theory of Vandalism," *Crime and Delinquency* 24 (July 1978), 309–21.

Alsop, Joseph. *The Rare Art Traditions: The History of Art Collecting and Its Linked Phenomena*. New York: Harper & Row, 1982.

Anderson, Robert C. "Paintings as an Investment," *Economic Inquiry* 12 (March 1974), 13–26.

Art & Auction. "Cultural Patrimony: Can Countries Protect Their Art While Free Markets Thrive?" *Art & Auction* 12 (February 1990), 128–33.

Bailey, Anthony. "The Art World: A Young Man on Horseback," *The New Yorker* 66 (March 5, 1990), 45–77.

Barnett, Catherine. "Of Masks and Marauders," *Art & Antiques*, October 1990, 98–109, 140–48.

Barron, James. "Swiss Extradite Khashoggi to U.S.," *The New York Times*, July 20, 1989, A5.

Bator, Paul M. *The International Trade in Art*. Chicago: University of Chicago Press, 1981.

Becker, Howard S. *Art Worlds*. Berkeley: University of California Press, 1982.

Belk, Russell W. et al. "Collectors and Collecting," *Advances in Consumer Research* 15 (1988), 548–53.

Beller, Thomas. "The Bronze Panther," *Connoisseur* 220 (January 1990), 95.

Bender, Marylin. "Investing: The Long and Short of It," *The New York Times*, February 3, 1985, F27.

Benjamin, Walter. *Illuminations*, Hannah Arendt, ed., Harry Zohn, trans. New York: Schocken Books, 1968.

Bennett, Philip. "Crimes Solved, Mexico Rejoices," *The Boston Globe*, June 15, 1989, 2.

Berger, John. *Ways of Seeing*. Middlesex, England: British Broadcasting Company and Penguin Books, 1972.

Berman, Avis. "Art Destroyed: Sixteen Shocking Case Histories," *Connoisseur* 219 (July 1989), 74–81.

Bickelhaupt, Susan. "In Rockport, Concern about 'Schlock Art,'" *The Boston Globe*, June 25, 1988, 1, 5.

Binder, David. "Met Officials Visit Rumania to Help with Damaged Art," *The New York Times*, January 19, 1990, C18.

Blowen, Michael. "Wilder's Latest: A \$33m Auction," *The Boston Globe*, November 15, 1989, 81, 88.

Bohlin, Virginia. "How to Tell Fakes from the Real Thing," *The Boston Globe*, April 10, 1988, A15.

The Boston Globe. "Four Men Arrested in Art-Theft Case," *The Boston Globe*, February 24, 1986, 44.

———. "US Details Drug Charges against N.Y. Priest," *The Boston Globe*, April 2, 1988, 3.

Brandt, Anthony. "Room for Cynicism: The Booming Antiquities Trade: It Is Only a Moral Issue, but Who Cares?", *Connoisseur* 220 (January 1990), 92–99, 116–17.

Brenson, Michael. "Are Museums Hospitable to Art and People?" *The New York Times*, August 21, 1988, H29, H30.

———. "Scholars Re-examining Rembrandt Attributions," *The New York Times*, November 25, 1985, C13.

Brooke, James. "Faced with a Shrinking Supply of Authentic Art, African Dealers Peddle the Illusion," *The New York Times*, April 17, 1988, H51.

Burke, William K. "Priam's Treasure: Too Good to Be True?", *The Boston Globe*, January 6, 1992, 31, 32.

Burnham, Bonnie. "Another Delaney Collection Scheme Exposed," *Stolen Art Alert* 3 (May 1983), 1.

———. *The Art Crisis*. New York: St. Martin's Press, 1975.

———. "Four Paintings: An Unresolved Case," *Stolen Art Alert* 1 (April 1980a), 2–3.

———. "Inside the DeShong Museum Thefts," *Stolen Art Alert* 1 (February 1980b), 2–3.

———. "Italian Culture and the International Community," *Stolen Art Alert* 1 (August 1980c), 2–3.

Burnham, Sophie. "As the Stakes in the Art World Rise, So Do Laws and Lawsuits," *The New York Times*, February 15, 1987, H1, H28.

Butterfield, Fox. "F.B.I. Releases Sketches of Art Thieves in Boston," *The New York Times*, March 22, 1990, C20.

Carter, Malcolm N. "The End of a Multimillion-Dollar Art Fraud," *Art News* 79 (October 1980), 100–105.

Cassidy, Suzanne. "Museums Study Safe Passage for Art," *The New York Times*, September 15, 1991, 55.

Ceram, C. W. *Gods, Graves, and Scholars: The Story of Archaeology*. New York: Alfred A. Knopf, 1951.

Chamberlin, Russell. *Loot! The Heritage of Plunder*. New York: Facts on File, 1983.

Chaneles, Sol. "The Great Betrayal," *Art & Antiques*, December 1987, 93–103.

Chira, Susan. "Art Inc." *The New York Times Magazine*, May 3, 1987, 38–39, 55–56.

Coggins, Clemency. "Illicit Traffic of Pre-Columbian Antiquities," *Art Journal* 29 (Fall 1969), 94–98.

Cohen, Daniel. "You Old Fakes," *Connoisseur* 217 (October 1987), 56, 58.

Cohen, Stanley. "Campaigning against Vandalism," in Colin Ward, ed., *Vandalism*. New York: Van Nostrand Reinhold, 1973a, pp. 215–57.

———. "Property Destruction: Motives and Meanings," in Colin Ward, ed., *Vandalism*. New York: Van Nostrand Reinhold, 1973b, pp. 23–53.

Collins, Glenn. "Is It or Isn't It? A Van Gogh Languishes in Limbo," *The New York Times*, July 8, 1990, H1, H31.

Corbett, Patricia et al. "Ethics: The Getty's Statue: Beyond Legality," *Connoisseur* 218 (October 1988), 202–10.

Cornell, Barbara. "A Display That Rings False," *The Boston Globe*, June 13, 1986, 2.

Cowell, Alan. "Underground Pollution Imperils Egypt's Relics," *The New York Times*, January 30, 1990, C1, C9.

Cremin, Ann. "Vandalism at FIAC," *Art & Auction* 13 (December 1990), 24–28.

Crossley, Mimi, and E. Logan Wagner. "Ask Mexico's Masterly Brigído Lara: Is It a Fake?", *Connoisseur* 217 (June 1987), 98–103.

Csikszentmihalyi, Mihaly, and Eugene Rochberg-Halton. *The Meaning of Things: Domestic Symbols and the Self*. Cambridge, England: Cambridge University Press, 1981.

Day, Virgie D. "Misfeasance, Malfeasance, and Theft Uncovered at Brigham Young University," *IFAR Reports* 9 (June 1988), 4–6.

Decker, Andrew. "Lost Heritage: The Destruction of African Art," *Art News* 89 (September 1990), 108–19.

———. "Real and Fake in the 'Zagreb Louvre,'" *Art News* 86 (Summer 1987), 151–58.

———. "A Tale of Money, Intrigue, and Old Masters," *Art News* 83 (February 1984), 55–65.

de Coppet, Laura, and Alan Jones. *The Art Dealers*. New York: Clarkson N. Potter, 1984.

DiMaggio, Paul, and Michael Useem. "Social Class and Arts Consumption," *Theory and Society* 5 (Spring 1978), 141–61.

Dornberg, John. "Art Vandals: Why Do They Do It?" *Art News* 86 (March 1987), 102–9.

————. "The Mounting Embarrassment of Germany's Nazi Treasures," *Art News* 87 (September 1988), 130–41.

Dryansky, G. Y. "Arts of the Restorer," *Connoisseur* 218 (April 1988), 108–13.

Dullea, Georgia. "At Sotheby's, the Resident Old Master Is the One Wielding the Hammer," *The New York Times*, June 22, 1990, B4.

Dunlap, David W. "Artist Ends Fight to Bar Removal of Sculpture," *The New York Times*, March 16, 1989a, B2.

————. "Moving Day Arrives for Disputed Sculpture," *The New York Times*, March 11, 1989b, 29, 32.

Duthy, Robin. "The Fortunes of Rothko," *Connoisseur* 215 (November 1985), 174–85.

————. "Investor's File: The Colourists: Scotland's Gift to Painting," *Connoisseur* 219 (January 1989a), 122–26.

————. "Investor's File: Degas: Mystery Man, Hot Property," *Connoisseur* 218 (October 1988a), 190–98.

————. "Investor's File: Jackson Pollock: America's Greatest Artist," *Connoisseur* 219 (August 1989b), 105–7.

————. "Investor's File: Status plus Value: Nineteenth-Century Watercolors," *Connoisseur* 218 (April 1988b), 164–73.

————. "Investor's File: Swedish Painting: A Lively Backwater," *Connoisseur* 219 (July 1989c), 98–101.

Elsworth, Peter C. T. "The Art Boom: Is It Over, or Is This Just a Correction?", *The New York Times*, December 16, 1990, F4.

Esterow, Milton. *The Art Stealers*, rev. ed. New York: Macmillan, 1973.

————. "Confessions of an Art Cop," *Art News* 87 (May 1988), 134–37.

Failing, Patricia. "Picking up the Pieces: The Case of the Dismembered Masterpieces," *Art News* 79 (September 1980), 68–78.

Faith, Nicholas. *Sold: The Rise and Fall of the House of Sotheby.* New York: Macmillan, 1985.

Feldman, Franklin. "Authenticity in Sales: British Art Dealers' Suit over Munter Decided," *IFAR Reports* 11 (November 1990), 4.

————. "New Decisions on Statutes of Limitations: Authentication and Art Theft," *IFAR Reports* 12 (February/March 1991), 3–4.

————. "Stolen Art Ruling," *Art Theft Archive Newsletter* 1 (January 1979), n.p.

Fine, Gary Alan. "Cheating History: The Rhetorics of Art Forgery," *Empirical Studies of the Arts* 1 (1983), 75–93.

————, and Deborah Shatin. "Crimes against Art: Social Meanings and Symbolic Attacks," *Empirical Studies of the Arts* 3 (1985), 135–52.

Fine, Rebecca L. "Reward for Returning Stolen Art: Incentives in U.S. Law," *IFAR Reports* 13 (July-August 1992), 4–5.

Freedberg, David. *The Power of Images: Studies in the History and Theory of Response*. Chicago: University of Chicago Press, 1989.

Frey, Bruno S., and Werner W. Pommerehne. "Art Investment: An Empirical Inquiry," *Southern Economic Journal* 56 (October 1989), 396–409.

Gamboni, Dario. *Un Iconoclasme Moderne: Théorie et Pratiques Contemporaines du Vandalism Artistique*. Zürich: Institut Suisse pour l'Etude de l'Art; and Lausanne: Les Editions d'En-bas, 1983.

Gardner, Paul. "That Shrinking Feeling," *Art News* 90 (January 1991), 124–27.

Gerard, Jeremy. "Art Magazines Compete for the Elegant Salon," *The New York Times*, June 6, 1988, D10.

Gillette, Joshua. "Man Charged with Stealing Back Bay Art," *The Boston Globe*, July 12, 1989, 56.

Glueck, Grace. "Donations of Art Fall Sharply After Changes in the Tax Code," *The New York Times*, May 7, 1989, 1, 32.

———. "Masterpieces Rise and Fall on a Tide of New Expertise," *The New York Times*, December 7, 1986a, H1, H35.

———. "Portrait of a Collector: Walter Annenberg," *The New York Times*, April 25, 1990, C13, C16.

———. "Rothko Art Dispute Ends Quietly after 15 Years," *The New York Times*, August 20, 1986b, 17.

———. "State Panels Explore Regulating Art Sales Like Commodities," *The New York Times*, January 16, 1991, C9, C14.

Golden, Daniel. "Hot Art," *The Boston Globe Magazine*, February 12, 1989, 16–19, 34–50.

Goleman, Daniel. "Prized Presents Offer Map of the Self," *The New York Times*, December 29, 1987, C6.

Goodrich, David L. *Art Fakes in America*. New York: Viking, 1973.

Goodwin, Derek V. "Raiders of the Sacred Sites," *The New York Times Magazine*, December 7, 1986, 65–67, 84–90.

Grampp, William D. *Pricing the Priceless: Art, Artists, and Economics*. New York: Basic Books, 1989.

Grant, Daniel. "Collecting Art? Beware the Wrinkles," *The New York Times*, November 29, 1987, F9.

———. "Uncertain Art: Getting Back What's Been Stolen," *The Boston Globe*, June 9, 1986, 45, 48.

Green, Peter. "Bad Czechs," *Connoisseur* 221 (June 1991), 74–79, 101.

Green, Timothy. *The Smugglers*. New York: Walker, 1969.

Greenfeld, Howard. *The Devil and Dr. Barnes: Portrait of an American Art Collector*. New York: Viking, 1987.

Greenhouse, Steven. "New Scandal in French Art World," *The New York Times*, January 2, 1989, H15, H20.

———. "Scandal over Heiress's Art Entangles a Louvre Curator," *The New York Times*, December 26, 1988, 1, 26.

Greenspan, Stuart. "Regulating the Art Business," *The New York Times*, August 31, 1985, 23.

Grimes, William. "The Antiquities Boom: Who Pays the Price?", *The New York Times Magazine*, July 16, 1989, 17–19, 24–26.

Haberman, Clyde. "Florence's Art Makes Some Go to Pieces," *The New York Times*, May 15, 1989, A3.

——— . "Italy Fears That Its Art Treasures Will Scatter in a Unified Europe," *The New York Times*, March 5, 1990, A1, C13.

Hamblin, Dora Jane. *Pots and Robbers*. New York: Simon & Schuster, 1970.

Hayt-Atkins, Elizabeth. "Masterminding Masterpieces," *IFAR Reports* 9 (January 1988), 3–4.

Haywood, Ian. *Faking It: Art and the Politics of Forgery*. New York: St. Martin's, 1987.

Heath, Dwight B. "In Quest of 'El Dorado': Some Sociological Aspects of Huaquerismo (Pot-Hunting) in Costa Rica," *Anales del Instituto de Geografia e Historia de Costa Rica, 1967–68, 1968–69*. Sa Jose, Costa Rica, 1971.

Hennessee, Judith. "Why Great Art Always Will Be Stolen (and Seldom Found)," *Connoisseur* 220 (July 1990), 41–47, 104.

Hess, John L. *The Grand Acquisitors*. Boston: Houghton Mifflin, 1974.

Hitchens, Christopher. *Imperial Spoils: The Curious Case of the Elgin Marbles*. New York: Hill & Wang, 1989.

Hofmann, Paul. "Italy's Endangered Treasures," *The New York Times*, July 30, 1989, XX35.

Honan, William H. "Artists, Newly Militant, Fight for Their Rights," *The New York Times*, March 3, 1988, C29.

——— . "Deciding How Diligent Art Collectors Have to Be," *The New York Times*, June 4, 1989a, E9.

——— . "Judge Orders Art Dealer to Return Rare Mosaics to Church of Cyprus," *The New York Times*, August 4, 1989b, A1, C25.

——— . "Lately, More Antiquities Can Go Home Again," *The New York Times*, January 25, 1993, C11, C16.

Hooper-Greenhill, Eilean. "Counting Visitors or Visitors Who Count," in Robert Lumley, ed., *The Museum Time-Machine: Putting Cultures on Display*. London: Routledge, 1988, pp. 213–232.

Hoving, Thomas. *King of the Confessors*. New York: Simon & Schuster, 1981.

——— . *Making the Mummies Dance: Inside the Metropolitan Museum of Art*. New York: Simon & Schuster, 1993.

——— . "My Eye," *Connoisseur* 217 (June 1987), 25.

——— . "My Eye: The Forgery Boom," *Connoisseur* 216 (November 1986), 41.

——— . "My Eye: 'Hot' Antiquities," *Connoisseur* 218 (July 1988), 19.

Hughes, Robert. "Sold!" *Time* 134 (November 27, 1989), 60–65.

Idzerda, Stanley J. "Iconoclasm during the French Revolution," *American Historical Review* 60 (October 1954), 13–26.

IFAR Reports. "A New Con Game," *IFAR Reports* 7 (July/August 1986), 5.

Jeppson, Lawrence. *The Fabulous Frauds: Fascinating Tales of Great Art Forgeries*. New York: Weybright and Talley, 1970.

Johnson, Kirk. "2 Are Convicted of Art Thefts at Warehouse," *The New York Times*, April 11, 1987, 31.

Jones, Alan. "Introduction," in Laura de Coppet and Alan Jones, eds. *The Art Dealers*. New York: Clarkson N. Potter, 1984, pp. 11–18.

Jones, Mark., ed. *Fake? The Art of Deception*. Berkeley: University of California Press, 1990.

Kane, Sid. "The Big—and Illegal—Business of Indian Artifacts," *The New York Times*, September 7, 1986, F13.

Katsh, M. Ethan. *Taking Sides: Clashing Views on Controversial Legal Issues*, 4th ed. Guilford, Conn.: Dushkin, 1991.

Katz, Jack. *Seductions of Crime: Moral and Sensual Attractions in Doing Evil*. New York: Basic Books, 1988.

Kaylan, Melik. "Who Stole the Lydian Hoard?" *Connoisseur* 217 (July 1987), 66–73.

Ketchum, Linda E. "Galleries Victims of Fraudulent Consignment Scheme," *Stolen Art Alert* 4 (November 1983), 2–5.

———. "Warehouse Thefts Plague Unsuspecting Art Collectors," *Stolen Art Alert* 5 (May 1984), 1, 3–5.

Kimmelman, Michael. "Getty Fulfills a Role, for Itself and the Public," *The New York Times*, June 3, 1989a, 13.

———. "Sotheby's to Break up a Robert Sketchbook," *The New York Times*, October 31, 1989b, C21, C28.

———. "When Art Takes Wing, Cross Your Fingers," *The New York Times*, March 7, 1993, H1, H33.

Kirkpatrick, Sidney D. *Lords of Sipán: A True Story of Pre-Inca Tombs, Archaeology, and Crime*. New York: Morrow, 1992.

Kleiman, Dena. "Behind Inflated Attendance Figures," *The New York Times*, February 21, 1987, 11.

Koning, Hans. "The Real Rembrandt," *Connoisseur* 216 (April 1986), 106–13.

Kristof, Nicholas D. "Tourists Threaten Buddhist Mural in Ancient Chinese Caves," *The New York Times*, November 21, 1989, C19.

Kurz, Otto. *Fakes*, 2nd rev. and enlarged ed. New York: Dover, 1967.

Lang, Gladys Engel, and Kurt Lang. *Etched in Memory: The Building and Survival of Artistic Reputation*. Chapel Hill: University of North Carolina Press, 1990.

Leary, Warren E. "Tomb in Peru Yields Stunning Pre-Inca Trove," *The New York Times*, September 14, 1988, A1, A18.

Leitch, David. *The Discriminating Thief*. New York: Holt, Rinehart and Winston, 1968.

Lessing, Alfred. "What is Wrong with a Forgery?", in Denis Dutton, ed., *The Forger's Art: Forgery and the Philosophy of Art*. Berkeley: University of California Press, 1983, pp. 58–76.

Lowenthal, Constance. "Fraudulent Fabergé," *IFAR Reports* 9 (October/November 1988), 4–5.

———. "Imported Pollock Seized," *IFAR Reports* 13 (October 1992), 2–3.

————. "Six Months in Prison for Buyer of Stolen Art," *IFAR Reports* 12 (February/March 1991a), 6.

————. "Unidroit Draft Convention," *IFAR Reports* 12 (August/September 1991b), 5–6.

Lyons, James R. "Auctions: Yes, It's Awards Time All Over Again," *Connoisseur* 218 (August 1988), 30–32.

McGill, Douglas C. "Art Galleries Told to Post Prices," *The New York Times*, February 10, 1988a, C17.

————. "Art People," *The New York Times*, January 15, 1988b, C25.

————. "Artworks by Soyer Are Stolen," *The New York Times*, December 23, 1987a, C10.

————. "The Case of the Purloined Goddess," *The New York Times*, October 9, 1986a, C25.

————. "Christie's Aide Says Chief Knew of Sale Lie," *The New York Times*, July 12, 1985a, C28.

————. "Christie's Chairman Quits in False Sale Case," *The New York Times*, July 29, 1985b, 1, 9.

————. "Everything Had Its Price," *The New York Times Book Review*, May 18, 1986b, 15.

————. "Expert on Miró's Style Detects Fake Artworks," *The New York Times*, January 14, 1985c, C15.

————. "Fake Art Prints: Big Business Getting Bigger," *The New York Times*, July 22, 1987b, A1, B5.

————. "False Bids Were Called, Christie's Jury Is Told," *The New York Times*, January 15, 1987c, C25.

————. "Getty, the Art World's Big Spender," *The New York Times*, March 4, 1987d, C23.

————. "Hundreds of Art Works Mildewing in Historical Society's Warehouse," *The New York Times*, July 10, 1988c, 1, 23.

————. "Japanese Investors Spur Higher Prices in U.S. Art Market," *The New York Times*, December 10, 1986c, A1, C23.

————. "Met Says Its Popular Cat Is Probably Fake," *The New York Times*, April 30, 1987e, A1, C25.

————. "An Out-of-Court Settlement Reached in Christie's Case," *The New York Times*, January 22, 1987f, C20.

————. "Pre-Columbian Works Could Be Fakes," *The New York Times*, May 20, 1987g, C19.

————. "Proposed Auction Rules Would Reveal No-Sales," *The New York Times*, April 10, 1986d, C17.

————. "Sotheby's Settlement Is Approved by Judge," *The New York Times*, August 15, 1985d, C15.

————. "Sweeping Reassessment in the Auction Trade," *The New York Times*, July 31, 1985e, A1, C20.

McIntosh, Mary. *The Organisation of Crime*. London: The Macmillan Press, Ltd., 1975.

McLeave, Hugh. *Rogues in the Gallery: The Modern Plague of Art Thefts*. Boston: David R. Godine, 1981.

Magnusson, Paul. "Rich Getting Richer, Taking Bigger Share of US Wealth, Study Says," *The Boston Globe*, July 26, 1986, 1, 4.

Malkin, Lawrence. "Investor's File: How the IRS Looks at Art," *Connoisseur* 219 (May 1989a), 170–74.

———. "Why Buy Art?" *Connoisseur* 219 (October 1989b), 166–70.

Marquis, Alice Goldfarb. *The Art Biz: The Covert World of Collectors, Dealers, Auction Houses, Museums, and Critics*. Chicago: Contemporary Books, 1991.

Mason, Donald L. *The Fine Art of Art Security: Protecting Public and Private Collections against Theft, Fire, and Vandalism*. New York: Van Nostrand Reinhold, 1979.

Menn, Joseph. "Fakes Flourish in Booming Art Market," *The Boston Globe*, July 23, 1987, 45, 48.

Meyer, Karl E. *The Plundered Past*. New York: Atheneum, 1973.

Miller, Judith. "Nine Paintings Stolen in Paris by 5 Gunmen," *The New York Times*, October 28, 1985, A1, C17.

Miller, Margo. "MFA Trustee Profits from Plunder," *The Boston Globe*, June 13, 1988, 10–11.

Mills, John FitzMaurice, and John M. Mansfield. *The Genuine Article: The Making and Unmasking of Fakes and Forgeries*. New York: Universe Books, 1979.

Mitgang, Herbert. "Old Copyright Treaty: New Shield for U.S. Artists," *The New York Times*, March 10, 1989, B7.

Mittlemark, Howard. "Fake African Art and the Passion for Authenticity," *The New York Times*, June 5, 1988, H22.

Molotsky, Irvin. "Artists Want Work Protected," *The New York Times*, October 1, 1987, C21.

Mydans, Seth. "At a California High School, Pygmalion in Reverse," *The New York Times*, June 12, 1989, A14.

Myers, John Bernard. *Tracking the Marvelous: A Life in the New York Art World*. New York: Random House, 1983.

Nagin, Carl. "The Peruvian Gold Rush," *Art & Antiques*, May 1990, 98–105, 134–45.

Nasar, Sylvia. "Fed Gives New Evidence of 80's Gains by Richest," *The New York Times*, April 21, 1992, A1, A17.

Neuffer, Elizabeth. "DEA Seizes Art Cache Owned by Alleged Drug Traffickers," *The Boston Globe*, November 20, 1990, 39.

The New York Times. "Christie's Chairman Admits to False Report," *The New York Times*, July 8, 1985, C13.

———. "Court Denies Claim to Items Found on Indian Burial Site," *The New York Times*, December 31, 1986, A15.

———. "Experts Err on a Carracci," *The New York Times*, December 10, 1987, C16.

———— . "Paintings Are Stolen in Ireland," *The New York Times*, May 22, 1986, C21.

———— . "Paris Art Thefts Meant Just as Spectator Sport," *The New York Times*, January 22, 1989, 14.

———— . "Price Tags on Art, Cont'd," *The New York Times*, May 1, 1988, H40.

———— . "Putting Price Tags in Art Galleries," *The New York Times*, September 18, 1988, 58.

———— . "Scholar Wins His Libel Case over Statue," *The New York Times*, December 8, 1989, C17.

———— . "2 Indiana Art Dealers Face Trial in Sale of Reputed Forgeries," *The New York Times*, November 6, 1986, A26.

———— . "U.S. Yields Stolen Artifacts to Ecuador," *The New York Times*, August 15, 1987, 11.

———— . "A Widow's Might Defeats the Louvre," *The New York Times*, December 14, 1988, C30.

Norman, Geraldine. "In China: A British Trade in Smuggled Art," *Connoisseur* 218 (May 1988), 172–76.

————, and Thomas Hoving. "The Getty Scandals," *Connoisseur* 217 (May 1987a), 98–109.

———— . "'It Was Bigger Than They Know,'" *Connoisseur* 217 (August 1987b), 72–81.

———— . "Scandals: Shady Business in the German Art Market," *Connoisseur* 22 (March 1991), 110–111.

O'Brien, Margaret I. "All about Art Recovery," *IFAR Reports* 11 (October 1990a), 8–10.

———— . "Arrests and Recoveries in Zürich Dutch Old Masters Theft," *IFAR Reports* 10 (June 1989a), 3–4.

———— . "The Baltimore Illusionist," *IFAR Reports* 9 (July/August 1988), 7–8.

———— . "Himalayan Hoard Recovered," *IFAR Reports* 11 (January 1990b), 3.

———— . "Wanted," *IFAR Reports* 10 (September 1989b), 6.

O'Connor, Robert. "8th-Century Chalice at Center of Dispute," *The Boston Globe*, December 27, 1986, 2.

Pancoast, Virgilia Heimsath. "Center Art Principals Given Prison Terms for Dali Print Fraud," *IFAR Reports* 11 (December 1990a), 7.

———— . "Deceptive Rodins," *IFAR Reports* 11 (October 1990b), 2–3.

————, and Constance Lowenthal. "Larionov Forgeries," *IFAR Reports* 9 (July/August 1988), 3–5.

Passell, Peter. "Vincent van Gogh, Meet Adam Smith," *The New York Times*, February 4, 1990, H1, H12.

Patterson, Jerry. "Valuations: Getting Your Masters," *Connoisseur* (August 1991), 102–5.

Pearson, Lynn Stowell. "Art Dealer Claire Eatz Convicted of Fraud and Sentenced to Six Years in Jail," *IFAR Reports* 6 (October/November 1985a), 6–9.

———— . "Current Trends in Art Theft," *IFAR Reports* 7 (June 1986a), 3–4.

————. "Henri Kuntz: Mastermind Behind Countless Thefts and Forgeries," *IFAR Reports* 7 (September 1986b), 4–5.

————. "Title Disputes at Auction Houses," *Stolen Art Alert* 5 (January/February 1984), 4–6.

————. "Tom Moscardini: Interview," *IFAR Reports* 6 (March 1985b), 6.

————. "Update on U.S. Cultural Property Act," *IFAR Reports* 6 (October/November 1985c), 9–10.

Pennington, Samuel. "Grant Wood Drawing Returned," *IFAR Reports* 6 (March 1985), 4.

Plenge, Heinz. "The Robber's Tale," *Connoisseur* 220 (February 1990), 76–85, 118.

Possehl, Suzanne. "Russian Art Objects Vanishing to the West in Smugglers' Bags," *The New York Times*, March 17, 1993, C15, C20.

Raab, Selwyn. "Fighting Fake Art: Victims' Shame and Muddled Law," *The New York Times*, July 23, 1987a, B1, B2.

————. "Where the Art is Selling," *The New York Times*, July 23, 1987b, B1, B2.

Rasky, Susan F. "Senate Panel Adopts Tax Break for Donations of Art to Museums," *The New York Times*, October 16, 1990, A1, B8.

Reif, Rita. "Animation Auction Is Questioned," *The New York Times*, October 17, 1992, 17.

————. "Auctions' Big Spenders: The Japanese," *The New York Times*, May 19, 1990a, 12.

————. "Businessman Identified as Buyer of van Gogh," *The New York Times*, May 18, 1990b, C28.

————. "Colonial American Desk Is Sold for $12.1 Million," *The New York Times*, June 4, 1989a, 36.

————. "Global Market Brings Auction Records," *The New York Times*, August 10, 1987, C18.

————. "Rewriting Auction Records," *The New York Times*, January 25, 1990c, C1, C10.

————. "A Stolen Rembrandt Drawing Is Identified," *The New York Times*, July 20, 1989b, C17.

————. "A $27 Million Loan by Sotheby's Helped Alan Bond to Buy 'Irises,' " *The New York Times*, October 18, 1989c, C15, C20.

————. "Which Washington, a $495,000 Stuart or a $3,300 Copy?", *The New York Times*, November 17, 1988, A1, C26.

Reynolds, Maura. "Queens Court Aide Held in Apartment Theft," *The New York Times*, March 3, 1988, B3.

Ribadeneira, Diego. "Rembrandt Is Sold for a Record $10.3m," *The Boston Globe*, December 11, 1986, 1, 11.

Riding, Alan. "Europe, Unifying, Has Fears for Its Art," *The New York Times*, December 28, 1992, C9, C16.

————. "French Museum Chief vs. Art Thieves," *The New York Times*, June 15, 1991, 13, 15.

Riley, Charles A., II. "The Confidence Game," *Art & Auction* 13 (June 1991), 118–23.

Robinson, John P. et al. *Public Participation in the Arts: Final Report of the 1982 Survey*. College Park: University of Maryland Survey Research Center, October 1985.

Robinson, Michael F. "Art and Money: Pitfalls Aplenty: Appraisals and Insurance," *Connoisseur* 220 (April 1990), 142–45.

Rockwell, John. "Islamic Art Collection Is Offered to Britain; Some Say, 'Refuse,' " *The New York Times*, February 15, 1993, C11, C14.

Rohter, Larry. "Marilyn and Virgin: Art or Sacrilege?", *The New York Times*, April 2, 1988, 4.

———. "Police Foil $18 Million Art Theft; Manhattan Dealer Seized with 2," *The New York Times*, January 6, 1986, A1, B3.

Rule, Sheila. "Museums in Need Warn Thatcher of Art Damage," *The New York Times*, July 27, 1989, C15.

———. "Restoring a Leonardo Drawing That Was Hit by a Shotgun Blast," *The New York Times*, November 8, 1988, C15.

Russell, John. "Conservators Endorse Sistine Restoration," *The New York Times*, April 16, 1987, C17.

———. "Disputed Greek Statue to Go on Exhibition," *The New York Times*, August 12, 1986, A1, C18.

———. "Italy Reclaims Its Treasures from the Past," *The New York Times*, June 26, 1988, H1, H18.

———. "Plots that Balzac Would Have Savored," *The New York Times*, January 15, 1989, H33, H35.

Saltus, Richard. "Peru Tomb Yields Ancient Treasure Trove," *The Boston Globe*, September 14, 1988, 1, 18.

Schaire, Jeffrey. "Notes from the Editor: Shades of Gray," *Art & Antiques*, May 1990, 12.

Scheff, Thomas J. *Being Mentally Ill: A Sociological Theory*, 2nd ed. New York: Aldine, 1984.

Schwartz, Louis B. "Theft," in Sanford H. Kadish, ed., *Encyclopedia of Crime and Justice*, vol. 4. New York: Free Press, 1983, pp. 1537–52.

Seldes, Lee. *The Legacy of Mark Rothko*. New York: Penguin, 1979.

Sereny, Gitta. "Forbidden Treasures," *Connoisseur* 213 (March 1983), 85–92.

Servin, James. "SoHo Stares at Hard Times," *The New York Times Magazine*, January 20, 1991, 24–29.

Shenon, Philip. "France Yields Art Linked to Marcos," *The New York Times*, January 8, 1988, A7.

———. "Interior Department Says 357 Pieces Are Missing from Its Art Collection," *The New York Times*, August 18, 1990, 10.

———. "Washing Buddha's Face," *The New York Times Magazine*, June 21, 1992, 18–21, 38–40.

Sherman, William. "The Drug Cartel: Fences, Informers, and Stolen Art," *Art News* 90 (March 1991), 122–27.

————. "The Marcos Collection," *Art News* 89 (October 1990), 154–63.

Sill, Gertrude Grace. "Art and Money," *Connoisseur* 220 (July 1990), 96–99.

Simons, Marlise. "Art with a Perfect Past, but an Indefinite Future," *The New York Times*, February 18, 1991a, 4.

————. "A Restoration Becomes a Criminal Case in Italy," *The New York Times*, May 25, 1991b, 13–14.

Simpson, Colin. *Artful Partners: Bernard Berenson and Joseph Duveen*. New York: Macmillan, 1986.

Singer, Mark. "Profiles: Wall Power," *The New Yorker* 63 (November 30, 1987), 44–97.

Smith, Charles W. *Auctions: The Social Construction of Value*. New York: Free Press, 1989.

Sox, David. "Master Forger," *Connoisseur* 218 (November 1988), 176–79.

Squassi, Florence. "U.S. & Cultural Property," *IFAR Reports* 13 (November 1992), 4–6.

Stein, Anne-Marie, as told to George Carpozi, Jr. *Three Picassos before Breakfast*. New York: Hawthorn Books, 1973.

Steiner, Wendy. "In London, Catalogue of Fakes," *The New York Times*, April 29, 1990, H37, H43.

Sterngold, James. "Some Big Japanese Art Purchases Are under Scrutiny for Scandal," *The New York Times*, April 23, 1991a, A1, D6.

————. "South Korea Seeks Return of Its Artworks from Japan," *The New York Times*, July 11, 1991b, C15, C16.

Stille, Alexander. "Art Thieves Bleed Italy of Its Heritage," *The New York Times*, August 2, 1992, H27.

————. "Thousands in Italy Protest Florence Bombing," *The Boston Globe*, May 29, 1993, 2.

Stolen Art Alert. "An Attack on Ancient Tikal," *Stolen Art Alert* 2 (September 1981), 1.

————. "Clouds Dispersed," *Stolen Art Alert* 3 (December 1982), 1–2.

————. "Deja Vu," *Stolen Art Alert* 3 (November 1982a), 1, 2.

————. "Delancy Collection Paintings See Daylight," *Stolen Art Alert* 4 (March/April 1983), 1–2.

————. "New Antiquities Law," *Stolen Art Alert* 3 (November 1982b), 2.

————. "A Successful Con Man Reappears," *Stolen Art Alert* 3 (October 1982), 2–3.

————. "UNESCO Convention Legislation Passed," *Stolen Art Alert* 4 (January/February 1983), 4.

Suro, Roberto. "Going Undercover for Art's Sake," *The New York Times Magazine*, December 13, 1987, 42–52.

————. "Italy Accuses Getty Museum on Sculpture Loan," *The New York Times*, August 11, 1988a, 11.

————. "Quiet Effort to Regain Idols May Alter Views of Indian Art," *The New York Times*, August 13, 1990, A1, A13.

————— . "A Race for Artifacts Pits Sicilians against Scientists and Officials," *The New York Times*, August 17, 1988b, C17, C19.

Swanstrom, Florence Squassi. "War Booty Is His Quarry," *IFAR Reports* 14 (January 1993), 5–7.

Sykes, Gresham M., and David Matza. "Techniques of Neutralization: A Theory of Delinquency," *American Sociological Review* 22 (December 1957), 664–70.

Tagliabue, John. "Art Thefts Soar in Eastern Europe," *The New York Times*, July 6, 1991, 13.

————— . "Vienna Sifts Claims to Nazi Art Cache," *The New York Times*, November 26, 1986, C11.

Taylor, John Russell, and Brian Brooke. *The Art Dealers*. New York: Charles Scribner's Sons, 1969.

Taylor, Robert. "The Costly Quest for Contemporary Art," *The Boston Globe*, February 12, 1989a, A1, A4.

————— . "Sizing Up the '80s: An Era When Cash Superceded Canvas," *The Boston Globe*, January 1, 1989b, 77, 86.

————— . "Top of the Art World Immune to Economics," *The Boston Globe*, November 13, 1987, 54.

Temin, Christine. "Galleries: Retailing the New Art," *The Boston Globe*, October 25, 1987, B1, B4.

————— . "The MFA and the Politics of Plunder," *The Boston Globe*, January 4, 1989, 37, 42.

Tomforde, Anna. "Austria to Allow Jews to Claim Artwork," *The Boston Globe*, December 9, 1985, 11.

Tomkins, Calvin. "The Art World: Peaks and Valleys," *The New Yorker* 63 (February 23, 1987), 114–17.

————— . "A Reporter at Large: Irises," *The New Yorker* 64 (April 4, 1988), 37–67.

Trustman, Deborah. "Abuses in the Reproduction of Sculpture," *Art News* 80 (June 1981), 84–92.

Tye, Larry. "A Motive, Recovery of Art Elude the Investigators," *The Boston Globe*, May 13, 1990, 1, 22.

Veblen, Thorstein. *The Theory of the Leisure Class*. New York: Modern Library, 1934.

Vogel, Carol. "The Art Market," *The New York Times*, January 3, 1992a, C25.

————— . "At Sotheby's, Managing the Art of Business," *The New York Times*, May 1, 1987, A26.

————— . "Sotheby's and Museum in Dispute over a Painting with a Murky Past," *The New York Times*, March 23, 1992b, C13, C15.

Walder, Linda J. "Fraud Proliferates as Art Investments Rise," *Stolen Art Alert* 1 (September 1980a), 2–3.

————— . "O'Keeffe Ruling Reversed Again," *Stolen Art Alert* 1 (August 1980b), n.p.

Walker, Richard W. "The Saatchi Factor," *Art News* 86 (January 1987), 117–21.

Warren, William. "In Thailand, Faking Art Is an Art in Itself," *The New York Times*, December 11, 1988, XX12.

Watson, Peter. *The Caravaggio Conspiracy*. New York: Doubleday, 1984.

Weil, Stephen E. " 'Repose,' " *IFAR Reports* 8 (August/September 1987), 6–7.

White, Harrison, and Cynthia White. *Canvases and Careers*. New York: John Wiley, 1965.

Wilkerson, Isabel. "Temple Lintel Pits Thais against an Art Museum," *The New York Times*, July 17, 1988, 14.

Wintersgill, Donald. "Dealers' Rings and Other Things," *Art & Auction* 8 (December 1985), 28–32.

Wolff, Janet. *The Social Production of Art*. New York: New York University Press, 1981.

Woodruff, John E. "Japanese Art Buyers Are Back, with Deeper Pockets than Ever," *The New York Times*, December 17, 1988, 15.

Wraight, Robert. *The Art Game*. New York: Simon & Schuster, 1966.

WuDunn, Sheryl. "China Is Fighting for Its Soul: Its Looted Antiquities," *The New York Times*, December 8, 1992, A4.

Yarrow, Andrew L. "London Art Dealer Is Criticized for Museum Accord Gone Sour," *The New York Times*, December 14, 1988, C21, C30.

Index

About the Author

JOHN E. CONKLIN is Professor of Sociology at Tufts University. He is the author of a successful textbook, *Criminology* (Fifth Edition will be published in 1995), as well as *Sociology: An Introduction* (1987, 1984); *"Illegal but Not Criminal": Business Crime in America* (1977); *The Impact of Crime* (1975); *Robbery and the Criminal Justice System* (1972); and editor of *The Crime Establishment: Organized Crime and American Society* (1973).